THE UNIFICATION OF
GREECE
1770–1923

THE UNIFICATION
OF
GREECE
1770-1923

DOUGLAS DAKIN

LONDON
ERNEST BENN LIMITED

First published 1972 by Ernest Benn Limited
Bouverie House · Fleet Street · London · EC4A 2DL

Distributed in Canada by
The General Publishing Company Limited · Toronto

© *Douglas Dakin 1972*
ISBN 0 510–26311–9

Printed in Great Britain

To

the memory of

Basil Laourdas

Preface

THE PRIMARY SOURCES of modern Greek history are vast and to a large extent either unexplored or inadequately studied. University historians in this field are still relatively few, not only in Greece itself but in centres of learning in Europe and America. Classical and Byzantine studies attract more scholars and research students than do the more recent periods of Greek history. In Greece itself university historians are so overburdened with teaching and administrative duties that the time they can give to the wealth of source materials around them is limited.[1] The result is that their output of published work, although of great merit, is neither considerable in bulk nor necessarily devoted to those themes on which long-term research needs to be done. Fortunately, however, there are many Greeks outside the universities who have an interest in modern history, and these—journalists, administrators, businessmen, politicians, and teachers—collect, study, and publish documents, build up private libraries which contain editions of rare books, and write articles and monographs of fundamental value and good scholarship. These collections of documents, and these monographs and articles, are usually published in small editions or are scattered in a multiplicity of periodicals, magazines, and newspapers. In this way new documentary sources (from central and local archives, from family papers and private collections) are daily brought to light and gradually become incorporated in the more general compilations on Greek history.

This present work, where it is not based on my own original research, or on the researches of my students (to whom I express my gratitude), is based either directly on the published collections, memoirs, monographs, and articles, or on the more general works of Greek and foreign historians who, besides using unpublished sources, have drawn upon the same type of material. To all these writers (and they are legion) I must express my gratitude and also my apologies if inadvertently I have failed to profit from their wisdom and their learning. In particular I must acknowledge a special debt to all those friendly and considerate Greeks who kindly send me copies of their publications. They are far too numerous to mention individually.

In my acknowledgement I will mention only four names. Yannis Yannoulopoulos has given me considerable help with much of the detail of this book. He has checked names and dates, and he has compiled for me the Appendices which, it is hoped, the reader will find useful, and he has put me right on many points. He also did much work on the preliminary stages of the maps, which were entrusted, in their final stages, to the expert hands

---

[1] Extensive material, principally diplomatic despatches and consular reports from the European archives—essential for the study of modern Greek history—is being collected under the direction of Dr E. Prevelakis by the Academy of Athens in the form of microfilms. This collection, which is already enormous, is expertly catalogued and indexed.

of Mr G. Davenport of the department of geography of Birkbeck College. I am most grateful to the Head of Department Professor Eila Campbell and to Mr G. Davenport for their invaluable help. Finally, I have to thank my friend Professor John Bromley of the University of Southampton for all the trouble he took in reading a very rough draft of this book. Had I been competent, or had I had the leisure to carry out all his suggested improvements, the result would have been infinitely better. As it is, I hope this book will serve to introduce students and general readers to the history of the unification of modern Greece. I have tried to do for modern Greece what others have done for modern Italy—to tell the story of how unification was achieved. My terminal dates are far apart: a glance at the table of contents will show that the Greek unification took over a century to achieve.

Note: Throughout this book, except where for obvious reasons or inadvertence I have compromised, I have used a phonetic spelling of Greek proper names and technical terms, using the letter 'i' as it is pronounced in French.

DOUGLAS DAKIN

Birkbeck College, London
August 1971

Contents

Appendices

Maps

CHAPTER 1

The Antecedents of Modern Greece

I. The Distribution of the Greek People under Turkish Rule

The Greeks of present-day Greece occupy some 50,000 square miles and number nearly 9 million. Half of them depend for their livelihood on the sea or on urban occupations. The rest of them get their living from the mountains, which form the greater part of Greece, or from the cultivable soil which constitutes only about a quarter of the total area. Their country is a relatively compact state: although innumerable islands (some of them at great distances from the mainland) and great mountain-ranges make for a somewhat scattered population, the Greek nation is remarkably homogeneous, the ethnic and linguistic minorities being very small.

One hundred and fifty years ago the picture was very different. There was no Greek national state. The Greeks (if we here define them as Orthodox Christians speaking Greek as their mother-tongue) were not then nearly so numerous; they were spread unevenly over the Ottoman empire; and in some regions they were outnumbered by other peoples—by Slavs, Albanians, Jews, Armenians, and the various kinds of Turks. Only in the Peloponnese, in continental Greece as far as the line Jannina–Thessaloniki, and in most of the islands were they in a clear majority. In these regions, however, they did not exceed 2 million. In Macedonia, except in the more southerly coastal plains, they were to be found in strength chiefly in the townships which they shared with the Turks and other peoples, or in certain villages scattered among the Slav-speaking villages and the Moslem communities. In Thrace they were again in strength in the towns and they enjoyed a predominance in the coastal areas. In Constantinople (in the province and the city) they numbered 300,000 in a total population of 880,000. Again in strength in the towns on the Black Sea, they were to be found in large settlements in Asia Minor, their total number here being about 1,800,000. They formed substantial colonies in the Danubian Principalities, in Russia, in Bulgaria, in Egypt, Palestine, and North Africa, but, wherever they were, relatively few of them lived more than fifty miles from the sea. Most of them dwelt, as they had always dwelt, on the coastal plains which were fragmented by high mountain-ranges. But although these mountain-ranges denied them land communications, the sea kept these mainland Greek communities in touch with one another and with those on the islands.

II. The Continuity of Greek History

The antecedents of the modern Greek nation, as indeed of all nations, are diverse. First of all Greece is an heir to the European Enlightenment and a residuary legatee to the economic development of seventeenth-, eighteenth-, and nineteenth-century Europe. Moreover, like other European nations, she is an heir to the classical world, both Greek and Roman. It is here, obviously, that she has a special position. Not only do her sons occupy much of the soil of classical Greece, but they have in some profusion the visible remains of classical civilisation around them. Certainly they owe the discovery and the preservation of these remains in some measure to scholars and archaeologists of other nations, who, along with the travellers of the eighteenth and nineteenth centuries, imparted to them a clearer picture of their classical ancestors. To some extent therefore the consciousness of the modern Greek of his classical ancestry is a product of Western scholarship. That consciousness, already evident when the Greeks prepared and fought their first War of Independence in 1821–33, became more pronounced when they established a small nation-state. As was only natural, they began to devote themselves to the study of ancient Greece and introduced classical studies into their educational system. For them the heroes of the ancient Greek world became the heroes of their nation, and they began to stress their classical ancestry. In doing this they failed perhaps to see their diverse antecedents in true perspective—a failure which is common enough in all the nineteenth-century nations, all of whom tended to select from the past just those facts which fitted preconceived ideas. This is not to say, however, that there is no continuity in Greek history. On the contrary, there is a continuity of race, language, and culture.

Despite the Roman conquest of the ancient Greek world, the Greek-speaking population survived. To a remarkable degree they imposed their culture on the occupying forces; and although they came to call themselves Romans, they remained unmistakably Greek. So important were the Greek people, so important was their homeland, in respect of wealth, population, and geographical position, that in A.D. 330 the Emperor Constantine made Byzantium the capital of the Empire. Except for certain regions where the legionaries from the West were settled in great numbers, here in the East the Greek language predominated and it more than held its own in those regions where the newcomers from the West married Greek women. That same language became the language of the Christian Church as it spread throughout the eastern portion of the Empire. It was in Greek that St Paul, a hellenised Jew, preached to the Philippians, the Ephesians, the Thessalonians, and the Corinthians. It was Greek in a popular form which was the language of the Gospels.

The question, however, whether the Greek popular language survived the Slav invasions of the eastern portions of the Empire has given rise to much dispute, especially among scholars outside Greece. According to Fallmerayer, whose findings were published in 1830 and 1836,[1] the Slavs who overran Greece in the sixth and seventh centuries so changed the ethnic character of the country that not a drop of pure Hellenic blood was left. Fallmerayer went on to say that for a time the Greek language disappeared in that region entirely and that, when it reappeared, its presence was to be accounted for by the activities of the Byzantine Church.

Now it is generally accepted that the Slav invasions (which came in the seventh and eighth rather than in the sixth and seventh centuries) had considerable effect: there was certainly a great reduction in the old Greek stock and there was much intermingling of the populations. But the theory that the Greek language disappeared and was later reintroduced by the Church requires the assumption of an absurdity—that the Greek Church had at its disposal an elaborate organisation of schools and a veritable army of teachers for teaching the Greek language to the Slavs. The enormity of this absurdity becomes apparent when one realises that the twentieth-century Greek state made very little headway in its attempts to substitute the Greek for the Slav language among relatively small Slav minorities in northern Greece. At the best it could merely establish Greek as a 'second' language in the schools. In the home the children continued to speak their mother-tongue. It is surely significant, too, that when the Greek missionaries Method and Cyril converted to Christianity the Slavs of Macedonia in the second half of the ninth century, they made no attempt to use the Greek language as the medium of instruction: instead they preached to the multitude in the Slavonic tongue, into which, using a modified Greek alphabet, they translated the liturgy. In any case, even if the Byzantine Church had been able to teach Greek to the Slav populations, the Greek it would have taught would have been a learned language, considerably different from the language that the inhabitants of the Morea and central Greece were speaking during the sixteenth, seventeenth, and eighteenth centuries. It follows then that there must have been an unbroken tradition of the Greek language. It follows also that the linguistic hellenisation of the Slavs (and the same is true of the hellenisation of the Albanians who entered Greece in the fourteenth century) must have come about from the intermarriage of the newcomers with an existing Greek-speaking population. It follows again

---

[1] J. P. Fallmerayer, *Geschichte der Halbinsel Morea wahrend des Mittelalters*, 2 vols., Stuttgart and Tübingen, 1830, 1836.

that the surviving Greek-speaking population must have been considerable. In support of this last contention there exists important evidence
which, though not unchallenged, must certainly outweigh the more dubious
exaggerations of chroniclers with no first-hand knowledge of the regions
concerned. There is evidence that in the eighth century thirty-two Greek
bishops officiated in the Morea. There is evidence also that in Korinth, a
region assumed to have been completely overrun by Slavs, the Greek
metropolitan bishopric survived; that at the close of the sixth century two
of the metropolitan bishops of Korinth were in correspondence with Pope
Gregory the Great; and that in A.D. 680 and again in 843, the Greek metropolitan bishop of Korinth attended oecumenical councils.[2]

Further evidence of the survival of the Greeks in considerable numbers
during the period of the Slav invasions is provided by the study of folklore.
Greek folklore contains various beliefs and practices which are known to
date from the pre-Christian era. These, which pertain to the pagan deities,
the Church failed to eradicate: it therefore had to tolerate them and
assimilate them. It is inconceivable that these beliefs and practices, having
disappeared, could after a lapse of time have been imparted to the Slavs,
who had their own folklore which, though containing kinds of belief to be
found in Greek and in other folklores, is readily distinguishable from the
folklore which is unmistakably Greek.

The Greek people with their language and their folklore survived not
only in the Peloponnese and central Greece, but also in a multiplicity of
eastern Mediterranean islands, in southern Macedonia, in the coastal regions
of Thrace, and in many parts of Asia Minor. In Asia Minor (and the same is
true of the islands) there was less mingling with other peoples. Although
foreigners in great numbers entered the Byzantine service and mixed with
the Greek aristocracy, and although Slavs and Armenians were settled in
that region, the mingling of the lower orders of the Greek population with
other peoples came relatively late and under different circumstances. It
came in the period following the Turkish conquests. Moreover, Greeks in
substantial numbers were islamised. These Greek converts (though some of
them continued to use the Greek tongue) were, on account of their new
religion, lost to the Greek nation.

III. The Byzantine Inheritance

Despite their links with classical times, the modern Greeks of the early
nineteenth century stood a long way from their forebears. Not only had the
racial stock undergone changes (especially outside Asia Minor and mountain fastnesses on the mainland), but the language, as spoken by the masses,
had been mutated in pronunciation, in vocabulary, and in syntax, there

---

[2] For recent surveys of the evidence, see the excellent articles, 'Byzantium and Greece'
by George Arnakis, and 'Observations on the History of Greece during the early Middle
Ages' by Peter Charanis, in *Balkan Studies*, vol. 4 (1963) and vol. 11 (1970).

being many loan words, not to mention numerous place-names, from the Slavonic and Albanian tongues. The popular language had become much simpler. Much closer to the written language of ancient Greece was the language of the Church and of the Byzantine administration. It was in this language that Byzantine scholars had kept alive the thought of classical Greece. True, to this thought most churchmen were fundamentally antagonistic, for it was hardly to be expected that God's chosen people occupying God's earthly kingdom could regard themselves as children of the gods of the ancient world. But although the mainstream of Byzantine thought was hostile to Hellenism, nevertheless the Hellenism of the ancient world was known to the theologians and the intelligentsia of the Byzantine age, and the very fact that churchmen, especially towards the end of the Byzantine period, went out of their way to denounce it, is proof that there were many among them who were drawing upon the store of classical literature of which the Church was the custodian. To that store those who cared to browse therein had the keys—the Greek language and a training in thought which, though Hellenistic rather than Hellenic, enabled those so trained to divine the wisdom and the artistic merits of the ancients. Indeed, from the days of Origen (d. 255), right through the Byzantine ages to the time of the Komnini and the Paleologi, there were frequent renaissances of classical ideas.

The revival of the old ideas became more prominent during the period of the schism between East and West (eleventh, twelfth, and thirteenth centuries) and during the age of the Turkish invasion (fourteenth and fifteenth centuries). Schism and invasion meant that the universality of the Empire was being destroyed in both its aspects—the spiritual and the temporal. To fit this fact new theories were developed; and many Byzantines began to see themselves not as heirs to the Romano-Hellenistic traditions of the West but as the successors of ancient Hellas. Foremost among them was Psellus (eleventh century) who based his philosophy on what he thought to be the ideas of Plato; and so widespread did his Neoplatonism become that three centuries later the holy synod, the citadel of the old traditions, anathematised those who subscribed to that philosophy. But this attempt to put back the clock was without effect. Early next century the new ideas became firmly entrenched in a more elaborate form, the Neoplatonist Pletho advocating the establishment of an Hellenic state based on the Peloponnese, continental Greece, and the nearby islands—an area considered to be the cradle of the Hellenic race and culture. These new ideas were reinforced by intellectual exchanges between East and West. In the West, during the twelfth and thirteenth centuries, Latin translations made chiefly from the Arabic versions of ancient Greek manuscripts had led to the adoption of Aristotelian philosophy, above all in the universities of Bologna and Padua. In the next century Italian scholars visited the East, while Byzantine teachers went to Italy, taking Greek manuscripts with them. After the fall of Constantinople in 1453 the flow of these manuscripts increased, and the Italians, having ransacked their own classical sites for the remains of antiquity, began to search the fruitful soil of Greece. The result of all this was the idealisation of classical Greece, though not necessarily an understanding of it, for the humanists' picture of ancient Hellas was much distorted by their study of Roman literature.

After the fall of Constantinople it was to the University of Padua that Greek scholars went. This university, which was Venetian and outside Papal control, welcomed students of Orthodox faith. From it the Neo-aristotelian philosophy flowed into Greece; from it came the teachers who staffed the patriarchal academy of Constantinople, refounded early in the sixteenth century. Here the great Aristotelian scholar Theofilos Koridalefs taught from 1624 to 1641 and from here later scholars went out to teach in academies founded in Epiros, Macedonia, Patmos, Athos, and Chios. It was this same academy which was to provide the education of the fanariots, those wealthy Greeks who gathered in the *fanar*, the Patriarch's quarter in Constantinople, and who were to provide administrative personnel for the Patriarchate and even for the Ottoman empire.

Although many Greeks had become, through the intellectual developments within the Byzantine Church, the heirs of classical Greece, yet the Church itself remained a stronghold of the Byzantine tradition. It looked upon the schism between East and West as the heresy of the West, and it regarded the Crusaders, who in 1204 had sacked Constantinople, as barbarians. The advance of the Turks it regarded as divine punishment for the sins of God's chosen people. Not until those sins had been purged would God relent and revive the pristine glories and universality of the Roman Christian empire in both its aspects—the temporal and the spiritual. Only through the Church would the Greek nation find absolution: only through the Church would the Holy City, the Emperor, and the Empire be restored. For this role the Church was well fitted. It possessed its own organisation and system of government, which extended into the temporal sphere. It had never been a mere department of the state. It had indeed benefited from the protection afforded by the secular power; it had benefited too, artistically and culturally, from the great wealth which derived directly and indirectly from the powerful Byzantine administration, but it had nonetheless its own existence: it had enjoyed at times an influence outside the range of Byzantine political power (for example in Russia); it had survived in regions where the writ of Byzantium had failed to run; it had survived the Latin conquest of Constantinople in 1204 and the partition of the Byzantine territories among the Frankish feudatories; and above all it had survived the Turkish conquest of Constantinople. Throughout the period of the Ottoman occupation it was to preserve the Byzantine heritage; and in doing this it was to preserve all that Byzantium had inherited from the ancient world. It may therefore be said that the modern Greeks stood in two relationships to ancient Greece. They were heirs of a renaissance which had given rise to a consciousness of their descent from the ancient Greeks— a renaissance which would not have been possible had there not been a continuity of language and in a restricted sense a continuity of race. They were heirs too of Byzantine Greece with its own tangled roots in the Hellenistic world, which in turn had origins in classical Greece. To Byzantine Greece the modern Greeks were undoubtedly closer than to ancient Greece, for Byzantine Greece, owing to the continuity of the Church, constituted the living past. As time went on, however, the revived memory of the classical age, reinforced by the ideas of the European Enlightenment, came to constitute, though by no means the exclusive, yet the stronger force in the history of modern Greece.

Between the two traditions, the Byzantine and the neo-classical, there was always a potential conflict—not only in the minds of most individual Greeks but also between groups of Greeks, the one group tending to stress the Byzantine tradition, the other the compound of classical tradition and Western ideas. But when we speak of the Byzantine tradition we must have in mind its cultural and ecclesiastical aspects rather than its political, for among the Greeks it was the cultural and ecclesiastical that survived. The political tradition passed into the keeping of the Ottoman Turks, who, in allowing the Greek Church to retain its power and privileges, consciously endeavoured to make their empire a successor to Byzantium. Hence under Turkish rule the Church found solace and protection and, although churchmen dreamt that one day a Greek ruler might return to Constantinople, in the realm of practical politics the hierarchy were mainly concerned with the task of preserving the identity of their Church and of ministering to the Christian populations. In other words, the Church endeavoured to preserve its oecumenical character and it continued to do so in early modern times. It was here that the conflict between modern Hellenism and Byzantinism arose. Whereas Hellenism stressed the unity of those speaking Greek (of those considered to be the descendants of the ancient Greeks), the Patriarchate usually emphasised the unity of all Christians in the Ottoman empire, including those who spoke Slav, Turkish, or some other tongue. But this conflict, whether it existed in the minds of individuals or as a tension between political groups, was not a struggle between mutually exclusive ideas: submerged in the Hellenism of Athens was the conviction that the Church had preserved the nation in Turkish times, while in patriarchal circles, much as it might be thought expedient that the Church should accommodate itself to the Turkish state, there developed a strong Hellenic feeling—a feeling that among God's chosen people the 'Greeks' enjoyed the place of honour. Hence instead of emphasising the conflict between Athens and Constantinople, one ought to think in terms of two forms of Hellenism, national Hellenism and ecclesiastical Hellenism, both with broadly common if somewhat ill-defined aspirations, but not necessarily in agreement on the measures of the hour. In what we call the 'Great Idea' (the *megali idhea*), the *Graecia irredenta*, there was always a lack of precision. The Greeks as a whole never seemed certain whether they should simply add acre to acre in expanding aggressively the national state, or whether they should adopt a longer-term policy of preserving and strengthening the Greek elements within the empire, so that on the collapse of Ottoman authority they themselves could substitute their own. But although all Greeks came to look upon the acquisition of Constantinople as the greatest prize of Hellenism and although certain Greeks elevated the *megali idhea* into a fantastic extravagance, there was never, in modern times, any serious aim to restore a Byzantine empire with its autocratic political tradition. Most modern Greeks merely envisaged a Greek state covering those territories where there were strong centres of Hellenism, including those regions where the Slav-speaking populations might be large, it being assumed that these would be content to remain within the patriarchal fold, to recognise the superiority of Greek culture, and even to aspire (as indeed they often did) to a Greek education and regard themselves as Greeks. The Greeks, though claiming a racial continuity with ancient Greece, never stressed race as the basis of nationality. Their conception of nationality, like that of most nineteenth-century nationalists, was Mazzinian: they stressed the elements of language, common history, and individual consciousness. Anyone who thought and called himself a Greek was, in general estimation, a Hellene.[3] The shape of his nose, the colour of hair, the measurement of skull were all irrelevances. What mattered was his soul, his mind, the way of thinking. The result was that Greek-speaking Albanians, Vlachs, Romanians, and Slavs were all eligible to become true Hellenes and many of them, particularly Albanians and Vlachs, figure prominently in the annals of Greek patriotism.

When during the course of the nineteenth century the non-Greek-speaking Balkan people discovered that they had their own culture and history, when moreover they began to strive for nationhood, the nationalists of Athens were compelled to restate the *megali idhea* in less extravagant terms; and the Patriarchate, too, had constantly to readjust itself to the changing Balkan scene. For the Patriarchate this process of adaptation was perhaps less difficult than for the Greek national state. There were at least historical precedents. In the Eastern Church, where the uniformity of doctrine had always been pronounced, administrative autonomy had been

[3] The word 'Hellene', however, was not fashionable in the late eighteenth and early nineteenth centuries, nor, for that matter, was the word 'Greek'. The early modern Greeks continued to call themselves 'Romans' and to designate their language 'Romaika'. In the eighteenth century the word 'Hellenes' in the popular language denoted a mythical people of great stature and superhuman strength who were thought to have lived in Greece in remote ages. When the word came into general use at the time of the War of Independence it denoted only the fighting men. The great leader Kolokotronis (see below, pp. 23–5) invariably addressed his men as 'Hellenes', and so did other leaders. Only later did they learn from scholars of the exploits of the ancient Greeks and to regard all Greeks as descendants of the Hellenes of ancient Hellas.

conceded to many regions. Separate patriarchates had been created at Antioch, Jerusalem, and Alexandria; the Russian Church had become independent in 1589; and earlier still there had been a Bulgarian patriarchate at Trnovo and a Serbian patriarchate at Pech. Over these Churches the Patriarch of Constantinople had no control, but he was recognised as a *primus inter pares*, and it was from Constantinople that the holy oil for the anointing of bishops was obtained. Hence when the Balkan nationalists demanded separate Churches, there was no fundamental reason why further ecclesiastical autonomies should not be granted. The Patriarch of Constantinople might well believe that autonomies were quite unnecessary and might therefore resist the demand for them, but in making concessions, he could console himself that the universality of the faith was unchallenged, and he and those around him could continue to dream that one day the Holy City would be Greek and that a Greek empire would be founded on the ruins of the Ottoman state.

IV. The Turkish Inheritance

The Ottoman Turks, who had helped the Greek emperors to regain Constantinople from the Latins in 1261, in the following century began their piecemeal conquest of the Byzantine Empire. In 1326 they overran Bithynia. Called in by the emperors to fight the Serbs, by 1354 they had established themselves on the European shore of the Dardanelles. In 1360 they captured Adrianople, which they made their capital. By 1380 they occupied Macedonia, though the city of Thessaloniki held out until 1430. In 1389 they defeated the Serbs, Bulgars, Vlachs, and Albanians at Kossovo. In 1393 they overran Thessaly. In 1430 they captured Jannina. In 1453 they seized Constantinople. Shortly afterwards (1456–57) they took the islands of Limnos, Imvros, Samothraki, and Thasos. Between 1456 and 1460 they established themselves in the Duchy of Athens. By 1461 they were in occupation of the Peloponnese, except for certain coastal areas held by the Venetians. In 1462 they took Lesvos and in 1470 they overran Evia (Euboea). In 1479 they seized the Ionian Islands, which, however, later passed to Venice.[4] Almost a century was to elapse before Naxos, Chios (1566), and Cyprus (1571) succumbed. Crete held out till 1669 and Tinos until 1715.

During all the period of their advance, the Turks had to contend with attacks from Venetians, Hungarians, Poles, and Persians. In 1698 they suffered defeat at the hands of the Austrians, Russians, and Venetians; and at the ensuing peace of Karlowitz they surrendered the Peloponnese to the Venetians and Azov on the Black Sea to the Russians. The Venetian victory, however, was short-lived: in 1715 the Turks invaded the Peloponnese, to which in 1718, by the treaty of Passarowitz, Venice relinquished her

[4] Zante in 1482, Kefalonia and Ithaka in 1500, and Santa Maura (Lefkas) in 1682.

claim. As for the inhabitants, they preferred Turkish to Venetian rule. Taxes were lighter; life was in many ways freer; and the relatively tolerant infidel was more welcome than the hated Roman Catholic.

Turkish rule did not deprive the Greeks entirely of their freedom. Throughout the period of conquest, the Turks sought the support of the Orthodox Christians in their struggles against the Latin West. They saw that, to repopulate Constantinople, they must call back the Christians who had fled to other regions. They realised, moreover, that the Christian peasantry and traders were the economic mainstay of many of the provinces they had conquered. These provinces they took over as going concerns. In them they acquired the landed estates and they established control of the cities. But they were never numerous enough to colonise all their extensive territories. Always out to islamise their empire as far as possible and being free from racial prejudice, they attempted to increase their scanty stock from the Christian populations. They therefore welcomed conversions, which were numerous enough, but they did not go out of their way to promote them: indeed the *Sheriat*, the Holy Law of Islam, forbade forcible measures; and most conversions came about from the activities of the *Bektashis*, one of the orders of dervishes, who themselves were heretics in the eyes of true Moslems. These *Bektashis* gave Christ a place of honour among their prophets; and, far from denying wine to their followers, they welcomed its consumption as a means of promoting religious fervour. They converted thousands in Asia Minor, in Albania, and in the Slav regions. It was, however, not unusual for these converts to retain at first some connection with their Christian faith. But having gone so far they frequently went the whole way and became strict Moslems. There was every incentive to do so. Although the Turks might tolerate the Christians, they did not regard them as full citizens or subjects. The law forbade them to carry arms; to dress like the Turk; and to ride a horse. The Christian infidel, who under Moslem law in theory had only the choice of conversion or death, must in practice pay a tax, the *haratch* (poll tax), for the privilege of living. His womenfolk were subject to the *droit du seigneur*. His property could be seized and his earnings, whether from land, commerce, or a profession, were subject to tithes and other taxes. It is not surprising therefore that many Christians should have chosen to become Turks. Their greatest incentive was the desire to avoid the tribute of Christian children (the *devshirme*), from whom the Sultans built up the corps of janissaries, a military brotherhood founded in the early fourteenth century. From this same source pupils were recruited for the Palace School, where they were trained for higher administrative office. Every four years officials visited each village and levied one in five of the boys between the ages of six and nine. It was not unusual for Turkish parents to 'sell' their own children to the Greeks so that these could enter the corps of janissaries or the Palace School; while it was not uncommon for Greek parents to mutilate their sons to save them from being carried off. Gradually the *devshirme* fell into disuse, the last known levy being at Naousa in 1705. By that time the janissaries, who had been permitted to marry, had become an hereditary, privileged, and seditious military caste.

Of the conversions to Islam no reliable statistical information is available.[5] That they were considerable, however, there is no doubt. Western Anatolia, which in the twelfth and early thirteenth centuries was entirely Greek, became during the two centuries 1260–1460 almost entirely Turk. In Cyprus and Crete Turks of Greek origin came to form substantial minorities. In Macedonia, Thessaly, and western Thrace Moslems became a majority, though it is not clear whether conversion or colonisation was the predominant cause. At all events, throughout the earlier period of the Turkish conquests the Christian population lost ground to Islam. That is why Greek and Slav blood flowed in the veins of many Turks.[6] That is why, too, by the end of the seventeenth century the Greek population was relatively sparse. From that time onwards conversions to Islam were rare. But if the Greeks did not increase appreciably and if in some regions they continued to dwindle, it was because large numbers emigrated. The movement to Russia gained momentum at the time of Peter the Great and continued throughout the eighteenth century. In Russia, Greeks were able to engage in commerce and to enter the army, the Church, and the professions. But Russia was not the only promised land: many Greeks went to Austria,[7] the Netherlands, Italy, France, England, and even to India.

But for the energy of the Greek Church (and the same is true of the Latin Church in western regions of the empire) the Christian population would have been reduced to an insignificant minority, or, at best, the whole of the Balkans would have become somewhat similar to parts of Albania or Bosnia where the Moslems predominated. Enjoying, however, a privileged position, the Greek clergy were able to keep within limits the loss of the Christian population to Islam—an achievement made possible by the extensive powers vested in the Greek Patriarch. To him the Turks gave precedence over the other patriarchs (those of Jerusalem, Antioch, and Alexandria) and authority over the Christian Slavs, thus making the Greek Patriarchate more truly oecumenical than it had been in the later Byzantine centuries. As early as 1394 the Bulgarian patriarchate of Trnovo was abolished and the dioceses brought under control of the Greek Patriarch, Gennadios Scholarios. In 1624 the metropolitan bishopric of Moldavia was subjected to the Patriarchate. In 1766 and 1767 the patriarchate of Pech and the archbishopric of

[5] It has been estimated that two-thirds of the Albanians left the Eastern Church. In an endeavour to prevent further losses and to compete with the Roman Catholics in reclaiming souls from Islam, during the eighteenth century the Patriarchate established in Albania some 200 schools.

[6] Of forty-nine grand viziers between 1453 and 1623 eleven were Albanians, eleven were Slavs, and six were Greeks, there being only five of pure Turkish origin.

[7] Out of some 120 banks and commercial houses in Vienna at the end of the eighteenth century about ninety were Greek.

Ochrid lost their independence. The result was that by the end of the eighteenth century the Greek Patriarch was the spiritual ruler of some 13 million Christians—of approximately one-quarter of the inhabitants of the Ottoman empire. To describe him, however, as the spiritual ruler is to understate his powers. He was in a large degree also a temporal ruler. He was the Ethnarch (*Millet-Bashi*), the leader of the eminent Roman nation. He was styled lord and despot of the Christians. He thus inherited the title of the emperors and with it he inherited also their emblem, the two-headed eagle, which he displayed upon his mitre. He was allowed to have his own imperial guard. Provided he paid the *peskesh* (a composition which increased as each successive Patriarch took office) he was exempt from taxation and was permitted to recoup himself by mulcting his Christian subjects.

This toleration of the Greek Church and the bestowal of powers upon it derived from the very nature of the East. In pre-Christian times rights of life, property, and worship had been recognised in return for economic, fiscal, and military services; and Constantine, in favouring the Christians, had followed that tradition—the same tradition that Mohammed the Conqueror was to follow in 1453. But the Ottomans, even more than their predecessors, were disposed to tolerate and to grant rights to their subject peoples. Since as Moslems they did not distinguish between the religious and secular authorities, they regarded their subject populations as nations or *millets*, and they looked upon the clergy of these populations as state officials. The Greek bishop in his judicial capacity held a position analogous to that of the *kadi*, or Moslem judge, particularly where marriage, divorce, and wills were concerned. In time, however, the Greek clergy came to exercise a judicial authority in excess of that which the Turkish system had at first allowed them. Christians usually preferred to submit their differences to the arbitration of their priests rather than go to the Turkish courts. Hence almost every conceivable kind of case was dealt with by the clergy, and the law they applied was Roman Law, which they learned from the *Exavivlos*[8] of 1345 or the *Nomocanon* of 1561. This law was by no means static. Under the Turks, as indeed under the Byzantines, the Church had extensive legislative powers and the flow of canonical edicts increased steadily in the Ottoman period. What is more, because of their sanctions (excommunication and aphorism), these edicts and the laws of the Church in general managed (though not in all cases) to hold their own with the customary law which had grown up in Turkish times and which in some regions had been codified.

Conflicts between the church law on the one hand and customary and Turkish law on the other were common in matters of family conduct and inheritance. The Church, for instance, made repeated but unsuccessful

---

[8] In 1741 the *Exavivlos* was translated into a simpler language and was published in Venice. Eight editions appeared in the next ninety years.

efforts to abolish the *trachoma* or the pre-marital dotation paid by the parents of a bride to the future husband of their own choosing, a practice which became more common with the increased affluence of the *rayahs*.[9] It was much the same with the *trimiria* or the disposal of the property of a deceased child who had inherited from a deceased parent, of which the Church claimed a share.

Where, however, the inheritance of land and goods generally was concerned, the Church, on the whole, made more headway. According to Turkish law, where there were no direct inheritors, all property passed to the Ottoman state, less any portion[10] bequeathed to the Church. To defeat this law, a *rayah* would donate in his lifetime all his property to the Church, in return for a usufruct (or use of the property) which could be bequeathed according to church law. The result was that much land passed out of the cognisance of the Turkish courts into that of the ecclesiastical tribunals, only, however, to pass in some regions under the jurisdiction of the communal courts applying customary laws.

Not infrequently the Church, in a matter where the Turks had granted it complete control, namely marriage, found that the faithful had recourse to Ottoman law. Marriage by *kepinion* (a temporary marriage performed by the *kadi*, usually between a Moslem and a Christian) became more and more common and continued into the nineteenth century in the unliberated regions. This practice was given a degree of recognition in the customary codes and was made legal by the first code of the Greek state in 1823. Marriage by *kepinion* had a great many advantages. Those whom the Church would not divorce could contract a new temporary marriage, arrange for alimony to be paid, and take advantage of certain rights of bequeathal which the Turkish law allowed.

The customary law with which the ecclesiastical law often came into conflict was the outcome of the arrangements by which the Turks left considerable powers of self-government to their subject peoples. Eventually the principal Greek lands had been divided into six major *pashaliks* or provinces—Morea (Peloponnese), Negropont (Euboea and the mainland opposite), southern Albania (including western Greece), Selanik (Thessaloniki and most of Macedonia), Crete, and the Aegean Islands (which were placed under the Kaptan pasha, the chief of the navy).[11] Each pasha appointed representatives in the districts into which his *pashalik* was divided. The whole system was designed primarily to maintain a military occupation, to collect taxes, and to provide a judicial administration, not only for the

---

[9] Originally this term was applied sometimes to the Sultan's Moslem subjects but more usually to his Christian peoples, denoting not so much the Sultan's cattle as the flock of which he was the good shepherd. By usage the term came to denote the downtrodden subject peoples.

[10] This portion was limited to one-third.

[11] Certain smaller areas were administered by governors directly responsible to Constantinople.

Sultan's Moslem subjects but also for the non-Moslems in so far as they were amenable to Turkish law.

The extent to which non-Moslems came under Turkish law and administration varied enormously from place to place. The islands Idra, Spetzes, Mikonos, Poros, the Dodekanese, Thira, and parts of Crete enjoyed almost complete autonomy, and so too did Zagorochoria and the Kefalochoria in western Greece, Meleniko in Macedonia, Smyrna and Aivali in Asia Minor, Souli in Epiros, and the Peloponnese, where towns like Kalamata and Argos were completely Greek and for the most part governed by Greeks, and where the mountain province of Mani was left to the rivalries of the families of Mavromichalis and Tzanetakis. Most of these regions had their own customary codes which regulated a vast field of human relationships and recognised practices in defiance of both the Orthodox Church and the Ottoman state. One such practice was that of fraternisation (*adelfopiia*), the creation of a fraternal bond by the performance of sacred rights, the object of which was the protection and promotion of individual and family interests. Needless to say, the practice facilitated conspiracy: it was used by Rigas Velestinlis, by the *Filiki Eteria*, and by parties formed in the first War of Independence. Despite its denunciation by the Church, its extension continued, as did a whole range of customary practices, some of great antiquity.

The local liberties of the Greeks and the precise way they were exercised have never been fully studied; but we know, in a general way, that a highly organised system of Greek local government existed side by side with the Turkish administration even in those regions where that administration was much in evidence. Throughout the Peloponnese the Greeks raised their own taxes to meet the demands of the Turkish treasury and to provide for the needs of local expenditure. Each large village or group of hamlets formed a community (*kinotis*). Groups of villages constituted districts (*eparchia*), the heads of which (the elders, known variously as *dimogerontes*, *proesti*, *prokriti*, *kodza bashis*) elected a part of the senate (*gerousia*) of the Morea, a body which included the higher clergy. This body advised the Turkish pasha and his officials: no additional taxation was levied without its approval. For the Turks this approval was important: in the Morea they were outnumbered by ten to one (approximately 400,000 to 40,000), and their rule depended on the upper-class Greeks. These wealthy Greeks, known as primates, held about 350,000 acres of land out of a total of just over one million. Possessing capital, stores, warehouses, and pack animals, they furnished most of the tax-farmers, and, as taxes were levied in kind, they were usually merchants as well as landowners. They lived like pashas; they had their own secretaries, priests, doctors, servants, tenants, and armed retainers, not to mention bands of brigands (*kapi*) whom they took into their pay. They were hardly distinguishable from the Turks: the only difference was that they went, not to the mosque, but to the church. Similar primates were to be found in Chios, which island paid to the treasury of the Validé Sultan (the Sultan's mother) a fixed annual sum; in Sfakia (in the south of Crete); and indeed in almost all the regions where Greeks were in strength. In certain districts these primates had large estates; in the mountain areas they possessed large flocks; and in the islands they owned the ships. Such Greeks of the lower orders who were not working on the Turkish and church estates or were not in professions, trade, or fishing, the primates engaged as share-croppers, labourers, shepherds, or as crews.

Not only did the wealthy Greeks enjoy self-government and local influence, but they had office in the central institutions of the empire. The Patriarch himself was virtually a minister of the interior for Christian affairs; and from the patriarchal quarter, the *fanar*, the Turks, as we have seen, recruited for their government departments educated Greeks who knew Western languages. From these fanariots were drawn the chief dragoman (interpreter) of the Porte (council of ministers)—a private secretary to the grand vizier and virtually foreign secretary for European affairs —and the dragoman of the fleet, who as secretary to the Kaptan pasha was virtually the governor of the islands, it being his responsibility to man the fleet, the crews of which, as distinct from the gunners, were usually Greek. From this same source—the *fanar*—were also drawn the two princes (hospodars) of Moldavia and Wallachia, who from the early eighteenth century were invariably Greeks. These (like the Patriarch) purchased their office. In other words they paid the tax revenue in advance. When they left to take up their appointments in the Principalities (where their first concern was to recoup themselves for their advances, to pay the high interest on sums they had borrowed, and to make a profit), they were accompanied by swarms of Greek officials. In these Danubian provinces the Greek was the Turk. His regime was hated by the natives, except by those who could profit from it or find pleasure in the court circles of Jassy and Bucharest, both of which towns contained Greek colonies and were centres of Greek culture. Outside these towns Greek culture had but little hold. The natives had their own language, their own traditions, and they much preferred their customary codes to Turkish and patriarchal law.

Besides depending upon Greek administrators drawn from the *fanar*, the Turks employed Greek *vekilidhes* (originally hostages) to report upon the conduct of the local Turks. Two such officials represented the Morea. They had direct access to the central government. Not infrequently they obtained the removal of a pasha and they often secured the redress of local grievances. The Sultan welcomed their reports. In his remoteness he was solicitous of the welfare of all his Christian subjects; but if, as so often, he failed to check misgovernment, it was because he had to rule a vast polyglot, multiracial, multi-religious empire by means of what had once been a sheer military machine and of local arrangements he had been powerless to supersede. Power and revenue in the extremities of the empire had passed into other hands. Morocco, Algeria, Tunis, Egypt, Syria, Mesopotamia, Arabia were all virtually independent. Hungary, Bukovina, and Transylvania had been lost to Austria. Territory on the Black Sea had been lost to Russia, who at the treaty of Kutchuk Kainardji in 1774 had acquired a form of protectorate over Wallachia and Moldavia. By the end of the eighteenth century the over-mighty vassal Ali Pasha had extended his power over Albania and parts of Macedonia and Greece, while another pasha, Pasvanoglou, held sway in and around the sanjak of Sofia.

V. Greece at the End of the Eighteenth Century

As a result of the treaty of Karlowitz, which granted to Turkish subjects trading rights in the Habsburg dominions; as a result moreover of the decline of Venice and Genoa and of Russian expansion on the Black Sea, the increasing trade of the Turkish empire became more and more concentrated in the hands of the Greeks, who had acquired in 1779 the privilege of flying the Russian flag and the protection of Russian consuls. So well based indeed and so far-flung had Greek trade become that, when during the revolutionary wars the British navy swept the French from the eastern Mediterranean, the Greeks moved into the first place as traders in the Levant. By 1813 they had at least 615 ships (some of the best American design) totalling 153,580 tons—ships which provided employment for some 17,500 sailors.

Along the trade-routes Western ideas had for long flowed into Greece, but by the late eighteenth century those routes had become broader and the ideas themselves had undergone change. The result was that the whole range of thought of the European Enlightenment flowed into the Levant. This thought, because of its predominantly utilitarian character, easily found a place among the Greeks, who were at once practical and prone to theorising. The trickle of Greek students seeking professional training in the West became a veritable stream. In the Greek lands and colonies abroad new schools were founded and the old ones were transformed—much to the discomfort of the Orthodox Church which feared the impact of irreligious opinions. Traders and returning students brought to Greece countless books, some of which were Greek translations (printed in Venice and Vienna) of Western works, while the homeland Greeks, like the plagiarists of Europe, rehashed the prevailing ideas in what purported to be original compilations. All this time the European philhellenes, who had begun to visit Greece in the seventeenth century and who towards the end of the next century were certainly numerous, inspired the naturally curious Greek to ponder upon the glories of his distant past. On a lower level the novelties of thought were circulated in the seaport taverns by hosts of seamen and even in inland centres by muleteers and pedlars. When at length the ideas of the Enlightenment were transformed into a creed of political revolution, they found a receptive audience among almost all classes of the Ottoman Greeks. Masonic lodges were founded among the Greek communities in the last decade of the eighteenth century. Liberty, equality, and fraternity appealed perhaps more to the Greeks than to any other people. Always prone to wishful thinking, and putting their own constructions on events in Europe, they imagined that the hour of deliverance was at hand. They hailed Napoleon as a would-be saviour. The Maniat women, it is said, hung his portrait above their household shrines.

Hitherto the Greeks had looked towards Russia as their saviour. Portraits of Peter the Great and pamphlets describing his exploits had been distributed in great quantities in Greece. At the time of Catherine the Great (1762–96), Russian agents in Greece talked of the restoration of the Byzantine Empire. Among these was Papazolis, a Russian artillery officer who came originally from Siatista in Macedonia. It was he who, in collaboration with the Orlov brothers, drew up optimistic plans for an insurrection in the Morea in aid of the Russian military operations of 1769 against the Turks. A zealous Greek patriot rather than a reliable Russian agent, he had promised to Catherine the support of the Maniats, whose signatures on documents he had forged and whose chieftains had in fact let him know that they could not operate outside their own mountain fastnesses. Hence when in February 1770 Theodore Orlov (who had been to Venice to recruit from the Venetian underworld crews for his Russian squadrons) arrived off the Peloponnese with a few ships, he was able to raise only two small legions of 200 men at Kalamata and 1,200 at Mistras. The larger legion managed to advance to Tripolitsa and its success led other Greeks (chiefly Ionians) to move against Patras, Kalavrita, and Gastouni. But nothing came of these operations. The Turks, who had called in Albanian irregulars, in March defeated the Greek rebels, and prevented the chiefs of Macedonia and Olympos, whom Papazolis himself had raised, from going to their help. The arrival of Russian reinforcements under Alexander Orlov merely served to prolong the struggle for a short period for, although the Russians established a base at Navarino, the thousands of Greek refugees who rushed there to escape massacre by the Albanians found the gates of the castle closed against them. In May, Orlov and his troops sailed from Navarino; and despite the provision of an amnesty in the treaty of Kutchuk Kainardji (1774) which ended the Russo–Turkish War, the looting of the villages and monasteries continued until 1779. That year the Turks expelled the Albanians who had become a law unto themselves. They defeated them at Tripolitsa where Greek chieftains combined with the Turkish forces to rid the country of these despoilers. During the nine years of upheaval, altogether between 20,000 and 30,000 Greeks had perished or had left their homeland.

The Greek chieftains and their bands (the klefts), who the Russians fondly imagined would create diversions in the Peloponnese and elsewhere, were later to provide, along with the sea-captains of the islands, the military forces which fought the first War of Independence. They were also to provide an ideological contribution to the Greek revolution. Behind them they had a long tradition of hostility to Turkish rule and their exploits, whether fact or fiction, had been extolled in song and fable—in a popular literature which was a great spiritual force among the people. True, the klefts often mulcted the villages, but at least they were Greeks, and they reduced considerably the marauding activities of the Albanians who in the second half of the eighteenth century were expanding westwards.

The klefts (or *haiduks* as they were called in the Slav regions and *pandours* in the Danubian Principalities) were bands of outlaws who, in the early days of the Turkish occupation, took to the mountains. As was their wont, the Turks made the best of conditions that they could not alter, and often employed these outlaws as *armatoli* (guards) in outlying fortresses or frontier-passes (*dervenia*). *Armatoli* had existed in Byzantine and Venetian Greece, and the Turks, on taking over territories, came sooner or later to some arrangement with these local forces and increased them by recruiting brigands. By the sixteenth century *armatoli* were to be found in Bosnia, Albania, Bulgaria, Macedonia, and in the regions south of the Aliakmon river as far as the gulf of Korinth. There were no *armatoli* in the Peloponnese. Here there were only klefts and *kapi*. These *kapi* resembled the *armatoli*, in that they pursued brigands: they were employed, however, not by the Turks but by the Greek primates.

Drawn usually from the Christians in the Greek regions and from the Moslems elsewhere, the *armatoli* were entrusted with the task of keeping away the klefts from the villages and from the defiles through which Turkish officials, military detachments, flocks, and caravans had to pass. Between these *armatoli* and klefts there were frequently battles, especially in the regions where the *armatoli* were drawn from Ali Pasha's Albanians. Indeed, it was upon these Albanian *armatoli* that Ali Pasha's usurpation of Turkish authority largely depended: and so hard did these legalised marauders press upon the Greek villages that many Greeks took to the mountains and became klefts. From the standpoint of the Turkish central administration there was little to choose between *armatoli* and klefts, and the same was to become true of that of Ali Pasha himself: the *armatoli* tended to slip from his control, and more and more he was obliged to recruit support from certain klefts, who thus became 'tame' klefts, as opposed to 'wild' klefts who remained a law unto themselves.

Klefts, *armatoli*, and *kapi* were often men of wealth. The Greek kleft Stournaris, for instance, controlled 120 villages, each, on an average, of seventy families. He himself possessed 8,000 cattle and his whole family 500,000, which were hired out to herdsmen for a rent in kind. From plots of cultivated land he received further rents. Altogether he maintained 400 fighting men (*pallikaria*) who were bedecked, like all the klefts and *armatoli*, with ornaments and amulets according to their rank. Stournaris and his kind, like the wealthy primates who employed the *kapi*, were lesser Ali Pashas—men who could carve out for themselves a territorial independence where the Sultan's writ ran only haphazardly and intermittently.

Although there are notable exceptions, the Greek klefts had no conception of a Greek national state, but they possessed at least some of the characteristics that made for a feeling of nationality. They had a rooted hatred of the infidel. They had a simple veneration for their Church and, though they sometimes dealt harshly with monasteries that failed to befriend them, they offered prayers in the little wayside chapels and called upon priests to bless their arms. Despite the misfortunes of those who had joined Orlov, they continued to hope that with Russian assistance they might free themselves from Turkish rule, and during the period of the revolutionary wars many began to think of fighting for liberty on a grander scale—even of a Balkan-wide rising in which the *haiduks* of Serbia and Bulgaria, and the *pandours* of Romania, would take part.

CHAPTER 2

The Prelude to the
First War of Independence

I. Rigas the Protomartyr

The developments within kleftic Greece, the whole impact of events in western Europe on the Balkans, and much more besides, become apparent in a study of Rigas, the traditional, but not the only, forerunner of the Greek revolution. The son of a merchant, Andonios Kiriazis, he was born *c.* 1757 in Velestino, near the ancient Ferai, later assuming the name of Rigas Velestinlis. Educated (according to one tradition) at Ambelakia or at Zagora (according to another), as a youth he entered the service of Alexander Ipsilantis, the dragoman of the Porte. When in 1774 his patron became the prince of Wallachia, he remained in Constantinople with the prince's sons to complete his education. Subsequently he travelled extensively. Towards 1780 he went to Bucharest to become the prince's secretary. Meanwhile in Wallachia Alexander had established a regular army of 12,000 men, nearly all of whom were Greeks. The officers of this army had formed a secret society, of which the prince's sons, Konstantinos and Dimitrios, who had gone to join their father, had become members. Following the discovery by the Turks of a plot in 1782, the two sons fled to Transylvania. The prince himself returned to Constantinople to clear his name. For a short while Rigas probably acted as secretary to Brancoveanu, a hellenised Vlach of distinguished family, and in 1787 entered the service of the new hospodar, Nikolaos Mavroyenis, who, it is said, appointed him governor of Craiova. In 1790, following the execution of Mavroyenis for alleged complicity with the Russians, he became secretary to Kirlianos, baron de Langenfeld, whom he accompanied to Vienna for a visit of several months. Already a good linguist, speaking French, Turkish, Arabic, German, Italian, Vlach, and Greek, he now began his literary activities. Wishing to enlighten his somewhat staid compatriots, he translated *L'École des amants délicats* into the popular Greek tongue; he compiled a work on physics; and he began to translate (but did not finish) *L'Ésprit des lois* of Montesquieu. He returned in 1791 to Wallachia, where, besides attending to his properties, he founded a commercial house, an enterprise which involved him in much travel. In 1794 he went on a visit to Trieste. By that time he had come under the influence of French revolutionary ideas. Later he became dragoman to the French consul of Bucharest and in all probability acted as secretary to the new hospodar, Michael Soutsos. In August 1796 he went again to Vienna. It was there that he published his famous pictorial and commemorative map in twelve sections showing the European portions of the 'Hellenic Republic' and a portrait of Alexander the Great, whose name was already a legend among the modern Greeks. There, too, he completed, with the help of his friend Vendotis, a translation of Barthélemy's *Le Voyage du jeune Anacharsis*, and he published his translations of Metastasio's *L'Olympe*, of Marmontel's *La Bergére des Alpes*, and of Gisner's *Le Premier matelot*.

Already in 1790 two Macedonian brothers, Georgios and Poulios Markidis-Poulios, had founded in Vienna the newspaper *Efimeris*, which purveyed a mixture of French revolutionary and Greek patriotic ideas. This newspaper, which circulated in Greece, Serbia, Bulgaria, and the Principalities, began to give prominence to the ideas of Rigas, who had become a friend of the two brothers; and it was from the printing-house of Markidis-Poulios that in October 1797 were issued no less than 3,000 copies of his revolutionary manifesto, a declaration of the rights of man, a constitution, and a martial hymn (*thourios*) calling on the Balkan Christians to throw off their chains. The rousing hymn was circulated throughout the Balkans and during the next two decades it was sung everywhere, even in the Turkish capital.[1]

In the preamble to the constitution, a powerful condemnation of Ottoman rule, Rigas stated that the Hellenic republic, though divided by mountains and rivers, and though embracing different races, tongues, and religions, was one and indivisible; and although he stipulated that the Greek language should be used for administration (Article LIII), he advocated that men of all races should have the vote and be eligible for administrative office (Articles VII–X). Among these races he included Turks, the lower orders of whom he assumed to be potential democrats and ready to throw off their shackles. He thus envisaged a Balkan–Asian state with a predominantly Greek culture and based on three historical precedents: the multiracial polyglot state of Alexander the Great with its Hellenistic culture; the multiracial Byzantine Empire (not that Rigas had much use for the Church, which in fact condemned his works); and the Ottoman Empire

---

[1] There also circulated several free Greek translations of the French *Marseillaise*. In 1810 Byron and Hobhouse obtained from their host, the primate Londos, an incomplete text of one of these translations. This Byron rendered into English ('Sons of the Greeks, arise!'). It is most unlikely that Byron's Greek text was the work of Rigas: it was in a learned form of Greek, whereas Rigas always wrote in a popular (demotic) language.

itself, again polyglot and multiracial. What he envisaged was a Turkish empire without the ruling Turks and without the 'Christian Turks', and he expressly stated (Article XXII) that the masses and not the primates were the true basis of the nation—the masses whose natural leaders were the educated Greeks or the Slavs and Romanians who had enjoyed a Greek education. These leaders, he hoped, would take over and eventually transform the theoretically centralised Turkish state into an efficient form of government. At no time did he pronounce for a federal state. Nevertheless, his democratic leanings and his knowledge of the diversity of the Balkan and Asiatic regions led him to envisage provincial legislative assemblies of two houses working in conjunction with a centralised legislature and executive—a design which in a sense was the very opposite of the prevailing Ottoman order, in which laws emanated from the centre and in which provincial executives went their own sweet way. To both the central executive and its provincial agents he denied the right to initiate legislation: legislation must be initiated in the local assemblies, and no legislative measure must be enforced in any region unless it had nine-tenths of the local vote.

Following the fashion of the day, he gave the judicial power an independent existence. The judicial system, however, he never worked out in detail, and we do not know how he proposed to draw the line between the civil and ecclesiastical jurisdictions, although he pronounced boldly for the election of judges. Similar egalitarian ideas coloured his other proposals, which were more democratic than his models—the French constitutions of 1793 and 1795. He envisaged, for instance, the emancipation of women and even proposed that women should do military service. Setting but little store by the rights of property, he thought of abolishing debts and of establishing a right to work and to social assistance. Needless to say, he contemplated a compulsory system of (Greek) education.

Like many Greeks, Rigas was much impressed by Napoleon's Italian campaigns of 1796–97, by the entry of the French into the Ionian Islands, and by General Gentili's call to the Greeks to remember their classical ancestry. He himself hoped to meet Napoleon and to offer him the assistance of a Greek *eteria* for what he imagined to be Napoleon's intended drive towards the East. Whether this *eteria* was anything more than the hope of making arrangements with groups of klefts and with merchant societies in various towns we do not know. Certainly Rigas had agents who distributed his literature. Certainly as a freemason he had many contacts. He was a member of the *Bons Cousins*, founded in Vienna in 1780, with lodges in Belgrade, Athens, Vidin, and elsewhere. But there is no evidence[2] for the existence of a highly organised conspiracy like the *Filiki Eteria* of later years.[3]

---

[2] Rigas had intended to go to Mani to raise the chiefs, but the Maniat chiefs had never heard of him.

[3] See below, pp. 29ff.

Rigas arrived at Trieste in December 1797 with a medical student Hadjivasilis (Christoforos Perraivos), having forwarded to one Koronios letters and copies of his manifesto and other literature in three large chests. But a fellow Greek, Ikonomou, opened the letters and gave them to the local governor, whereupon the Austrian police, who had already been keeping a close watch, arrested Rigas along with seventeen others (chiefly Macedonian Greeks), and took him back to Vienna. An inquiry established (it revealed no details) that the prisoners belonged to a conspiratorial organisation. Those with Austrian citizenship were expelled and their property confiscated. The eight Turkish nationals, among them Rigas, were handed over (quite illegally) to the Turkish *kaimakami* of Belgrade, the Austrians hoping in return to obtain the extradition of certain Austrian Polish refugees in the Principalities. The Porte, aware that Ali Pasha and others had plans to rescue the prisoners on their journey from Belgrade to Constantinople, ordered the *kaimakami* to fake the accidental death of Rigas and his seven associates.[4] The sequel was that on 24 June 1798 the eight victims were strangled. Their bodies were thrown into the Sava; it was announced that they had perished while attempting to escape. The story is that before he perished Rigas said: 'This is how brave men die. I have sown; soon will come the hour when my nation will gather the ripe fruit.'

After Rigas's death certain other Greeks endeavoured to obtain the support of France. In 1800 Stamatis, a Greek employed by the French commercial agency of Ancona, reported to Talleyrand that there had been formed a revolutionary society consisting of Greeks from Epiros and the Morea. In 1806 a so-called 'second' *eteria*, which included klefts in the Ionian Islands, was founded in Italy and planned to obtain Napoleon's aid. Among these klefts was Theodoros Kolokotronis of Leondari. This famous warrior had amassed wealth by sheep-stealing and by marriage to a wealthy primate's daughter,[5] but when in 1804 Veli, one of the sons of Ali Pasha, had begun to subdue the Morea, he had been forced to flee. That same year (when the Russians were in the ascendency in the islands) he had composed a memorial to Tsar Alexander I asking for assistance for the mainland Greeks. After the Tilsit Peace of 1807, which had brought the French back to the islands, he planned to go to Paris to offer Napoleon support against Ali Pasha who, as a result of J. P. Morrier's and Colonel Leake's missions, was in alliance with the British. The purpose of these missions was to persuade Ali to assert his independence and fight the French. But Ali would

---

[4] These were E. Argentis and Koronios of Chios, Dr Nikolidis of Jannina, the brothers P. and J. Emmanuil of Kastoria, Torountzis of Siatista, and Karatzas of Nicosia.

[5] In order to appear respectable Kolokotronis styled himself *armatolos* of Leondari, but he was in fact a *kapos* serving the wealthy primate Deliyannis of Karitaina. The famous patriot Vasili Petmezas served the primate Zaimis of Kalavrita in a similar capacity. Koliopoulos ('Plapoutas') and Stamatelopoulos ('Nikitaras'), later important leaders during the War of Independence, were also *kapi*.

not go so far as this: when in 1809 Lord Byron visited Jannina, he indeed found the 'Old Lion' favourably disposed towards England, but Ali let it be known that he disliked the British dealings with his enemies, the klefts 'those evil men', and he continued to intrigue with the French, who, like the British, treated him as an independent power.

II. The Rise of Ali Pasha of Jannina

Ali Pasha was a life-long intriguer. Born at Tepeleni in 1744, he was a friend and an enemy to everyone—a friend one moment, an enemy the next —and the tangled story of his life became interwoven with the history of the Greeks. He was brought up by his mother, a relative of Kurd Pasha of Berat. Sheep-stealing, which he began at the age of fourteen, brought him wealth and enabled him so to increase the strength of his bands that he became a man to be reckoned with. Relatives and foes he murdered with a studied impartiality and complacency, his sole aim being to increase his wealth. A number of these murders he represented to the Porte as politically desirable, and for his services he was appointed by Abdul Hamid I guardian of the passes of Rumeli and governor of Thessaly. Here he quickly became the permanent robber and thus established a kind of law and order. For these further services the Sultan appointed him in 1786 pasha of Trikala and two years later added the sanjak of Jannina to his *pashalik*. Leaving his son Veli in charge of Trikala, he concentrated on his new domain in Epiros. Making friends with some and despatching others, he brought the unruly Albanian beys under his control. He next turned his attention to the Christian clans (*fares*) of Souli, in the mountains above Jannina—clans which had governed themselves for more than a century, which lived by raiding the villages in the plains below, and which on several occasions had been stirred up by Russian agents to tie down Turkish forces in their neighbourhood. Afraid, however, to make a direct assault upon these expert and hardy warriors, he invited them to join him in an expedition against the beys of Argirokastro. To humour Ali and to find out what he was really up to, the Souliots sent a token force, which, however, Ali seized as hostages, offering their leader Tzavellas his liberty if he would help to reduce his kinsmen. Tzavellas, leaving his own son as hostage, obtained Ali's permission to return to Souli for consultations. Once free, he and the Souliot chief of chiefs, Georgios Botsaris, sent a letter of defiance to Ali, who, much incensed, attacked the Souliot village of Kiafa. Here, however, his forces were badly mauled; and he had to free the hostages, and pay a large ransom, to get back his men who had been taken prisoner. Later, taking advantage of the feuds that raged among the Souliots and having won over Botsaris, whom he appointed *armatolos* of Tzoumerka, in 1799 he made a further, yet unsuccessful, attempt to reduce Souli. In 1802, having informed the Porte that the French were running arms and money to the Souliots, he received imperial supplies and the assistance of the pashas of Delvino and Berat for a third attack. This time he managed to establish a blockade, and the Souliots, being short of food and ammunition, agreed to evacuate their homeland and to live in Parga, whence most of them left for Corfu to enter the service of the Russians and later of the French. As a reward for this achievement Ali was appointed beylerbey of Rumeli (Bulgaria, Macedonia, and Thrace), while his son Veli became pasha of the Morea.

Ali now set to work to reduce the *haiduks*. He was so successful that the Porte, fearing he was becoming too powerful, ordered him back to Jannina. He went willingly, for the task of reducing Rumeli was not profitable, and in any case he was much more interested in Berat and the Ionian Islands. Berat he soon acquired. He drove out Ibrahim Pasha; denounced him as a traitor; and was appointed in his place. Meanwhile Veli had dispersed the klefts of the Morea who had organised a confederation under the famous Zacharias. Here, however, he quarrelled with Ali Farmakis, chief of the Musulman Albanian family of Lala, who made a compact in 1809 with Theodoros Kolokotronis, the successor of Zacharias.[6] These two hoped to obtain the assistance of the Souliots, and of Albanians under Hasan Tchapari, and to overthrow the two tyrants, Ali and Veli. This was the occasion when Kolokotronis planned to go to Paris to seek Napoleon's support. But General Donzelot, the French governor of the Ionian Islands, offered to spare him the trouble: he would obtain Napoleon's authority to provide the two allies with 500 French artillerymen, with 5,000 Greeks who were in French pay, with a regiment from Corsica, with funds to recruit further Albanians and Greeks, and with adequate transport. He would have the Porte informed that the rebellion was not against the Sultan but against the usurpers, Ali and Veli. Furthermore, should the revolt prove successful, France would establish a democratic government composed of twelve Christians and twelve Moslems.

Supplied with French money, Farmakis and Kolokotronis recruited in Epiros 3,000 of Ali Pasha's enemies. But the British occupation of Zante in October 1809 changed the whole situation. Kolokotronis became a captain in the Duke of York's Greek Light Infantry, a regiment raised by Major Richard Church,[7] who had led the British landing force at Zante. It was no longer to Russia or to France that he and fellow-spirits looked for salvation, but to Great Britain. So too did the Greeks assembled in Parga, where the inhabitants, menaced by Ali Pasha, hoisted the British flag.

[6] In 1807, Kolokotronis, responding to invitations from the Russian admiral Seniavin, had assembled with other klefts, including Macedonians, in the northern Sporades. Here they adopted a Greek flag—a white cross on a light blue background. Assisted by the British frigate *Sea-horse* (Captain John Stuart), they made attacks on Ali Pasha's partisans on the mainland.

[7] Later General Sir Richard Church who in 1827 became the Generalissimo of Greece (see below, pp. 56–7).

III. Osman Pasvanoglou and Konstantinos Ipsilantis

While Ali Pasha was carving out for himself a satrapy in the western half of European Turkey, Pasvanoglou (born in 1758 at Kirsu in Bosnia) was acquiring independence in the eastern half, to which region his grandfather and father had moved to hold respectable minor office in the Turkish administration. Osman, a born rebel, was disinherited by his father. Becoming a bandit, he enlisted the services of disgruntled janissaries. These unruly and inefficient military men were hostile to the *Nizam-i-Djedid* of 1792—the reform programme of Sultan Selim III, an enlightened despot who, like his Western counterparts, wished to modernise his army, increase his revenues, and destroy vested interests. Among those vested interests were the janissaries, who combined their local tyrannical activities with shopkeeping and petty trading. In all the regions where they operated they were detested. When the Serbs rebelled in 1804 under the leadership of the wealthy pig-seller and warrior Karageorge and the *haiduk* Glava, it was not primarily against the Ottoman administration but against the tyranny of that hereditary caste. In this rebellion they received some support, not only from the klefts of Olympos and Macedonia and from Konstantinos Ipsilantis, hospodar of Wallachia, but also from certain Moslem *spahis*. The last thing that the Serbs, the Sultan, and Ipsilantis wanted was to see Pasvanoglou, who had become pasha of Vidin, established in Belgrade with the help of the janissaries, or to extend his influence into Wallachia.

Although Pasvanoglou met with opposition from Ipsilantis and the Serbs, and although he recruited Moslem bandits and unruly janissaries, he had nevertheless been a friend of Rigas who in his *thourios* (lines 88–95) gave him an honourable mention. From Rigas he had taken some of his ideas: he appealed to the downtrodden and discontented Moslems and to the Greek Christians, to whom he promised a return to the privileges of Suleyman the Magnificent: and he had the support of Grigorios, the metropolitan of Vidin. Not that he would have fitted into Rigas's Hellenic republic, which logically would have swept his tyranny away.

Much closer to Rigas in political thinking was his old fellow-student, Konstantinos Ipsilantis, who, in spite of his complicity in the conspiracy of 1782, had become chief dragoman of the Porte and later hospodar of Wallachia. Like his father Prince Alexander, he planned to make the Principalities into a westernised, independent state, and he hoped one day to take Constantinople. Feeling his way through the labyrinth of Turkish-Balkan politics, which were so intricately bound up with the changing fortunes of the European powers, in 1802, as a result of Russo-Turk negotiations in which he had a hand, he secured a *hatti-sherif* whereby, in extension of her powers under the treaty of Kutchuk Kainardji, Russia acquired the right to overrule Turkish decisions to depose the hospodars, whose term of office was to be seven years, and to make representations concerning taxation and privileges in the Principalities direct to those governors. Thus assured of seven years' tenure, he began to strike out an independent line. He did not rely solely on Russia. He maintained good relations with Austria and Prussia, and he did not go out of his way to offend the French. His first task was to curb Pasvanoglou, with whose enemies he made alliances; his second, to recreate his father's army which had not survived the Austro–Russian–Turkish War. Here, however, he encountered not only opposition from Selim III but also from the Tsar, who least of all wanted an independent power upon the Danube. For a while he was content to send some aid to the Serbs, and when eventually Selim forced him to despatch an envoy to persuade them to lay down their arms, he tried putting them up to demand strict terms, but because of lack of support from both Russia and Austria they made (April 1805) only moderate proposals—an elected hereditary prince as governor, a fixed levy of taxation, and the expulsion of the janissaries together with the band of Pasvanoglou from the province of Belgrade. In vain did Konstantinos appeal to Russia to collaborate with Austria and to send aid to the Serbs, in order to forestall the French, who might use them in an attempt to expand eastward from their bases in the Illyrian provinces. Of these intrigues the Turks gained knowledge, but Konstantinos, knowing he was in danger, managed to escape to Russia, whose armies subsequently restored him, and forced the Porte to nominate him as prince of Moldavia. He now sent food and military supplies to the Serbs; he encouraged them to massacre the Moslems of Belgrade; and he planned to assist them with an Hellenic legion composed of Vlachs, Christian Albanians, Bulgarians, and Greeks. But he found great difficulty in obtaining volunteers and all he managed to send to Serbia was a relatively small body under Georgakis Olimpios.[8] In August 1807, following differences with the Russian generals, he retired to Kiev, never to return to the Principalities. Two months later the Serbs accepted autonomy under a native prince—an arrangement guaranteed by France and Russia, who following the Tilsit Treaty were in alliance. So ended for the time being the fanariot intrigue in the Serbian provinces. By that time Selim III was no longer Sultan: rebel forces had marched on Constantinople and, having massacred members of the reformist faction, had forced Selim to abolish the *Nizam-i-Djedid* and to abdicate.

IV. The Ionian Islands

Following the retirement of Konstantinos Ipsilantis and the conclusion of the treaty of Tilsit, schemes for a general Balkan rising were less prominent. The Serbs, hoping to do better for themselves, continued the struggle more or less on their own, and, so successful were they, that in 1812 they freed the *pashalik* of Belgrade. But in 1813 the Turks defeated Karageorge, who fled first to Austria and then to the Russian province of Bessarabia. In 1815 the

[8] Olimpios was the 'blood' brother of Karageorge and later married his widow.

Serbs revolted again, this time under Milosh Obrenovich, who negotiated a settlement which left him supreme in the Serbian principality. Meanwhile the Greek klefts had thrown in their lot with the British, who, after taking Zante, had seized Kefalonia, Ithaka, Kithira, and Lefkas, where Kolokotronis fought with great distinction. Greeks in great numbers from the mainland wanted to join the British service. According to Major Church, six to eight thousand could have been recruited within a few months. Church himself was overwhelmed with applications. One chieftain promised that his *pallikaria* (brave young men) if taken into British pay, would win for him the fame of Miltiadis, Leonidas, and Themistoclis. Another chieftain offered five hundred men from eastern Greece, while four hundred Spartans, citing their illustrious ancestry, clamoured to be taken on. The klefts indeed had gone a long way since Kolokotronis's father, Konstantinos, had joined the revolt of 1770. As Kolokotronis himself tells us in his *Memoirs*, they had had their eyes opened. In the old days, he says, many Greeks had thought that Zante was in France!

When Major Church went on sick leave in 1812 (he had been wounded at Lefkas) he carried a memorial from the Greeks to the British government asking for assistance in freeing their country. But Church and his Greek friends were to be disappointed. Three months after the signing of the first peace of Paris, the British government, in deference to the protests of the Turks, disbanded the Greek regiments.[9] Kolokotronis was downhearted. He tells us: 'I then saw that what we had to do, we must do without any hopes of help from the foreign powers.' But other Greeks, and the philhellene Church, at least had hopes that the Ionian Islands would be maintained as an independent state, even if under the protectorate of a great power. In a memorandum to the British delegation at the Congress of Vienna, Church stated that the nation that controlled the Ionian Islands would ultimately influence the destiny of Greece: and that, as the Greek nation possessed some five hundred ships, the power with influence in independent Greece would ultimately dominate the whole Levant: if England did not elect to become the protector of the Greeks, then it would be Russia who would play the role. In another memorandum which he submitted in January 1815 to Castlereagh, the British foreign secretary, he let it be known that important Greeks from the islands and the mainland were hoping for British protection.

After the 'Hundred Days' Castlereagh and his colleagues, who had earlier been prepared to see the Ionian Islands pass to another power, except France and Russia, made a determined attempt to acquire control over them. Here, however, their efforts met with some opposition from the Russian minister Count John Kapodistrias, who had been given by the Tsar a more or less free hand in negotiations concerning his native islands.

---

[9] A second Greek regiment had been formed in 1812. It had given assistance in the capture of Paxos and Parga.

Like Church, Kapodistrias believed that these islands were likely to become the precursor of a Greek nation-state. He himself came from Corfu. Born in 1776 and having studied medicine at Padua, in 1800 he had become first secretary of state in the newly-established Septinsular republic. He subsequently rendered useful service to the Russians who came to occupy the islands. When after Tilsit the islands had again passed under French control, General Berthier had pressed him to enter the French service, but he had much preferred to keep the links he had formed with the Russians. In 1809 he entered the Russian diplomatic service, and for a time was political officer with the Danube army. In 1814 he was appointed by the Tsar plenipotentiary to the Congress of Vienna. He subsequently attended the negotiations in Paris in 1815 and it was here that he made a determined fight to secure the complete independence of his native islands. He met, however, with strong resistance. Many thought that these islands, if left to themselves, would only pass under Russian influence. There was, as a consequence, every chance that they would be given to Austria, or to an Austrian nominee. To avoid this unsatisfactory solution, he suggested the compromise (which was adopted) that they should be constituted a republic under the protectorate of the British crown. In the treaty of 15 November 1815, however, neither the status nor the constitution of the islands was clearly defined, and the British, once they were in control, administered them as a crown colony. Nevertheless, in theory they were an independent Greek state, and as such they were a beacon to the mainland Greeks, ever reminding them of their nationality and opening out to them a vista of freedom.

V. The Filiki Eteria (The Friendly Society)

In 1807 Choiseul-Gouffier, formerly French ambassador at Constantinople, had, along with certain distinguished Greeks, founded in Paris the 'Greek-Speaking Guest House'. Its object was to organise a Greek rising against the Turks. In 1811 Count Romas, an Ionian Greek, had founded a masonic lodge at Corfu, which in 1812 became the Grand National Lodge of Greece, there being other lodges in Lefkas, Paris, Moscow, and elsewhere. The one in Moscow was known as *Athena* and it was said to have been a continuation of Rigas's *Eteria*. Like another society, *Phoenix*, which Alexander Mavrokordatos is said to have founded during his exile in Russia, it put forward to Napoleon plans for the partition of Turkey. All these societies indirectly gave rise to yet another, the *Filiki Eteria*, which was founded in Odessa in mid-1814 by Athanasios Tsakalov, son of a rich fur-dealer in Moscow and formerly a member of the 'Greek-Speaking Guest House'; by Nikolaos Skoufas, a merchant of Odessa and a member of the *Phoenix*; and by Emmanuil Xanthos, a native of Patmos, formerly an agent of the rich merchant house of Xenis and a member of a lodge in the Ionian Islands.

In forming this society these three men consciously imitated Rigas: they conceived of a conspiracy covering the whole field of Hellenism and including all Balkan Christians. Needless to say, they also drew upon their own experiences of freemasonry, but they did not follow slavishly the organisations already known to them.

In the autumn of 1814 Skoufas and Tsakalov (Xanthos was absent) drew up an organisation of four grades, above which there was to be a supreme authority, composed of several anonymous persons. Later a more elaborate scheme was made and the title *Filiki Eteria* was chosen, but during the two years 1814–16 the conspirators initiated not more than thirty members, chiefly from the Greek merchant class in Russia. The most important of these was Nikolaos Galatis, who was promised membership of the highest grade provided he initiated Count John Kapodistrias, whose relative he claimed to be. At the time Kapodistrias shared with Nesselrode the general direction of Russian foreign affairs, and he was certainly the predominant partner.

Already at Vienna in 1814–15 he had displayed his Hellenism by joining the Philamuse Society, which had been founded in Athens in 1813 and which had as its object the cultural regeneration of the Greek nation. He was not, however, so optimistic as Adamantios Korais, the foremost Greek scholar, who lived in Paris and who was busy attempting to restore to the current Greek language the lustre of ancient Greek. Whereas Korais believed that the Greeks had merely to recapture their classical heritage to regain their freedom, Kapodistrias, who was much closer to political reality, was counting on the outbreak of a Russo–Turkish war. This war he did not expect to take place immediately, for he realised that Russia, as a member of the European Concert, had obligations and interests in western Europe. Nor did he favour, indeed he feared, a spasmodic Greek revolt which was likely to have dire consequences for the Greeks; and it is doubtful whether he ever thought in terms of a Greek rising to establish a national state. All he seems to have envisaged as practical politics was an eventual Russo–Turkish war leading to an improved status for the Orthodox Church under the guarantee of Russia, or, at the most, principality status for those regions where the Greeks were in strength.

Great indeed was his alarm when Galatis informed him of the aims of the *Filiki Eteria* and asked him to become its president. 'Anyone who thinks of such an undertaking', he said, 'must be mad.' But the Tsar, to whom he reported the approach, insisted that Galatis should remain in St Petersburg, so that more might be learnt about the conspiracy. Galatis, who talked freely, was subsequently arrested. Papers found on him showed that a conspiracy of some sort existed. This information came to the ears of the British ambassador and the British government hastened to inform the Turks. All this alarmed Kapodistrias, who feared the Porte might begin its own inquiries with unpleasant consequences for many Greeks. He represented to the Tsar that the whole affair was of no importance and that Galatis was a romancer, who should be sent back to Ithaka. He wanted to hush matters up and allow the work of preparation to proceed quietly, undisturbed by the indiscretions of hare-brained conspirators like Galatis.

On his way back, Galatis, though supposed to be under the eye of General Pini, the Russian consul at Bucharest, contrived to initiate two important persons in the Principalities—Levendis, a Russian dragoman at Jassy, and Theodoros Negris, the secretary-general of Kallimachi, prince of Moldavia. Levendis then initiated Georgakis Olimpios and through him Karageorge, who promised (May 1817) that if he got back to power in Serbia he would prepare a revolt to coincide with a rebellion in the Morea and, with the help of one Hadjimichali, a revolt in Bulgaria. When, however, Karageorge returned to Serbia, Milosh Obrenovich contrived his murder (night of 12/13 June 1817) and sent his head to the Sultan.

In March or April 1818 the *eterists* transferred their headquarters to Constantinople where Skoufas worked incessantly until his death from illness the following August. It was he who organised the 'apostles' to take charge of initiations in specified areas.[10] Among these were many able men: 'Anagnostaras' (Panayotis Papageorgiou) (Ionian and Aegean Islands); Antonis Pelopidas (Peloponnese); Ilias Chrisospathis (Mani and Messinia); Georgakis Olimpios (Serbia); Dimitrios Vatikiotis (Bulgaria); Gabrial Katakazis (Russia); Ipatros (Egypt); Konstantinos Pentedekas (the Principalities[11]); and Christodoulos Luriotis (Italy). Kamarinos Kiriakos was given the special mission of enrolling Mavromichalis (Petrobey)—a task accomplished in August 1818.[12]

Those enrolled by the apostles in turn enrolled others, thus setting in motion a snowball which became an avalanche. There were, apart from the supreme authority, four civilian grades and two military grades of *eterists*. The lowest grade (*vlamis*) consisted of simple and illiterate people, who were given only the vaguest information in return for their oath and a monetary contribution. The next grade (*sistimenos*) was recruited from the lower classes (clerks and small traders). These recruits too took the oath, paid a higher subscription than the *vlamides*, and were given further information. The third and fourth grades (*ierefs*—priest; and *pimin*—shepherd) were reserved for rich and educated Greeks. The lower military grade was called *afieromenos* (a dedicated one) and the higher grade was known as

---

[10] The *eterists* did not follow the freemason organisation of lodges or cells which sent off offshoots but, as they themselves claimed, the system of Christ, the system of apostles.

[11] Galatis too was active in the Principalities. To get money, he would threaten to expose people to the Turks. When attempts were made to restrain him, he threatened to expose the whole conspiracy. The supreme authority took the threat seriously and arranged for his murder.

[12] Some of the 'apostles' were old *kapitanei* ('Anagnostaras', Chrisospathis, Farmakis, Vatikiotis, Olimpios). Others were merchants (Pentedekas, Krokidas, Pelopidas, Kamarinos, Luriotis). Ipatros was a former priest. Katakazis was a secretary in the Russian embassy at Constantinople.

archigos (leader). Initiation was an elaborate procedure. There was a solemn ritual during which the initiate was instructed in the use of secret signs. As for the oaths for the different grades, that for the lowest grade was the simplest. The initiate swore in the name of justice, of truth, of the country, and in the name of the Father, the Son, and the Holy Ghost to keep the secrets of the *Eteria*. From 1820, however, most of the elaborate ritual was dispensed with: the main object of the *eterists* was to recruit as many people as possible in the shortest possible time.

From the ample (but incomplete) records of enrolments, it is evident that by early 1820 the *eterists* had brought together hundreds of leading Greeks of all sorts—rich merchants from many centres; intellectuals steeped in Western ideas; shipowners and sea-captains; parish priests, monks, and certain higher clergy; teachers and landowners; and klefts, *kapi*, and *armatoli*. In other words the *eterists* 'pre-mobilised' the resources and manpower of the Greek nation scattered far and wide throughout and even outside the vast territories of the Ottoman empire; to enrol a kleft or a primate was to enlist a private regiment, which in time could absorb men from the villages (shepherds, woodcutters, builders, and artisans). To enrol a merchant was to raise funds or yet more regiments. And to enrol the monks was to enlist couriers, even warriors (for many of them were to fight), and, more important still, to obtain as strongpoints numerous fortified monasteries.

The chief reason for the success of the *eterists* was that they created the impression that their movement was sponsored by Russia, that the leader was Kapodistrias, and that they had the blessing of the Patriarch.[13] So firm was this impression that a cautious realist like Petrobey (Mavromichalis) had ceased his feuds with the families of Grigorakis and Troupakis in order to join, that wily fanariots had been enrolled, and that the timid in high places, out of fear that they would be confounded with the Turks when the day of reckoning came, had become compromised. The enrolment of Russian consuls (most of whom were of Greek extraction) seemed to prove that the hidden hand was Russia. The truth was, however, that at the beginning of 1820 the higher authority consisted only of the founders Tsakalov and Xanthos, the merchants Sekeris, Paximadis, and Komizopoulos, the 'apostles' Levendis and Anagnostopoulos, the fanariot Manos, the archimandrite Dikaios (Papaflessas), and the intellectual Gazis. It was not long before this truth became widely known, and these leaders, fearing that the whole structure would collapse like a pack of cards, made a second approach to Count Kapodistrias. To him they sent Xanthos, who, in the course of two meetings, explained the organisation of the society, its great extent, and its illustrious membership. Kapodistrias was sympathetic, but

---

[13] Farmakis's attempt to enrol the Patriarch Grigorios failed. Grigorios as Ethnarch was mindful of his obligations to the Turks, and he did not want a repetition of the disaster of 1769–70. All the same he expressed some sympathy with the *eterists*.

he made it clear that he did not approve of a conspiracy that was likely to miscarry. Moreover, he was well aware of the Tsar's opinions. When in 1819 he was about to visit his family in Corfu, Alexander had made it clear to him that he did not want a war with Turkey; and in Corfu he had counselled all those (including Kolokotronis) who had flocked to see him to have patience. To Xanthos, who now asked for arms and money, he replied that the Greeks must wait until the diplomatic situation had changed; they must wait until there was another Russo–Turkish war (he was here referring to a possible war arising out of the disputes over the execution of the treaty of Bucharest of 1812); and he refused to accept Xanthos's argument that a spontaneous Greek rising was inevitable. Nevertheless, Xanthos came away from his conversations with Kapodistrias with the impression that, though Russia was not likely immediately to assist the Greeks, perhaps God and the Tsar would eventually help those who helped themselves.

Failing to find a leader in Kapodistrias, Xanthos, without the authority of the *eterists*, approached Prince Alexander Ipsilantis, whose younger brothers, Nikolaos and Dimitrios, had been the first fanariots to join the conspiracy. Born in 1792 at Constantinople, Alexander had gone with his father to St Petersburg, where he attended the military school of cadets of the Imperial Guard. He had fought at Kulm (where he lost an arm) and he had later become a general and aide-de-camp of Tsar Alexander. Earlier attempts to enrol him in the *Eteria* had failed, but he now succumbed to Xanthos's pleading. Before he accepted the offer of the leadership, he consulted Kapodistrias, who raised no objection but advised him, before committing himself, to seek the Tsar's blessing. This he did. Alexander I raised no absolute objections: indeed he probably counted on Ipsilantis to control the movement, to avoid precipitate action, and to ensure that the military preparations were thoroughly made. Writing to Alexander's successor, Nicholas I, on 14 January 1828, shortly before his death, Ipsilantis, looking back upon the events of some seven or eight years before, stated:

> I thought that my hour had come and, following the advice of Kapodistrias,[14] I accepted [the offer of the leadership of the *Eteria*]. It was at the beginning of the year 1820, at the time when the Ottoman Porte had declared war without mercy against Ali Pasha of Jannina.

VI. *Ali Pasha and the* Filiki Eteria

In November 1818 Ali Pasha had informed his old acquaintance, Paparrigopoulos, dragoman at the Russian consulate at Patras, that he knew of the existence and the secret signs of the Greek conspiracy, which is believed to be Russian-sponsored. At the time, he was planning to make his territories

---

[14] Kapodistrias always denied that he encouraged Ipsilantis, even at a later date when it might have been to his personal advantage to have posed as the originator of the Greek revolution. It is not improbable that Xanthos had given the impression that Kapodistrias had sent him specially to offer the leadership to Ipsilantis.

more independent of the Porte, and he was anxious to obtain not only Russian support but any other assistance that might be going. In 1819 he approached Kapodistrias, who was then at Corfu, only to be advised to remain loyal to his master and just to his supporters. Later Ali asked Paparrigopoulos to go to Russia to see the Tsar on his behalf, saying that he himself had already been initiated into the *Eteria* by Manthos Ikonomou, a brother of one of his secretaries, Christos Ikonomou. On being questioned Paparrigopoulos denied the existence of a conspiracy. He knew that, while the *eterists* had enlisted Greek personnel in Ali's service (the secretaries Christos Ikonomou and Alexis Noutsos, the physician John Kolettis, and several of the klefts and *armatoli*), they had refrained from recruiting Albanians and that it was most unlikely that they had initiated Ali Pasha himself. Nevertheless, he visited Stroganov, the Russian envoy at Constantinople, who, however (like Kapodistrias), was not much interested in Ali's plans. But despite this reaction of his superiors, he wrote to Ali saying that he might look forward to Russian support. By this time Ali was in revolt against Sultan Mahmud, who was determined to bring his unruly vassal to heel, and Paparrigopoulos evidently wished to encourage Ali to continue his resistance to the Porte. His efforts met with some success. Ali himself made approaches to the Greeks. He convened his Greek secretaries and said he would assist their organisation. He entered into correspondence with Ignatios, an *eterist*, a former bishop of the Principalities who was in exile in Pisa. But the Greeks, though ready to encourage Ali to resist, had no wish to become involved with him. They knew at any moment he might betray them.

The story goes that Ali had sent agents to Constantinople to murder his enemy at Court, Ismail Paso Bey. The attempt 'failed': it is not improbable that the whole incident was staged by the would-be 'victim' who, shortly afterwards, was nominated pasha of Jannina and Delvino in place of Ali. Not to be outdone, Ali, posing always as a faithful subject, warned the Porte of the existence of the Greek *Eteria*, the implication being that it would be safer for the empire if he himself remained in power. To this warning the Constantinople Turks paid not the slightest heed. They were accustomed to hearing of Greek conspiracies. To them Ali was the immediate danger. Hence they persisted in their plans to remove him. Ali turned to the Greeks, the Serbs, and the Montenegrins. He summoned the Greek klefts and primates to a conference at Preveza, promising them arms, pay, and booty. He next called a conference of Greeks and Moslems. Besides promising pecuniary rewards, he offered to grant a constitution and he asked Metternich of all people to send him one. Among the Greeks were many *eterists*: they saw the need to humour Ali, realising full well that as long as he was in revolt against the empire he would provide such a diversion that their own plans would stand a better chance of success.

In July 1820 the Porte ordered Ali to present himself in Constantinople

within forty days. This he failed to do, whereupon imperial forces under
Ismail Paso Bey moved against him and his sons. These forces compelled
Veli to abandon Lepanto, and Mouktar and Salih to quit Berat. The better
to defeat Ali at the centre of his power, Sultan Mahmud engaged the
services of the Souliots, who helped the imperial forces to seize Preveza.
Veli was taken prisoner. His brothers Mouktar and Salih were captured at
Argirokastro. The Souliots then went on to assist the Ottoman armies in
the siege of Jannina. Here, however, they fell foul of certain local beys and
agas, who had joined Ismail Paso Bey. Ismail ordered the Souliots to leave.
Ali learned of this, for he had many spies in the imperial camp. He made an
alliance with his old enemies (27 January 1821): he would give them back
Souli, their forty villages, their old fortress of Kiafa, and money for their
families in the Ionian Islands.[15]

Alexander Ipsilantis was fully informed of these negotiations by the
eterist Alexis Noutsos, a counsellor of Ali Pasha. Since taking the leadership
he had set great store by Ali Pasha's rebellion. He ordered Kolokotronis to
encourage the Greek klefts to join the Souliots, but at the same time to
impress upon them the need to ensure (and this they did in December
1820) that towns and fortresses taken from the imperial forces should be
garrisoned by those who could later be expected to declare for the Greek
rebellion. In this way he hoped to seize a province which would be close to
supplies at Corfu and which would provide a salient for operations.

---

[15] Employing the good offices of the Greek metropolitan of Arta, the Turks endeavoured,
but without success, to win back the allegiance of the Souliots.

CHAPTER 3

The Outbreak of the Greek Revolt

I. The Decision to Begin the Revolt in the Principalities

Ipsilantis wished to begin the rebellion as soon as possible—before the Turks crushed Ali Pasha. He therefore rapidly reorganised the *Eteria*: he concentrated on enrolling Greeks of importance rather than the lower orders which, when the day came, would in any case follow their local leaders; he increased the number of local treasuries; and he began to draw up military regulations to provide a firmer discipline. He endeavoured moreover to enlist Obrenovich, for it was his plan to use Serbian territory as one of his routes to the south. On 5 November he wrote to Obrenovich saying that the Greeks would revolt on 27 November in Constantinople and in Greece, and that he himself would arrive in Serbia between 2 and 7 December with supplies and money provided Obrenovich would send troops to Bulgaria. But to this approach Obrenovich showed every reserve.

Ipsilantis, besieged with planners, had always been torn between an entirely Hellenic plan of action and one that envisaged Balkan co-operation. One plan which he was inclined to favour was that of capturing the Ottoman fleet and of taking Constantinople. But this became known to the Turks[1] and was to provide the pretext for the massacres of April 1821. He came, however, to prefer a Balkan plan, and therefore the failure of Obrenovich to respond was a great blow to his unduly optimistic mind. (At the same time he was counting on Russian help when there was no valid reason to suppose that it would be forthcoming.) He was, moreover, unduly optimistic in counting on the Bulgarian chiefs to play an important role once the rebellion had begun. Strange to say, however, in view of what transpired, he attached no military importance to the Principalities, which he regarded merely as a source of provisions and of financial aid. He was well aware that, although Michael Soutsos, hospodar of Moldavia and an

---

[1] It was the British ambassador who informed the Porte, and it is said that he obtained his information from one Asimakis.

eterist, had allowed the *eterists* to work openly, the Greeks of the Principalities were too affluent and pleasure-loving, or, if poor, too intent on improving their social positions, to think in patriotic terms. What is more, he and his fellow-*eterists* realised that the non-Hellenic people of the Principalities were hostile to fanariot rule. Hence they were prepared to accept the view of Perraivos: instead of wasting energy in the Principalities, considerable attention should be paid to Epiros, to Macedonia and Thessaly, and above all to the Morea.

At the meeting of leading *eterists* at Ismail in October 1820, Perraivos had doubted the readiness of the Moreots to take up arms, but Ipsilantis had insisted that something must be done while Ali Pasha occupied the Turks' attention. He considered, along with most others, that the *eterists* had been betrayed and that, if something were not done quickly, all would be lost. He had therefore issued on 21 October proclamations to the *eterists*, calling on them to throw off the Turkish yoke. He intended the revolt to begin in Mani on 20 December. Later, however, he had changed his mind. He had decided not to proceed to Mani but to raise the revolt in the Principalities and to bring the date forward to 14 November 1820. He had learned that preparations in the Morea were lagging. He was also under pressure from the Moreots to create a diversion; otherwise the Turks would act against them before they could move. Later still, discounting somewhat the reports of betrayals, he had postponed the rising for the spring. As optimistic as ever, he began to count upon Russian aid: he surmised that this would be the sooner forthcoming in the Principalities, and all the more certain, if he were to provoke the Turks into breaking the treaties, which stated that their forces should not cross the Danube without the Tsar's permission. He therefore gave orders to Savvas Fokianos and Olimpios to prepare for an attack on Bucharest and Jassy; he implored Obrenovich to rise against the Turks in Serbia;[2] and he called upon the leaders in Constantinople to put into action the preliminary plans for seizing that city. Having bribed the Cossack sentries he himself crossed the Pruth near Skouleni on 5 March 1821. Years later he explained to Tsar Nicholas, in a misleading letter written just before he died:

> Count Kapodistrias, whom I consulted, agreed with me, found that my plans and preparations were good and appropriate, and counselled me to proceed with their execution without showing any hesitation with regard to their success which seemed to him to be linked with the policy of Russia.

His army, however, consisted of only 4,500 men. It included Serbs, Bulgarians, Montenegrins, Moldavians, and 700 Greek students who composed

---

[2] To Obrenovich he sent via the trusted *eterist* Aristidis Papas a draft of treaty. Papas was taken by the Turks and killed. Obrenovich at no time showed any desire to assist Ipsilantis. Indeed, he appealed to the Serbian people, through a pastoral letter of the archbishop of Belgrade, to remain quiet.

the 'Sacred Battalion'. It had only four cannon and very few cavalry. It could, however, count on assistance from Olimpios, who had 1,500 followers in the vicinity of Bucharest.

II. The War in the Principalities

Ipsilantis's decision to gamble and to make his heroic gesture in the Principalities at the earliest possible moment had been prompted by the news sent to him by Olimpios that Tudor Vladimirescu, a wealthy man of peasant origin, Olimpios's former friend and chief of Tsernetsi, had revolted in January 1821 not against the Turks but against the fanariot administration and the local landowners (boyars), with the avowed aim of social and agrarian reform. Born in 1770 Vladimirescu had served with the Russians in 1806 and had taken part in the Serbian insurrection of 1811. He had quarrelled with Olimpios in 1817, but in 1819 had negotiated with him. It is doubtful, however, whether he was a member of the *Eteria*. Early in January 1821 Olimpios made a convention with him, probably on behalf of Ipsilantis, and certain *eterists* gave him funds. But he had no intention of fighting solely for Greek ends. His chief aim was to get rid of fanariot rule, to substitute a native governor for the Greek princes, and to convene a national assembly representing all classes of the population. Enjoying considerable support among the peasantry and suspicious of the political designs of the leading boyars, he no doubt dreamt that he himself might one day gain the place of honour as leader of the Romanian people.

The *eterists*, unable to prevent Vladimirescu's revolt, had to try to use it for their own ends. Olimpios, despite orders from Soutsos (whose bodyguard he commanded) to put down these rebels, unfolded to Vladimirescu the plans of the *Eteria* and implored him to support the Greek rebellion. But Vladimirescu wanted to know first what the Russians were doing, and he subsequently visited Ipsilantis to find out the truth. Failing to obtain satisfaction, he passed information to the Turks, thus forcing Ipsilantis to detach troops to keep watch on this would-be enemy's army of 3,000 men concentrated in Bucharest.

By that time Ipsilantis's desperate venture was already doomed. Tsar Alexander, who was at the Laibach congress and under the influence of Metternich, publicly denounced the Greek rebellion and deprived Ipsilantis of his Russian rank. The Patriarch, under pressure from the Porte, excommunicated him. Later the Tsar sanctioned the entry of Turkish troops into the Principalities. Already the plan to attack Constantinople had failed. Ipsilantis wavered; he ignored the advice of Olimpios; spent countless hours in futile discussions with subordinate commanders; and, being ignorant of guerrilla tactics, always hankered after a set-piece campaign.

Towards the end of May Olimpios seized Vladimirescu at Golesti and executed him for his treacherous dealings with the Turks, but imperial forces in three formations were closing in on the rebels. Yannis Koloko-tronis was forced to abandon the monastery of Notsetoul, thus exposing the chief Doukas, who withdrew towards the Austrian frontier. These with-drawals, combined with the desertion of Savvas Fokianos, exposed Ipsi-lantis, advancing towards Rimnik, to the full strength of the Turks. Ipsilantis decided to make a stand at the village of Dragatsani on the river Olte, but he failed to carry out the battle plans prepared by Olimpios, while the subordinate commanders struck out on their own. The Greeks were routed. The 'Sacred Battalion' was annihilated and those few who escaped owed their lives to a brave counter-charge made by Olimpios. Ipsilantis crossed the Austrian frontier. On 15 June, despite a promise of safe-conduct, he was seized by the Austrian authorities and cast into a dungeon at Mugats Castle, where, broken-hearted, he was illegally held for seven long years. He died in the arms of the patriot Lasanis in January 1828, his last conso-lation being the news that Kapodistrias was on the way to take up office as first president of Greece.

Olimpios, because of his former relations with the Serbs, had not dared to think of seeking refuge in Austria. Instead he joined up with his old com-panion Farmakis and together they fought successful skirmishes which compelled the Turks to keep large forces in the field. They were at length discovered holding the monastery of Sekoul on a precipitous height. Here Olimpios and his men blew themselves up. Farmakis held out longer in another part of the building. An Austrian agent arranged a cease-fire and capitulation; but the Turks broke faith. Farmakis and other chiefs were humiliated and tortured, and were then sent to Constantinople where they were put to death. Thus perished two of the great sons of the Greek nation; and thus ended a campaign ill-prepared and ill-conducted from the outset, redeemed only by the outstanding but almost futile heroism of hardened chiefs and of unseasoned young idealists. Ipsilantis had lived in a world of fantasy. None of the things on which he had counted had come to fruition: there was no attack on Constantinople, no help from Russia, no assistance from Vladimirescu, and no widespread support from the Serbs and Bulgarians.

III. The Outbreak in the Morea and in Other Parts of Greece

Alexander Ipsilantis had sent his brother Dimitrios to take military com-mand in the Morea. Dimitrios's long-delayed arrival, however, was not directly connected with the outbreak of revolution there. In the Morea, events, though not completely uninfluenced by those in the Principalities, took their own course. The bolder *eterists* had wanted to act before it was too late. They had sent urgent messages to Alexander Ipsilantis not to delay the day of reckoning and these appeals had certainly influenced him and his entourage.

Shortly after the rising in the Principalities, but not because of it, the Turks of Tripolitsa, intending to seize important Greeks as hostages, had invited the primates to discuss the problem of Ali Pasha's intrigues. To these they still attached far more importance than to what they knew of the *Eteria*. They feared that Ali might make a bid for Greek support. Suspecting the worst, many primates, chiefly from Achaia, made excuses for their non-appearance in Tripolitsa. At the time they probably knew nothing of the outbreak of revolution in the Principalities. But while they were waiting for news, one of their number forced their hand by an act of brigandage which may or may not have been connected with other widespread risings throughout the Peloponnese, led by impetuous leaders like Dikaios Papaflessas, who were firmly convinced that if they acted, they would receive help from Russia. Murders of Turks began as early as 30 March. On 2 April Mani rose and the next day Petrobey laid siege to Kalamata, near which on 5 April some 5,000 Greeks assembled to receive the blessings of the Church; and on the following day, 6 April (25 March, O.S.), according to tradition, the metropolitan bishop of Patras, Germanos, raised the flag[3] of revolution at the monastery of Agia Lavra near Kalavrita, where the primates were waiting to hear whether the Russians were on the move before taking a final decision to defy the Turks.[4] This 'event' at Agia Lavra is celebrated as the beginning of the Greek revolution.[5]

Before long all the Morea was in arms and no less than 15,000 Turks perished. On 16 April the Christian Albanian chiefs of Dervoenchoria (villages in eastern Greece) rose against the local Turks. Joined by the peasantry of Boeotia and Attica, they seized the towns of Salona, Livadhia, and Talanti, and, had they shown more enterprise, they might have taken Athens. Before April was out the islands of Spetzes (15 April), Psara (18 April), and Idra (28 April), which were to provide most of the ships and the crews of the Greek navy, had joined the revolution and had assembled a fleet under Yakoumakis Tombazis. Already the island of Samos had revolted. Western Greece, however, was to wait for nearly two months. In Epiros the *eterists*, surrounded by strong Turkish forces, had been unable to move and, unlike the Souliots, had been reluctant to join Ali Pasha.

In Chalkidiki, Thessaly, and Macedonia the rising was likewise delayed.

---

[3] It was not, however, the flag of the *eterists*. Exactly what the flag was is a matter of dispute. It has even been questioned whether there was a flag at all.

[4] A few primates and three prelates had met at Vostitsa in January: they had sent out agents to Kapodistrias, to Ignatios, to Constantinople, and the islands in the hope of obtaining precise information about plans and of learning whether Russian help had been definitely promised.

[5] In his *Memoirs* (p. 25) Xanthos states that immediately after the outbreak of the revolution in the Principalities, he sent Stamatios Doukakis to Greece by way of Constantinople with letters and proclamations of war for delivery to the apostles of the *Eteria* in Greece. He sailed from Constantinople on 13 March in the ship of Georgios Prasinos, which reached Mani, with news of the outbreak of the revolution in the Principalities, several days before the Maniats laid siege to Kalamata. (See V. P. Panayotopoulos, *The proclamation of the Messinian Senate to the Courts of Europe* (in Greek, Athens, 1957).)

Here the leader was the apostle Emmanuil Papas, the chief cashier of the *Eteria*. He had landed as early as 23 March on Mount Athos at Vatopedi and had gone on to the monastery of Esfigmenou, a revolutionary head-quarters where the head, Nikiforos Iviritis, was an *eterist*. Hundreds of monks from Athos rushed to join him, most of them ready to carry arms. From Esfigmenou, Papas sent out orders to the *eterists* of northern Greece to rise in revolt, but before their leaders responded the Turks, with the example of the Peloponnese already before them, seized hostages and Greek property, and attacked the towns. Thousands perished in Thessaloniki, and it was to take over half a century for the Greeks of the city to recover from the blow.

Early in June, however, Papas, still based on Esfigmenou and holding other strongpoints, defeated the Turks at Ierissos. Reinforced by chieftains and hoping others from Olympos and Vermio would join him, he advanced towards Sedes near Thessaloniki, only to be driven back by strong Turkish forces. He held out for some time at Kassandra, but lost the support of the clergy; towards the end of the year he was obliged to take ship. Worn out and broken-hearted, he died on the voyage to Idra. The rebellion of the chiefs of Olympos and Vermio came much too late to save him. These too were in their turn defeated. Hundreds of them perished in April 1822 at Naousa, where many of the women threw themselves over the falls of the river Arapitsa rather than be massacred or sold into slavery. Shortly after-wards the Macedonian revolutionaries gave up the struggle, but like the men of Chalkidiki they had tied down and had inflicted heavy casualties on the Turkish forces which would otherwise have been employed in the Peloponnese. Following their defeat, many of the Greek warriors (old Karatasos of Veria and Nikolaos Kasomoulis of Serres, for example) made their way southwards to fight in the Morea and western Greece.

In the Morea, following the general rising, military operations were centred around the chief towns and fortresses in which the survivors of the 40,000 Turks had taken refuge. Two strongholds, Monemvasia and Navarino, the Greeks soon captured, and then turned their attention to Tripolitsa, a walled city. Here, amid a population swollen by Turkish refugees, were 4,000 Moslem Albanians who had been sent by Khursid Pasha to reinforce the garrison. Around this town the Greeks, under the supreme command of Dimitrios Ipsilantis, had concentrated some 12,000 men.[6] Although Ipsilantis meant something to the rank-and-file, for his brother had appointed him leader of the *Eteria*, the chiefs, who wished to get their hands on the fabulous booty of Tripolitsa, wanted to get rid of him. Kolokotronis and Petrobey therefore persuaded him to go to the gulf of Korinth to intercept a Turkish force said to be advancing to relieve the beleaguered city. These two had been negotiating with the Albanians, who

[6] With them were the first philhellenes, Thomas Gordon, Ipsilantis's chief of staff, and the Frenchman Raybaud, who had already served in northern Greece.

little desired martyrdom in the service of the Turks. The lesser chiefs got wind of this, and, fearing they might be deprived of the spoils, captured the town by assault on 5 October, killing no fewer than 8,000 people. It is often said that had greater clemency been shown, the Greeks could have arranged for the capitulation of most other towns.

Meanwhile, from the Turkish point of view the chief danger was still Ali Pasha. True, in Constantinople and Asia Minor, as in Thessaloniki, there had been massacres of the Greeks: the authorities had moreover seized the Patriarch Grigorios and other higher clergy and had put them to death. But for political and economic reasons the Sultan, though welcoming demonstrations of bigotry, made attempts to curb it: he feared not only a diminution of his taxable subjects but also the hostility of the powers, above all of Russia; and he therefore supported the grand vizier, Halet Effendi, who, in his determination to crush Ali Pasha, ignored the Greeks, even to the extent of allowing them to consolidate their gains. Eventually the Turks declared a Holy War, but the main object here was to discourage Moslems and above all the partisans of Ali Pasha from co-operating with the Christian klefts.

As soon as he had heard of the Greek revolt, Ali Pasha had sent his counsellor, Alexis Noutsos, on missions to the Greeks. Noutsos's plan was to create a Greek–Albanian state under Ali's sovereignty. But he soon saw that the Greeks had other ideas, and he himself passed over to the Greek revolution, becoming a counsellor of Alexander Mavrokordatos who had arrived in Mesolonghi to plan operations in western Greece. Nevertheless, a Greek–Albanian alliance was signed at Peta on 1 September 1821, between the Greek chiefs on the one side and the Souliots and their Albanian allies on the other. The Greek aim was to save Ali for a price—the freedom of the villages which he had made into *chifliks* (domains) under his direct control. Ali was counting on this combination to attack Khursid, so that he himself might make a sortie. But Mavrokordatos, who feared that at any moment Ali might come to terms with the Turks, persuaded the Souliot Botsaris not to take the risk, but to join other Greek chiefs who were besieging Arta.

The Albanian Omer Pasha Vrioni, sent by Khursid to relieve Arta, attempted to dissolve the alliance of the Greeks, the Souliots, and anti-imperial Albanians. Vrioni told the Albanians that Ali was as good as lost and that the Greeks were not fighting for Ali, but on their own account. To check this information the Albanians sent agents to the Greek regions. They learned that mosques had been burned, and, what is more, that the Greeks lacked arms and munitions. They therefore decided to join Vrioni and to turn against the Souliots, who managed however to slip away and to get back to Souli without great losses. But despite this increase in Albanian support, Ali Pasha was driven back to defend himself in his last stronghold of Itch-Kalé in Jannina. Here he threatened to blow himself up unless he were allowed to present his case to Sultan Mahmud. Khursid (and it says much for Turkish chivalry) granted him an armistice provided he gave up his fortress and retired to the little monastery of Agios Panteleimon on the island in the lake of Jannina. This Ali was prepared to do, and Khursid sent to him delicacies and musicians to while away the time of waiting. But from Constantinople came the order that Ali must die. On the night of 5 February Khursid sent troops to the island. A brief struggle ensued, Ali was shot, and his head was sent to Constantinople. His colourful career belongs to Greek as well as to Turkish history. His court was Greek and had been the centre of a Greek renaissance. His rebellion had encouraged the Greeks to revolt and, by tying down large Turkish forces, he had enabled the Greeks to get a firm footing in the Morea.

CHAPTER 4

The Progress of the Revolution

I. The Arrival of the Fanariots

The *Eteria* had not only failed to promote a general Balkan rising, but it had shown signs of fragmentation even within the narrower bounds of Hellenism. The factions which the leading *eterists* had brought together, though their leaders might sometimes speak the language of Western revolutionaries, were fundamentally hostile to westernised institutions. They had revolted for a variety of reasons—their sense of nationality in its Turkish setting, their veneration for the Church, their ingrained conspiratorial habits, their hostility to central authority, their fears of being left out when the day of reckoning came, their desire for gain, and above all their hopes of seizing land. The Greek upper classes wanted Ottoman society without the Turks, while the lower orders desired to improve their lot, to own and increase their holdings, to escape exactions, and to move up the social scale. Between rich and poor there was a latent conflict, but there was never a united front of the lower orders against the upper classes. The poor had no leaders of their own; they were not a uniform mass; and there were no intellectuals to tell them that they were. In so far as they had leaders they followed local worthies higher up the social scale to whom they were tied by the complex bonds of Greek society.

How exactly they were to replace the vanished Turkish authority was a problem of which the indigenous Greeks had only hazy notions. This was a task closer to the hearts of the Greeks of the dispersion, above all the fanariots. But these well-meaning people, who had no local roots, could only find a niche by coming to terms, each one after his own fashion, with Greek society and by exploiting those struggles between the *kapetanei* (the klefts and *kapi*) and the primates, and between the different areas of Greece, which had arisen following the early successes of the revolution. The state of war had given the *kapetanei* a power and prestige much greater than they had enjoyed under the old regime. In the Peloponnese the *kapi* had been

44

employed at great cost by the primates to lead the revolutionary bands. Deliyannis had spent a fortune on his former henchman Kolokotronis, but Kolokotronis, like other *kapetanei*, found war a profitable enterprise and had ceased to be a docile general. He had established control over the villages, on which he imposed contributions, and it was not long before he and others like him became important political figures. But although he was a law unto himself, he was intelligent enough and popular enough to think on a national scale. The same is true of lesser men like General Yannis Makriyannis, whose first military employment had been financed by one of Ali Pasha's minions. He too became a politician of some importance and like Kolokotronis had a hearty dislike of civilian politicians. Nevertheless, the very existence of indigenous Greeks who could think on a national scale made it possible for the outsiders to persist in their efforts to create a nation-state.

Among these outsiders was Dimitrios Ipsilantis, who had arrived, at long last, in June 1821. Though physically insignificant, he was popular, for he was thought to represent Russia in whom the wishful-thinking Greeks still placed some hope. Moreover, in their struggle against the primates, the *kapetanei* wanted his support, and had he been more ruthless, less of an idealist, and more willing to compromise, he might have succeeded. Of greater stature and of infinitely more finesse was the fanariot Alexander Mavrokordatos, formerly secretary to his uncle Karatzas, prince of Wallachia, with whom he had gone into exile in 1818, after Karatzas's enemies had branded him as a danger to the Porte. Leaving Marseilles on 10 July 1821, he had arrived in a ship carrying French, Italian, and Greek volunteers, with military supplies bought by Karatzas. He soon realised that the Morea was no place to get a footing and proceeded with Ipsilantis's blessing to western Greece, having arranged that Theodoros Negris,[1] another fanariot, should go to Salona in eastern Greece. In western Greece Mavrokordatos, though inclined towards civilian parties, had some backing from the *kapetanei* who imagined that the funds he carried were an instalment of more to come. The local primates, not to be outdone, backed him in the hope that he would usefully employ the military and keep them under control. His military ventures, however, met with scant success. His expedition to relieve the Souliots and to enlist their services for Greece suffered defeat at Peta in July 1822, and a raiding party sent by sea to Epiros retired with its mission unfulfilled.[2]

II. The National and Regional Assemblies

Although Mavrokordatos had based himself on western Greece, he believed

---

[1] Negris (1790–1824) was a westernised Greek who disagreed with other *eterists* and left the Principalities to take up an appointment in the Turkish embassy in Paris. On his way to France by ship he had learned of the outbreak of the Greek revolution and decided to make his way to the Peloponnese.

[2] By a treaty of 28 July 1822 the Turks allowed the Souliots to leave their homeland and to become refugees in the Ionian Islands.

that a central authority should be created. He had no intention of allowing this authority to derive from the *Eteria* and to come under the exclusive control of Ipsilantis and the *kapetanei*. With Ipsilantis he was prepared to collaborate to a certain extent, while Ipsilantis, who agreed that a central authority should be created, was willing to negotiate with Mavrokordatos. Both wished to avoid a head-on clash. The result was that with the blessing of Ipsilantis and the assistance of Negris, Mavrokordatos drew up at Zarakova, where the primates had assembled, an instrument of government. This provided for a national parliament consisting of those nominated by the primates of the Morea and of representatives of other regions; a senate of twenty-four members similarly chosen to serve a term of one year under the presidency of Ipsilantis; and ephors to serve a one-year term as district administrative officers. The *kapetanei*, however, disliked this scheme and they even threatened to massacre the primates. They were prepared to accept a temporary measure to which Ipsilantis agreed: that the Morea only should be administered by a senate of five primates, in effect the Peloponnesian senate of Turkish days. Meanwhile Ipsilantis was endeavouring to set up an administration of the islands on the basis of the *Eteria*, his object being to involve all the islands in addition to Idra, Spetzes, and Psara, in the cost of providing ships. In this, however, he met with no success.

After the failure of the Zarakova assembly, Mavrokordatos convened in November an assembly of western Greece consisting of thirty members. This body established an administration based on the Turkish pattern. The ephors and *kapetanei* elected a senate of ten members who, under the presidency of Mavrokordatos, were to serve for one year. Real authority, however, rested with the *kapetanei*: they controlled the police and each administered his own district as he pleased. Much the same was true of eastern Greece, where Negris convened at Salona an assembly of seventy-three members, some of them representatives from Thessaly, Epiros, and Macedonia. This assembly established a senate known as the *Arios Pagos*. In theory this body supervised the existing communal administrations, but, as in western Greece, these took their orders from the *kapetanei*.

All three regional assemblies had envisaged the convention of a national assembly (*vouli*). But when on 1 December 1821, following further efforts by Ipsilantis to promote national unity, a so-called national assembly met at Argos, its twenty-four members were nearly all primates from the Morea. Nevertheless, it was this body which entrusted to a committee, the active members of which were Mavrokordatos, Negris, and the Italian philhellene Gallina, the task of drawing up a constitution. This, known as the provisional constitution of Epidavros (or Piada), was dated 1 January 1822. According to its provisions the primates and respectable citizens were to elect for one year ephors for each village or township, the numbers varying from one to five according to the size of the population. These ephors were to elect representatives (five from each district). What in fact Mavrokordatos and Negris did (for all the democratic and revolutionary principles announced in the constitution) was to allow the oligarchy of the primates to replace the Turks. Even the districts they envisaged were simply the old Turkish *kazas*. The only innovation was to establish four of the *kapetanei* as military advisers to the senate. For the rest, the constitution mostly followed the French constitution of August 1795. But it was no slavish imitation of that model. Although it gave to the judiciary an independent function, it merged the functions of the legislature and executive. The executive, a body of five elected in a special assembly, could revise legislative acts, while the legislature could review the acts of the executive. Both bodies were to be served by eight ministers, who, like their departmental civil servants, were to be appointed by the executive. As a body these ministers had no independent power and, as they were debarred from being deputies, they had little or no political influence. They were, in fact, merely heads of departments in a rudimentary civil service. If power resided anywhere, it resided in the executive of five, who represented the Morea, western Greece, eastern Greece, and the islands, with Mavrokordatos as its president. Negris, though a deputy, received the less important offices of foreign affairs and president of the ministerial council. He enjoyed also the high-sounding but empty title of chancellor of state.

What the constitution did, behind a façade deliberately fashioned to impress Europe,[3] was to organise anarchy. In place of the various higher Turkish officials, it attempted to substitute a series of committees on which vested Greek interests were represented. At the same time it left intact, indeed it gave a form of legality to, the existing regional governments—the senate of the Peloponnese, the assembly of western Greece, and the *Arios Pagos* of eastern Greece. These, arenas for fierce rivalries, were soon to undergo changes. In the Peloponnese power passed into the hands of Kolokotronis; in western Greece first Georgios Varnakiotis, an *armatolos* from Akarnania, and later the Souliot Markos Botsaris came to the fore; while in eastern Greece the kleft Androutsos ('Odysseus', E. J. Trelawney's friend and brother-in-law) left the *Arios Pagos* and called together his own assembly. But although we know in much detail the story of these local rivalries, we do not know precisely how government was carried on. We do not know how the bands and ships were set moving, how expenditure was controlled, how officials were chosen and their conduct watched over, or how the former Turkish lands were taken over. Nor do we know how far the real initiative rested with the central and the larger regional administration, or how far it remained with local bodies and local leaders, who, at their leisure (and the War of Independence was a most leisurely affair), managed

[3] In July 1821 Count Kapodistrias had sent Mavrokordatos and the primates a memorandum advising them to satisfy the European powers by setting up a strong central government based on the existing local administrations. Little did Kapodistrias then realise that this was a contradiction in terms.

by negotiation to contrive some degree of co-operation. The only thing that is reasonably certain is that the vast record of laws and instructions does not describe what actually happened. The historian George Finlay[4] tells us— and he was in Greece at the time—that Greece continued to be governed by her Turkish institutions, but unfortunately he never explained precisely what he meant.[5]

III. Military Events, 1822–24

The Turkish campaigns of 1822 and 1823 were attempts to relieve the fortresses of Methoni, Koroni, Patras, Rio, Rumeli, Nafplion, Negropont, Chalkida, Karistos, Vonitsa, Zitouni (Lamia), and Athens. These were massive structures built mainly by the Franks and Venetians. All of them were on or near the sea. The Turkish navy, however, was neither large enough nor competent enough to undertake this task alone. Hence considerable land forces had to be employed, and these had necessarily to advance as two separate forces, the one through the western gates of the Makrinoros and the other through the eastern gates of Thermopylae. As these forces advanced southwards through the broken coastal plains, they must control the routes that lay between them, guard each defile that lay behind them, and then, if the Morea were to be entered, the western army must either be transported across the gulf of Korinth or link up with the eastern army to force the defiles of the Korinthian isthmus.

For two successive years the Turks attempted this task only to find that the lines of communication were much too long and the campaigning season much too short. They always lost time in mustering unruly Albanian forces in the west. They were constantly harried by the Greek bands, past-masters in guerrilla warfare. In 1822 the western army was held up by Mavrokordatos's campaign and, although it was victorious at Peta (July 1822), it was too short of supplies and too poor a match for the Greeks when at length it tried on Christmas Day to take Mesolonghi. That same year the Greek expedition to Chios (authorised by Ipsilantis out of rivalry to Mavrokordatos) delayed not only the advance of the eastern army but also the operations of the Turkish fleet, which subsequently suffered losses at the hands of Konstantinos Kanaris, a sea-captain from Psara and an expert in the use of fireships. The eastern army under Dramali Pasha, which was allowed by Androutsos to proceed unmolested, arrived too late to save the Acropolis of Athens, which had surrendered to the Greeks on 21 June.

---

[4] George Finlay, a philhellene who arrived in Greece in 1821, lived in Athens after the War of Independence. He wrote on the whole span of Greek history, from the Roman conquest. Volumes VI and VII in the Tozer edition (see Bibliography), dealing with the Greek revolution and the reign of Otho, were originally published separately in 1861.

[5] G. Dimakopoulos has produced an excellent study (see Bibliography) of the attempts of the Greeks to create a regular system of government and of their failure to do so. He rightly points out, however, that these attempts, despite their failure, kept before the Greeks the idea of national unity, without which they could never have survived to enjoy independence.

Although that army subsequently took Akrokorinth, it was defeated by Kolokotronis, Ipsilantis, and Dikaios in the *dervenakia*—the defiles between Korinth and Argos. Of the 23,000 who had entered the Morea with Dramali, 17,000 perished including the pasha himself.

In 1823 the Turks, wishing to avoid the perils of the isthmus and the *dervenakia*, sent their main force against western Greece, intending to transport it by sea across the gulf of Korinth. But both the naval and military preparations were delayed by a great fire, the work of unruly janissaries, at the arsenals of Constantinople. The eastern army was further delayed by the activities of the chiefs of eastern Greece and it suffered heavy losses in the passes of Elikon and Parnassos at the hands of Androutsos. In November the Turks surrendered Akrokorinth and then retreated northwards. The western army had already suffered a severe defeat on the night of 21/22 August at Karpenisi, at the foot of Mount Veluchi, with the result that only very weak forces managed to approach Mesolonghi and these, having suffered heavy losses on 11 December 1823, retreated to Arta.

The next year the Turkish effort was on a much smaller scale. The Sultan, having realised the difficulties of operations from the north, had called upon his vassal, Mohammed Ali of Egypt, to land forces in the Morea. But these forces under Ibrahim Pasha, Mohammed Ali's son, had first to subdue Kasos and Psara and to form a base in Crete. These preliminary operations took some time, and it was not until December 1824 that Ibrahim, constantly harassed by the Greek squadrons, obtained a footing in Crete. The Greeks, however, failed to take advantage of the respite thus gained. They missed the opportunity to seize the fortresses of Methoni and Koroni, salients which were likely to facilitate Ibrahim's task. With the pressure on them removed, their political quarrels became so intense that they began fighting among themselves.

IV. The Civil Wars of 1824 and 1825

Owing to the calls of military operations, the provisional government set up by the constitution of Epidavros had been prolonged to March 1823, when a second national assembly met at Astros. No regular elections had been held. The assembly was simply a gathering of those leaders who chose to attend or who were afraid to stay away. Its main task was to revise the constitution, which had satisfied no one. The principal revisions made were: the substitution of a suspensive veto for the absolute veto of the executive on the resolutions of the legislature; the granting to the legislature of a voice in the appointment of higher civil servants; the replacement of the war and navy ministers by two committees representing various regions; the abolition of the foreign ministry and chancellorship, whose duties were allocated to a general secretary of the executive. Following further, irregular, elections Kolokotronis became vice-president of the executive, with

Petrobey as president, Mavrokordatos became secretary-general, and Orlandos, representing the island interest, became president of the legislature. In theory the legislature was supreme, but, since the chieftains of the executive had their own armies, in practice it counted for nothing. Orlandos, a primate from Idra, resigned in disgust. For a short time Mavrokordatos took his place, but, being disgruntled and in danger, he fled to Idra. Ipsilantis no longer counted. Having been outwitted by Mavrokordatos, he was generally discredited, the more so as it was realised that no help could be expected from Russia. His place as leader of the 'military-democratic' factions had been taken by Kolokotronis, who, rich in booty and revenues from the villages, was able to buy the support of the lesser Moreot chieftains. Except for moments of bravery and patriotic example in the field, Ipsilantis was henceforth to play only a minor role in Greek affairs.

After Panos Kolokotronis[6] had tried to coerce the legislative assembly, many of its members left Astros and established themselves at Kranidhi, where they appointed a rival executive with Koundouriotis from Idra as president. The schism was the result of new alignments based on regional rather than on class interests. On the one side were the primates and chieftains of the Morea, temporarily in alliance; on the other were the maritime classes, the Greeks of western Rumeli, and men like Mavrokordatos, who were remnants of a national party. It was not long before the two governments were at war, squandering the slender resources of the nation precisely when advantage should have been taken of the weakness of the Turks. Outside the struggle, for the most part, were the men of eastern Greece, where the warring factions paid no heed to either government.

In December 1823 the legislature managed to dismiss Petrobey and in January appointed Koundouriotis as president of the executive. It also prolonged its own existence until October 1824. The elections had been delayed and it was not until September that a quorum was obtained. Throughout the early summer civil war raged between the Moreot chieftains and the government of Koundouriotis. All attempts to establish a congress of conciliation at Salona, in which Androutsos, Yannis Gouras (lieutenant of Androutsos), and Negris hoped to play leading roles, came to naught, and the body that assembled there in April was merely a revival of the former *Arios Pagos*. In June, however, John Kolettis, a Vlach from continental Greece and former physician to Ali Pasha, organised Rumeliot troops under Panoutsos Notaras and Makriyannis, who succeeded in driving the Moreots out of Nafplion. But for the influence of the primates Zaimis, Londos, and Sisinis, who were temporarily in alliance with the government of Koundouriotis, Kolokotronis might have been seized and put to death. But the last thing these primates wanted was the predominance of the island or the

---

[6] The eldest son of Theodoros Kolokotronis; he married the daughter of Bouboulina, the famous woman sea-captain.

Rumeliot interest; and they were generous enough to realise that not only they themselves but the nation also would still have need of Kolokotronis.

An assembly which met in Nafplion in October 1824 reappointed Koundouriotis as president of the executive and Mavrokordatos as general secretary. Included in the executive of five was Kolettis, their rival, but indispensable because of his influence with the Rumeliot chieftains. These nominations, however, satisfied neither the chieftains nor the primates of the Morea who, not to be outdone, tried to enlist the support of Petrobey, Androutsos, and Gouras. Petrobey and Androutsos remained aloof, however, and much depended upon Gouras, who had become powerful in eastern Greece. But eventually Kolettis won him over to the government party. In December he defeated Nikitas Stamatelopoulos, Kolokotronis's nephew, and the primate Andreas Londos, and early in 1825 he overcame Georgios Sisinis, who along with Anagnostis Deliyannis and Theodoros Kolokotronis were taken prisoner.[7]

The imprisonment of Kolokotronis meant that the Greek nation, despite the extraordinary powers conferred on Koundouriotis, was in no position to meet the threat from Ibrahim Pasha, who in February and March 1825 landed two strong forces at Methoni. Belated attempts organised by the executive to contain the Egyptians were unsuccessful. Koundouriotis and Mavrokordatos were discredited. The former, in poor health, resigned and the executive, despite protests from Mavrokordatos, released Kolokotronis from prison and appointed him field marshal. Meanwhile the legislative body had established two committees of its own: one to organise the struggle against Ibrahim and the other to provide for the defence of Nafplion. The situation was critical. Despite resistance from Kolokotronis and much determined action on the part of some seventy Greek vessels to impede supplies and reinforcements for the Egyptians, Ibrahim's troops began to fan out in the Morea, destroying crops, animals, and dwellings. Towards the end of June they threatened Navarino. Ibrahim, however, was short of supplies; and once again that sincere patriot Ipsilantis came forward with the gallant Makriyannis and some 250 men to defend the fortified mills of Lerna which commanded the road leading northwards to Argos. Ibrahim and his 7,000 men were forced to retreat. They were fortunate to escape disaster; Kolokotronis was just too late to catch him in the defile of Parthenion.

V. The Act of Submission, June–August 1825

In the hour of peril, the wishful-thinking Greeks expected Europe to repay its long-standing debt to Greek civilisation and to come to their aid. Right from the beginning of their struggle they had hoped that Europe and

---

[7] Gouras later imprisoned his rival and old friend Androutsos in the Acropolis of Athens. For the intrigue which led to this event and for the part played at this time by Edward J. Trelawney, see my *British and American Philhellenes*, pp. 90ff.

America would bless their enterprise. On 6 April 1821 Petrobey had issued an eloquent appeal. Later that year the *Arios Pagos* of eastern Greece, in drawing up a constitution, had made provision for a king; and it was hoped that the powers would choose him from a European ruling house. In 1822 the Greeks had sent to the congress of Verona, initially convened to discuss the Greek question, a delegation to propose a monarchy for Greece; but the powers turned it away. Nevertheless, men of all parties in Greece, despite their strong republican habits, continued to think in terms of monarchy. Wishing to appear respectable and conservative revolutionaries, they thought it politic to dangle a Greek crown before the eyes of the European Concert.

Very few Greeks continued to place hopes in Russia, whose policy was generally discredited. Of France, who for long had backed Mohammed Ali, most Greeks were exceedingly suspicious and there was a widespread predilection for Great Britain. The founding of the London Greek committee in 1823; the raising of the first Greek loan in England; the formal recognition in March 1823 of Greek blockades by Canning; the very elevation of Canning to the British foreign office; Canning's policy in Spain, Portugal, and South America; his antagonism to the so-called Holy Alliance; the arrival of the British philhellenes in Greece; and above all the second Greek pilgrimage of Lord Byron—all these had led most Greeks to discount the declared British policy of strict neutrality. What is more, those same Greeks chose to forget the British government's unwelcome offer (made unofficially early in 1823) to promote a mediation between Greeks and Turks on the basis of principality status for Greece—a proposal which, in more elaborate form (three principalities), was embodied in a Russian memorandum of January 1824 for discussion at a projected conference of the powers at St Petersburg. This Russian proposal would have given the Greeks a form of autonomy in an area larger than the one they had freed; but it was highly unpopular in Greece and served only to convince the Greeks that Russia was about to betray their cause and that every effort must be made to enlist the sympathies of Canning.

In December 1824 Canning rejected a Greek appeal (of 24 August) for intervention, saying in effect that Britain could intervene only if both Greeks and Turks requested mediation, but adding, as if to soften the blow, that Britain would not force upon the Greeks a settlement not to their liking. He himself favoured Greek independence provided the Greeks themselves won it. His military intelligence suggested that they would do so. Austrian intelligence pointed the other way, for it came from subservient consuls in touch chiefly with the Turks. Hence, for different reasons, Metternich, the Austrian minister, and Canning waited upon events, both wishing to avoid a war between Russia and Turkey. Canning calculated that Russia would be reluctant to act alone. He also calculated that the growing English interest among the Greeks would prevent Russia from having a predominant influence in regenerated Greece.

The development of the English interest in Greece, so essential to Canning's policy, was not unchallenged. Despite official French neutrality, General Roche, agent of the Paris Greek committee, and the philhellene Jourdain had, in collusion with the Vitalis brothers, wealthy merchants from Zante, formed a French party. Its aim was to place an Orleanist on the throne of Greece. This French intrigue was largely a reaction against an earlier move to establish John Kapodistrias as ruler of Greece—a move which had no connection with Russia: neither Kapodistrias nor his promoters had any illusions about Russia; they knew that the Russian memorandum of January 1824 was unpopular in Greece; and they counted largely on Franco–British rivalry to work for the benefit of Greece. The chief bond that united them was their abhorrence of the Moreot chieftains and their rivalry to Mavrokordatos, whose own policy was substantially the same. Mavrokordatos had connections with both the English and the French interests, and for a time he even toyed with the idea of a Franco–Russian alignment on the Greek question.[8] His policy, in short, was to stimulate the rivalries of the European Concert in such a way as to benefit Greece.

The English interest, which had its origins in Byron's last journey and in the activities of the philhellene Edward Blaquiere, was developed by Lord Guilford, by his pupil Trikoupis, and by a committee of Zantiots, who enlisted the support of Kolokotronis. As time went on, it came to have a greater following, among the leading Greeks, than that of either the Kapodistrians or of the French party; and even Mavrokordatos became entangled in it, if only because he did not want to see the French party monopolised by his rival Kolettis. Encouraged by the British naval commander, Commodore Hamilton, the pro-English Greeks circulated a petition requesting for the Greek nation the sole protection of Great Britain. This petition, the so-called Act of Submission, was dated 30 June 1825 and was sent to England. It was subsequently approved by the legislative assembly on 1 August and a further copy was taken to London in a Greek ship—much to the annoyance of Kolokotronis, who resented the act's becoming a government measure. Not to be outdone, the French connection sent in February 1826 an address to the duc d'Orléans asking him to accept the Greek crown for his son, the duc de Nemours. Ipsilantis, Nikitas, and Kolokotronis, who had changed party, had already signed an act of submission to Russia.

During the winter of 1825–26 the three Greek 'parties' prepared for the third national assembly, which eventually came together at Epidavros in April 1826 under the presidency of Notaras. This assembly appointed a governmental committee of eleven members, and a legislative committee of thirteen. The governmental committee, under the presidency of Zaimis, created or rather recognised local committees which already existed, thus

---

[8] This was the plan of Theobald Piscatory, a philhellene and later French minister at Athens. He was counting on the help of a small Russian connection which had been formed by the old Psarian Greek Varvakis, one of Orlov's veterans of 1771.

maintaining the fiction that Greece was a centralised state. The legislative committee was to concern itself with expected negotiations with the European powers and to continue the attempts, first begun in 1824, to find a Western military commander. In August 1825 Lord Cochrane's services as naval commander had been secured in principle, and the decision had been taken to devote the proceeds of the second London loan (7 February 1825) to the provision of a steam fleet. But the search for a military commander had met with no success, Charles James Napier, formerly the British resident of Kefalonia, having decided that he would not play second fiddle to Lord Cochrane.

Meanwhile military and naval operations had continued in a confused and desultory fashion. By January 1826 Ibrahim was concentrating strong forces around Mesolonghi, but the inhabitants and garrison held out until their desperate and fateful sortie on the night of 22–23 April. Thereafter Ibrahim turned his attention to Tripolitsa, which the Moreots were besieging. Although he entered and provisioned the town, he was unable to crush the Greek bands, which inflicted heavy losses upon his columns throughout the summer of 1826. By the end of the year he had lost 16,000 out of his original 24,000 men: of the survivors many were sick; and food and ammunition were in short supply. That same year a revolt of the janissaries and plague and fires in Constantinople so disorganised the Turks that in October they signed with Russia the treaty of Akkerman, by which they recognised Russian possession of certain Asiatic frontier forts, granted an improved status to Serbia, and agreed to native rulers for the Danubian Principalities. Nevertheless, despite the spirited operations of the Rumeliot chieftain Karaiskakis, the Turkish general, Kiutaya, managed in August to take Athens, though he was unable to dislodge the Greek garrison in the Acropolis.

VI. The Protocol of April 1826 and the Treaty of London, July 1827

Canning had no use for Metternich and a profound suspicion of the French. He rejected Wellington's proposal that Britain should align herself with France and Austria to deter Russia from making war on Turkey and decided to co-operate with Russia. He calculated that Lord Cochrane's projected expedition, consisting of six steamships and various other vessels, would strengthen the English interest in Greece, and he therefore decided to get the Greeks, whose request for a British protectorate he had rejected, to ask for mediation. This Greek request was not immediately forthcoming. Nevertheless he began negotiations with the Lievens,[9] which he followed up by sending the duke of Wellington on a special mission to St Petersburg. The result was the protocol of 4 April 1826. Greece was to be an autonomous

[9] Princess Lieven counted for more than her husband, the Russian ambassador, in these negotiations which began at Seaford in December 1825.

though tributary state, but no boundaries were indicated. The Sultan was to have 'a certain share' in the nomination of its sovereign. Mediation was to be offered to, but not forced upon, the Turks. If they refused, the two powers were to be free to continue their intervention either jointly or separately, but in the event of a Russo–Turkish war, the Greek settlement was to follow the lines laid down. The protocol was to be communicated to the Courts of Paris, Vienna, and Berlin with the request that they should become parties to and guarantee the final transaction in concert with Russia, but not with England. This protocol was certainly a stick to beat the Turks with. As Canning explained, his policy was 'to save Greece through the agency of the Russian name upon the fears of Turkey, without a war'.

Canning had quit the European Concert at the congress of Verona in 1822. He had refused to join it at St Petersburg in 1824. Now it was his policy to reconstruct it under British leadership. He therefore went to Paris in September 1826 to try to persuade France to take part in the mediation and thus to provide additional restraint on Russia. The French demanded a five-power treaty and a guarantee of the Ottoman empire, but Canning strongly objected. Months passed by. Eventually in March 1827 Russia proposed a treaty with a secret clause providing for the use of force if necessary to compel the Turks to accept mediation. Canning, who became prime minister in April 1827, was quick to realise that force, or at least the threat of force, could not be excluded; he therefore drafted a treaty, which, with some amendments, was signed in London on 6 July 1827 by Russia, France, and Britain.

The first article stated that the three powers would demand the consent of both Greeks and Turks to an armistice, whereupon the powers would negotiate a settlement on the basis of the establishment of Greece as an autonomous, though tributary, state under Turkish suzerainty. A secret article stated that if the Turks did not accept the proffered mediation, the allies would send consuls to Greece, and that if one or other party should refuse the armistice, the powers would jointly prevent collisions, without, however, taking part in hostilities. A week later instructions were sent to the allied naval commanders in the Aegean: if the Turks refused and the Greeks accepted the armistice, the admirals were to treat the Greeks as friends and intercept supplies from Egypt and the Dardanelles. They were to take care, however, to prevent these measures from degenerating into hostilities and were to resort to force only if the Turks persisted 'in forcing the passages which they had intercepted'. Thus Canning had intended, in his own words, a 'peaceful interference, recommended by a friendly demonstration of force'. He died shortly after the treaty was signed.

Meanwhile in Greece the third national assembly of Epidavros, upon which the fall of Mesolonghi had had a sobering effect, had pronounced in favour of negotiations for a settlement. This assembly represented principally that old combination of Kolokotronis, Londos, and Zaimis which had been defeated in December 1824. It was not long, however, before Kolokotronis was again at loggerheads with his former allies and he joined forces with Koundouriotis who was in conflict with the majority of the Idriot primates. Reinforced by Sisinis, they called in February 1827 their own assembly at Kastri (Ermioni). As a counter-move the old government convened its supporters at Egina. These divisions resulted principally from personal and regional animosities—from a struggle for power. There was no division on policy, for all factions had come to accept British mediation, which they realised implied a settlement by England, France, and Russia. Each faction was out to dominate the government that would be called upon to deal with those powers. Kolokotronis in particular now wanted to bring Kapodistrias to Greece. He realised, however, that this could be done only with the concurrence of the English interest, and to cut out Mavrokordatos and Zaimis he made attempts to bring his old friend Major (now General Sir Richard) Church to Greece as military commander.

Church arrived near Kastri on 9 March 1827. Eight days later that professional liberator and breezy sailor Lord Cochrane arrived. Their first task was to compose the quarrels. This they did. Broadly speaking they formed an alliance between the English and the Kapodistrian interests, which were not mutually exclusive. The two assemblies agreed to meet at Damala (Troezene). Here the deputies proclaimed Count John Kapodistrias as president of Greece for a period of seven years, appointing a provisional government of three to carry on until his arrival. All the other leaders had been found wanting and had been involved in the interminable civil strife that had paralysed the nation. Kapodistrias by way of contrast had remained aloof. A legened had grown up about him. He had never stooped to intrigue; and his diplomatic experience would be a great asset in handling the negotiations with the powers. Throughout the winter of 1826–27 his stock had improved, and many of the English interest had come to support his nomination. Nevertheless, although the Greeks had decided to concentrate the executive function in one man, they designed at Damala a new constitution to limit his powers. His ministers, who were liable to impeachment by the legislature, were to countersign all state documents. To the legislative body (elected for three years with one-third of members retiring annually) he was denied access except at the opening and closing of each session. He had no right of dissolution and he had no absolute veto on legislation. Indeed, the new constitution, to which was attached a bill of rights, showed, if anything, an even greater aversion to a strong executive than did its predecessors.

The assembly at Damala appointed Cochrane as chief admiral and Church as generalissimo. On assuming their commands these two attempted to co-ordinate Greek operations which, with money and supplies provided by the European philhellenes, had been carried on spasmodically throughout 1826 and during the early part of 1827. In particular they attempted to increase the scale of operations for the relief of the Acropolis of Athens. Church managed to muster some 3,000 troops, and he was hoping for support from Tzavellas whose bands numbered a further 7,000. But Cochrane's interference with Church's land forces led to a severe defeat between Athens and the sea on 6 May 1827 and to the surrender of the Acropolis about a month later. Thereafter Cochrane sailed about to no purpose, but Church began to build up forces at Akrokorinth and the Moreots continued to harry Ibrahim in the Morea. Such was the situation when news of the treaty of London arrived in Greece.

Church and Cochrane, in collaboration with the Greek government, which had accepted the armistice on 2 September, planned three expeditions —one to Chios, one to Thessaly, and the third to western Greece, where news of the treaty had caused the chieftains to declare their readiness to renew the struggle. They had rightly calculated on the Porte's refusal to accept mediation and they wished, in anticipation of allied intervention, to rekindle the revolt and claim extensive boundaries. Meanwhile the Egyptians planned to send reinforcements to the Morea in order to crush the Moreots before the powers could intervene. On 9 September these reinforcements arrived in Navarino Bay, where a Turkish squadron was already anchored. These forces became the concern of the senior allied naval commander, Admiral Codrington, who had been informed by Stratford Canning, the British ambassador at Constantinople, that the allied instructions meant that the admirals were to intercept supplies—in the last resort 'by cannon shot'. Fearing that the Moslem fleets would sail out of Navarino to carry war to other parts of Greece, Codrington saw Ibrahim, explained to him his instructions, agreed to wait while Ibrahim consulted the Sultan and Mohammed Ali, and promised to prevent Church and Cochrane from operating in western Greece. But Church and Abney Hastings, a naval captain commanding a steamship, had begun operations in and around the gulf of Korinth. The Moslem fleets consequently left Navarino for the scene of action, but were driven back by Codrington with only four ships. To prevent a repetition of this sortie, Codrington, who later asserted that owing to bad weather he could not maintain a watch from outside Navarino, decided to enter the bay with the three allied squadrons and to anchor within the arc formed by the Moslem ships stationed in three curving lines from shore to shore. Had the Moslems waited till nightfall of 20 October (the day Codrington entered), they might have wrought havoc with fireships; but they began action in daylight, and in the firing-match that ensued they lost sixty out of eighty-nine vessels and 8,000 men.

Such was the 'untoward' event of Navarino—an event so unwelcome to the British government, which was never quite certain whether to blame Canning or Codrington. There were many who believed that Codrington had exceeded his instructions, but as Codrington himself was the chief source of information for what happened, it was not easy to make a case against him. Moreover, the weak parts of his 'defence' were never probed:

he was never asked why he permitted Church and Hastings to continue operations, or why he did not wait, before entering Navarino, for Ibrahim to receive instructions from Constantinople and Alexandria; and he was allowed to make much of a report (unconfirmed at the time) that Ibrahim intended to devastate the whole Morea. When at length he was recalled, the pretext was his failure to institute a blockade, which as a non-belligerent he had no right to do. Though he was punished ostensibly for neglect, everyone knew that the real case against him was his impetuosity, which gained for him, whatever his fellow-countrymen may have thought about him, the eternal gratitude of the Greek nation. Church bells rang in all the villages and huge fires were lighted on the mountains, but Greece's problems were far from settled.

Despite their defeat the Turks showed no sign of yielding and even repudiated the convention of Akkerman. The allies, influenced mainly by Wellington, Canning's successor, remained inactive until the Tsar, impatient of delays, declared war on Turkey in April 1828. After the Canningites had left the English ministry, however, Wellington became more co-operative with his two allies. In May 1828 he agreed to a conference, which in July drew up instructions for the allied ambassadors who were to meet at Poros. These instructions suggested four different frontiers for consideration, the most favourable being the line Volos–Aspropotamos and the least favourable confining Greece to the Morea. He further agreed that French troops should be employed to expel Ibrahim. It was understood that they were not to operate north of the gulf of Korinth and should be withdrawn as soon as their task was done.

VII. The Arrival of Count John Kapodistrias, January 1828. The War in Western Greece

But for the good tidings of Navarino it is very doubtful whether Kapodistrias, the president-elect, would have gone to Greece. On receiving official news of his election, he had not accepted the honour immediately: he had wished to ascertain whether the powers approved his nomination and to go to St Petersburg to ask permission to resign from the Russian service. He hoped, moreover, to raise a loan sanctioned by the assembly of Damala and to collect ample funds from the European Greeks. In neither of these two aims did he succeed. He was not enamoured of the constitution under which he was called upon to rule, and he knew only too well that the Greeks were engaged in fierce party struggles. For the party leaders, whom he labelled Christian Turks (primates), Robbers (*kapetanei*), Fools (intellectuals), and Children of Satan (fanariots), he had nothing but contempt. His own ideal was a nation of farmers and peasants under paternal rule and the French civil code—in other words a democratic society but not a democratic state. From the moment he arrived in Greece, he violated the constitution. On 30 January 1828 he transferred the powers of the legislature first to a council (*panhellinion*) appointed by himself, and later to an even more docile senate. He filled many offices with Ionian Greeks and he appointed non-local men as prefects. He delayed calling a national assembly, which should have met in April 1829, and when at length he convened it in July, he packed it with his nominees. Little wonder, then, that he was to arouse considerable opposition from a combination of factions which called themselves the constitutional party. He enjoyed, however, some standing among the lesser Greeks of all regions and he had the support of Kolokotronis and other *kapetanei*. It can therefore be said that he consolidated a national party, which in the less tangible form of the secret Phoenix Society[10] had been taking shape before his arrival.

Although he tended to despise all Greeks as individuals, in his sentimental and abstract way he had the good of Greece at heart, and he certainly approved the nationalist aims of the Greek revolution. He had, moreover, a deep religious sense, indeed a sense of divine mission, and it was perhaps not to be wondered at that he wanted the Church in nascent Greece to be a department of his paternal state. This state he wished to be as large as he could persuade the powers to sanction. He was therefore intent to ensure that when the boundaries came to be settled the Greeks should be under arms over the greatest area of territory possible. This idea had already occurred to others. Immediately after Navarino, Cochrane had gone to assist the French philhellene Fabvier in operations (which in fact ended in disaster[11]) in the island of Chios, while General Church and Captain Hastings had begun a campaign in western Greece, where many of the chieftains were anxious to join those who had kept the flicker of revolt alive. Church formed a base at Dragomestri, with the intention of seizing the gulf of Arta and the 'gates' of Makrinoros. This, he calculated, would lead to the fall of the chain of twenty-five fortified Turkish posts between that region and Mesolonghi. But Hastings favoured operations against Mesolonghi itself and Church, who was dependent upon him for naval assistance, agreed to the plan, which Kapodistrias also favoured. In these long-drawn-out and unsuccessful operations Hastings lost his life (June 1828).

Church reverted to his former plan and established a second base at Mitika. To this venture Kapodistrias, who had his own connections with the chiefs of western Greece, promised support, but by August had changed his mind, hoping that General Maison's 8,000 French troops would clean up Rumeli as well as the Morea. Further, he had become antagonistic to

[10] Not much is known about this society. Its early members were Metaxas, Nikitas, Kanaris, Kolokotronis, Rangos, and Perroukas, who were chiefly responsible for calling Kapodistrias to Greece. During the Kapodistrian regime it expanded its membership considerably, and it certainly remained active for some time afterwards. In all probability it was transformed into the Philorthodox Society (see below, p. 72).

[11] Cochrane gave up his command in January 1828, and formally resigned it the following November.

Church, whom he identified with the growing opposition to the government. Nevertheless he did not recall Church: he still wanted the revolution to continue in western Greece, and indeed in eastern Greece, where Ipsilantis was in the field. With the allied protocol of 18 November 1828, which placed the Morea and the Cyclades under a provisional guarantee of the allied powers, he was far from happy and he feared that Wellington might follow up this move by adopting Metternich's proposal that a small independent Greece should be established before the Russians gained successes in their war with Turkey.

Church, who considered his own mandate from the Greek nation as good as the president's, carried on without regard for Kapodistrias. In March he took Vonitsa; in April he seized Karvassara, having been joined by the powerful chief Iskos of Valtos[12]—events which led the Albanians to evacuate the chain of the posts on the supply-line to Mesolonghi. Through certain Albanian chiefs he had already negotiated the capitulation of Mesolonghi itself, but it fell to the president's brother, Agostino, to make a triumphal entry into this shrine of the Greek revolution, leading an army which had never fired a shot in western Greece. Thoroughly disgusted, he made on 6 April 1829 what he hoped would be a dramatic resignation of his command to the Greek nation; but only through his friendship with Kolokotronis did he get a silent hearing from Kapodistrias's packed assembly. Altogether he had been given an uncommonly bad deal. Had Kapodistrias afforded him even moderate support, he could easily have won for Greece Thessaly and much of Epiros.

Meanwhile in December 1828 the conference of Poros had recommended for Greece the Arta–Volos frontier, the inclusion of Samos and Euboea, but not Crete; an hereditary prince; and an annual tribute payable to the Sultan at the moderate rate of £60,000. But these recommendations found no favour with Wellington, who pointed out to the British representative at Poros, Stratford Canning, that the original object of the treaty was to pacify the Levant and not to create a power capable of making war on Turkey. Later, however, in a protocol of 22 March 1829, Wellington agreed to the Arta–Volos line, not as a settlement to be imposed, but as a basis for negotiations with the Turks. The Russians signed this protocol too, calculating that the Turks would not accept it and that the whole situation would eventually be changed by their armies. These calculations proved to be correct. In June Silistria fell and on 20 August Russian troops reached Adrianople. This advance alarmed both Wellington and the Turks. The Turks hastened to accept the treaty of London, suggesting that Greece should consist of the Morea and Cyclades. For a brief moment, Wellington, like the French, thought of creating a Greek empire to replace fallen Turkey

---

[12] Iskos had rebelled against the Turks in 1821, had joined Mavrokordatos in 1822 (with the rank of general), but had subsequently made a truce with the Turks. He had rejoined the Greeks in 1824 but had renewed his truce in 1826.

as a buffer to an expanded Russia; but he did not realise that the Russians had changed their policy—that they had decided to preserve Turkey as a senile neighbour. Not until he received news of the peace of Adrianople (14 September 1829) was he fully aware of their moderate terms: a frontier advance at the mouth of the Danube; a new system under Russian supervision in the Danubian Principalities; commercial privileges; a war indemnity; the extension of Serbian privileges; and the acceptance of the protocol of March 1829. After this, Wellington dropped all ideas of a large Greek state and worked for a small, entirely independent Greece, shorn of the western provinces that General Church had won.

Much, however, was likely to depend upon the choice of ruler. This Kapodistrias had fully realised, and he had proposed to the Poros conference the name of Leopold of Saxe-Coburg, thinking that this nomination would reconcile Wellington to larger boundaries. Leopold had long coveted the Greek crown, but he was likely to insist upon an adequate and a reasonable financial arrangement, and was therefore acceptable to Kapodistrias, who certainly meant to use him for Hellenic ends. But if the three allied Courts were determined to keep the boundaries small, then Kapodistrias would, in the last resort, work through Russia for vassal status and better boundaries.

For the Greek crown there were at least six other possible candidates and it was Russia's policy to encourage France and England to run rival nominees, in the hope of making the final choice herself. At length, however, in a protocol of 3 February 1830, the powers decided on Leopold: he was acceptable to England because of his dynastic connections; to Russia because he wanted large boundaries for Greece; and to France because there was a chance he would marry an Orleanist princess. But in offering him the crown, they abandoned the favourable Arta–Volos frontier and substituted the more southerly Aspropotamos–Zitouni (Lamia) line, and they excluded both Samos and Crete from the proposed Greek kingdom. All this and much more besides Leopold found unsatisfactory, but he accepted the offer in principle intending to revise the terms. In the subsequent negotiations, however, he overplayed his hand: he went so far as to tender his resignation, which he fondly imagined would, owing to Russian and French policy, and to the power of the British opposition, be refused. Much to his own surprise, however, and much to the sorrow of Kapodistrias and of the majority of Greeks, his resignation was accepted with alacrity. What he had failed to realise was that Wellington's parliamentary position was strong and his diplomatic hand was by no means feeble.

The story that Kapodistrias deliberately frightened Leopold away from Greece, that he was throughout the tool of Russia, and that he aimed to be a hospodar of a Russian-made principality in Greece is sheer legend—legend which had its origins in English philhellenic and official circles and which was perpetuated by the nineteenth-century historians and by those who have based their story on them. The truth is that Kapodistrias was never exclusively attached to Russia any more than Mavrokordatos was exclusively attached to England, or Kolettis to France. Like Mavrokordatos he always worked for a European solution of the Greek question, and if at times he was driven to draw closer to Russia, it was because of British hostility towards him and because of the excessive finesse of the French, who in the main, however, were favourable to him. After all, like Mavrokordatos, he understood in a general way the working of the European Concert. What he was not able to do was to ensure that its intricate manoeuvres would always work for what he considered to be desirable for Greece.

But Leopold's sacrifice was not made in vain. His withdrawal, along with the July revolution in France, delayed the settlement until a new British government came to power. With the minimum of fuss, Palmerston, the new British foreign secretary, agreed to the Arta–Volos frontier; but Greece lapsed into anarchy and civil war. Kapodistrias, who had made a genuine attempt to abolish Greek parties by including opponents within his administration, was faced with an opposition growing daily more truculent. By October 1829 only servile partisans remained with him. Up to that time opposition leaders like Mavrokordatos had shown much forbearance: they did not want to discredit Greece in the eyes of the powers or deter a European prince from accepting the crown; and they continued to hope that the powers would choose a sovereign who would dispense with Kapodistrias's services. Hence they were at first content merely to discredit the president in the eyes of France and Great Britain, spreading the story, transmitted by the philhellenes to their governments, that he had sold himself to Russia, that he planned to incorporate the Ionian Islands in the new Greek state, that he was aiming to perpetuate his presidency, and that he would drive the Francophil and Anglophil constitutionalists into exile. These stories were certainly believed in London. The French government, on the other hand, tended to discount them. What they feared was not that Kapodistrias would remain but that he might throw in his hand out of sheer despair and that utter chaos would reign in Greece.

Following Leopold's withdrawal and the July revolution in France, the opposition to Kapodistrias's regime began to take on the semblance of a national party, to which some cohesion was given by governmental countermeasures and by the encouragement afforded by the French and British representatives (residents) accredited to Greece. Basically, however, the opposition was personal and regional, and it eventually manifested itself in three local rebellions—that of Mani, that of Idra, and that of Talanti in eastern Greece. These rebellions forced the president to seek the support of the Russian admiral Ricord[13]—a development which seemed to prove more

[13] Ricord had succeeded Heyden as commander of the Russian squadron stationed in the Aegean under the terms of the treaty of London, 1827.

clearly than ever that Kapodistrias was sold to Russia. But although at times he contemplated resignation, he still half hoped that the powers, in concert, would find a solution for Greece; and he was prepared, if only to prevent utter confusion, to carry on his work, even to act as regent until the sovereign prince arrived. His brave struggle, however, was brought to an untimely end on 9 October 1831: he was assassinated by Georgios and Konstantinos Mavromichalis as he was entering the beautiful little church of St Spiridhon in Nafplion.

VIII. The Settlement: the Arrival of King Otho, 30 January 1833

The senate appointed a provisional triumvirate consisting of Agostino Kapodistrias, Kolokotronis, and Kolettis. The Kapodistrians hoped thus to prevent Kolettis from joining the Maniats, the Idriots, and the followers of Mavrokordatos. They counted, moreover, on the rivalry between Kolettis and Kolokotronis to give Agostino the upper hand. But what they had really done was to weaken their position. Kolettis not only had the Rumeliot *kapetanei* at his beck and call but he made a bid for the support of the constitutionalists. Having established his independence, he was joined by the Moreot primates and the Idriots, and it was not long before he set up his own triumvirate (himself, Koundouriotis, and Zaimis) at Perachora, which Mavrokordatos joined as a secretary of state. But this combination was quite unstable. Mainly through the persuasions of Dawkins, the British resident, who feared that Kolettis would establish French influence in Greece, Zaimis, Mavrokordatos, and many others joined the Kapodistrians. As in early 1827, what in fact took place was a *rapprochement* between the Kapodistrian and the 'English' parties.

Civil war again resulted. As in 1824, Kolettis sent his Rumeliot troops into the Morea. In April 1832 they entered Nafplion and forced Agostino to resign. Following negotiations between Kolettis, the senators, the foreign residents, and various other interests, it was agreed that a governmental commission of seven and a cabinet of five ministers should be appointed. In this administration most parties were represented. Once again it was evident that the Greeks, though always apt to fly at one another's throats, could arrive at a compromise when tempers had cooled down: they were never divided on principle; the labels they gave themselves were always misleading. No Kapodistrian was absolutely opposed to a constitution and no constitutionalist despised naked power whenever he got the chance to wield it.

On 26 July 1832 the national assembly of Pronia met—a symbol of the new-found unity. It abolished the senate, proclaimed an amnesty, and declared itself a constituent assembly. But this intention to make a new constitution was frustrated, at Dawkins's instigation, by the Rumeliot *kapetanei*, who dispersed the assembly. Once again chaos reigned. The governmental commission had no power outside Nafplion. Power continued to reside in the provincial centres where, even in the Morea, the Kapodistrians were often in the ascendant.

Amid the inter-factional strife, debate centred on who should have the place of honour when the sovereign prince arrived. The seventeen-year-old Otho, second son of the philhellene King Ludwig of Bavaria, had already been nominated, and the choice had been approved in the assembly of Pronia. This nomination, first agreed in February, had been confirmed in a treaty of 7 May 1832 between Bavaria and the protecting powers. Until the king came of age, three regents appointed by his father were to rule in his name. The Bavarians were to provide an army of 3,500 men. Its cost, like that of the indemnity (£462,000), was to be paid out of a guaranteed allied loan of £2,400,000. Greece was to be an independent country with the Arta–Volos frontier (Crete and Samos excluded) under the guarantee of the powers. As no formal guarantee treaty was concluded with Greece, it was never certain what the purpose of the guarantee was. The powers had put on record that they would not permit Turkey to reconquer Greece; and they had given, for what it was worth, an undertaking to Bavaria that, if Otho went to Greece, as far as they themselves were concerned he could stay there. They did not, it seems, see the need to make provision for a situation in which the Greeks themselves might wish to depose him.

In November, the Kapodistrians and certain others made a determined effort to take over the government. They stole the official printing-press and issued proclamations. They set up a military commission and established a senate. Hostile to Otho, and unaware of Russia's support for him, they elected Admiral Ricord as president of Greece. The three residents called in French troops[14] to restore order and thus frustrated the plot. But when Otho arrived off Nafplion in a British frigate the wranglings still continued, and it was not until 6 February 1833 that it was fitting for him to step ashore. He was the idol of the moment and the symbol of Greek freedom, so long delayed by Greek strife and the tortuous diplomacy of Europe. But the 750,000 Greeks within Otho's kingdom were not completely free: Greece was under a protectorate exercised by Bavaria on behalf of the three protecting powers, who had a claim to interfere and did so frequently throughout the nineteenth century. Outside the Greek kingdom were over 2 million Greeks still under Turkish or British rule. All this presaged a stormy future, as did the conflicting principles upon which the settlement of 1832 was based. Implicit in the treaty of May 1832 was the unconstitutional power of Otho; but in a London conference proclamation of August 1832 the powers had called upon the Greeks to rally round the throne and to assist Otho in giving the kingdom a definitive constitution.

The Greece that Otho went to rule was in one sense primitive and yet in

[14] General Maison's troops had remained in Greece with the reluctant agreement of the British government.

another politically advanced. It was primitive because of the poverty of the soil, the lack of raw material, and the devastations of war and civil disorders. Restoration was bound to take years; economic progress was bound for decades to be slow. The greatest asset was the sea, but time was required before the Greeks could develop their mercantile marine.

During the war they had lost their grip on trade; their larger ships had been converted into men-of-war; commercial capital had been spent on supplies; and in the old commercial centres of Turkey trade had passed into other hands. Even when after several decades Greek commercial shipping revived, the greater part of it was not based on Greece itself but on Turkish and other foreign ports. Its economic effect on the small Greek kingdom was consequently limited. Greece therefore long remained an under-developed country and was described, officially, as such until a decade or so ago. But despite its poverty and economic backwardness, the small Greek nation-state was to enjoy a vigorous political and cultural life and Athens was to become a centre of Hellenism no less important than that which remained in Constantinople.[15]

[15] See below, Chapters 6 and 17.

CHAPTER 5

The Greek Kingdom 1833-62

I. The Regency, 1833–35

The three regents appointed to rule on Otho's behalf were Count Joseph von Armansperg, leader of the Bavarian constitutional party, Professor Ludwig von Maurer, formerly Bavarian minister of justice, and Major-General Karl Wilhelm von Heideck, who had already served Greece with distinction. To these three were attached Karl von Abel to act as secretary and Johann Baptist Greiner to provide a link with the ministers. As under the previous regime the ministers were eight in number. They formed a purely executive body. The regents had no obligation to consult them and there was no legislative assembly to whom they were responsible, for the Bavarians, whose principal aim was to curb the Greek factions, had no intention of following up the call of the London conference to the Greeks to assist their king in framing a definitive constitution or of honouring a pledge given by Bavaria in July 1832 to convoke a constituent assembly.

Instead of a constitution there was to be a Western-type civil service manned at the higher levels by Bavarians and specialists from other countries. An army of 5,000 recruited in Germany was to keep order and carry out public works pending replacement by Bavarian troops. Into this army it was intended to incorporate Greek regulars, irregulars, and volunteers, the plan being that each regiment should consist of three Bavarian and three Greek companies. To absorb some 2,000 irregulars who showed no enthusiasm for the dress, weapons, and discipline of the regular army, ten battalions of *chasseurs* were to be formed. For these battalions, however, less than fifty recruits came forward. Most Greek irregulars preferred to take to brigandage, and some even crossed into Turkish territory, where they were certainly more at home. About 800 veterans were enticed by the pay into joining the *chorofilaki* (gendarmerie), but some 400 vacancies remained unfilled, and recruits had to be found from other sources. This failure to absorb the old irregulars compelled the regents, who wished to get a grip on the provinces, to quarter army detachments in all the chief fortresses.

In the provinces the regents retained in essentials the Kapodistrian system. These provinces (nomarchies) were ten in number and were divided into some forty-two districts (eparchies). The nomarchs and eparchs were chosen by the crown and were posted to places where they had no local influence. They could be transferred or dismissed at a moment's notice. The only men who held important office in their own localities were the mayors of the *dhimi* (demes). These, some 400 of them,[1] were chosen with care. Existing mayors and their councils drew up electoral rolls and elected new councils. Each council, in conjunction with a small body of electors, chose three candidates. From these the crown, in the case of larger demes, and the minister of the interior, in the case of lesser ones, selected the mayor who served for three years unless summarily dismissed in the meantime.

The nomarchs, eparchs, and mayors were under the scrutiny of the bishops, local treasurers, gendarmerie commanders, medical officers, and chief engineers, all of whom had direct access to higher authority. All local officials were in fact a check upon one another, and in theory all government was centralised. In practice, much initiative rested with the councils of the demes which provided for most of the essentials of government. The main preoccupation of the central authority was to increase the yield of taxation in order to meet the deficit, the interest on state loans, and the Turkish indemnity. Radical reform was out of the question; and all the government could do was to reduce the size of the tax farms (thus enabling former subcontractors to hold leases), to allow leaseholders to pay in instalments (thus encouraging small capitalists to make higher bids), and to hold auctions for leases in public and under the scrutiny of state officials, the aim being to eradicate traditional chicanery and to prevent loss of revenue. This last motive underlay the reform of expenditure. A central board of control was established under the French official A. J. F. de Régny. This body not only watched over central spending but scrutinised the transactions of the provincial treasuries. It attempted, moreover, to check illegal sales of public lands and to inquire into the irregular purchases and appropriations that had already taken place. The Bavarians, who wished to create a class of peasant proprietors, were intensely interested in the land question, and they subscribed fully to the principle, laid down during the revolution, that all those who had served Greece should be given land. In 1833 only about one-sixth of Greek peasants were freeholders. These paid a tax of 10 per cent. The rest were tenants. Those who farmed on the national domain paid a rent of 25 per cent of annual produce. In June 1835 the Bavarians promulgated a law providing for vouchers valued at 2,000 drachmai to be allocated to all heads of families qualified to obtain land. Each recipient then bid at

[1] The numbers of the demes and eparchies varied throughout the Othonian period.

auctions for the land he wanted, up to a maximum of 40 stremmata (approximately 10 acres). On the land acquired he was liable for thirty-six years to a tax of 180 drachmai (the equivalent of about 9 per cent of the value of his property).

The regency was also faced with the problem of the Church, which, during the revolution, had been severed administratively from the Patriarchate. On this issue the country was divided. Although it was generally agreed that the Church in Greece should not return to its former relationship with a Patriarchate, under the influence of the Turks, there were many and perhaps a majority of Greeks who, recognising the great role of the mother Church in the history of the Greek nation, wished to retain close ties with Constantinople. For this there were, as we have seen, the precedents of Byzantine times. The patriarchs of Jerusalem, Antioch, and Alexandria, although autonomous, had recognised the leadership of the Patriarch of Constantinople; and the close relationship between the mother and daughter Churches was regulated by canon law. But the Bavarians, with the connivance of westernised and liberal Greeks, pronounced for an Erastian or Gallican relationship between Church and state. Maurer, a Protestant totally ignorant both of the democratic structure of the Orthodox Church and of the extent of its traditional independence of the temporal authority, readily adopted the ideas of the Greek theologian Farmakidis who, like Korais, had long advocated placing the clergy under government control. In an act of 4 August 1833 the king (although a Roman Catholic) was declared head of the Church. In this capacity, he was to be assisted by a synod of five clergy of his own choice. Although in matters of doctrine and liturgical practice this synod was to be autonomous, nevertheless it could meet only in the presence of a royal commissioner and its decisions were subject to royal approval. It could communicate with the clergy only through the ministry of religion and it was expressly forbidden to have relations with any authority outside the kingdom. This meant that it could have no dealings with the Patriarch or with Russia.

No sooner had the new ecclesiastical order been promulgated than the Patriarch issued a challenge by appointing a bishop to the see of Zitouni. In reply, the regents called an assembly of all Greek bishops, not only of those holding sees (there were fifty-six sees of which nineteen were vacant) but also of those who had fled from Turkey. All pronounced in favour of the royal act. Called together at short notice, some were afraid of being dismissed and others were hoping to obtain the vacant sees. If only they had had opportunity to confer amongst themselves, there would probably have been a majority of dissenters. Some did indeed propose certain revisions, basing their case upon canon law, but these, like the revisions suggested by the synod, were completely ignored by the regents.

It was not long before the government began to employ the royal supremacy to divert the wealth of the Church into the coffers of the state. A series of acts suppressed three-quarters of the 524 monasteries and most of the nunneries—all those houses which had only six inmates or less. Nearly a thousand monks were thereby forced either to give up their vocation or to seek entry into the remaining houses. The holy treasures were sold and the income from the properties of the suppressed houses were turned over to the government. A great outcry ensued, for the monasteries, although in decline during the war, remained a part of the democratic religious and communal life of Greece; and no wonder there were rumours that the Bavarians were trying to force the nation to become Roman Catholic.

These rumours were spread by the growing body of opponents to Bavarian rule, above all by the so-called Napists (former Kapodistrians and pro-Russians), whose leaders (Kolokotronis among them) the regents had passed over in filling the offices of state. Not that the regents were out to favour other factions. Their policy was to recruit for office men of moderate views, no matter what party they had hitherto supported. Similarly, they endeavoured to display impartiality towards the representatives of the protecting powers. But this attempt to maintain a balance failed not only because of their own shortcomings, but also because party leaders and foreign envoys did not view governmental and political problems in such simple terms, and indeed could never believe that the regents, who were known to intrigue against one another, were above suspicion. The result was that the whole regency period, indeed the whole reign of Otho, was one of bewildering party conflict in which the foreign envoys, out to maintain the influence of the countries they represented, became entangled. Around these envoys the Greeks tended to group themselves and to form British, French, and Russian parties. But such combinations were never stable; the Greeks frequently changed their allegiances; and the relationships between the representatives of the protecting powers were for ever shifting.

Although in the administration formed in April 1833 only one leading French partisan, Kolettis, had been included, the regents were driven more and more to lean towards France, if only to steer clear of the rivalries of the Russian and British envoys and their followers. In any case, Russia and Britain had interests in the eastern Mediterranean which clashed with those that the Bavarians envisaged for Greece—the recovery of Greek trade and its expansion. Furthermore, the regents wished to retain the French army in Greece until such time as Bavarian troops arrived; and they also had hopes that Otho would marry the daughter of Louis-Philippe. Towards France they were forced a step further when the Napists, having organised political brigandage and having raised in their newspaper, *Chronos*, the cry that the Church was in danger, appealed to the Tsar to have the three regents withdrawn. Quick to strike back, the regents arrested three leading Napists and put the two key ministries (interior and justice) into the hands of the two Francophils, Kolettis and K. Schinas.

Armansperg, who had always objected to the collegiate nature of the regency, was already intriguing in Munich to bring about the recall of his colleagues Maurer and Heideck. Supporting this intrigue were Dawkins and his Russian colleague, Katakazi. Lord Palmerston, too, was pressing Munich. King Ludwig finally gave way. Following a rebellion of the Maniats in the summer of 1834, when Bavarian troops were roughly handled, he recalled Maurer and Abel, thus leaving Armansperg supreme.

Armansperg himself, however, soon ran into difficulties. First of all he had to contend with Kolettis, who not only endeavoured to crush opposing factions but stirred up brigandage to show that his services were indispensable. Kolettis had friends at Court—General Lesuire, the minister of war, and Heideck. He enjoyed also the support of Dawkins, who had found that his formerly friendly Russian colleague had become thick with Armansperg. When, however, Sir Edmund Lyons arrived as the first British minister to Greece, Armansperg was able to recover his balance and to scotch the intrigues of certain Bavarians for his recall. Encouraged by Lyons, he boldly demanded the removal of Kolettis, the control of appointments in the royal household, the power to sign all state papers, and the right to preside at cabinet meetings. Although he did not get his own way completely, he at least got rid of his enemies and he was in a position to ensure that the ministers were his own partisans. He shared his authority with a newly-created council of state of twenty members, drawn from outside the ranks of factious leaders; and he created his own following by bestowing offices and granting favours. The Greek attached considerable importance to office. During the war so many provincial worthies had been impoverished that to acquire office was often the only alternative to brigandage. Office, moreover, gave prestige and, what was more, protection from enemies. All Greek parties were then, as in the years to come, largely based on office-holding, and what Armansperg did was to play Greek party leaders at their own game. One of his main objects was to prevent a union of Napist and Kolettist factions. Towards this end he prevailed on Otho to form a House-hold Regiment, which gave a place of honour and a small pension to some 800 veterans; he caused certain Napists to be appointed aides-de-camp to the king; and he had Kolettis posted to the Paris legation.[2] In so far as he leaned towards a 'foreign party', it was towards the English. Although he was careful not to make his preference too pronounced, through Lyons he obtained from Palmerston an advance of one million francs in respect of the guaranteed loan of 1832 and, in return, he frequently accepted for ministerial and administrative employment the nominees of Lyons, who also secured preference for British investment in the projected Bank of Greece. Through Armansperg, Lyons worked for reconciliation of French and British interests, in accordance with Palmerston's policy of maintaining in Greece a 'British-led' constitutional party as a means of thwarting what was

[2] Mavrokordatos was sent to Munich and later Vienna; Trikoupis was posted to the London legation; and Metaxas was sent first to Cairo and later to Madrid.

imagined to be the Russian policy of creating a Russo–French alignment in Greece. So influential was Lyons that the historian Finlay could say that he and Armansperg were the rulers of Greece.[3]

In his pursuit of reconciliation and appeasement Armansperg failed to face up to the real tasks of government. He allowed his friend Lasanis to distribute land in excess to political supporters; he posted men with local influence to become nomarchs and eparchs; he permitted *kapetanei* to raise followers at the expense of the villages; and he never seemed to realise that these favoured *pallikaria* stirred up trouble merely to be able to prove that they could keep order better than westernised troops. Against his mis-government the French were the first to protest, and like the Russians, who were trying to have Armansperg recalled, refused to give guarantees for a loan. Among the Greeks a strong opposition encouraged by French and Russian agents began to form, the Russian envoy, Katakazi, going so far as to finance the newspaper *Sotir*, which, of all things, demanded a constitu-tion. Eventually in February 1837 Otho, on his return from a visit to Munich, appointed Ignaz von Rudhart, a subservient Bavarian bureaucrat, to suc-ceed Armansperg. In the following December he decided to become his own prime minister and to establish paternal absolutism.

At the end of November 1836 Otho had married Amalia of Oldenburg—an event of which the Greek ministers had learned, much to their con-sternation, from the European press several weeks after it had taken place. Earlier plans for Otho's marriage with one of the Tsar's daughters had fallen through. To that marriage the Tsar had been ready to give his consent provided Otho became Greek Orthodox. But to this condition King Ludwig, under pressure from the Papacy, had been unable to agree. If, however, the Greeks failed to obtain a Russian queen of the Orthodox faith, they cer-tainly found in Amalia a first lady who was a staunch philhellene. Under the tuition of Filippos Ioannou, she quickly learned the Greek language and she became a devotee of the *megali idhea*. She dressed in Greek fashion; she showed great concern for the welfare of the families of the veterans of the War of Independence; and she came to take an interest in all affairs of state. As time went on her influence over the somewhat weak-willed Otho became decisive. She frequently interfered in governmental matters and it was this interference, combined with outbursts of temper, that made her unpopular with the foreign envoys and Greek ministers.

II. Otho's Personal Rule 1837–1841: the Megali Idhea

Otho was good-looking, he loved Greece, he had good intentions, and he had an excellent memory for faces and administrative details. Yet he was

---

[3] Lyons, however, was not alone. He took most of his ideas from General Sir Richard Church, who had become a citizen of Greece, a councillor of state, and the military governor of Rumeli.

hardly the man to impose paternal rule upon the politically cunning and possessive Greeks. Although he chose his royal cabinet (*anaktovoulion*) from all parties, he raised up too many enemies by leaving out important people and by allowing patronage to fall into the hands of two Napists, Glarakis (minister of interior), and Paikos (minister of justice). Aided by Katakazi, who was more Greek than the Greeks, these ministers managed to infiltrate Napist office-holders into all the institutions of Church and state and to secure a firm grip on the provinces. But although the Napists were entrenched in the government, they were hostile to Otho and, being well organised, they were more to be feared than the loosely-knit liberal opposition. It was they who were behind the Philorthodox plot,[4] which came to the knowledge of the government towards the end of 1839. The plan was to seize the king and queen and offer them the alternatives of Orthodoxy or abdication. At the same time there were designs to liberate the Greeks of Epiros, Thessaly, and Macedonia. This plot placed Otho in a quandary. If he got rid of the Napists he would have to employ liberals who would demand a constitution. He therefore proceeded with caution, and waited for the plot to fail. He had come round to the view that the whole conspiracy was primarily irredentist and that the attempt against the throne was the work of one or two individuals of no great consequence.

That there were irredentist movements at this time in Greece there is not the slightest doubt. These had been stimulated by the Near Eastern crisis of 1838–40, when it seemed that Mohammed Ali of Egypt might advance from Syria and deal a mortal blow to the Ottoman empire. All Greeks of consequence were aware of the concern of the European powers at this development and of their rivalries in finding a solution for the problems it raised. Of these rivalries each had a simplified yet vivid picture and his own facile opinion how best Greece could utilise them to realise the *megali idhea*. Otho himself, like his aspiring subjects, had, as a result of the tense political atmosphere in which he lived, his own version of the diplomatic moves required by Greece to exploit the situation. He was a convert to the Great Idea and was hardly less oblivious of the inadequate resources of his kingdom for its attainment than the coffee-house politicians in the capital and small townships.

In order to counteract the supposed designs of Russia and the equivocal policy of France, who backed all comers, the Austro–British alignment within the European Concert had by July 1839 obtained agreement on a collective Note, stating the intention of the powers to pursue a collective policy towards the Turkish empire. This prompted the Cretan leaders to petition the protecting powers on 10 August for the *enosis* (union) of their island with Greece. To Otho this appeal was highly acceptable in principle. It conflicted, however, with the more immediate need for a commercial

---

[4] A Philorthodox Society, probably a continuation of the Phoenix Society, had been founded in June 1839. One of its members had betrayed the plot to the government.

treaty with the Ottoman empire. Sultan Mahmud, who died earlier in 1839, had put up trade barriers against his former rebellious subjects and, although individual Greeks had indulged in profitable smuggling, the Greek state had as a consequence only a very moderate taxable trade. But despite the conflict between irredentism and the need for the trade treaty, Otho and his advisers planned to exploit the Near Eastern situation for both ends. To do this necessitated the goodwill of either Great Britain or France, for at this time it was almost beyond hope to get the backing of both. Great Britain tended to favour for Crete an autonomous status which in the view of certain Greeks, Kolettis for example, meant that Crete would become, like the Ionian Islands, virtually a British protectorate. Hence in the discussions that arose many were in favour of leaning towards France. At the time, however, neither the Near Eastern policy of France nor the policy of Great Britain towards France was known to the Greeks. It was not, as they thought, British policy to exclude France from the Concert of the European powers: rather it was British policy to force France to enter the Concert— an aim which Palmerston finally fulfilled on 13 July 1841 when the Straits convention was signed. Nevertheless, the Greeks rightly sensed that French and British policies were in conflict, not only upon the Eastern question but upon every other diplomatic issue. They therefore, each according to his fancy, placed their hopes in either one or other of the two contestants; and the result was that the Greco–Turkish commercial treaty came in for such fierce criticism that Otho dared not ratify it. In any case the treaty itself left much to be desired. It withheld from Greece the right to give Greek citizenship to Greeks who were Ottoman subjects; and it gave Turkey the power to prevent Greeks from emigrating to the Greek national kingdom.

The dispute became fiercer when the Turks, in revenge for the non-ratification of the treaty, excluded Greek ships from entering Turkish ports and imposed severe restrictions upon their Greek subjects. Needless to say, these measures stimulated Greek irredentists to call for action, and to dream of making war on Turkey in company with France and Mohammed Ali. Many imagined that Kolettis would return from France with ample funds and a promise of French military support. Even Otho himself was caught up in this wishful thinking, and his illusions were not dispelled until Sir Charles Napier threw Mohammed Ali out of Syria and until Thiers resigned on 20 October 1840. Already, however, the bolder irredentists in Greece had taken the field. John Velentzas, a follower of Kolettis, had collected bands in Thessaly; the patriotic monk Ilarion was organising from Mount Athos a conspiracy in northern Greece; and the famous kleft Tsamis Karatasos had turned up in Thessaloniki. Away to the south in Crete, the chiefs were busy preparing a revolt, and near Athens the patriot Makri-yannis of the first War of Independence was in the thick of some plotting.

This situation called for a rebuke from the representatives of Great Britain, Austria, and Russia who, as a result of Palmerston's diplomacy, were acting in concert on the Eastern question. Lyons did the talking and he took the opportunity to demand that Greece should aim at constitutional government and carry out a number of reforms. To these demands Otho, hoping for financial assistance and diplomatic support for a revised trade treaty, and under pressure from the crown prince of Bavaria, a spokesman of Austrian diplomacy, who was on a visit to Greece, paid some attention. One result was that on 22 February 1841 he appointed Mavrokordatos as his foreign minister.

III. The Ministry of Mavrokordatos, July–August 1841

It is extremely doubtful whether Mavrokordatos was the leader of an English party. He was certainly not subservient to Lyons. First and foremost he was a Greek. In a general way he saw that Greek policy, both internal and external, had to be adjusted to the constantly shifting relations of the great powers. Moreover, it is doubtful whether he had a party at all. He certainly had 'friends' who for one reason or another moved in English circles, cronies of the indefatigable Lyons, who breathed the air of Greek intrigue; but he had other 'friends' who were not particularly pro-English. Like any other leading Greek politician, he found that the most he could do was to build up a coalition and, if his writ as a reformer was to run, that coalition must extend to the provinces, where local clientèles and local coalitions were entrenched. This was no easy task. The local worthies did not often appear in Athens. As often as not negotiations had to be conducted through the friends of local leaders on a visit to Athens or through emissaries sent into the provinces. It was through such a system that the regents, Armansperg, and Glarakis had attempted to govern on Otho's behalf; and it was this same system, in essentials, that obtained (even when Athens had grown larger and had become a parliamentary centre) throughout the nineteenth century. No matter whether Greece was an absolute monarchy or a crowned democracy, the problem of government remained substantially the same—that of keeping together a coalition on a nationwide scale.

Like many Greeks with Western experience and learning Mavrokordatos hoped to build up a professional bureaucracy and to subject it to constitutional control, or, more strictly, to the rule of law. He was not a doctrinaire democrat, and he attached much more importance to systematic administration than to the kind of parliamentary assembly that Greek political society was likely to produce. In the first place he wanted to put the powers of the crown into commission and then at some later date to introduce a more democratic machinery. He therefore proposed the appointment of a prime minister presiding over a cabinet which should determine policy. This cabinet would replace the *anaktovoulion*. Instead of a parliament there would be a large council of state which would exercise control in fiscal matters. From all these bodies the Bavarians would be excluded, and the Bavarian officers would be removed from the army.

Mavrokordatos's programme met with no enthusiasm from Lyons, who was still pressing for a representative constitution, and it aroused, as was to be expected, the hostility of Otho, who meant to be king in deed as well as name. In choosing Mavrokordatos he was hoping to enlist the services of a bureaucrat, a 'Greek Bavarian', a salaried administrator who had no private interest in Greece. Such a role, however, Mavrokordatos was unlikely to accept. He had taken the precaution before returning to Greece to obtain the blessing of both Palmerston and Guizot. To Guizot he had promised to include pro-French Greeks in his government and even to arrange for the recall of Kolettis. When shortly after his arrival in Greece in June 1841 he was faced with appointments made by Otho which conflicted with his own manoeuvres to form a broad-based government, he threatened to resign, knowing that Otho was unlikely to be able to form another government. Otho at length gave way, and though Mavrokordatos made some concessions on certain appointments, he had at least managed to form an 'all-party' government.

But despite this initial victory, Mavrokordatos held office for barely six weeks. For one thing, the French deserted him. Guizot had sent Piscatory to Greece on a special mission (June–September 1841) to press the claims of Dimitrios Christidis, a leader of the pro-French factions. Otho, wishing to free himself from Mavrokordatos, seized the chance to appoint Christidis as minister of the interior, promising to assist him in carrying out certain reforms which Mavrokordatos had demanded in vain. Mavrokordatos resigned in disgust. Christidis thus became a kind of successor to Kolettis. By exercising the patronage at his disposal, he gave the whole administration a somewhat pro-French character. Nevertheless Otho, always under the influence of other factions at Court, prevented him from having matters all his own way. In any case this pro-French coalition was unstable. Palamidis (successor to the ageing Deliyannis as head of the Peloponnesian interest), Makriyannis (of the Rumeliot interest), and many others went over to the 'Russian' and 'English' opposition which once again, in view of the growing French ascendancy, had drawn together. The growing opposition was vociferous in the flourishing Athenian press. It accused Christidis of failing to introduce reforms, of allowing the Bavarians still to monopolise power and office, of leaving the Orthodox Church in jeopardy, and even of preventing the return of Kolettis.

IV. The Revolution of 15 September 1843

Otho was soon to find himself deserted by the French. Guizot, greatly disappointed that the Christidis regime had neither enhanced French prestige in Greece nor embarked upon a programme of reform, aligned himself with

Britain and Russia. What is more, he denied financial help to Greece. Otho therefore resorted to various expedients; he made a levy on office-holders; he reduced the number of offices; and he curtailed spending generally. These measures annoyed many Greeks and yet failed to satisfy the powers, which met in conference in London on 5 July 1843, and fixed the annual interest and repayments of the Greek debt at 3,635,922 francs, assigned revenues to meet this charge, and installed an agency to control Greek expenditure. To the Greek mind these measures deprived Otho's monarchy of its *raison d'être*: Otho was to be tolerated only if he could obtain from the powers financial support for Greece.

As time went on the hostile faction formed a vast conspiracy, which was joined by all those who, for one reason or another, had become dissatisfied with the government. In this conspiracy the prime movers were Andreas Londos, Andreas Metaxas, and Konstantinos Zografos. They had the support of army officers, disgruntled because a reduction in the military establishment had been made, not at the expense of the Bavarians, but to the disadvantage of the Greeks. The original intention was to stage a revolt on 25 March (Independence Day) 1844. Believing that their secret had been betrayed, they brought the date forward. In August 1843 they implicated three military commanders: Nikolaos Skarvelis (Athens infantry), Dimitrios Kallergis (Athens cavalry), and Spiromilios (director of the military school). Makriyannis, who had a large personal following among the *kapetanei*, had already joined the conspiracy.

On the night of 14 September Kallergis and Skarvelis threw troops around the newly-built palace, while crowds were organised to shout in the square that lay in front of it. Otho's orders that the troops should be dispersed by the household guard were disobeyed. After some delay, Otho appeared on the balcony overlooking the square. In response to popular demands he promised that, if the troops withdrew, he would consult his cabinet, the council of state, and the protecting powers. But the military commanders refused to withdraw. Instead Kallergis presented Otho with a constitution. At 3 a.m. on 15 September the council of state assembled in the palace and after some deliberation presented to the king draft decrees for the convocation of a national assembly, for the institution of a provisional government, and for an expression of gratitude to, and appropriate decorations for, the conspirators. These decrees Otho (on the advice of the diplomatic corps, with Lyons playing a leading role) accepted, albeit reluctantly. Thus ended the almost[5] bloodless revolution of September 1843, as a result of which the hated Bavarians were sent packing.

V. The Constitution of 1844

Otho accepted a tripartisan cabinet of seven who had been recommended by

[5] One gendarme on duty outside the house of Makriyannis was killed.

Makriyannis, later joined by Mavrokordatos and Kolettis on their return to
Greece.[6] Many had feared that he would abdicate, that civil disorder would
follow, and that Greece would earn the disapprobation of the powers. The
British, French, and Austrian representatives had all counselled moderation.
They feared that if Otho departed, Russia, with the help of the Napists,
would attempt to impose a king of Orthodox faith and thus succeed either
in making Greece a Russian satellite or in plunging the country into civil
war. Russia, however, did not at this juncture seek any advantage. She
recalled Katakazi for his share in the conspiracy; and having pronounced in
favour of monarchical institutions for Greece, she left it to France, Britain,
and Austria to preserve the Bavarian dynasty. This they did. They worked,
not through the government as a whole, but chiefly through Metaxas,
Kolettis, and Mavrokordatos, the last two of whom had not been directly
concerned in the revolution. Their strong support of this conservative
grouping paralysed the two extremes—those who wanted to carry the revolution further, and those like Gennaios Kolokotronis who wished to organise
a counter-revolution.

Such was the situation when the elections for a constituent assembly
were held. Of these elections—how the local factions worked, how far they
were linked with parties in Athens, to what extent armed clientèles exerted
pressure—very little is known. It is probable that some provincial factions
came to the verge of civil war. What is certain is that in the end the better-
organised Napist faction concentrated on the elections and avoided recourse to arms. The Napists, however, did not obtain a majority. Of the 243
deputies returned, it was not clear where the allegiance of a large number
lay and it took some time before they began to show their colours. Broadly
speaking, the Mavrokordatos-Kolettis coalition emerged as a large minority
which, on being joined by Metaxas and his friends, became a majority. The
opposition consisted chiefly of the Makriyannis group, of a number of
groups which followed the former pro-French leader Palamidis, a rival of
Kolettis, and even of disgruntled Napists who followed Michael Schinas.
This opposition had no agreed programme of action. Each faction was content to denounce the alleged machinations of Otho's 'advisers'—Mavrokordatos, Kolettis, and Metaxas—and the interference of foreigners, while
followers of Schinas made a demand for the improvement of the status of
the Church.

The constituent assembly, which opened on 20 November 1843, appointed a committee of twenty-one to frame the constitution. This committee, dominated by Mavrokordatos, Kolettis, and Metaxas, confined its
deliberations to strictly constitutional issues and avoided such problems as

---

[6] Three were Napists—Andreas Metaxas (prime minister and foreign affairs), Schinas
(religion), Kanaris (marine). Two were pro-French—Palamidis (interior) and Mansolas
(economy). Two were pro-English—Londos (war) and Leon Melas (justice). Mavrokordatos
and Kolettis were without portfolios.

land and pensions. Article I of the draft constitution declared Orthodoxy the official state religion; it granted toleration to other creeds but forbade them from engaging in proselytising activities. Article II affirmed that the Church in Greece, though having dogmatic unity with other Orthodox Churches, was autocephalous. These articles were debated in the assembly on 15–17 January 1844. It was then that Schinas attempted to gain for the Church freedom from the interference of the secular power, to reduce the king's role to that of protector, to place the authority of the synod and of the church canons above that of the minister of religion, and to safeguard clerics from the jurisdiction of the secular courts. He also demanded that the autocephalous Church should be recognised by the Patriarch. Eventually a compromise was reached. A vague phrase was inserted stating that there was to be no interference with the established Church. Also included were words to the effect that the Church in Greece would maintain the canons and holy traditions of the Orthodox Churches. There were other compromises. The synod was to be composed of bishops, but its independence was not specifically stated. As for the headship of the Church, this was vested in Christ, the position of the king being left without precise definition.[7]

Article III, debated on 20 January, defined Greek citizenship. This was a highly contentious matter, for apart from a general hostility to the Bavarians (whose numbers were never large), there was extreme bitterness on the part of those who had fought in the War of Independence and had given freely of their wealth, towards the Greeks (the *neilides*) who, after 1827, had rushed in to seize lucrative office, to favour their friends, to buy up the land, to lend money at usurious rates, and generally to exploit a people whom they had had no share in freeing. On these Makriyannis vented his wrath: he called them the filth of Constantinople and Europe, accusing them of grabbing the best property, of living in luxury, and of imprisoning the veterans or of turning them into slaves. He found a good hearing. Numerous petitions, demanding a long period of residence as a necessary qualification for citizenship, were sponsored in the assembly as amendments. On this issue he had the support of Palamidis, who even called in irregular troops to threaten the deputies. But in the assembly Makriyannis and Palamidis eventually collected only 59 votes, Mavrokordatos and Kolettis having skilfully mustered support for a proposal which made eligible for public employment all those who had lived in Greece before 1827 or who had taken up arms against the Ottoman empire. From this provision army and naval personnel were exempted, and so were teachers.

---

[7] Article II ran as follows: 'The Orthodox Church of Greece, acknowledging for its head our Lord Jesus Christ, is indissolubly united in doctrine with the Great Church of Constantinople, and with every other Church of Christ holding the same doctrines, observing invariably, as they do, the holy apostolic and synodal canons and holy traditions. It is self-governed, exercising its governing rights independent of every other Church, and administering them by a holy synod of bishops.'

Non-combatant emigrants of the period 1827–32 were to be eligible for office after two years of residence, those of the period 1832–37 after three years, and those of 1837–43 after four years.

Another contentious question was that of the upper chamber or senate. On this issue the drafting committee had been divided and a majority, ignoring the advice of Lyons and Piscatory, had opposed the principle of life tenure. Eventually, however, a compromise was reached and it was agreed that for a trial period of ten years senators should enjoy life membership. But when this matter came up before the assembly, it was for long doubtful whether even an elective second chamber would be accepted. Finally the decision to establish a senate was taken and a proposal for life tenure was carried by the narrow margin of 20 votes.

An even more serious issue was that of the succession. Otho had no children. Luitpold, his younger brother and heir, had stated his intention to remain a Catholic and to bring up his family in the Catholic faith. Although the treaty of May 1832 had not specified that Otho's successor should be of the Orthodox faith, most Greeks had always hoped that one day their monarch would be a member of the national Church. This opinion prevailed among the representatives of the national assembly who, backed by Russia, succeeded in framing Articles XL and XLV which provided that every successor to the Greek throne, or any regent, must belong to the religion of the Eastern Orthodox Church of Christ.[8] These provisions Otho after much hesitation accepted: had he not done so, he would certainly have been deposed.

When on 7 March the constitution was presented to Otho for approval, he demanded certain changes. These were not at all to the liking of the opposition which, mustering nearly 40 per cent of the votes in the chamber, threatened to withdraw and to set up their own assembly. This threat was effective: Otho gave way and a situation which might have led to civil war was averted. Greece, equipped with parliamentary institutions which were more democratic than any to be found in Europe, embarked on her history as a constitutional monarchy. But the party strife remained much as before. The harmony that had been maintained with difficulty in the national assembly quickly disappeared and the collaboration of Mavrokordatos, Kolettis, and Metaxas was to be replaced by their conflicts. The old 'parties', the coalitions of clientèles, came into their own again. Only in a very minor way did the parliamentary system impart to them discipline and cohesion, or endow them with principles. Indeed, the new constitution, by providing senatorial and assembly seats and by enhancing the powers of patronage, stimulated and even complicated the party struggle.

[8] Mavrokordatos succeeded, however, in gaining for Otho the concession that Queen Amalia should become regent in the event of a minority.

VI. The Parliamentary Dictatorship of Kolettis

Throughout the summer of 1844 the French and British envoys endeavoured to exploit the victory for constitutionalism. Piscatory went so far as to provide for Kolettis a bodyguard (the leader of which was a brigand) and Lyons, not to be outwitted, used secret service funds to finance a similar service for Mavrokordatos. At the elections, which were fiercely disputed, no leader was returned with a clear majority. Subsequently, however, Kolettis managed, by negotiations, to increase his following among the deputies, and after the resignation of Mavrokordatos on 16 August 1844, he was summoned by Otho to form a government. He was then able, by promises and bribery, to build up a majority. Not until that majority had been secured did he face the chamber of deputies. In the chamber he further improved his position by declaring invalid, during the scrutiny of returns, the elections of many opponents.

It was not long before he had fashioned out of the least stable and often least desirable elements in Greek political life 'the system', as it was called —a mixture of the methods of his former patrons, Guizot and Ali Pasha. By means of patronage and corruption, and by constant interference with the processes of law, he managed to get under control the nomarchs, eparchs, demarchs, gendarmerie officers, tax officials, and law officers throughout the greater part of Greece. In keeping his grip upon the provinces he had recourse to brigands who continued to play an important role in Greek political life. Certain politicians were themselves brigands in that they had their own armed followers, and others made arrangements with brigands who worked upon their own account. Brigandage, although denounced by westernised Greek liberals, was not generally considered to be a pernicious occupation. Local brigands had social standing, and certainly considerable power. At any rate, Kolettis could not ignore them, and he employed them either directly or indirectly through his followers, who had brigands in their pay. Similarly he took great pains to gain support within the army. He dismissed General Church from his office of inspector-general, and appointed in his place General Gardikiotis Grivas, an old henchman of Ali Pasha, who could be counted upon to place friends in the military commands.

In all these ways, Kolettis, true to his old Turkish training (and he continued to dress as a Turk), made a farce of the constitution, being content and crafty enough to preserve its forms. Nevertheless, he had the approval of a well-paid press and he enjoyed much popular support, for in his speeches he was profuse in his love for his fellow-countrymen, to whom he promised the realisation of the Great Idea. It is not surprising that he won the 1847 elections and that he established what was virtually a parliamentary dictatorship. With Otho and Amalia he found great favour, and being pro-French, he was all that the French government could want. At first he enjoyed, too, the support of Metaxas and the pro-Russians, but these later deserted him when he showed no signs of relaxing the state control of the Church.[9]

Needless to say, Kolettis found a fierce opponent in Lyons, who intrigued against him and plied the British government with long reports on the iniquities of his regime. So hostile did Lyons become that Otho and Amalia tried to get rid of him: they asked their relatives to have a word with Queen Victoria; and in the end many European celebrities, including Metternich, were trying to engineer the recall of the British envoy. But the time was not propitious. The Anglo–French *entente* was fragile and was to disappear almost completely when Palmerston returned to office in July 1846. Palmerston drew up a long memorandum for Prince Albert, who had been approached by the Bavarians on the subject of Lyons's conduct. Kolettis, he contended, had governed Greece 'corruptly, illegally, prodigally, unconstitutionally and tyrannically'. He went on to say: 'In the Foreign relations of the Country Mr Kolettis seems to have three leading objects in view, aggression towards Turkey, subservience towards France, and insult towards England.' Palmerston's attitude was that as long as Piscatory stayed in Athens Lyons would stay there too. Well briefed by Lyons, he began to take a firmer line in Greece. When at Easter 1847 an Athenian crowd plundered the Portuguese consul, Don Pacifico, a Maltese Jew and British subject, he demanded compensation and took the opportunity to raise certain unsettled British claims against the Greek government. This affair dragged on until 1850. In that year Palmerston, losing all patience, sent a large British fleet to the Piraeus to seize the tiny Greek fleet and blockade the port. This gesture, although it forced the Greek government to pay some £8,000, earned for him the wrath of Europe, and the humiliation of having to accept French mediation.

By that time Kolettis was no more. He had died in September 1847. His successor, Lieutenant-General Tzavellas, remained in office until March 1848, having put down a revolt in western Greece—an essentially Greek affair unconnected with the revolutions which were to break out in Europe in 1848–49. Indeed the year 1848 was unusually quiet in Greece. Piscatory was recalled and French influence declined with the dethronement of Louis-Philippe in February.[10] In May Stratford Canning, British ambassador in Constantinople, went on a special mission to Greece. His finding was that Lyons had been unreasonable and in March 1849 Lyons was transferred to Berne, his place in Athens being taken by Thomas Wyse. Stratford Canning failed, however, to persuade Otho to send for Mavrokordatos or any of the constitutionalist politicians to form a ministry. Instead, Georgios

[9] In 1849 a new approach to the church problem developed both in Athens and Constantinople and, following protracted negotiations, the Patriarch recognised the Church of Greece, which was restored to full communion with the other Orthodox Churches.

[10] The revolution in Bavaria brought about King Ludwig's abdication in favour of Otho's elder brother, Prince Maximilian.

4

Koundouriotis followed Tzavellas, and was himself followed by Admiral Kanaris (until December 1849) and by Antonios Kriezis, who remained in office until May 1854.

VII. Otho and the Megali Idhea

Relations with Turkey had become strained when in January 1847 the Turks refused to permit the visit to Constantinople of General Karatasos, one of Otho's aides-de-camp and a colourful character from Macedonia who had led bands in Thessaly in 1841. These relations remained unsatisfactory and Otho vainly waited for upheavals in Europe to provide the opportunity, despite a deficit of 2 million drachmai, to attack the Turks. His opportunity did not come until 1853—the fourth centenary of the fall of Constantinople. That year Prince Menshikov arrived at the Porte with instructions to obtain for Russia a protectorate over all the Orthodox subjects of the Ottoman empire. Although a three-year-old dispute concerning the Holy Places was quickly settled, the somewhat ambiguous demands of Menshikov for a Russian protectorate were rejected by the Porte, and the Russians, to show that they meant business, in July 'by force, but without war' occupied the Danubian Principalities. This turn of events, combined with the recent changes of regime in France, where Louis Napoleon, who was thought to favour nationalist movements, had in 1852 established the Second Empire, led Otho and many of his entourage to believe that the divinely-ordained hour of Greek expansion had arrived. His aunt, Archduchess Sophie of Austria (a power behind the imperial throne), assured him that Austria favoured the union of Thessaly with Greece. What he failed completely to realise was that Great Britain and France would react strongly to encroachment upon the Ottoman empire and, ignoring completely the presence of their fleets in Besika Bay whence they would be able to enter the Straits and support the Turks, he encouraged the formation of Greek bands, which infiltrated into Thessaly. At the same time he moved the Nafplion garrison and artillery from Athens to the northern frontier, despite strong representations from the British and French governments that they would not tolerate any attack upon the Ottoman empire. He appealed to his brother Maximilian of Bavaria to supply him with funds; and it was generally believed in Athens, where war fever ran high, that Otho himself would join his troops at the frontier in readiness to invade Thessaly, already infiltrated in some strength by irregular bands.

Meanwhile the Turks, under strong pressure from Stratford Canning, and in answer to Russian demands for a bilateral treaty, had made a unilateral statement (somewhat misleadingly named the 'Turkish Ultimatum') which confirmed in perpetuity 'the ancient privileges of the religion professed by H.M. the Emperor of Russia'. This 'ultimatum', however, was rejected by the ambassadors in conference at Vienna, who proposed a compromise, known as the 'Vienna Note', which they believed would be acceptable to the Tsar. In this Note the ambassadors suggested that the Turks should reaffirm their adherence to the treaties of Kutchuk Kainardji and Adrianople and that the existing state of affairs 'concerning the Christian religion in the Ottoman Empire' should not 'be modified without previous understanding with the Governments of France and Russia'. This proposed compromise, which would have made those two powers the guarantors of Turkish good faith, was accepted by Russia, not, however, without the interpretation that it gave Russia a protectorate over the Sultan's Orthodox subjects. Nevertheless, the Tsar, on learning that the Turks had rejected this interpretation, was ready to climb down. He was prepared to accept the Austrian foreign minister's project (the Buol project) which consisted of a gloss to the Vienna Note, to the effect that Russia would not herself exercise the protection of the Christian cult but would merely ascertain that the Sultan fulfilled his obligations towards his Christian subjects as laid down in the treaties. This reasonable compromise Napoleon III was ready to accept; but the British cabinet, under pressure of opinion hostile to Russia, rejected it and on 8 October instructed Stratford Canning to move the fleet to Constantinople. On 4 October the Turks had demanded the evacuation of the Principalities within fifteen days. The Russians failed to comply. Skirmishes began and the Turks managed to achieve enough success to encourage them to send a fleet into the Black Sea. Here on 30 November they met disaster in the so-called Sinope massacre at the hands of a much more powerful Russian squadron. This event prompted Napoleon to call for Anglo–French action to sweep the Russian flag off the Black Sea. The British government was quick to act. It instructed the fleet to protect the Ottoman flag and to require all Russian warships to repair to Sebastopol. On 6 February 1854 Russia broke off diplomatic relations with France and England. Three weeks later the two Western powers demanded that Russia should evacuate the Principalities. They received no reply, and on 28 March declared war.

In January the Greeks, who had infiltrated strong bands into Epiros, Thessaly, and Macedonia, and had raised the standard of revolt at Radovitsi near Grevena, freed a number of Macedonian villages from Turkish rule. Leading the bands were several of the old warriors of the War of Independence who had resigned their commissions—Theodorakis Grivas, Kitsos Tzavellas, Yannis Rangos, Andreas Iskos, Sotiris Stratos, Georgakis Varnakiotis, and others. Some of them laid siege to Arta, while a band under Grivas reached the outskirts of Jannina. Altogether the Greek insurgents in Epiros were two thousand strong and many volunteers were on their way. So serious was the situation that the Porte despatched an army of 3,000 to Preveza to reinforce the Turkish garrisons. In Thessaly the Greeks were at least two thousand-strong. Here again they were led by the old warriors of the War of Independence, or by the local *kapetanei*.

The last thing that France and Britain wanted was that Otho should declare war on Turkey in support of the irregular bands. In February 1854 Napoleon, recalling France's services to Greece, plainly informed him that an attack on Turkey would be tantamount to an attack on France. Otho replied that as the only Christian king in the Near East he had a sacred mission and that God in his greatness would never abandon the Christian cause. In adopting this fatalistic attitude he had every encouragement from Amalia, who was made of sterner stuff than Otho and who was already receiving funds from her relations in Russia. The British and the French, however, were not prepared to stand any nonsense. They threatened to enforce their financial rights arising from the loans and in May they occupied the Piraeus, forcing Otho to declare neutrality and to institute a new ministry under Mavrokordatos. But the Greek irregulars had already suffered a reverse. At the end of April they were defeated at Petra and forced to retire to their own frontier. Their lack of organisation was to blame for this defeat; and they lost an opportunity of presenting the Western powers with a *fait accompli* which would have had the blessing (for what it was worth) of Austria and Prussia.

Otho, who much to his chagrin discovered that the French and British forces of occupation were highly popular in certain circles in Athens, refused to lie low. Along with Amalia he intrigued against Mavrokordatos—so much indeed that the British at least considered the necessity of a change of dynasty. Otho might have saved himself the trouble. In September 1855 a court scandal (a rare occurrence at Otho's Court) led to the resignation of Kallergis, the minister of war. Mavrokordatos found himself unable to carry on the government. He therefore brought to a close his long and crowded political career. Dictatorial while in office—a characteristic shared with many of his fellow-Greeks—he was yet reasonable in opposition and a parliamentarian of a very high order. He had never been able to get on with Otho. Otho, who was stubborn, meticulous over details, and yet indecisive, had found him an intolerable servant and had preferred always to choose his ministers from the old soldiers, from the more effusive and warmer Greeks, and from those less westernised—men who worried less about administration and constitutional niceties, but were happy to serve their king and to bask in the sunshine of the Court.

With Mavrokordatos gone, the new British envoy, Wyse, thought the time had come for the powers to take a firm grip on Greece, but Palmerston, who had replaced Aberdeen in February 1855, would have none of this, for he feared there would be too many repercussions both at home and abroad. Not that he would have been sorry to see Otho go: he and Napoleon considered a scheme whereby Prince Carignano, the cousin of their ally the king of Sardinia, would be given the crown of Greece and marry the duchess of Parma, who would then cede Parma to Sardinia. But he was not prepared to move until a scheme had been agreed. Otho was therefore able to call upon Dimitrios Voulgaris, a primate from Idra, to form a ministry—a man

who had no aptitude for administration but who nevertheless was an influential politician. Dressed in the old style, he spent much more time in the
cafés among his cronies than at work. Against his maladministration both
Wyse and his French colleague Mercier made frequent complaints, but
Otho took no notice. In February 1857 the protecting powers appointed a
commission to inquire into the administration of the finances. This commission worked for two years and then produced a report. Otho, however,
completely ignored the valuable recommendations which this report contained.

In November 1857 Voulgaris's ministry gave way to that of Athanasios
Miaoulis, son of the admiral. During the earlier part of this new ministry,
Otho, despite the activities of the foreign representatives, was popular in
the country at large. The allied troops had been withdrawn; Greece was
beginning to make some commercial progress; a new Athens was growing
around spacious squares (a development in which Amalia took much interest); and, despite continued brigandage in certain provinces, it seemed
as though the country was settling down. But in 1859 the scene suddenly
changed. The events of that year in Italy and the activities of Italian agents
in Greece gave a fresh stimulus to the *megali idhea*.

Despite his sympathy with Greek irredentism, Otho became identified by
a growing opposition with the oppressors of the Italians—the Court of
Austria—and his new-found popularity vanished. The volatile Greeks
noted with disappointment that both France and Great Britain favoured
only the Italians, and casting round for an explanation of their own fall from
grace, they attributed the disdain for Greece to the ineptitudes of their
dynasty. Comments in the press were most unflattering. Hoping to counteract this unhappy trend, Otho and his entourage began to canvass the idea
of an attack on Turkey. This brought a sharp reaction from the powers, and
when questioned in the chamber, Otho's government had to admit that
there was nothing to be done except to observe a strict neutrality towards
the Porte. With the successes of Garibaldi and his 'Thousand' in Sicily,
with the spectacle of Bavarian volunteers fighting for the Bourbon dynasty
(Queen Maria Sophia of the Two Sicilies was Otho's niece), and with the
proclamation of Victor Emmanuel as king of Italy in January 1861, feeling
in Greece became more than ever hostile to Otho's rule. By March the
situation was serious. During the Independence Day celebrations the usual
royal portraits were absent, and Garibaldi was the hero of the hour.

Once again Otho took up the plan for an attack on the Ottoman empire.
This time he aimed to create a Balkan league consisting of Greece, the
Danubian Principalities,[11] Montenegro, and Serbia—an idea long canvassed
in the Balkans by Canini, a Venetian who had taken refuge in Greece in
1848, and indeed by Mazzini who, in his *Slavic Letters* of June 1857, had
assigned to the Hellenes a leading role in forming a confederation to replace

[11] These had been united in 1859 following their partial liberation in 1856.

Turkey as the barrier against the Muscovite empire. The plan in question was first put before the Serbian government by Koundouriotis, Otho's foreign minister. The four powers were to prepare their military forces, conduct intensive propaganda in those parts of Turkey inhabited by their brothers, and which they hoped to annex, and to send out agents to preach fraternity between the different peoples. The Serbs were favourable in principle, but they would not agree to a four-nation pact, fearing that it would not remain secret. Moreover, they wanted to know first what French reactions would be and yet were unwilling themselves to take soundings in Paris. Meanwhile, indeed for the past two years, Otho had been in secret correspondence with Garibaldi and had even offered him a command in the Hellenic army. He was hoping that Garibaldi would co-ordinate an attack on Venetia from the east with a Balkan rising against the Turks.

But Otho's plans (even had they been feasible and even had there existed the national strength to back them) did not mature fast enough to improve his position. Opposition to his rule continued to increase. During the years 1860–62 a new generation of politicians and citizens appeared upon the scene, many of them products of the University of Athens, many of them members of the growing trading, commercial, and professional classes, and many of them widely travelled or educated abroad. These, combining with the diehards among the older politicians, created a more vigorous and more enlightened opposition to Otho's authoritarian rule. This opposition found much support among the Greeks of the dispersion and certainly much sympathy in the European press.

CHAPTER 6

The Revolution of 1862
and the Change of Dynasty in Greece

I. The Revolution of 22 October 1862

One of Otho's greatest difficulties had always been the question of the succession, which came up for consideration intermittently throughout his reign. During his visit to Bavaria in 1850–51, he had discussed the problem with his family, but no decision had been reached. In 1852 the matter had been taken up by the protecting powers, who had gone on to make a treaty with Bavaria and Greece: Otho's successor was to profess the Orthodox faith; if he were a minor, Queen Amalia was to act as regent. But this treaty provided no real solution. The Bavarian signatory had declared that the heir need not change his religion until the throne was vacant and the Greek delegate had stated that Greece could not recognise any arrangement not expressly sanctioned by the Greek constitution. Since none of the Bavarian princes had adopted the Orthodox faith, there was in fact no heir. In such a case the constitution provided that the king, with the consent of two-thirds of the chamber and the senate, should nominate his successor. But Otho, believing that an Orthodox heir living in Athens would merely become the centre of an opposition to himself, refrained from following this procedure.

By 1861, when events in Italy had led to an anti-dynastic movement in Greece, the whole question of the succession had become acute. The Russian government, fearing that the Greek dynasty was in danger, pressed Otho, in his own interest, to have the question of the succession settled. This advice Otho was unwilling to accept immediately, but at the end of the summer he went to Karlsbad, leaving Amalia as regent and intending to discuss with his family the vexed problem of an heir. The outcome was that he invited the two sons of his brother Luitpold to visit Athens, in the hope that their presence would calm down the populace. But when they reached Corfu, they learned that on 13 February 1862 the 900-strong garrison at

Nafplion had revolted, and they therefore returned to Trieste. Against the rebels the government assembled loyal irregulars under the command of the Swiss philhellene General Hahn. These drove the insurgents back within the walls of Nafplion. For the next few months the regime somehow managed to survive and on 14 October Otho and his queen left Athens for a tour of the Peloponnese, intending to listen to the grievances of the people. But two days later a revolt broke out in Vonitsa, which was followed on 18 October by an insurrection in Patras. Otho hastened back to his capital only to find, when off Piraeus on 23 October, that the previous day the government had been overthrown by Voulgaris; that a provisional government had that morning declared Otho's reign ended and Amalia's regency abolished; and that this government had announced that a national assembly would be convoked at once to elect a new king and draw up a constitution.

Upon receiving this news Amalia was all for returning to Kalamata, where the royal couple had enjoyed a great welcome, there to await the arrival of ships and friendly forces. But Otho was in less hurry; he wanted further information; and he stayed to receive the foreign representatives. These advised him to leave at once, saying that as the nation as a whole had risen against him, he would not be safe anywhere in Greece. He then accepted the offer of Scarlett, Britain's new representative since the death of Wyse, of a passage to Venice in a British ship. Before leaving he sent out a proclamation stating, not that he was abdicating, but that he was leaving Greece to avert a civil war. He expressed his genuine love for Greece—a love he retained until his dying day (26 July 1867), when he insisted that the Testament should be read to him in Greek. Such was the sad end of one who had ruled Greece for nearly thirty years and who had not been a total failure. In making many friends in Greece he had inevitably made enemies, and one sometimes wonders whether Leopold of Saxe-Coburg would have done much better.

II. The Change of Dynasty

The quest for a new sovereign was to prove reminiscent of the attempts to find a king some thirty years before, with this difference, however: that many who had seen how Otho had fared were not prepared to be considered. But even before Otho was deposed there had been much speculation concerning his successor. Prince Alfred, the second son of Queen Victoria, had visited Greece as a midshipman in 1859. He had made a good impression; and it was rumoured that he would, to begin with, be given a separate kingdom, consisting of the Ionian Islands, Crete, Epiros, and Thessaly, and that, when Otho died, he would unite the two Greek states. It had also been rumoured that Otho's successor was likely to be the duke of Leuchtenberg, a nephew of the Tsar, who was related to the houses of Bavaria and Bonaparte and who was Orthodox in religion. These rumours embarrassed the

British and Russians. Both feared to come off second best and preferred the continuation of Otho's rule; but once the revolution had taken place, both realised that any attempt to restore Otho would be out of the question[1] and endeavoured, while publicly avowing a policy of neutrality, to steal a march upon one another. All this time France, though suspicious of British influence in Athens, was deeply involved elsewhere in Europe and needed British support: she therefore gave Russia no real assistance.

Both Russia and Britain paid scant respect to the two international agreements concerning the Greek throne which laid down the exclusion of members of their reigning families as candidates and the need to find an Orthodox successor. The British were not interested in an Orthodox successor. Palmerston certainly favoured Alfred, but unable to press openly for him because of Queen Victoria's objections, he nevertheless kept him in the running lest failure to do so would clear the way for Leuchtenburg, whom the Russians, on the assumption that he was not a member of the imperial family, hoped to establish as a Bavarian. Throughout the long negotiations that ensued Palmerston held a strong card, the Ionian Islands, which he had already offered to Otho on condition he would refrain from aggression against the Turks. This offer Otho rejected: he was more interested in the unredeemed Turkish Greeks than in the Ionians, who were intriguing on their own with the Italians, and who were likely to be just as difficult for him to rule as they had been for the British. But the majority of Otho's subjects welcomed the possibility of adding to Greece their Ionian kinsmen, and consequently the pro-British factions were throughout the crisis always in strength. The Greeks forgot that 'Alfredakis' came from a pro-Turkish country and fondly believed that Great Britain was only pro-Turkish because she was anti-Russian; once 'our Alfred'[2] were installed in Athens, Great Britain would be a convert to the Great Idea (just as she had become a convert to Italian unity) and would bestow upon Greece, in addition to the Ionian Islands, loans and trade, Epirus and Thessaly, and even Constantinople. So hard did the Russians (and they had the lukewarm support of the French) press for Leuchtenburg after Britain's 'first choice', Nicholas of Nassau, had been ruled out by France, that Palmerston encouraged the Greeks to clamour for Alfred, despite Queen Victoria's ruling. This forced the Russians to withdraw Leuchtenburg in return for the formal withdrawal of Alfred (4 December 1862). The Greek government, however, in response to popular clamours, had decided to hold a plebiscite, and in

---

[1] Palmerston ruled that Article IV of the treaty of May 1832 gave no guarantee to Otho personally: what was guaranteed was the nationhood of Greece and not the Bavarian dynasty. He went on to say that the Greeks had the right to change the dynasty—a principle to which Queen Victoria, despite her Hanoverian antecedents, subscribed with considerable remorse.

[2] Sir Richard Church used his influence on behalf of Alfred. His Athenian neighbour, the historian Finlay, thought Gladstone would be a better choice, for he had 'learning enough to confound the professors and calculation to confuse the merchants'.

mid-December Alfred was elected by 230,016 votes out of 244,202. To console the Greeks, Palmerston not only offered them the Ionian Islands but intimated that he would recommend to the Sultan the cession of Epiros and Thessaly, providing their choice of a sovereign was satisfactory to England.

It was no easy task, however, for Palmerston to assist them in their choice of a man who satisfied all his conditions—no connection with France or Russia, liberal views, and some experience in administration. One such man was Ernst, duke of Saxe-Coburg-Gotha, nephew of King Leopold, but like his uncle in 1830 he made demands which were too exacting. Meanwhile the French backed the duc d'Aumâle, Louis-Philippe's fourth son who was betrothed to a Leuchtenburg; but Palmerston let it be known that he found the 'hen bird' of that house just as objectionable as the 'cock'. Numerous other candidates were considered.[3] At one point Gorchakov, the Russian foreign minister, endeavoured to revive the Bavarian claims, but he failed to persuade the Bavarians to announce a candidate who would adopt the Orthodox faith, and when he later urged that Otho should formally abdicate in favour of his nephew Ludwig, he met with no response.

When almost at the end of his tether, Palmerston came forward with the name of Prince Christian William Ferdinand Adolphus George, the second son of Prince Christian, the heir to the Danish throne, and brother of Princess Alexandra, who was to marry Prince Albert Edward of Wales. Queen Victoria had no sympathy for his family (Glücksburg) and she underrated his intelligence, but she did not definitely oppose him. Napoleon III favoured him. Tsar Alexander II, deserted by France who was backing the revolution in Poland, could offer no firm resistance. Any difficulties in the way of Palmerston's latest move were made by Prince Christian. The Greeks, carefully managed by the British and eager to settle the business quickly, came out in George's favour. On 20 March 1863 they acclaimed him in their national assembly and appointed a deputation of three to go to Copenhagen to offer him the crown. But the members of the deputation, Zaimis, Kanaris, and D. Grivas, who were political rivals, were without authority to make a settlement and did not arrive in Denmark until 25 April.

Meanwhile Prince Christian was attempting to drive hard bargains with the powers—the abdication of Otho,[4] the extension of the Greek frontier in Epiros and Thessaly, a civil list of at least £50,000, recognition of Prince

---

[3] Among them were: duke of Oldenburg; duke of Aosta (son of Victor Emmanuel); Prince Napoleon; Prince Oscar of Sweden; Prince Ferdinand of Portugal; Prince Henry of the Netherlands; Prince Alexander of Hesse Darmstadt; Prince Philippe, count of Flanders; Prince Ernst of Leiningen; Prince William of Baden; prince of Carignano; Ludwig, son of Luitpold of Bavaria; Prince Augustus ('Gusty') of Coburg; Ferdinand-Maximilian, future emperor of Mexico; Leopold of Hohenzollern-Sigmaringen; and Prince Waldemar of Holstein Augustenburg.

[4] Prince Christian was logical in pointing out that his own succession in Denmark depended on an instrument similar to that on which Otho had held the Greek crown and that while Otho was free to abdicate, he could not lawfully be deposed.

William's rights of succession to the Danish throne, retention of his Lutheran faith, his continued sojourn in Denmark until he had attained his majority, the replacement of the old Greek army by a new army which should take an oath of allegiance not to the constitution but to the king personally, and the provision of a British naval squadron which should be put at William's disposal. All these demands were supported in the Danish press, which suggested that, as William would be making a great sacrifice, the protecting powers should show their gratitude by supporting Denmark in the vexed Schleswig-Holstein question, which was then approaching a crisis. There was, however, one ray of hope: the young William was keen to go to Greece.

Following protracted negotiations in London, Munich, and Copenhagen, and following a threat by King Frederik VII of Denmark that he would overrule his heir Prince Christian, a protocol was drawn up on 5 June between Denmark and the three protecting powers recognising the election of William as king of Greece. A final settlement was reached in the treaty of London of 13 July 1863. Frederik accepted for the son of his heir the hereditary sovereignty of Greece offered by the Greek national assembly in the name of the Hellenic nation (Art. I); Prince William should bear the title 'George I, King of the Greeks' (Art. II); Greece under his sovereignty and under the guarantee of the three powers was to form a monarchical, independent, and constitutional state (Art. III); the Ionian Islands were to be added to the Hellenic kingdom when such a union proposed by Great Britain should have been given the assent of the Ionian parliament and of Austria, France, Prussia, and Russia (Art. IV); these islands when united to Greece were to be comprised within the terms of the third article (Art. V); the crowns of Greece and Denmark were never to be united on the same head (Art. VI); King George's successors must belong to the Orthodox faith (Art. VII); King George, subject to the agreement of the Greek national assembly, was to attain his majority before completing his eighteenth year (Art. VIII); a *dotation personelle* was to be provided from funds owed by Greece to the protecting powers and the Ionian government was to be recommended to provide £10,000 annually towards the civil list (Art. IX, X, XI); and the powers were to use their influence to obtain general recognition of the new king, whose arrival in Greece the king of Denmark was to do all he could to expedite (Art. XII, XIII).

At no point in these negotiations did the British endeavour to make King George an exclusively British agent. Nor was there (as is sometimes asserted) any secret arrangement pledging King George to pursue a pacific policy towards the Turks. True, it was generally understood that he should go to Greece to put an end to chaos and uncertainty, and not to pursue the policy of the Great Idea; and his title, changed by a protocol of August to 'King of the Hellenes', was, despite its apparent ambiguity, intended to denote that he was sovereign only of those within the boundaries of the

Hellenic state. Indeed it was on that understanding that the title had been sanctioned by the Turks, who had rejected Russell's proposal—'King of the Hellenic Nation.'

King George's departure for Greece was delayed because it was uncertain whether the Ionian parliament, which was not truly representative of the people, would vote for union with Greece. But the new king decided to take a risk. Having visited his three patrons, Queen Victoria, Louis Napoleon, and the Tsar, he arrived in Greece on 30 October 1863. While he was on his way, a newly-elected Ionian parliament voted for union with Greece, Austria and Prussia having already intimated that they had no objections to offer.

III. Greece in 1863

The Greece which young King George went to rule was, to all outward appearances, not so vastly different from that to which the young Otho had gone thirty years earlier. In the countryside life went on much as before— the fixed round of the seasons, lambing, the sowing, the harvesting, and the many religious festivals essential to the Orthodox religion. For most Greeks life revolved round the Church and round the hospitable but poverty-stricken homesteads. For them the real events were the saints' days, births and baptisms, betrothals and marriages, sickness, death and burials,and the comings and goings of brigand bands and tax officials, between which there was but little to choose. Of the outside world, of political events in Athens, and of occasional disorders in the provinces, these village Greeks had only the knowledge that came from hearsay or from the reading-aloud of a newspaper by one of their number who might be lettered. Then, as now, and during the days of the Turkish occupation, the meanest Greek thirsted for news. Whether this news was fact or fiction, he was in no position to judge; nor could he have judged whether his own repetitive toil and his unrecorded efforts to scrape together a little money for himself were of greater or lesser historical importance than the much bruited political activity of the economically unproductive Greek in the thick of Athenian politics.

Both toil and politics have their place in Greek national history, but in the writing of a story which is based on records, the political activity of the relatively few (an activity which has indeed its own separate interest) tends to predominate over the hundreds of repetitive village histories, which though imperfectly known owing to a paucity of record, nevertheless must be given emphasis, even though they can be presented only in general terms. Life in the villages, despite the permanence of outward forms, was undergoing gradual change which, while always remaining gradual throughout nineteenth-century Greece, was certainly important. The little money scraped together by the more fortunate and the thrifty resulted in small investments in land or in the purchase of goods produced by the slowly expanding local industries or circulated by a slowly expanding commerce.

During the first decade or so of Otho's reign the villages and homesteads that had been destroyed during the War of Independence had been gradually rebuilt and the devastated olive groves had been replanted. Moreover, much of the land had passed into the ownership of the peasantry, in some degree as a result of governmental action but probably more often by prescriptive occupation. In some regions, partly owing to emigration,[5] there was land to spare and much of it passed into the hands of those who were able to create relatively large estates and farms. Altogether about 16 per cent of the rural population was composed of peasant proprietors. The rest were share-croppers, the normal holding of a family ranging between 10 and 25 acres.

Agricultural practice, however, had not changed. Except for those commodities which through the system of rents, tithes, and taxation in kind passed into commerce, or which the peasants took to the local markets, most agricultural production was consumed by the producers under what was chiefly a regime of subsistence agriculture. The old wooden plough which merely scratched the soil was still almost everywhere in use; broadcast and uneven sowing continued as before; springtime inundations and summer drought frequently destroyed or reduced the yield of crops; and the custom of leaving the soil fallow for considerable periods further diminished agricultural output. Much of the growing crop was wasted while it awaited the assessment of the taxation official, and further losses of grain occurred when the crop was belatedly transported by pack animals to a communal threshing floor, which might be many miles away. Roads, even wide tracks, were few and far between, and wheeled traffic almost nonexistent. During the whole of Otho's reign only about 150 miles of road were built. Hence, even where it was relatively easy to produce a surplus of grain, there was little incentive to do so, with the result that several of the towns on the sea were supplied not from their own hinterland but from foreign surpluses transported by ship.

Another impediment to agriculture was the heavy interest-rate of mortgage loans, which might be as high as 24 per cent. This, along with the relatively heavy rates of taxation and tithes, and the wasteful methods of collection, prevented even the more enterprising from amassing capital and from making improvements. Hence there was hardly any export of agricultural production. The one exception was the export of currants, which rose in value from about 3,500,000 drachmai in 1845 to nearly 18 million in 1865.

The lack of considerable agricultural production and of export meant that industry was confined almost entirely to domestic trades. Even the manufacture of dyed cotton-thread at Ambelakia, which had flourished in Turkish days, had declined, owing to the competition of the cheaper

---

[5] Between 1834 and 1836 some 60,000 Greeks emigrated to Turkey.

English-made thread in the markets of central Europe. Only in a few coastal towns were factories established and these were very small. In shipping, however, the national Greeks made some headway in Otho's reign. During that period they more than made good the losses of the revolution and they began to regain, following the development of southern Russia, an important share in the Black Sea trade. The transition to steam was to cause some recession, but in the next reign the problem of competing with shipowners of the more industrialised countries was to be solved on traditional lines— by co-operative enterprises in which the small Greek owners formed partnerships to buy vessels discarded by European firms.

Despite the lack of industrial development in all the Greek towns and villages, a certain amount of building went on throughout Otho's reign. Public administrative buildings, hospitals, schools, and churches (some of them the gift of wealthy Greeks who had left their place of birth), and private houses and villas were erected around public squares, into which ran tree-lined thoroughfares. This was particularly true of Athens, which on becoming the capital of Greece in December 1834 had been merely a township of a few thousand inhabitants,[6] with a very small church, many squalid buildings, but with a few reasonably solid pleasant Turkish houses on and near the area now called Plaka. By 1855 its population had risen to 30,000 and its seaport, Piraeus, which in 1833 had consisted only of a monastery, a customs-house, and a few fishermen's houses, by that year housed some 6,000 people. In Athens itself the roads which today form the centre of the city had begun to take shape, a development encouraged by Queen Amalia. The university, established by a decree of 31 December 1836, had opened in May 1837 in a large house in Plaka with fifty-two students. Its present classical building (architect, Christian Hansen)[7] was begun in 1839, opened in 1841, and finished in 1862. The palace, overlooking the open space which from 1842 became known as Constitution Square, was begun in 1836 and completed in 1843. On another side of the square a rich Greek from Trieste, Antonios Dimitriou, began to build in 1842 a sumptuous home (architect, Theofilos Hansen) which later housed the French archaeological school and which in 1875 became a hotel (now the *Grande Bretagne*). Between 1846 and 1852 the wealthy Greek Arsakis built a school which bore his name (Arsakeion; architect, L. Kaftantzoglou) and which today houses the magistrates' court of Athens. Other buildings of importance were the Academy (architect, Theofilos Hansen), built in 1859 alongside the university; the metropolitan church (architects, Theofilos Hansen and others), begun in 1842 and completed in 1862; the English

---

[6] Estimates vary from 4,000 to 12,000.

[7] Christian Hansen (1803–83) was a distinguished Danish architect who arrived in Greece shortly after Otho. He assisted Saubert and Ross in the reconstruction of the temple of 'wingless victory' on the Acropolis. His brother Theofilos Hansen (1813–91) first went to Greece in 1838 and became a professor in the Greek polytechnic. Later he became a distinguished architect in Vienna.

church, consecrated in 1843; the house of the philhellene duchesse de Plaissance (architect, Kleanthis), built between 1840 and 1848 and which now houses the Byzantine museum; the Planetarium (architect, Theofilos Hansen), built between 1842 and 1846 from funds provided by Baron Sina; the Eye Hospital (architect, Kaftantzoglou), a building in the Byzantine style begun in 1847 and completed in 1854 as a clinic of the university;[8] and the Catholic church of St Dionisios, on which work began in 1857. All this time fanariots and wealthy Greeks of the dispersion built for themselves homes in Athens and summer villas on the lower slopes of Mount Pendeli. One particularly imposing house, built (1839–45) by Kleanthis for the banker Theodoros Rallis, later became the British legation. Athens, though still small, thus gradually became a city of some character and an intellectual centre of the westernised brand of Hellenism, in which the intelligentsia for the most part not only studied and glorified their Greek classical ancestry, but embellished their ingrained nationalism with the revolutionary and liberal theories of Europe.

It was the growing intelligentsia and above all the younger generation which had, as we have seen, become highly critical of Otho's effete and autocratic rule; and it was that same intelligentsia which was to provide many of the political figures of the constitutional regime of King George I. It produced on a smaller scale that kind of intellectual opposition to government which had faced Charles X and Louis-Philippe in France. Indeed, Athens with its press and its cafés had become the miniature Paris of the Levant. Here a growing body of literary men imitated in verse and prose, and especially in prose, the outstanding French writers. Here too, as in Paris, there were political and literary cafés. Between 1835 and 1870 the most famous was the 'Beautiful Hellas' (*Orea Ellas*) situated at the junction of the streets Aiolou and Ermou.[9] Here journalists and politicians talked; here they read their newspapers, of which in 1863 there were over twenty published in Athens, to say nothing of periodicals, pamphlets, and occasional broadsheets. Until the promulgation of the revolution of September 1843 Otho had kept a firm control of the press. But after that date, although the press law was tightened up in June 1850 and although between 1857 and 1862 attempts were made to stifle those newspapers which attacked Otho's regime, the press certainly flourished. All this time a vigorous intellectual life developed. Theatrical productions, which began as early as 1836, became more frequent and led to a Greek theatre of outstanding merit. The following year the Greek archaeological society was founded. By 1842 a well-stocked bookshop was to be found in Athens. The National Library had already opened in the church of Agios Eleftherios, where it remained until 1863. In 1840 Ross the archaeologist began work on the

[8] The military hospital (1834–36) was built outside Athens, in the district known as Makriyanni.

[9] It was not until later that *Zacharatos* and *Gambetas* became important.

Acropolis. It had rightly been decided to make this eminence, with the Parthenon and other ancient buildings, the cynosure of the city and to reject the idea of building there King Otho's palace.

Led by the university, which by 1863 had close on a thousand students, a Greek education system began to take shape. By 1860 there were eight gymnasia, with some 1,300 pupils, and 87 Hellenic (secondary) schools with close on 6,000. Primary schools, which in 1830 had numbered 71, by 1860 had reached the figure of 598 (for boys) and 70 (for girls), the total number of pupils having risen from nearly 7,000 in 1830 to over 45,000 in 1860. In addition to these, there were specialist schools which trained recruits for the army, the merchant navy, and the Church. Broadly speaking, educational progress had been sufficient to meet immediate needs. It failed, however, to satisfy the Greeks of that day, who prized education highly and who were prone to attribute to it miraculous powers.

CHAPTER 7

The Constitution of 1864:
The Acquisition of the Ionian Islands

I. Party Conflicts in 1863–64

When King George of the Hellenes arrived in Greece, he found he had to deal with four principal parties. One of these was headed by Voulgaris, the leader of the insurrection of 1862. A second party was that of Alexandros Koumoundouros, a Maniat lawyer and a man of exceptional intelligence, who, as minister of finance in the first ministry of Voulgaris, had been lavish in his use of patronage. The third party was that of Thrasivoulos Zaimis of Kalavrita, a son of the determined hero of the War of Independence but himself a timid politician who favoured moderation both at home and abroad. The fourth party was that of Epaminondas Deligiorgis, a lawyer and deputy for Mesolonghi, and an orator of some power who found support among young officers and students with Western, liberal ideas.

These four parties, coalitions of personal groups, continued the traditions of the old clientèles and failed to become parties based on principles. More important than a party programme was to be in office before an election and thus, by the use of government patronage, to secure some sort of majority at the polls. Indeed all parties, and the groups which composed them, competed for the honour of achieving ends on which they were all generally agreed. On domestic issues they bickered endlessly over trivial matters. On national policy they all subscribed to the *megali idhea*, but quarrelled violently about the means and the timing of its fulfilment. Some favoured a momentary policy of friendship with Turkey, of conserving and developing the national resources, and of seeking, for the time being, the aggrandisement of Greece by diplomatic means. Others, however, who in their various ways looked for quicker results, encouraged secret societies and insurrectionary movements against Turkish rule. It was this policy that Koumoundouros supported, as indeed occasionally did Voulgaris and Deligiorgis. All believed

97

that the acquisition of the Ionian Islands would open an era of annexation, and each after his own fashion was firmly convinced that the European situation was developing favourably for Greece.

These speculations on foreign policy and the intense political disputes which had preceded the long-delayed arrival of the king meant that the task of constitution-making had been much neglected. When the king arrived, the old constitution of 1844 was still in force. By a resolution of 22 October the assembly had provisionally vested in the new king the royal prerogatives and executive power of that constitution (Articles XXII–XXXVI). By that same instrument, however, the assembly had excluded from the royal veto all constitutional matters—a denial of the crown's constituent power. This situation the young king accepted in his proclamation of 30 October, when he acknowledged that he had been chosen sovereign by the Greek people and pledged himself to observe the constitution.

It was no easy task to play the role of constitutional king before a new constitution came into force. Until the constitution was promulgated the national assembly could not be dissolved and elections held; and, according to a ruling of the assembly, the constitution could not be promulgated until it had received the approval of the Ionian deputies, whose entry to the assembly could not take place until the treaty of annexation of the islands by Greece had been concluded. Even though the powers had signed among themselves a treaty on 14 November, the clauses providing for the neutralisation of the islands were not acceptable to Greece.

In view of this confusing situation the king, acting on the advice of his Danish adviser, Count Sponneck, decided to form an all-party cabinet. Voulgaris, who promised to undertake this task, promptly selected his own friends, thus giving rise to a ministerial crisis reminiscent of the early days of Otho. In this crisis the foreign envoys were soon involved: Scarlett, the British representative, supported Voulgaris; the French began an intrigue to bring back to Greece the Greek ambassador to Paris, Kallergis (one of the leaders of the revolution of 1843), to replace Sponneck as adviser; and the Russians with a similar aim in view foisted Colonel Skarlatos Soutsos on the Court as grand marshal.[1] Scarlett, however, had a strong card to play: he let it be known that Britain had not yet definitely ceded the Ionian Islands and would do so only if she considered the situation in Athens to be satisfactory.

Despite Scarlett's strong support Voulgaris found himself faced with a growing opposition. Colonel Dimitrios Botsaris, a diehard Othonist, had been chosen by the Italian (formerly Garibaldian) committee to raise revolt in Epiros and Thessaly. It was hoped that he would have the support of Theodoros Grivas's armed bands and that there would be diversionary risings in Serbia and the Principalities. The plan was not only to attack

[1] The Russians were working also through Vernardakis, a rich merchant from St Petersburg.

Turkey but to bring about the restoration of the Bavarian dynasty in Greece. In Athens itself the Othonist organisation, the 'Sacred Struggle', accused Voulgaris of allowing Greek affairs to be directed by Scarlett. Crowds of Ionians who had gone to Athens demonstrated in the streets, accusing Voulgaris of delaying the treaty of Union. On 8 March 1864 the garrison at Mesolonghi mutinied against the officers appointed by the government. Voulgaris appealed to the powers for assistance. The French and Russian envoys, Bourée and Blontov, contrived that Scarlett should have the odium of sending a British ship to the scene of the troubles. Meanwhile Sponneck, greatly incensed with Voulgaris, prevailed upon the king to dismiss him. One result was the formation of a new cabinet under the aged Admiral Kanaris, composed chiefly of friends of France and Russia. Another result was the determination of Voulgaris and Scarlett to bring about the fall of Sponneck.

Hoping to settle the problem of the constitution as soon as possible, Sponneck sought the help of Edward Erskine, who in June 1864 replaced Scarlett as British envoy. Sponneck hoped that Erskine would withdraw his support from Voulgaris and facilitate the making of a constitution based on conservative principles. But Voulgaris, who had some inkling of what was going on, could play Sponneck at his own game: he suggested to Erskine that if he himself were permitted to form a neutral ministry, then he would ensure a conservative constitution which would provide for a senate nominated by the crown for life; once the new constitution was working with himself firmly in the saddle, he would then get rid of Sponneck. But this plan was soon rendered impracticable: on 19 September the assembly ruled by 213 votes to 62 that there should be no senate; and the British government, in new instructions to Erskine, made it clear that he should not meddle in the internal affairs of Greece. Thus thwarted, Voulgaris withdrew his following from the assembly—a move which led Koumoundouros to reconsider his position. He offered to leave the government and to support a Voulgaris ministry, which would then have a majority in the assembly.

Faced with this intolerable situation, Sponneck began to think of a *coup d'état*. With some encouragement from the French, but none whatever from the British and Russians, he prevailed upon the king to tell the assembly that if the constitution were not completed within ten days, he himself would take matters into his own hands. This bold move a triumph for Sponneck—was not without effect. On 29 October the constitution was voted.

The new constitution, based on the Belgian constitution of February 1831 and therefore principally on the French constitution of 3 September 1791, created a 'royal republic'. The king was to exercise 'no other powers than those explicitly conferred upon him by the constitution and the special laws made in pursuance thereto'. He had no powers of revision. These were vested in specially elected revisionary assemblies. He had no power to initiate or veto constitutional changes. Indeed, when the constitution was launched, he had no share other than to sign it formally and to swear to abide by it. Nevertheless the king, and here the constitution differed from the French constitution of 1791, had the right to appoint and dismiss ministers and to dissolve parliament—a right which, owing to the instability of party coalitions, he had frequently to exercise. Although in theory the constitution rested on the principle that the people were the sovereign power, it was not always clear which of the parliamentary factions truly represented the national will. The result was that the king, though lacking in extensive constitutional powers, enjoyed considerable influence, which Greek politicians made use of when it suited them to do so or denounced when it worked against them. Not infrequently, in order to get business done or to bring foreign policy within limits prescribed by the European powers, the king found himself forced to govern through minority or even extra-parliamentary ministries. This exposed him to much criticism and eventually gave rise to a widespread but essentially sporadic anti-dynastic feeling.

II. The Ionian Islands

The treaty ceding the Ionian Islands to Greece was concluded by the three protecting powers with the government of Greece on 29 March 1864. This treaty established the perpetual neutrality of the islands and obliged the Greeks to recognise this principle. It further provided that the islands should contribute to the king's civil list and it made final the earlier agreement that an annual dotation to the king should be made out of the annual payments which Greece owed to the protecting powers. Finally, it provided that contracts between the Ionian Islands and foreign powers should be maintained by the Greek state and the pensions due to British and former Ionian subjects should become a charge upon the Greek treasury.

The acquisition of these islands added to Greece an area of 1,813 square miles and a population of 236,000, bringing the total to about 1,400,000. To the annual revenue of the Greek state these islands brought an increase amounting to approximately 4,600,000 drachmai. This sum, however, hardly covered administrative costs. Nor did the islands add immediately to the military and naval strength of Greece except in so far as they furnished recruits and crews. As we have seen, these islands were neutralised and they could not therefore be used as bases for the small Hellenic navy. On the other hand, they did not present Greece with a problem of defence: they had been included in the guarantee to Greece and they were therefore secure from other powers who might have designs upon them. All that the Greek state was required or allowed to do was to maintain police forces to preserve law and order.

Despite the fifty years of British rule and in some measure because of it, the islands had been the scene of considerable disorder. Ever since the day of their freedom from Venetian rule there had been, especially in Corfu, a conflict between the nobility and the lower orders. Successive British high commissioners had based their rule upon the sycophants among the higher classes. According to the constitution of 1817, drawn up by Sir Thomas Maitland (1816–23), the lower house of forty members had been elected from lists drawn up by a primary council consisting of ten nobles, and it had been subjected to a strict control by a senate composed of the creatures of the high commission. Maitland's efficient and ruthless rule had encountered opposition from the Kapodistrian family, which led a section of the nobility hostile to those sycophants who had feathered their own nests. Maitland's rule had been highly unpopular, especially when during the early years of the Greek War of Independence he applied the British policy of neutrality so strictly as in practice to favour the Turks. This neutrality, combined in some measure with intrigue in favour of the 'English party' in Greece, was continued by Sir Frederick Adam (1823–32), who again (much to the annoyance of the philhellene Colonel Napier, the resident officer in Kefalonia) sided with the nobility. More liberal was the Tory peer Lord Seaton (1843–49) who, because of his share in passing the British Reform Bill in 1832, had been well received by the Ionians. His handling of disturbances in 1848, similar to those in Europe at large, was considerate. Whereas in Greece itself there was no 'Revolution of 1848', in the Ionian Islands liberal intellectuals, with some support from the lower orders, had come within the full blast of the European revolutionary movement. Seaton made concessions to their demands and it was these concessions—free press, the right to vote extraordinary expenditure, the free election of municipal authorities—that were embodied in the new constitution of 1849, which came into force under his successor, Sir Henry Wood (1849–53). This constitution tripled the electorate, which elected by secret ballot forty-two members to a biennial assembly. It retained, however, a senate, whose members were chosen by the high commissioner from among the members of the lower house.

In the first parliament elected according to the new electoral laws eleven radicals were returned. These advocated *enosis* (union) with Greece, and in the new parliament they tabled a proposal, noisily advocated in the radical press, to that effect. True, the majority of the deputies consisted of moderate reformers and there was a small party which gave full support to firm British rule; the many disturbances throughout the islands and particularly in Kefalonia were not so much anti-British as agrarian. Nevertheless, the radicals were gaining strength, and they were able to increase their following by denouncing as tyranny the undoubted brutality which the administration used in dealing with subversives.

Only gradually did the British government come to realise that the sole alternative to *enosis* was martial law and that to govern these troublesome islanders with an iron hand was not only unprofitable but a constant embarrassment. As a naval base the islands were not essential, indeed superfluous to a power which held and had developed Malta. Right from the beginning the British presence had been prompted chiefly by a desire to deny them to another power. If they could be neutralised by international agreement, then there could be no valid reason why they should not be handed to Greece. To the British the goodwill of Greece, or at least a paramount influence in Greece itself, was more important than to retain these islands, which in a nationalistic age were regarded as indisputably Greek.

In 1859 Gladstone was sent on a special mission to the islands to replace the high commissioner Sir John Young (1855–59). His visit was very brief: he failed to convince the Ionians that what they needed was reform, not union with the misgoverned state of Greece. Those Ionians like Konstantinos Lomvardos and his followers found it quite illogical that a nation which had shown so much sympathy to the Italians should be so niggardly in its attitude to Greeks. Despite their respect for Gladstone's classical learning and his emotional interest in the Greek Orthodox Church, they persisted in their demand for *enosis*; and Gladstone himself, although later in parliament he continued to defend the British protectorate, decided that the Ionian Islands were no place for him. He therefore handed over to Sir H. K. Storks (1859–64), who was to be the last high commissioner.

The failure of Gladstone's mission, which was soon to be followed by the Italian war on Austria, led to increased demands for *enosis*. There the matter rested until in 1862 Palmerston seized the opportunity to barter these islands for the establishment of a dynasty in Greece favourable to British interests—a policy strongly favoured by Queen Victoria, who wanted to make the Greeks 'less likely to throw themselves into the arms of Russia'. At a cabinet meeting on 8 December 1862 Palmerston brought his colleagues round to his views, which had already received some prominence in *The Times*. To the queen he wrote describing the union of the islands with Greece as 'a natural arrangement', and he went on to say:

> While Otho misgoverned Greece it would have been an injury to them to have subjected them to his misrule: now that a brighter prospect is opening upon Greece the annexation of the seven Islands would be a benefit to them and to the Greek kingdom.

Whether or not *enosis* was an unmixed blessing to the islands and to Greece is difficult to say. There were many Corfiots and other islanders, from all classes, who looked with sadness upon the withdrawal of the British officials and garrison since it touched their pockets and social position. Titles of nobility were disdained in Athens. No longer would there be receptions at the Residency, which had given colour and importance to the lives of the more affluent families. The higher clergy, always appreciative of

British respect for Saint Spiridhon, were loth to pass under the control of the Athenian synod and thus to lose a large degree of independence granted by the Patriarchate of Constantinople. Officials of all ranks no longer enjoyed the security they had known for many years. Shopkeepers' profits diminished and the roads and pavements fell into disrepair. For Greece, however, the islands were to provide illustrious recruits to the ranks of the intellectuals[2] and politicians. As for the politicians, their intrusion was half-welcome, half-resented by those who had hitherto dominated the political scene in Athens. (In July 1864 sixty-six deputies entered the Greek national assembly.) Those from Corfu were in the main radicals and, like Lomvardos, staunch upholders of the Great Idea: those from the other islands were more usually conservatives. They all made their contributions to Greek political life but they did not bring about any very noticeable changes in it. They reinforced the already well-established constitutionalism of the greater majority of Greek politicians, but they made it no more disciplined that it was already.

III. The Retirement of Count Sponneck

On 28 November the national assembly was dissolved, but the parliamentary elections were delayed until 28 May 1865. During the interval there were the usual ministerial crises, the usual interference of the representatives of the powers, and continued attempts to get rid of Count Sponneck. Russell, the British foreign secretary, had protested in Copenhagen about Sponneck's behaviour, and King Christian IX, anxious to retain British goodwill, had sent his brother, the prince of Glücksburg, to Greece to examine the situation. This interference the young king resented. He called together his ministers and informed them that, while for the moment he would retain Count Sponneck, his intention was to rule Greece solely in co-operation with the representatives of the nation. Such, too, was the tenor of an audience he gave to the three envoys of the protecting powers.

At the elections of 28 May 1865, Koumoundouros, despite his use of patronage, was defeated, and the king called upon Voulgaris to form a government. During the long-drawn out scrutiny of the parliamentary returns, however, Deligiorgis changed sides, thus enabling Koumoundouros to remain in office until towards the end of October, when he was defeated on a tax bill. On being asked to form a government Voulgaris stipulated that Sponneck should be dismissed. The king turned to Deligiorgis, but he too would not agree to serve until King George promised that Sponneck would leave Greece, the agreed time of his departure being the spring of 1866.

---

[2] In a sense the Ionian scholars, artists, and men of letters (Solomos, Kalvos, and others) had always belonged to Greece, even though politically they had been citizens of another state.

Although the new government consisted of Anglophils and liberals, and was therefore to Erskine's liking, it quickly failed in face of an alliance between Koumoundouros and Voulgaris. A ministerial crisis followed, during which there were angry demonstrations in Athens. On 13 November 1865 there were threats against the palace and Count Sponneck. The king gave way. He sent for Voulgaris and informed him that Sponneck would leave Greece immediately. Voulgaris accepted office, whereupon all disturbance ceased. He remained in office barely two days. Hoping to placate Gobineau, the new French envoy and a staunch philhellene, he included Kallergis in his government as minister of war. This appointment led to the defection of Deligiorgis. But when the king sent for Koumoundouros, Deligiorgis and Voulgaris became reconciled. After a few days of confusion Deligiorgis undertook to form a government with the support of Voulgaris. But this government lasted barely a fortnight. The king then exhorted Voulgaris and Koumoundouros to form a coalition: this they did under Benizelos Roufos, without taking portfolios themselves. Meanwhile, on 21 December, Count Sponneck had left Greece.

Although the count's departure reduced the tension between politicians and the king, it did not lead to political stability. Successive coalitions remained principally negative in aim, their chief object being to keep rivals out of office. Once formed, they never lasted. Even the patronage at the disposal of the government was not at this time sufficient for any one leader to secure a stable majority. Hence there were recurrent ministerial crises which produced a state of paralysis. In a sense government hardly existed. There could be no firm foreign policy, no prospects of reorganising the army and the fiscal system, and no chance of carrying out a social and economic legislative programme. Nevertheless the king, much as he regretted this state of affairs, and much as he abhorred the frequent interference of the foreign envoys, did his best to carry on the function of a constitutional monarch—a role he had accepted when he went to Greece.

IV. Negotiations with Serbia

On his way home to Denmark, Count Sponneck saw Drouyn de Lhuys, the French foreign minister, and Lord Cowley, the British ambassador at Paris, and impressed upon them the need of French and British support for the Greek dynasty. The Russian government, and subsequently the Danish royal family and government, had approached the two Western powers in the same sense. The outcome, however, was a British proposal to speak firmly to King George and the politicians in Greece. This move delighted Gortchakov, the Russian foreign minister, as it fitted into his general policy of forming a Russo–French *entente*, of detaching Vienna from Paris, and of compelling Austria to seek understanding with Prussia, thus obviating the danger of a Polish revolution.[3] He proposed that the three powers should occupy Greek territory. To such extensive intervention, however, both France and Great Britain were opposed. So too was King George. On being informed by Gobineau, he showed great resentment at the Danish moves in London. He instructed Roufos, the prime minister, to make public his resolution that he would tolerate no interference either from the powers or from his family, which earned him much applause in Greece. Meanwhile in Athens, Erskine, acting more or less on his own, had proposed a controlled loan to the Greek state, the formation of a non-party government, and a foreign military force to keep law and order. Needless to say, Gobineau opposed these schemes, which he knew would only drive the Greeks into the arms of Russia, who would represent the whole affair as an Anglo–French manoeuvre. Eventually, however, on 30 January 1866, Erskine received precise instructions. He, and his colleagues, were to preach moderation to the Greek king and politicians. Hence, when finally on 2 February a *démarche* was made, it was quite innocuous. But King George still showed much resentment and, as it was followed up by threats from Erskine in his conversations with the Greek politicians, it raised an outcry in sections of the Athenian press.

Next day, determined to show he was master in his own house, the king dissolved the chamber. This move pleased the Russians. They wanted the king to be free from French and British intervention; they wanted him to marry a Russian princess; and they wanted him to bring Greece freely into the Russian sphere of influence. They were anxious, too, in pursuance of Article XII of the treaty of July 1863, to secure the recognition of King George by other powers. Here, however, Gortchakov overreached himself. Austria (who opposed Russian policy in the Principalities and in the duchies of Schleswig and Holstein) let it be known that the moment was inopportune.

Erskine's conduct widened the breach between the French and British envoys in Athens. This was further widened when Kallergis arrived on 8 May 1866 from Paris to assume office at Court. Immediately on his arrival he established an understanding with Voulgaris, Deligiorgis, and Koumoundouros, the hope being that they would form a coalition government and prepare for war. Claiming to have the confidence of Victor Emmanuel and of Napoleon III (the claim was not fantastic), he began to denounce the king for his subservience to Great Britain and his hostility to the Great Idea. In this he merely displayed his ignorance: King George had never opposed the Idea itself: what worried him was the optimistic and irresponsible plans of its adherents, the lack of financial stability, and the chaos and weakness of the army. He doubted, moreover, whether Kallergis had specific instructions from Napoleon.

[3] His reasoning was that civil war in Germany would lead to foreign intervention, which in turn would lead to a Polish revolution.

On 17 May King George saw Kallergis and appealed to him not to interfere. In reply Kallergis offered to accept office as foreign minister in a new government, stipulating that the king should write personally to Napoleon and to Victor Emmanuel. The king would have none of this. He continued Roufos in office, and consulted the foreign envoys about the existence of factions which claimed to have French support. To them he pointed out his difficulties—his need for money, attacks upon himself by irresponsible politicians, the hectoring of second-rate men, the necessity of keeping parliament prorogued. In reply Erskine and Gobineau (but not the new Russian envoy, Novikov) advised a return to a parliamentary administration. King George therefore sent for Koumoundouros, Voulgaris, and Deligiorgis, and appealed to them yet again to form a coalition government. This request Voulgaris rejected. The king then asked Koumoundouros and Deligiorgis to form a ministry. Negotiations between these two broke down. Eventually on 21 June 1866 Voulgaris and Deligiorgis agreed to serve, the latter taking office as foreign minister.

During this crisis Koumoundouros revealed to Deligiorgis that his envoy Michael Antonopoulos had conducted secret negotiations in May with Ristich, the Serbian agent at Constantinople. These were not of immediate importance, but they were part of a developing situation in Europe which had important repercussions throughout the Balkans.

CHAPTER 8

The Second War of Independence: The First Phase of the Cretan Revolution 1866-69

I. Crete during the Period 1830–66

In 1830 the Turks had placed Crete under Egyptian rule, this being Mohammed Ali's reward for his services to the Ottoman empire in the struggle against the Greeks. This rule fell even more heavily upon the Moslems than upon the Christians, the result being that the population of the island, which in 1821 numbered 289,000, had shrunk by 1840 to 129,000. After Mohammed Ali's defeat in 1840 Crete passed again under Turkish control, and during 1841 Cretan Christians and Cretan Moslems tried to exploit the situation and to improve their lot. Whereas the Moslems were content to request reduction in taxation and administrative reform, many Christian leaders demanded union with Greece. Encouraged by a 'Cretan Committee' which had been set up in Athens, the Cretans of the region of Sfakia (Sfakiots) revolted. Yet, although these Sfakiots rose in strength, they were unable to stand up to vastly superior Turkish forces.

For the next fifteen years Crete remained quiet, during which time an Albanian governor ruling on behalf of the Sultan showed more severity towards the Turkish beys than towards the Christians. Faced with heavy exactions, many of the Moslems sold their estates and left the island. As a consequence more and more land passed into Christian hands—a development which had already begun at the time of the Egyptian occupation. What is more, the Christian population of Crete steadily increased. Whereas in 1821 there had been 160,000 Moslems to 129,000 Christians, by 1866 the ratio stood approximately at 60,000 to 200,000. For this growing Christian population conditions had improved, at least in theory, following the promulgation in 1856 of the *hati-i-humayun*, a reform programme, the

Sultan's thanksgiving (as it were) for the salvation of his empire during the Crimean War. But the local Turks failed to implement these reforms and in 1858 the Christians began to voice complaints. These did not go unheeded. The Porte, fearing that the Cretans, if not pacified, would revolt, issued a decree which not only confirmed but extended the scope of the reforms of 1856. There the matter rested until 1866. In the meantime, the governor of Crete, Ismail Pasha, had attempted to whittle down the rights of his subjects; and once again the Cretan Christians had begun to complain.

In 1866 the Cretan leaders were divided. Some of them were content to demand a degree of autonomy and specific reforms – reduction of taxes; courts and the use of the Greek language in litigation; schools; roads; and a rural bank. Others, envious of the Ionian Greeks, were determined to seize their chance to bring about *enosis* with Greece. They judged the moment opportune. They considered that the Porte had revealed its weakness by its failure to maintain its rights in the Danubian Principalities, which had been granted autonomy at the conference of Paris in 1856. They had seen that during the intervening decade the Romanians, with some support from the European powers, had gone a long way towards independence. More recently they had seen that the Turks, following the fall of Cuza in February 1866, had been unable to carry out their threat to reoccupy the territories in question—that instead the Porte had been faced with the decision of the powers, reached in conference at Paris in March, to offer the Romanian crown to Prince Charles of Hohenzollern-Sigmaringen. They had heard, too, that the Serbs considered the moment propitious to demand the control of the Danubian fortresses of Sabac, Belgrade, and Ada-Kale. Finally they had sensed that Austria had given up her traditional policy of upholding the integrity of the Ottoman empire and that she was now inclined to favour the aspirations of the subject Christian peoples. This wishful thinking, however, was not restricted to the Cretans. If anything, the national Greeks were even more optimistic, and it was they who to a very large degree had encouraged the Cretans in their demand for *enosis*.

During the decade 1856 to 1866 the Cretans had received constant encouragement not only from Koumoundouros but also from the Russian consuls, Dendrinos at Chania and Mitsotakis at Candia (Iraklio). These two had led the Cretans to hope that they would receive support from Russia, who might possibly (and this did indeed happen) enlist the sympathies of France.[1] Likewise the Greek consul held out hopes of material support (for what it was worth) from Greece. The Roufos government, however, which had been formed in February 1866, was likely to be timid. Voulgaris was inclined as usual to keep in step with Great Britain and, although Koumoundouros had pro-Russian leanings and was anxious to help the Cretans, the whole governmental situation in Greece for the

---

[1] France, although at first hostile to the Cretans, in late 1866 and early 1867 aligned with Russia in return for support on the Luxembourg question (see below, pp. 113–14).

moment restricted him. But bolder spirits were to be found outside the government. The Cretan Renieris, a governor of the National Bank of Greece, formed in 1866 the so-called 'central committee', which raised funds, ammunition, and volunteers for Crete. With this committee Koumoundouros, Kallergis, and others in governmental circles had connections; and they certainly gave it some encouragement, but they were always able officially to deny their complicity in the Cretan revolution.

II. The Outbreak of the Cretan Revolution

Towards the end of April 1866 the Cretan leaders (with the knowledge of Dendrinos) met at Omalos and on 27 May, after long discussions, drew up a petition to the Sultan asking for the abolition of newly-imposed taxation and of other measures taken in violation of the decree of 1858. This petition they circulated to the foreign consuls with explanatory notes. In the notes addressed to the British, French, and Russian representatives, it was stated that the Cretans desired an autonomy or hegemony similar to that which obtained in Samos. On the following day many (in fact the majority) of the Cretan leaders signed a secret address to the monarchs of these three powers, requesting *enosis*—a procedure which showed that the Cretans themselves were divided. These moves Ismail Pasha considered subversive: he informed the European consuls on 29 May that, if the Cretan representatives did not disperse, he would take appropriate measures to remove them. But instead of dispersing, the Cretans, who were receiving encouragement from Christos Zimbrakakis, the minister of war in the Voulgaris–Deligiorgis government that had taken office in June, established at Apokorona a 'general assembly' and informed the foreign consuls on 3 August that they had no choice but to defend themselves with arms against the forces (8,000 Turks, 6,000 Egyptians)[2] which the Porte had despatched to the island.

By that time the Turks had concentrated in the castles, while the insurgent Greeks in relatively small bands were roaming the mountains, raising supplies and volunteers. Skirmishing began towards the end of August. Early in September the executive committee of the Cretan assembly declared the abolition of Turkish rule and the *enosis* of Crete with Greece. This same committee went on formally to request the good offices of the powers—a request supported by the Greek minister at Constantinople and by King George himself, who let it be known that rich Greeks had sent him funds, that 10,000 muskets were available in Greece, that friendly Garibaldians would rush to Crete, and that he himself might be forced to lead a popular cause. The powers had already begun to consider a commission of

[2] The despatch of these troops gave some credence to the rumour that Crete would be restored to Egypt in return for a down payment and annual tribute—a plan which Moustier, the French ambassador at Constantinople, had proposed to the Porte and which was obviously connected with French policy towards the Suez canal.

inquiry. Russia and France had shown a desire to intervene more actively; but Stanley, the British foreign secretary, who was anxious to avoid raising fundamental issues in the East at a time when the Western powers had many problems in Europe, was strongly opposed to moves which might only play into the hands of Russia. Indeed, it was already clear by September 1866 that the Russians had embarked on a forward policy. They were certainly sending arms to Crete, and intercepted letters showed that Dendrinos was giving the Cretans all the encouragement he could. But Russian activity was hardly so deliberate, hardly so much a part of a grand design, as the French and English imagined. Gortchakov remained fundamentally timid. He merely wished to appear less anti-Greek than his French and English colleagues.

With a view to forestalling possible intervention by the powers, Aali Pasha, the grand vizier, appointed Mustafa Kyrtli Pasha as extraordinary commissioner to Crete to inquire into the conditions of the Cretans, it being the intention to make a few concessions. But when Mustafa invited the Cretans to state their grievances, they demanded (on the strength of the encouragement given to them by the central insurrectionary committee in Athens) union with Greece. This development alarmed King George, who informed the Turks, through the British legation in Athens, that only if they made concessions to the Cretans would he himself have a chance to work for the maintenance of peace. It also alarmed the French. Moustier, who was recalled from Constantinople to succeed Drouyn de Lhuys as foreign minister and who passed through Athens at the end of September, made it clear to the king, Kallergis, and Voulgaris that Greece could expect no support from France. From that moment, much to the disappointment of Gobineau, French influence waned in Athens, where the press loudly accused Napoleon and his ministers of bad faith.

By the beginning of October the insurrection had spread throughout the island, the Cretans having taken heart during September after their victory over the Egyptians at Vrises. Lieutenant-General Panos Koroneos (a military adventurer and patriotic agitator) and Colonel Ioannis Zimbrakakis (brother of the minister of war) had already left Greece for Crete with some 800 volunteers. The Greek government itself, and especially the minister for war, urged the king to grant leave to army officers so that they could go as irregulars to Crete. The Greek press regaled the population with stories of Turkish atrocities. There were rumours too that Greek organisations were stirring up trouble in other Turkish provinces. These rumours were not unfounded. The central committee, which had established branches in Constantinople, London, Manchester, and Liverpool, did not confine itself to buying arms for Crete. It was preparing for revolts in Epiros and Thessaly to take place not later than March 1867. Nor was the central committee the only organisation. About this time a *filiki eteria* was formed under the leadership of the metropolitan bishop of Athens, its principal aim being to raise a patriotic loan of 25 million francs. The Greeks were in no mood to listen to counsels of moderation from the French and British envoys. They took heart from the knowledge that *The Times* was hostile to British policy, from the pro-Greek attitude of the Vienna press (a somewhat unexpected development),[3] and from Gortchakov's vague threats that, if the Turks broke off diplomatic relations with Athens, Greece would not be left alone. When on 24 October the Cretan insurgents and Greek volunteers were defeated at Vafe near Sfakia and the Sfakiots indicated their intention to make submission under a promised amnesty, the central insurrectionary committee, on the advice of the Russian envoy, Novikov, pressed the government to support an insurrection in Thessaly and Epiros. To this pressure the Greek government responded. Troops under Skarlatos Soutsos, Spiromilios, and Konstantinos Smolenskis were sent to the northern frontiers; and further supplies of ammunition and yet more volunteers (including Garibaldians and European philhellenes) were transported to Crete. These moves encouraged the Cretans who declared on 16 November their determination to continue their struggle of liberation.

This act of defiance infuriated Mustafa Kyrtli Pasha. He attacked the headquarters of Koroneos in the convent of Arkadi. After two days' fighting the brave defenders, like those at Mesolonghi some forty years before, blew up their powder magazines. On this occasion 450 Turks perished along with over 400 Greeks. The Greeks, everywhere outnumbered (the Turco–Egyptian forces were at that time somewhere in the region of 45,000 men), could hardly afford such losses. Nevertheless, although short of supplies, owing to the Turkish blockade, they managed to carry on, and by their constant guerrilla operations they presented the Turkish empire with a formidable financial and military problem over the next three years. The guerrillas (under the general command of Zimbrakakis, Koroneos, Michael Korakas, and Chionoudakis) could rarely concentrate large forces. Much of their energy had necessarily to be devoted to the protection of their families, a number of which, however, they were able to send to Greece for safe-keeping. Despite supplies from Greece and elsewhere, food was always in short supply and so was ammunition. Nevertheless, they took a steady toll of the Turkish regulars. When these attacked the villages which were the centres of the Greek organisation, they were frequently caught either on their way in or on their way out by the Cretan bands, and it is said that one Turkish general who managed to devastate in all some 600 villages, lost in killed and wounded at least 20,000 men.

III. Diplomacy and the Cretan Question

The fall of Arkadi, which was followed by systematic devastation and atrocity on the part of the Turks, aroused the sympathy of Europe and

---

[3] After her defeat in Italy and Germany, Austria had begun to seek influence in the Balkans. From Trieste arms were being sent to Crete.

rendered the Cretan affair (indeed the Eastern question in general) the most urgent European problem. To Ignatiev, the Russian ambassador at Constantinople, the moment seemed appropriate for fashioning a Balkan alliance against the Ottoman empire. Russia herself would refrain from active intervention: banking on the non-interventionist attitude of Great Britain, she would promote a policy of non-interference among the other European powers; but at the same time she would work quietly behind the scenes, giving the Balkan Christians moral support and unity of action. She would promote an alliance between Greece and Serbia and establish centres of action throughout the Balkans.

Prince Michael of Serbia, hoping to profit from the Cretan revolt, had on 29 October sent to the Porte his long-contemplated demand for the evacuation of the Danubian fortresses. In September he had made a treaty with Montenegro. He had, moreover, started military preparations in readiness for a general rising in the Balkans in the spring. He had already concluded with Romania a treaty which had probably been signed in May 1865. This treaty he cited when he opened negotiations[4] in May 1866 with Greece, the result of which was the Serbo–Greek alliance of 26 August 1867. In January Charilaos Trikoupis, who had become foreign minister in the new Koumoundouros government at the end of December 1866, began negotiations with Romania. Three principles were agreed upon immediately: common action by the Balkan Christians; the settlement of the Balkans according to nationalities; and agreement among the four Christian states (Serbia, Greece, Romania, and Montenegro) on the action to be taken and the military preparations to be made. But no alliance resulted from these negotiations: the Romanians were not convinced that the Cretans were capable of prolonged resistance; they doubted the ability of Greece to put sufficient forces in the field; and they were mindful, too, of their own instability and lack of military organisation. A similar fate befell Greece's attempts to form an alliance with the viceroy of Egypt and with Prince Nicholas of Montenegro.

Intelligence of these Balkan moves and the knowledge that Russia was behind them spurred on the Western powers, and particularly France, to find a solution to the Cretan question before it developed into the Turkish problem, with all its implications and dangers. Napoleon III, in view of his Rhenish policy and the existence of the Prusso–Russian *entente*, hoped to find a solution based on nationality which would satisfy Russia and thus afford France some advantage in the West. On 8 December 1866 he threatened the Porte that serious consequences would follow if Crete were not given principality status within three weeks. But British pressure on the Porte was much more cautious: the foreign secretary, Stanley, admitting that Great Britain could not defend the conduct of the Greek government

[4] These were a resumption of the negotiations which had been broken off in 1861 (see above, pp. 85–6

in Crete, merely implored the Porte to show moderation and not to put itself in the wrong. Gortchakov none the less seized the opportunity to go much further: he informed the Turks that the only basis of tranquillity in their empire was to be found in the granting of autonomy to all the Christian peoples. This policy he hoped to combine with the formation of an Austro–Franco–Russian *entente*, but he had to abandon it, for he discovered that the Austrian minister, Beust, was likely to press for the acquisition of Bosnia and Herzegovina. With France, on the other hand, he found the going easier; and it was agreed that both should propose to Great Britain that Crete should be given autonomy. But this solution found no favour with Stanley, whose rigid attitude placed Napoleon in a dilemma: if he acted in concert only with Russia, Russia might try to set the pace. He therefore merely instructed Bourée at Constantinople to urge Aali to give autonomy to Crete and to cede the Danubian fortresses to Serbia, if only to prevent the formation of a Serbo–Greek *entente*. But even this friendly advice caused much concern to Aali Pasha, who complained of it to the British. Stanley, however, was able to reassure him that the dismemberment of the Ottoman empire was no part of British policy. On the strength of this assurance Aali decided to give way on the issue of the Serbian fortresses and to stand firm on Crete—a move which had the effect of interrupting the Serbo–Greek negotiations.

This separation of the Greek and Serbian problems facilitated Moustier's aim of forming a Franco–Russian *entente* in such a way as not to give Russia too free a hand in her dealings with the Slavs. On 23 January 1867 he proposed to Gortchakov that Greece should not only annex Crete but should be given favourable frontier rectifications in Epiros and Thessaly. Gortchakov, however, wanted autonomous regimes under the guarantee of the great powers for all the Balkan Christian peoples and he wished to know more about French plans in Western Europe. Nevertheless, fearing that Moustier would do a deal with Austria (who would acquire Bosnia and Herzegovina), he subsequently showed signs of going a long way to meet the French demands. This policy annoyed Ignatiev, who wanted Russia to seize the initiative and to solve simultaneously the Slav and Greek questions under an arrangement whereby the Serbs would obtain Bosnia and Herzegovina. Showing contempt for, and disloyalty to, Gortchakov he revealed the French plans to the Turks; he advised them not to give way; and he made it clear to them that the protecting powers were by no means in unison. Yet Moustier persisted with his plans for intervention. He found support from Austria, from Italy, and even from Bismarck, whose idea was to divert the attention of France from the Rhineland to the Near East. Towards the end of March Ignatiev, under instructions, took part in an intervention of the powers at Constantinople, and Bismarck let the Turks know that any concessions made to France would only raise demands from Russia. He rightly calculated that the Turks, who would count on the non-participation of Great Britain, would reject the *démarche* out of hand.

For a while Moustier's attention was diverted to the Luxembourg problem in the West, but in the second part of April he again endeavoured to persuade the Turks to make concessions to the Greeks, arguing that the Greeks, if reconciled, would prove useful to Turkey in combating the Slavs. Hearing of this move Gortchakov endeavoured to substitute a general intervention of the powers, only to be thwarted once again by the British and by the refusal of Austria to join in any *démarche* from which Great Britain abstained. Subsequently the Austrians changed their attitude, and on 15 June France, Russia, Italy, Prussia, and Austria handed to the Porte a collective Note requesting a full inquiry into the affairs of Crete. This Note produced no effect: Ignatiev had convinced the Turks that the move was the result of a French design, the ultimate aim of which was to deprive them of Crete. Months passed by. A Russo–Turkish *rapprochement* promoted by Ignatiev led to nothing. Protracted negotiations ending in a four-power declaration, from which the British and Austrian governments abstained, on 30 October had no effect.

IV. The Greco–Serbian Negotiations of August 1867

Meanwhile, the Koumoundouros government, with the king's approval, had announced its intention of improving relations with Turkey. But their real policy was to gain time, to damp down risings in the Balkans, and to prepare for war in the spring. They continued to send arms and volunteers to Crete, having purchased for their transit the vessels *Arkadi*, *Enosis*,[5] and *Crete*. A somewhat similar policy was being pursued in Crete itself. The Cretan national assembly had appointed a provisional government of eight, which, in order to gain the sympathy of the European consuls, induced the Cretans under arms to make a pretended submission, demanded the release of influential Cretans, and gave much publicity to Turkish atrocities. These moves merely prompted the Turks to redouble their efforts to subdue the island. In April 1867 they sent to Crete General Omer Pasha with 15,000 reinforcements including cavalry and artillery. But on 6 May the Cretans inflicted a heavy defeat on him, and one month later (6 June) repeated this performance. In revenge Omer burned the villages, massacred the inhabitants, and on the night of 18–19 July attacked Sfakia, the chief base of the Cretan resistance. Trikoupis sent the powers a strong protest at this barbarity, and the Russians and French responded by sending naval squadrons to the island to evacuate the surviving Christian families.

The provisional government of Crete now requested the Athens government to send them a further thousand volunteers. This request coincided with Serbian moves for the resumption of negotiations for a Serbo–Greek alliance, and it led the Greek government to consider seriously a declaration

---

[5] The Greeks of Great Britain contributed to the cost of these two vessels.

of war on Turkey as the only way of solving the Cretan problem. Everything depended on the Serbian alliance, and this in turn depended on the purchase of munitions for the four new Greek battalions formed in May 1867, on the acquisition of warships, and on a loan. Ignatiev continued to press for this alliance and Tsar Alexander II had emphasised its advantages to King George, who had gone to Russia for his betrothal to the Grand Duchess Olga.

In August Trikoupis sent his friend Petros Zanos (ostensibly to consult the famous physician Dr Friedmann) to meet at Volslau spa near Vienna a Serbian delegation headed by Prince Michael himself. At the same time the Austrians, hoping to counteract Russian influence in the Balkans, were offering Bosnia and Herzegovina to the Serbs in return for a promise to uphold the *status quo* elsewhere in the Balkan peninsula. Prince Michael, however, doubted the sincerity of the Austrians. In any case, he much preferred a Balkan alliance. Earlier in the year he had negotiated an agreement with agents of the Bulgarian revolutionary 'benevolent society' for the creation of a Serbo–Bulgarian state (Yugoslavia) which would include Bulgaria, Thrace, and Macedonia. This he followed up by concluding on 26 August 1867 a treaty of alliance with Greece consisting of seventeen articles. Serbia was to furnish 60,000 men: Greece was to provide 30,000 men and also as large a naval force as possible. Hostilities were to begin in March 1868. If in the meantime Turkey attacked one of the allies, then the other should come to its assistance with all available forces. The aim of the alliance was to free all the Christians of the Balkans and of the islands of the Archipelago, but if it were not possible to undertake this extensive programme, then at least neither partner was to lay down arms until Epiros and Thessaly had been won for Greece, and Bosnia and Herzegovina for the prince of Serbia. It was further understood, although not expressly set down, that if the Serbs acquired Old Serbia, then Greece would acquire Macedonia. On the other hand, the treaty expressly provided (Article VII) that the wishes of the peoples taking up arms should be respected and that confederated states might be established.[6] These peoples, and especially the Albanians, Romanians, and Montenegrins, the two powers were to endeavour to bring into the alliance.[7] Neither Serbia nor Greece was to make agreements with foreign powers unknown to one another. A military treaty was to be concluded. The alliance was to be secret and ratifications were to be exchanged within six weeks.

In forwarding the text of his treaty to King George, who was still in St Petersburg, Koumoundouros made it clear that if the king refused to accept it or if he subsequently declined to sign a declaration of war on Turkey,

---

[6] By a separate instrument it was agreed that Crete should be left out of account in determining territorial negotiations between the two parties.

[7] Neither Romania nor Montenegro formally joined the Serbo–Greek alliance, though Serbia herself made an alliance with Romania in January 1868.

then the government might be faced with a national revolt against the monarchy. Despite this warning the king at first withheld his signature. He knew that Greece was not prepared for war; he feared the hostility of Great Britain in the event of war; and he had good reason to believe that Gortchakov was not only opposed to war but was even likely to abstain from intervention in Crete. Furthermore, he was well aware that Serbian forces were not so strong as they appeared to be on paper: there was a shortage of good officers; and the supply and medical services were almost non-existent. Following further representations from Koumoundouros, however, King George signed the treaty with two important reservations: that preparations for war should be made 'as soon as possible' and that both parties should give an undertaking not to provoke Turkey into aggression. It was not until January 1868 that ratifications were exchanged, and it was not until the following month that the military convention envisaged in the treaty was concluded.

V. Governmental changes in Greece, December 1867–April 1868

In the hope of avoiding intervention by the powers Aali Pasha had gone to Crete in person. On 6 October he offered an amnesty and a new system of administration. These offers the Cretans, acting on the advice of Koumoundouros, rejected. Nevertheless, Aali proceeded to reorganise the administration. He constituted Crete into a single *vilayet*, divided into five provinces and twenty districts. The *vali* (or governor-general) was to have two assessors, one Christian, one Moslem, and a mixed council of administration, partly elected, partly *ex-officio*, including the Greek metropolitan bishop. The *mutessarifs* (provincial governors) were, if Christian, to have Moslem assessors, and, if Moslems, then Christian assessors. Like the *vali*, each of them was to be assisted by a mixed administrative council, and all official correspondence was to be conducted in both Greek and Turkish. All districts were to have a council of elders (*dimogerondia*). These were to elect forty delegates to a general assembly which was to include twelve other delegates from the three principal towns. No fresh tax was to be imposed; the tithe was to be remitted for two years and then levied at only half-rate during the next two. To make his scheme palatable, Aali disbursed generous bribes, and he arranged for food convoys to be sent to the villages.

It was at this juncture (24 November) that King George and Queen Olga returned to Greece.[8] A week later (2 December) Koumoundouros received a vote of confidence, 97 votes to 52, in the chamber. He then obtained, on 13 December, approval of bills for extraordinary credits amounting in all to over 9 million drachmai to cover expenditure on munitions and armaments, naval vessels, public safety, and aid for the Cretan refugees. His aim was to force upon the king an aggressive foreign policy, a plan he had persisted with despite the withdrawal of Russian support the

[8] They had been married at St Petersburg on 28 October.

previous October and the attempts of Novikov to bring about the fall of his government. The king was in a quandary. He was opposed to an aggressive policy and yet he could hardly dismiss a ministry which had a firm parliamentary majority. But although he signed papers sanctioning the extraordinary credits, he endeavoured to persuade Koumoundouros to dismiss from his government the warlike ministers, Grivas and Lomvardos. Koumoundouros resigned on 28 December. The king then sent for Voulgaris who, unwilling to form a coalition with Deligiorgis, demanded a dissolution, which the king refused. The king then persuaded Aristidis Moraitinis, a non-party man, to form a government with Petros Deliyannis, the Greek ambassador at the Porte, as foreign minister. But this administration did not last long. The king had therefore to fall back upon Voulgaris and to grant him a dissolution, the new elections being arranged for 2 April 1868.

Voulgaris was prepared to adopt a more moderate policy towards Crete: publicly he demanded administrative autonomy for the Cretans; but privately he solicited from the protecting powers pressure which would force Greece to abandon the Cretans to their fate; and he put up Captain Voloudakis, one of the Cretan leaders, to appeal to the British for mediation. To this appeal the British replied that the Turks had already published an amnesty: if the Cretans cared to avail themselves of it, Great Britain, in concert with other European powers, would strongly recommend the Sultan to treat them 'with leniency and consideration'.

On the island there were chieftains who still wanted union with Greece and who, encouraged by the Greek, Russian, and American consuls, were determined to keep the insurrection alive, even if it meant provoking the Turks into taking reprisals. One act of provocation resulted on 15 June 1868 in a massacre of Christians in the villages around Iraklio. This event had repercussions in Greece. When on 16 July the new parliament met, the opposition demanded that the government should assist the Cretans. But Deliyannis (who was still foreign minister) persisted in his efforts to persuade the Cretan assembly to appeal to Great Britain for mediation. Meanwhile in Crete other plans were under consideration. Under the influence of the Russian consul acting on new instructions, many, including chieftains, were demanding not *enosis* but autonomy under a foreign prince. This new policy the Russians were now suggesting in Athens: the Grand Duchess Alexandra, mother of Queen Olga, had on a visit to her daughter endeavoured to persuade King George to dismiss Voulgaris (whom the Russians regarded as a tool of Britain) and to appoint a government favourable to the scheme now mooted. But to King George this proposal was sheer madness: even though Russia gave armed support to Greece, the Greek and Russian navies would be no match for those of France and England.

By this time the Greek king held the upper hand in Athens. The Greco-Serbian alliance no longer counted. On 10 June 1868 the prince of Serbia had perished at the hand of an assassin. This event left Serbia under the weak rule of Prince Milan; it inaugurated a conservative Serbian foreign policy: it deprived Serbia of the support of Prince Nicholas of Montenegro, of Russia, and of fellow-Slavs generally: it embittered Serbian internal politics for over three decades: and it left the country weak and generally discredited. For the immediate future it led to an estrangement between Greece and Serbia. The Greeks felt that the Serbs had merely used the occasion of the Cretan revolt to free themselves from the Turkish garrisons.

VI. The Greco–Turkish Crisis of December 1868–January 1869: the Collapse of the Cretan Rebellion

Although the new situation imposed caution upon the Greek government, the central committee in Athens continued to send supplies and volunteers to Crete and the Greek parliamentary opposition still clamoured at least for a clear statement of policy. Tension increased when it came to be realised that the Turks were no longer attempting to pacify the Cretans by concessions but had gone back to a plan of subduing them by force. The new situation (along with the rumour that Gladstone was likely to take office in England) prompted Voulgaris to change course. He adopted towards Turkey a policy of aggression, which was soon evident when volunteers for Crete were openly enrolled in the streets of Athens and when a band of two hundred[9] in Greek uniform under the Maniat chieftain Dimitrios Petropoulakis left for the island on 19 November under the gaze of the Athenian public. Against this overt act of hostility on Greece's part, Aali Pasha protested to the powers. On 2 December the Ottoman government decided to expel all Greek subjects from Turkish territory. The British envoy, Sir Henry Elliot, advised the Turks to be more cautious. Ignatiev, however, who accused Elliot of encouraging the Turks in their new policy, counselled Deliyannis to disregard Turkish threats and to trust to the intervention of the powers at Constantinople—an intervention which he hoped to initiate but which, owing to the attitude of Elliot and Bourée, turned out to be not so forceful as he had wished. All that the Turks would do was to postpone action against Greece on the understanding that the powers would within five days cause the Greek government to mend its ways. But the advice of the powers to Athens had no effect. On 9 December the Greek government rejected all the Porte's demands. Two days later the Turks delivered an ultimatum to Athens, stating that diplomatic relations would be broken off if the Greek volunteers did not leave Crete within five days and if the Cretan refugees were not returned to their homes. On 15 December the Greek government rejected this ultimatum and the next day the Turkish minister demanded his passport.

[9] Further batches, transported by the *Enosis* to Crete, brought the strength of the band up to one thousand.

It was at this juncture that a Turkish squadron under Hobart Pasha (an English ex-naval officer), after an exchange of gunfire, drove the Greek transport *Enosis* into the harbour of Syra. When called upon by Hobart to arrest this vessel, the Greek governor of the island refused to do so without express orders from Athens. But the Greek government, instead of sending an authorisation for the arrest of the *Enosis*, despatched a fleet to Syra with orders to demand, under threat of force, that Hobart Pasha should immediately quit Greek territorial waters. French intervention prevented a conflict. Hobart agreed to move away from the entrance of the harbour. He remained, however, in the vicinity and as a consequence the *Enosis* was unable to leave. His action prevented the Greeks from sending further volunteers and ammunition to Crete to reinforce Petropoulakis who, after suffering defeats at Kissos, Agios Vasilios, and Askifos, was forced at the end of December to surrender unconditionally. This marked the end of hostilities in Crete.

Meanwhile the three protecting powers endeavoured to find agreement on some form of intervention to prevent a Greco–Turkish war. Gortchakov, who wanted pressure exerted on Turkey as well as on Greece, asked Bismarck to propose the convening of a six-power conference under the provisions of the twenty-third protocol of the treaty of 1856. This proposal was acceptable to France and Austria, and eventually the British agreed to it on certain conditions. These conditions were the subject of considerable discussion, but it was finally arranged that a Greek delegate should attend the conference *à titre consultatif*.

The conference opened in Paris on 9 January 1869. The Turks had already announced that they would expel Greek ships from the Ottoman ports and from their territories all persons who, having become naturalised Hellenic subjects, refused to resume their original Ottoman nationality. The Greeks, on their side, demanded the annexation of Crete and a favourable rectification of the northern Greek frontiers. They also demanded that their representative to the conference should be placed on an equal footing with his Turkish colleague. This demand, though favoured by Russia and Great Britain, was rejected.

One of the first acts of the conference was to demand of both Greece and Turkey the observance of the *status quo* while the conference was sitting. To this demand the Turks promptly agreed, but there was no reply from Greece. The powers then drew up a declaration of the general principles upon which the future relations between Turkey and Greece should be conducted. Greece should not allow armed bands and armed vessels, intended for warlike operations against a neighbouring power, to be assembled within her territory. Turkey should accept a Greek undertaking to return the refugee Cretan families to Crete. She should follow normal judicial procedure in obtaining recompense for damages done to Ottoman subjects, and she should abandon the contemplated measures against Greek subjects in

Turkey. To this declaration the Porte gave a not unfavourable reply, but despite strong pressure by all the powers, no answer was immediately forthcoming from Athens. Here the declaration had given rise to a ministerial crisis. On 2 February Voulgaris resigned; Deligiorgis refused to join any government formed with a view to accepting the dictates of the powers; Zaimis laid down most stringent conditions,[10] which King George could not accept; and Spiridhon Valaoritis failed to form a ministry. Calling the representatives of the protecting powers to the palace on 4 February, the king explained his difficulties and intimated that if they could not help him, he would have to go to Paris to consult the conference. Next day, however, Zaimis formed a government and on 6 February this government accepted the declaration of the powers. At the same time it issued a proclamation to the people expressing in vague terms Greek sympathy for the Cretans and accusing the Voulgaris government, by its neglect of material preparations, of responsibility for Greece's inability to pursue her natural and rightful policy. Yet this face-saving interlude did not hold up the settlement. On 18 February diplomatic relations between Greece and Turkey were restored. By this time all the Greek volunteers had returned from Crete and the Cretan families had been repatriated. By 22 February the island was pacified and the blockade had been lifted.

[10] These were: right of dissolution; complete liberty of action; acceptance of the declaration of the powers to be accompanied by a declaration of Greek rights; a proclamation to the people explaining how the government had been forced to yield to the European powers.

CHAPTER 9

The Greeks and the Slavs 1870-85

I. The Origins of the Bulgarian Question

During the period of tension with Greece over the Cretan question, the Turks, in their struggle with Hellenism, began to encourage the claims of the Bulgarians for a national Church. These claims (which had their antecedents in the Middle Ages) were one of the many signs of a Bulgarian cultural awakening and nationalist movement, both of which, owing much to the example of the Greeks, Serbs, and Romanians, became pronounced about the middle of the nineteenth century. Since the 1820s the Bulgarian clergy had made occasional demands that Bulgarians and not Greeks should be appointed to the Bulgarian bishoprics. But it was not until 1856 that there was much reason to hope that they would get their way. That year a Turkish reform edict (the *hati-i-humayun* of 18 February) provided for the reorganisation of the non-Moslem *millets* (or nationalities) and it was this measure that aroused the expectations of the Bulgarian church movement. None the less, renewed requests for the appointment of Bulgarian bishops and for some degree of 'national' autonomy were constantly thwarted by the Greek Patriarch on the grounds that canon law recognised no national distinctions. But in March 1860 the Bulgarian community in Constantinople, by announcing that its church services were held with the permission of the Sultan, and not with that of the Patriarch, set an example of revolt which was followed by some thirty communities in the Bulgarian provinces. What is more, the rebels appointed Bishop Ilarion Stoyanovich as head of the so-called Bulgarian Church. Alongside this movement was the design long favoured by Austria and France to create a Bulgarian uniate Church which, like the eighteenth-century uniate Churches in Transylvania, recognised the supremacy of Rome while remaining Orthodox in dogma and ritual. This uniate movement, although it did not really amount to much, alarmed the Russians, above all Pan-Slavs like Ignatiev, who feared Catholic penetration of the Balkans. On the other hand, Ignatiev and the Pan-Slavs were none too happy about the Bulgarian church movement. They feared a schism in the Orthodox Church and the last thing they wanted was to alienate the Patriarch. All the same, out of respect for brother-Slavs in general, they felt obliged to show some sympathy towards Bulgarian aspirations.

In July 1860 the Patriarch offered concessions—the appointment of a number of Bulgarian bishops and the use of the Bulgarian language in churches and schools. These concessions Stoyanovich rejected: he wanted nothing less than an autocephalous Church. In 1867 the Patriarch Grigorios VI offered to recognise an autonomous Bulgarian Church in the territory between the Danube and the Balkan mountain—an offer which Ignatiev urged the Bulgarian leaders to accept. But these leaders, who had their eyes on Rumelia and Macedonia (a territory already coveted by the Greeks), refused this offer: they hoped to gain more from negotiations with the Turks, who, in view of developments in Crete, had shown signs of favouring the Bulgarian Slavs. Ignatiev worked hard to promote a compromise. He persuaded the Porte to establish a mixed Greek–Bulgarian commission which under his guidance produced a plan for a Bulgarian national Church of seventy-four dioceses, thirty-seven of which would be administered by the Patriarch, twenty-five by the head of the Bulgarian Church, four by the Serbian Church, and eight jointly by the Greeks and Bulgarians. This plan the Patriarch rejected. To end the dispute the Turks (encouraged by the British representative at Constantinople but not by Ignatiev) issued on 11 March 1870 a *firman* (decree) establishing in seventeen dioceses in the first instance an autonomous Bulgarian Church under an Exarch elected by a synod. This same decree provided that further dioceses could be added to the Exarchate wherever the inhabitants voted for union by a two-thirds majority. The Patriarch at length took a firm stand against the execution of this measure. In February 1872 he declared the new Bulgarian Church heretical and later excommunicated the Exarch and his bishops.

The effect upon the Greeks of their defeat in Crete and of the establishment of the Bulgarian Exarchate was immediate. Behind these two blows they discerned the perfidy not of Albion but of Russia. They had come to realise that Russia was out to exploit Hellenism in favour of the Slavs and above all of the Bulgars. They therefore endeavoured to gain the support of France and Great Britain for a new policy of friendship with Turkey. They even resented the separate attempts of Russia (Gortchakov wanted to revive Russian prestige in Greece) to compel the Porte to recognise the Greek nationality of some 300,000 former Ottoman subjects who had obtained by devious means certificates of Greek naturalisation. On this issue the Turks, wishing to forestall an intervention by the three great powers, met the Greeks half-way: they established mixed commissions of inquiry which worked sufficiently slowly as practically to leave untouched the *status quo*.

II. Brigandage and the Frontier Problem

It was to France and England again that the Greek government turned for help in solving the problem of brigandage, which became acute after the return of the volunteers from Crete. Many of these volunteers had been former outlaws and brigands. They had been promised an amnesty, that is to say a place of honour in society, after their return from what had been hoped would be a successful war. This promise, following the defeat, no government could fulfil, and no government was strong enough to suppress these professional patriots, who had returned to the fringe of politics in Greece to operate more energetically than before. At the elections of 28 May 1869 they were more than usually in evidence, for they were employed by the political factions to put pressure on the villages and thus to influence the voting.

The problem of brigandage was closely related to that of the frontiers. On the frontiers the Turks employed Albanian irregulars. Greek brigands, when pursued by Greek troops, usually sought refuge with the Albanians, among whom they had friends and relatives. In response to representations by the British, Aali Pasha undertook to remove the Albanian irregulars and to surrender outlaws to the Greek authorities. This he did at his leisure; and in November 1869 Zaimis considered the moment opportune to introduce a bill organising national forces for the suppression of brigandage. But this bill was rejected. Brigandage continued and its existence was dramatically brought to the notice of Europe when on 11 April 1870 a party of English and one Italian diplomats were kidnapped and held to ransom by a brigand band, the Arvanitakides, near Marathon. Following confused negotiations with the brigands, from which intricate political manoeuvring was never absent, and movements of troops, the brigands killed their prisoners at a place called Dilessi.[1] As was to be expected, the affair led to the usual ill-concerted representations of the powers, the British limiting their demands to a judicial inquiry, which they subsequently dropped. It also led to the resignation of Zaimis in July and to yet another ministerial crisis. Deligiorgis headed a government until December 1870. Then Koumoundouros, with the support of Zaimis, formed an administration which announced its intention to concentrate on internal problems and to maintain neutrality in foreign affairs. Nevertheless, when in January 1871 a conference on the Black Sea question opened in London,[2] Koumoun-

---

[1] A detailed account of this incident will be found in J. R. Jenkins, *The Dilessi Murders* (London, 1961) which, however, exaggerates the international importance of the whole affair. A briefer account which puts the matter in its Greek and European historical perspective will be found in Dontas, *Greece and the Great Powers 1863-1875* (Thessaloniki, 1966), pp. 164ff.

[2] During the Franco–Prussian War of 1870 Britain and Russia had worked towards preventing disturbances in the Near East initiated by Greece. Gortchakov was particularly anxious that the Balkans should remain quiet while he developed his plans for the abrogation of the Black Sea clauses of the treaty of Paris of 1856. Rumours of these plans had encouraged certain Greeks, above all Deligiorgis, to hope that the whole Eastern question would be reopened and afford Greece an opportunity to resume a policy in accordance with the Great Idea.

douros repeated the demand for a rectification of the Greco–Turkish frontier as a means of stamping out brigandage. The rectification he demanded
was substantial. But this demand was firmly rejected by all the powers who
had remained in concert when at the London conference they formally
abolished the Black Sea clauses of the Paris treaty of 1856.

As a result of this rebuff Koumoundouros turned his attention to internal
affairs—to the improvement of the administration and finances, the development of mineral resources, and the extirpation of brigandage. On 31
October, however, he was defeated over a mineral concession to a Franco–
Italian company. Following negotiations, Zaimis formed a ministry but
was defeated on precisely the same issue. Voulgaris next formed a government, only to be defeated on a budgetary matter. Further elections giving
Voulgaris a majority were held in March 1872. In July, however, he was
defeated in parliament. Deligiorgis then took office (20 July 1872). Enjoying
the sympathy of Britain and Russia, he secured a settlement of the concession problem in favour of Greece. Having won the elections of February
1873 and enjoying the support of the king, who dissolved the chamber in
order to protect him from hostile alignments among the opposition parties,
he embarked on attempts to balance the budget by reducing expenditure on
the foreign ministry, the navy, and the army. He took also some effective
steps to put down brigandage and he persuaded the king to set up commissions to inquire into the departments of government, with the aim of
breaking up old parties by getting rid of placemen and by introducing into
the civil service members of the growing commercial and professional
classes. But this measure brought about his downfall. The opposition parties united and in February 1874 he lost his majority. He had been in office
nineteen months—much longer than any of his predecessors in King
George's reign.

After yet another protracted ministerial crisis, Voulgaris, under pressure
from the king, promised to form a coalition with Koumoundouros and
Zaimis. But this coalition survived only a matter of weeks, and the plan to
form a coalition under Voulgaris and Deligiorgis miscarried. At the end of
April the king sent for Koumoundouros, who made exorbitant demands,
which amounted to complete control of foreign and domestic policy: he
denounced the foreign policy of Deligiorgis, who, he said, had left Greece
with only Turkey as a doubtful friend; he proposed to establish better
relations with Russia; and he laid down his plans for the reorganisation of
the civil and military services. These demands the king rejected. He dissolved the chamber, and insisted that, pending new elections, Voulgaris
should remain in office.

In the elections of 5 July 1874 Voulgaris obtained some sort of majority
and when the new chamber met in October, he was able to pass a bill sanctioning a loan of 26 million francs from the Bank of Greece. Yet when he
proposed to reduce the army, which he considered at 14,000 men to be

much too large, he encountered opposition, for by that time there were fresh signs of unrest among the Ottoman subject people and the opposition parties were able to provoke popular demonstrations. Voulgaris was generally accused of having won the election by fraud, and the king, under pressure, dismissed him (April 1875). This marked the end of Voulgaris's long political career. It marked too the beginning of a new era in Greek politics. Not that this new era was vastly different from the old, but there was clearly some change of pattern.

III. Charilaos Trikoupis

The new pattern began when the king, who himself had become more mature and more influential, in May 1875 after some hesitation called upon the young politician Charilaos Trikoupis, son of Spiridhon Trikoupis of the War of Independence, to form a government. This Trikoupis agreed to do but he insisted that free elections should be held. At the polls of August 1875, the first 'free' and 'honest' elections ever held in Greece, he and a small personal following obtained seats. The new chamber contained a majority of deputies of the old regime, but there were many new men and some of these joined Trikoupis's following. Trikoupis, however, could muster no majority over the opposition factions, which closed their ranks to elect Koumoundouros as president of the assembly, the voting for which office usually indicated the state of parties and the party alignments. Trikoupis resigned and at the end of October Koumoundouros, who had not held office for four years, formed a government with Alexandros Kontostavlos, an Anglophil and moderate, as foreign minister. Trikoupis's resignation was fully in accordance with the king's speech of 23 August, which Trikoupis himself had written. This laid down the principle of *dedilomeni*: no leader should take or continue in office unless there were clear indications that he commanded a parliamentary majority.

Koumoundouros, who had sensed a change in Greek political life, maintained the policy proclaimed by Trikoupis: internal reform and neutrality in foreign affairs. He and Kontostavlos resisted all Russian attempts to re-establish influence in Greece, and although he condoned and perhaps secretly encouraged those who advocated Balkan co-operation against the Turks, he refused to be drawn officially into any adventure, and adopted a policy of 'wait and see'. He had come to realise that Moslem Turkey was less immediately dangerous to Hellenism than Russian Pan-Slavism. He therefore quietly dropped the Great Idea and followed, with the blessing of Great Britain, a less adventurous course. Greece was thus able, within the confines of her limited resources, to concentrate on domestic problems and to apply liberal ideas, to which the successive constitutional crises of the old order had given supporters and some refinement.

IV. The Foreign Policy of Greece 1875–78

Events in the Balkans were taking a turn which no Greek government could ignore. In July 1875, following a failure of the harvest the previous year, a widespread revolt broke out in Herzegovina and later spread to Bosnia, two provinces where Moslem landowners and tax-collectors oppressed the peasantry, of whom some 42 per cent were Orthodox Christians and 18 per cent Roman Catholics. To some extent the revolt had been encouraged not only by Russian but by Austrian agents, and it is generally recognised that Emperor Francis Joseph's tour to Dalmatia the previous spring may have inspired the insurgents, who had drawn up a petition complaining of Turkish misrule and requesting his protection.

But neither Andrassy, the Austrian minister, nor Gortchakov wished to see the Balkans ablaze; they were anxious to preserve the *dreikaiserbund* which aimed at composing their Balkan difficulties; and they therefore persuaded the Turks to send a commissioner to Herzegovina to investigate grievances. But Turkish attempts to pacify the provinces were to no avail. Andrassy therefore drew up a reform programme (the Andrassy Note) which was approved by the powers and accepted by the Turks, but which the insurgents rejected because there was no mention of a guarantee. In May 1876 ministers of the *dreikaiserbund* drew up a more elaborate programme of reform known as the Berlin Memorandum. But this the British government refused to countenance, chiefly because it had not been consulted and because a reply had been peremptorily asked for within two days.

That same month the Bulgarians revolted and the Serbs, despite Prince Milan's lip-service to neutrality, were becoming restive. Milan sanctioned the formation of a new ministry which included Ristich, who counted on the strength of Pan-Slavism to force the Tsar to assist the insurgents. On 30 June Serbia declared war on Turkey and was joined in July by Montenegro. Serbs and Montenegrins invaded Bosnia and Herzegovina. Both powers (and Russian Pan-Slavists too) looked towards Greece for support. In July the Russian representative in Belgrade asked the Greek ambassador whether the Serbo–Greek alliance of 1867 was still valid; and Phillipon, an influential member of the Russian holy synod, was sent to Constantinople and Athens in the hope of improving Russo–Greek relations. Shortly afterwards the Tsar sent his brother-in-law, the Grand Duke Alexis, to Athens to enlist the sympathies of King George; and in October Prince Milan sent an envoy to Greece to discuss the revival of Serbo–Greek co-operation. But the Greeks held it inadvisable to begin an adventure until the Slavs were fully committed. Koumoundouros, while remaining basically in favour of co-operation among the Balkan powers, had continued Deligiorgis's policy of maintaining correct relations with Turkey. In reply to a second approach from the Serbs in February 1876, he had made it plain that Greece was totally unprepared for war. Secretly, however, unknown to the king and the foreign minister, he kept in touch with private negotiations which were going on between Greek and Serbian nationalist organisations. These negotiations were in the hands chiefly of Leonidas Voulgaris,[3] who was in touch with the Macedonian chieftains, with General Ignatiev, and with a Serbian army officer, Veher. In March 1876 he met the Serbian politician Miliutin Garashanin. The two agreed to encourage revolts in Epiros, Macedonia, and Thessaly, and thus to force the hand of the Greek government. Voulgaris, however, was able to send only a few men to the north to prepare a rising. But even this limited activity the Greek government found inopportune and instructed the consul at Thessaloniki, Konstantinos Vatikiotis, to advise the chiefs of Olympos not to move. With this policy Koumoundouros was outwardly in agreement. In May 1876 he sent out a circular to the Greek foreign missions stating that it was the intention of the government to remain neutral and to act as a mediator if a favourable opportunity arose; and when towards the end of June the Serbs, finding themselves hard pressed, asked for Greek help in accordance with the 1867 treaty, he replied that, as that instrument had not been renewed after the death of Michael Obrenovich, it was no longer valid. Nevertheless, hoping to profit from the situation, he pressed the Porte to ban Circassian emigration into Epiros, Thessaly, and Macedonia, and endeavoured to obtain sanction for the linking-up of the Greek railway system with the European network.

Like Greece, Romania held aloof from the war, and the Bulgars, Serbs, and Montenegrins were left to face the Turks alone. The Serbs, who mobilised one-sixth of their population, were heavily defeated and lost over one-tenth of their troops in killed and wounded. In Bulgaria the Turkish irregulars, the *bashi-bazouks*, wreaked vengeance, destroying villages and massacring over ten thousand. But despite these salutary lessons to would-be destroyers of the Ottoman empire, there were many Greeks who clamoured for war, fearing that the Slavs would reap all the fruits of a Turkish defeat which was bound to result as soon as Russia entered the war. On 1 October at a great rally near the Acropolis, speakers who included the Greek historian Paparrigopoulos denounced the government for failing to make adequate military preparations. To this and to other pressures Koumoundouros nearly succumbed, but Trikoupis, Zaimis, and Deligiorgis were firmly set against adventures, hoping to secure rewards from Great Britain for good behaviour, like the Serbs and Romanians who had profited from their aloofness during the Cretan crisis of 1868. Gladstone, however, as part of his somewhat belated 'Bulgarian atrocities' campaign began to talk of the need for establishing Christian autonomies in European Turkey. This caused the moderates to have doubts and all the supporters of the Great Idea, their passions inflamed by the governmental opposition, demanded action more vociferously than ever. All this time

[3] Not related to Voulgaris the former prime minister.

King George threw his influence onto the side of caution, but as his government could command a mere majority of five, the whole situation hung in the balance.

In July Russia and Austria had reached agreement at Reichstadt. They agreed that if Serbia and Montenegro were defeated, then the *status quo ante* should be restored, and if successful, then they themselves would together work out territorial changes in detail.[4] One result was that Russia sent Turkey an ultimatum which forced the Porte to sign, on 1 November, an armistice with Serbia and Montenegro. This was followed on 12 December by a conference at Constantinople. At this conference Lord Salisbury easily reached agreement with Ignatiev. Serbia was to lose no territory and Montenegro was to retain territory she had overrun in Herzegovina. Bulgaria should be divided into eastern and western provinces and these two provinces, along with a Bosnia–Herzegovina province, were each to be given a provincial assembly, a local police force, and a large degree of autonomy. This proposed settlement the Turks rejected: they had been encouraged to do so by the British ambassador, Sir Henry Elliot, who had the backing of the British prime minister, Disraeli, and his foreign secretary, Lord Derby.

Russia, realising that the Constantinople conference was doomed to failure, did another deal with Austria: in the event of a Russo–Turkish war Austria would remain neutral and, at the end of hostilities, would annex Bosnia and Herzegovina. Russia should regain the area lost in Bessarabia in 1856, in return for which she accepted the principle that no large Slav state should be formed in the Balkans. In March 1877 Russia persuaded the powers to sign the London convention, which stipulated that Turkey should introduce certain previously offered reforms, to be supervised by the foreign representatives. The Turks, hoping to stage another Crimea, turned the idea down. The situation, however, was not quite the same as it had been two decades earlier. France and Britain were not in alliance and Germany and Austria were less antagonistic to Russia. Hence when Russia went to war in April 1877, in spite of Disraeli's warnings not to occupy Constantinople, the Straits, Suez, or Egypt, she met with no hostility from Europe. The Russian forces advanced rapidly towards the end of June. It was not until they reached Plevna that they were halted.

With the Russians forging ahead, certain factions in Greece were pressing for action and fervent military preparations were begun, including schemes for employing foreign instructors. Even the king began to waver and even Trikoupis,[5] when pressed by the British minister for an assurance of Greece's peaceful intentions, replied that independent nations could not

[4] Parts of the Reichstadt agreement were later subject to dispute. Andrassy thought it had been agreed that Austria would get the greater part of Bosnia and Herzegovina. Gortchakov understood that all but a small part of Bosnia would go to Serbia and Montenegro. Both understood, however, that no large Slav state should be created in the Balkans.

[5] Trikoupis had become foreign minister in the coalition government formed by Admiral Kanaris in June 1877.

bind themselves to remain neutral in all circumstances. The Greek government had built up forces, some 35,000 men, at Lamia near the northern frontier, while Greek irregulars were making raids into Epiros and Thessaly. Vatikiotis, the Greek consul in Thessaloniki, reported that Greek intervention would be welcomed by the Slav-speaking patriarchists, particularly as the Turks, aware that Greek bandsmen had appeared in Macedonia, were arresting Greek notables just as they had done in 1869 at the time of the Cretan revolution. The Turks had rightly suspected that the Greeks had revolutionary committees preparing for action should the opportunity arise.

In accordance with government instructions Vatikiotis advised these committees to show restraint, but at the same time he began to send them arms. Meanwhile bandsmen continued to arrive in Thessaly and Olympos from Greece, among them the well-known klefts Panayotis Kalogeros and Karapatakis. These arrivals were the results of the work of the patriotic organisations in Athens—the 'National Defence', the 'Fereos' (after Rigas), and the 'Brotherhood'—and of Voulgaris who had at his disposal funds from Russia, who was in close touch with Koumoundouros, Kalligas, and Renieris, and who planned to excite revolts in Epiros, Thessaly, Macedonia, Albania, Crete, Thrace, the Rhodope mountains, Asia Minor, Samos, and Cyprus.

Working from a base on Olympos, Kalogeros, and Karapatakis mounted attacks on the Turks in Thessaly and Macedonia. It is doubtful, however, whether their operations were sponsored by the committees in Athens. In June 1877 the Kanaris government merged these committees into a new central committee under Kalligas in order to control them and to prevent them from acting prematurely. In July the central committee authorised Voulgaris to organise a band which could be sent to Macedonia should circumstances become favourable. Accordingly, Voulgaris set up a camp on Salamis. He enrolled 150 volunteers and began to train them with the help of the French officer Séril and certain Macedonian veterans like Exarchos, whom he recalled to Greece. His aim was eventually to train and arm one thousand men. But the failure of the Russians to overcome the Turks at Plevna led the Greek government to lose all enthusiasm for Voulgaris's venture. He was instructed to close down the camp and to disperse the volunteers, some of whom, however, joined small bands organised by the Greek committees, and found their way to Thessaly and Macedonia.

The repeated failures of the Russians to take Plevna had inculcated caution among the Balkan peoples generally despite protracted Russian efforts to bring them into the war. Only the Romanians, who in any case had been more or less involved from the outset, and who hoped to qualify for compensation for the territory they were likely to lose in Bessarabia, responded to the blandishments of the Russians. But in January 1878 the Russians, having taken Plevna, advanced towards Adrianople, the Serbians again made war on Turkey, and the long restive Cretans broke out in open revolt. The Greek king, who had been on tours of inspection of his troops and who had become much more bellicose than his government, informed the French minister that he would abdicate if Greece came out of the crisis devoid of honour and territorial gains. On 7 January 1878, he called up 10,000 men of the second reserve. Just over a fortnight later the Kanaris coalition government resigned. For three days (26–28 January) mobs roamed the streets of Athens, cheering the king, stoning the houses of the chicken-hearted politicians, and demanding that Grivas, who controlled many ir-regulars in western Greece, should be made prime minister. Whether it was these demonstrations that caused him to change course, or whether it was the news of armistice negotiations on the Russo–Turkish front, Koumoun-douros formed a government and obtained (31 January) from the chamber the authority to occupy Thessaly.

That same day the Turks and Russians concluded an armistice, under which Russian forces were to occupy territory to within 10 miles of Con-stantinople, but not the city itself. Of this provision the British government were not aware when on 12 February Disraeli, who had for some time been under pressure from the queen to have it out with the Russians, ordered the British fleet up the Straits to the Sea of Marmara. Meanwhile on 2 February 25,000 Greek troops with twenty-four field-guns and 400 cavalry had crossed into Thessaly, while Deliyannis had issued a circular to the powers stating that Greece wished merely to protect her nationals and not to wage war on Turkey. About the same time the Cretan revolutionary committee proclaimed *enosis* with Greece.

The powers protested against these actions and Deliyannis, seeking an excuse, asked the foreign ministers to press him to recall the Greek troops from Thessaly. This they did, and the Greek government, having learned on 3 February of the Russo–Turkish armistice and realising that the Turk-ish fleet was free to attack the coasts of Greece, issued on 6 February orders for the recall of the troops. Some, however, refused to leave and joined up with the irregular bands. As a reward for this prompt action, Koumoundouros and Deliyannis hoped to gain British support in any settle-ment made by the powers. Nevertheless, they connived at the revolutionary activities in Macedonia. After the fall of Plevna in December 1877, the Greek consuls, Vatikiotis of Thessaloniki and Logothetis of Monastir, helped by Joachim, metropolitan bishop of Thessaloniki, and the bishops of Kitros and Ierrisos, had begun to co-ordinate local efforts in accordance with a plan worked out in Athens. This plan provided for a seaborne band to disembark in the region Olympos–Katerini, to recruit local fighters, and then to cross the Aliakmon river to raise rebellion near Veria, Naousa, and Edhessa. Another band was to disembark on Chalkidiki, and a third at the mouth of the Struma river, whence it would proceed towards Nevrokopi and Meleniko. Other bands were to move from Thessaly and Olympos to co-ordinate the activities of local bands in Servia, Kozani, and Kastoria.

The intention was that these should extend operations northwards to Prespa, Ochrid, Monastir, and Morihovo. To facilitate all these operations stores of arms and ammunition were established in the Macedonian towns, a courier system was organised, and a whole network of intelligence was set up with Thessaloniki as the centre. So far was the organisation advanced and so enthusiastic were the members that the Greek consuls strongly urged the government to act lest Macedonia be lost for good and all to the Bulgarians.

In Athens the responsibility for the Macedonian front had been delegated by the central committee to a body known as the committee of Macedonians, its members being Stefanos Dragoumis, Paschalis, Pantazidis, Papazisis, and Chalkiopoulos. Voulgaris had been excluded, for he was considered too Slavophil. All the same, he had a hand in Macedonian affairs, and in January 1878 he set out with a band of 150 men intending to disembark at Katerini. Rough seas obliged him to put in at Pilion, whence he returned to Athens. Here he obtained cash and supplies, and leading a newly-constituted band he participated in a rising in Thessaly in March 1878. On 27 February Lieutenant Christos Dubiotis with 500 men (the 'Olympos Army') had gone to Litochoro where on 3 March 1878 the rebels proclaimed a provisional government of Macedonia, with Evangelos Korovagos, a local doctor, at its head. Meanwhile the bishop of Kitros, assisted by the chiefs Evangelos Chostevas and Panayotis Kalogeros, had raised revolt in the region of Pieria. But all these revolts met with only limited success. Dubiotis wasted time in trying to negotiate the surrender of Katerini instead of boldly assaulting that city and in attacking a Turkish (Circassian) stronghold outside the main area of operations. True, the rebels were well received by the local populations and volunteers came forward in great numbers, but the supplies of rifles and ammunition were much too small to stage a really effective rising.

It was not long before the Turks hit back with more than their usual efficiency. Troops under Asaf Pasha were concentrated in the region of Katerini; Litochoro was captured and burnt down; ammunition intended for Dubiotis was seized. A Turkish navy patrolled the coast from the mouth of the Aliakmon to that of the Pinios, thus preventing Greek reinforcements from landing. Dubiotis was forced to retire into Thessaly and in May, following an amnesty, he returned with other leaders to Greece. He had waited in vain for an insurrection in Chalkidiki and for a spontaneous rising in western Macedonia, which would have prevented the Turks from advancing from Kossovo to Olympos and Thessaly. The trouble was that there had been no co-ordinated action and this was because at the outset the bands had been planned not to launch a general rising but merely to assist the intended movements of the Greek army.

When at length western Macedonia revolted, the rebels acted independently of those elsewhere and with little or no direction from the Monastir consulate. To begin with, they drove away Albanian marauders, and their victories stimulated recruitment. A series of successful raids during June and July 1878 on Turkish posts at Kozani, Kastoria, Prespa, Pisoderi, Florina, Monastir, and Morihovo increased the supply of arms and ammunition and hence further recruits. Rich Greeks supplied money, and eventually the rebellion reached considerable proportions.

It was not, however, until August 1878 that Koumoundouros began officially to encourage the revolt in Macedonia. He then instructed the Greek consuls of Thessaloniki and Monastir to give the rebels all the assistance they could. Up to that time, ever since he withdrew the regular troops from the north, his position had been ambiguous. As a politician who gained much support from the upholders of the Great Idea, he at least had to allow the patriotic committee plenty of scope, and although he counted on Austria and British opposition to Russia to provide a solution not altogether unfavourable to Greece, he could never be sure that Britain and Austria, in looking after themselves, would go so far as to promote the interests of Greece. In any case, he wanted the Greek organisations in the unredeemed areas to remain intact and ready to act when called on to do so. Moreover, it is not improbable that for a long while he had underestimated the military value of the local populations and had therefore done nothing to co-ordinate and synchronise their efforts.

V. The Treaty of San Stefano: the Congress of Berlin

That the support of Great Britain was of vital importance was brought home to the Greeks when they learned of the peace terms of the treaty of San Stefano, which Ignatiev imagined could be imposed upon the Turks. Serbia and Montenegro were to be completely independent, with substantial increases of territory. Romania, who was also to achieve independence, was to be compensated with a part of Dobrudja in return for that part of Bessarabia she was to cede to Russia. Russia, as an alternative to a full financial indemnity, was to gain from Turkey the territories of Kars, Batum, Ardahan, and Bayazid. For Greece there was to be no gain of territory. All the spoils in Macedonia and Thrace were to go to Bulgaria, who was to be made autonomous under an elected prince, her territory stretching from the Danube to the Aegean, and Lake Ochrid to the Black Sea, excluding Constantinople, Adrianople, and Thessaloniki. Had this treaty been sanctioned by the powers, both Greece and Serbia, and particularly Greece, would have been hemmed in, and probably at the mercy of a Balkan power whose own efforts to free herself had not been particularly energetic. To the average Greek it was simply preposterous that a pocket of Slav population should, because it suited Russian Pan-Slav sentiment and Tsarist imperialism, be allowed to spread as a political force into regions where the Greeks were in strength and where they provided the more civilised elements. To

Greeks and Serbs alike the San Stefano treaty was the final proof of Russian treachery and sharp practice. But when the Serbs protested at St Petersburg that Serbian peoples were being handed over to another power, the reply was that Serbian interests were nothing as compared with those of Russia which required the creation of a big Bulgaria.

Fortunately for the Greeks and the Serbs, the San Stefano treaty was to the liking of neither Great Britain nor Austria. Nor was it wholly satisfactory to Bismarck, for it was likely to give rise to a struggle which in its repercussions might be harmful to Germany. As for the Russians at St Petersburg, they realised from the outset that Ignatiev, who had negotiated the treaty, had gone much too far; but they clung to it in the hope that by staking high claims, any concessions they made to Britain and Austria would leave Russia with substantial gains, particularly if, as they thought, Bismarck would give them some support. For these reasons, they were ready to take part in a congress to be held at Berlin. Before it met they started preliminary negotiations with Austria and Great Britain, who also negotiated with one another. Russia agreed that a reduced Bulgaria might be divided into two parts, and Britain accepted in principle a Russian advance in Asia. In return for Austrian support, the British agreed to back an Austrian solution for Bosnia and Herzegovina. Despite these agreements in principle, however, the whole treaty was open to revision at the congress (which sat from 13 June to 13 July) and nearly every clause was strenuously contested.

In response to Greek protests the British government replied that it 'was prepared to exert all its influence to prevent the absorption into a Slav state of any Greek population'; and Lord Salisbury pressed in vain for the admission of Greece to the congress, where Greece received no effective support except when British and Greek interests happened to coincide. The British for their part accepted a Russian advance into Asia by allowing Russia to acquire Kars, Ardahan, and Batum (as a primarily commercial port). They also agreed to guarantee Turkey against any further advance. On 4 June they acquired a lease on Cyprus, a predominantly Greek island which in 1821 had risen in sympathy with the Greeks of the Morea.[6] At the time, the Cypriots were glad to exchange Turkish for British rule in what has proved to be a forlorn hope that one day, like the Ionian Greeks, they would be united with the Hellenic kingdom.

At the congress Deliyannis, who was only to be heard and to have no vote, limited Greek claims to Crete, Epiros, and Thessaly. But the congress decided that Crete should remain Turkish on condition that the Turks should apply the 'Organic Law' they had promulgated in 1868 and that administrations based upon that model should be applied to Macedonia, Thrace, and the greater part of Epiros. In vain did the Cretan Christians

---

[6] Certain jingoes in England cited Richard I's conquest of Cyprus from its Greek ruler in 1191 as a justification for its acquisition. Since 1191 Cyprus had never been in Greek possession. Richard sold it in 1192 to Guy of Lusignan, whose dynasty ruled it until in 1489 it became a Venetian colony. As we have seen, it was taken by the Turks in 1571.

demand that, if they could not have union, they should pass under British protection like the Cypriots. The most that Salisbury did positively for Greece was to support the French delegate's proposal that the Porte should be invited (not compelled) to allow a Greek northern frontier running from the mouth of the river Pinios in eastern Thessaly to the river Kalamas in Epiros. This proposal, with Disraeli's consoling words that Greece had a future and could afford to wait, were all that the Greeks took away from Berlin.

Nevertheless, there was the real consolation for Greeks and Serbs that Greek and Serbian Macedonia had not been assigned to a large Bulgaria. The congress, mainly through British insistence, divided the area assigned to Bulgaria in the San Stefano treaty into three parts: Bulgaria, north of the Balkan mountain, which was to be autonomous under its own elected prince; eastern Rumelia, south of the Balkan, to be placed under a Christian governor nominated by the Sultan but approved by the powers; and Macedonia, to remain as before under direct Turkish administration. This meant that the Bulgaria of the congress of Berlin was cut off from the Aegean Sea and was barely one-third of the Bulgaria of the San Stefano treaty.

The treaty of Berlin left all the Balkan nations profoundly dissatisfied and, what is more, it focused their attention on Macedonia—Bulgaria, because it was a part of a prize nearly won; Serbia, because her principal expansion must be towards the south-east now that Austria had acquired the right to occupy and annex Bosnia and Herzegovina; and Greece, because of the numerous Slav- and Greek-speaking patriarchists who lived in that region. Moreover, the treaty, indeed the whole crisis of 1875–78, had a profound effect upon Greek public opinion and upon those responsible for foreign policy: it had become clear (although a few still adhered to the old ways of thinking) that the Great Idea could not be carried into effect by a general and concerted Balkan rising. Greece was now faced with a Bulgarian advance, which appeared to be backed by Russia.

It is no wonder, then, that following the disappointments of the congress of Berlin and in view of the likely Turkish refusal to rectify the frontiers, the Greek government should have begun to give more decided support to the Greeks in Macedonia. Not that Athens could throw caution to the winds. Quite obviously the small Greek army could not challenge the Ottoman empire alone and there could be no hope whatever that by declaring war the Greek government could count on the support of any great power. If, however, Macedonia were in revolt, there was just a chance that the Porte might be more amenable to Greek pressure, particularly if that pressure were supported by the European Concert.

Exactly how much material assistance the Greek government gave at this juncture to the Macedonian Greeks is not known, but what is certain is that the encouragement given by the Greek consuls led them to increase the tempo and the scope of their operations. By the middle of August 1878 they had liberated completely the region of Pisoderi, where they had about 1,500 men under arms. Their next main objective, it seems, was Monastir. Indeed, so serious had the situation become that the Turks sent to Macedonia fifteen battalions of Asiatic troops to reinforce the garrisons and the local levies. These troops were hard pressed and suffered heavy casualties. But in October they gained some respite. The severe Macedonian winter set in earlier than usual, and the Greek bands withdrew to more clement regions, leaving many of the villages to the mercy of the Turkish soldiery. When the spring came, the Greek government had changed its policy: negotiations over Epiros and Thessaly were in progress and it was deemed inadvisable to jeopardise these by encouraging the bands to return to Macedonia. Meanwhile, however, Bulgarian irregulars had entered this contested province, which was later to become the scene of the third Greek War of Independence.[7]

VI. The Acquisition of Thessaly and Arta, 1881

After the congress of Berlin, the Porte raised endless difficulties over the rectification of the northern Greek frontier, which the thirteenth protocol provided for. Regarding this protocol merely as a suggestion and not an obligation, the Turkish military experts on a Greco–Turkish frontier commission which met at Preveza objected to the line proposed by the Greeks on the grounds that it was strategically unsatisfactory; and they encouraged protests from the Albanians, who, with a heightened national consciousness and a newly-formed Albanian league to back their efforts, had presented petitions to the congress of Berlin, contesting Greek claims to southern Epiros. Largely owing to Salisbury's initiative, the whole question was subsequently transferred to a conference at Constantinople. Here again, however, the Porte displayed a dogged resistance to Greek claims, in spite of Salisbury's argument that the old frontier of 1832 had always been defective, that it was a source of weakness to the Sultan, and that it had encouraged brigandage which had been detrimental to Greco–Turkish relations.

In April 1879, however, Turkish procrastination led to the establishment of a London Greek committee, presided over by Lord Rosebery and supported by Gladstone, Dilke, and Granville. The English Liberals, who had freely criticised Disraeli's 'Peace with Honour' as a peace that passed all understanding and as the honour that is common to thieves, were committed to an anti-Turkish policy. Hence when in April 1880 Gladstone came to power, Greek hopes were raised once more. In May, King George paid visits to Paris and London, where he reminded Gladstone of promises he had made to Deliyannis. Even Trikoupis (who had taken office in March) had renounced his wonted moderation, and was all for occupying the territory that had been 'assigned' to Greece in the thirteenth protocol of the

7 See below, Chapter 12.

Berlin congress. This time it was King George who, in view of this reading of the European situation, advised caution and throughout June and July, while he was visiting Berlin and Copenhagen, he sent numerous telegrams to Trikoupis opposing mobilisation. But the prime minister ignored them. So bellicose had Trikoupis become that King George appealed to the powers to calm him down.

Eventually, however, the powers agreed to convene a conference at Berlin, at which Greece but not Turkey was represented. Here an Anglo–French proposal envisaged a frontier from the crest of Olympos to the mouth of the river Kalamas which would have given Jannina to Greece. As fate would have it, however, a ministerial crisis in Paris led to a change in French foreign policy and this encouraged the Turks to reject the frontier proposal outright. Great was the anger in Athens and great too was the disappointment of King George who, under strong pressure from Trikoupis, on 20 July signed a decree of mobilisation, authorising him to publish it when he considered the moment opportune. This he did on 5 August, having ascertained from Lord Granville, the British foreign secretary, that Great Britain had no objection.

On 17 October 1880 King George returned to Athens. New elections had favoured Koumoundouros, who formed a new government on 25 October. He did not, however, rush into war. He still hoped, as did King George, that the powers would put pressure on the Porte. Not until January 1881 did he begin to act more vigorously. He called up reserves and spread the rumour of a Greco–Serb *entente*. At the same time he issued threats to Turkey and encouraged Albanian insurrections against Turkish rule. His actions were not without effect. Towards the end of February the powers, fearing war might break out, convened yet another conference of ambassadors at Constantinople. Here, at the instigation of Bismarck, once again playing the role of 'dishonest' broker, the Turks offered to cede Crete to Greece in lieu of Epiros and Thessaly. But this offer the Greeks, who knew they would get Crete in the course of time, rejected out of hand, and amid popular rejoicing began to send forces towards the frontiers. Eventually the Turks, under pressure from the powers, offered to cede Thessaly and part of Epiros. Koumoundouros accepted this proposal on 12 April, only to be denounced by the opposition, which organised demonstrations in favour of the 'Berlin line'. But although he delayed the final settlement in the hope of improving it and sent Ioannis Gennadios to replace Andreas Koundouriotis as envoy to Constantinople, he agreed to the terms of conventions concluded between the six powers and the Porte on 24 May 1881. These powers had realised that the Turks would fight rather than cede the Kalamas line, because they were determined to retain Preveza, the main port of Jannina commanding the entrance to the gulf of Arta.

The new line fixed a Greek frontier running from slightly to the north of the Vale of Tempe to the gulf of Arta in the west. Thus Greece was to annex almost the whole of the potentially rich plain of Thessaly, but in Epiros only the district of Arta. The frontier excluded Olympos in the east and Jannina in the west. Strategically, from the Greek point of view, it left much to be desired. Although in the west the Greeks were to gain Punta which faces Preveza, they did not attain an easily defensible line. In the east they were excluded from the Karalik defile, which, however, they were to secure in 1882 following frontier incidents and the subsequent award of a mixed commission.

In Athens Trikoupis and the opposition denounced Koumoundouros as a traitor for accepting the proposed settlement, which was made final in the Greco–Turkish convention of 2 July. Nevertheless Greece, for the cost of mobilising (the money was raised by two loans and by the issue of paper currency), had acquired approximately 213,000 square kilometres of territory and an additional population of 500,000. All this time the Cretan Greeks had remained quiet in the interest of the general good. They had nevertheless reaped some benefit from the treaty of Berlin. In October 1878, in pursuance of its undertaking to the powers, the Porte extended the 'Organic Statute' of 1868 by granting concessions—a provision known as the Halepa pact. This provided for an annual assembly in which the Christians had a majority of 49 to 31. It provided also for a governor-general, for several years an Orthodox Turkish subject, and a Moslem assessor. It proclaimed freedom of the press; made Greek the official language of the assembly and the law courts; and laid down that half the surplus revenue should be spent on roads, harbours, and other local improvements. Indeed, as a result of the Halepa pact the Christians were more contented than the Moslems.

VII. The Crisis of 1885

After the acquisition of Thessaly and Arta, Trikoupis hoped to be able to concentrate his attention on internal affairs. He believed that Greece needed to put her house in order, improve her finances, build roads and railways, expand her production and trade, and reorganise her military forces. In March 1882 he turned down the proposal of Montenegro for a Balkan alliance and at the beginning of 1883, despite King George's inclinations to the contrary, refused to give any real response to Serbian approaches for an anti-Turkish combination. Although he did not reject the advances of the Slavs out of hand but instead endeavoured to remain on good terms with his Slav neighbours, he was highly suspicious of Pan-Slavist designs, which might do irreparable damage to Greece, and he therefore endeavoured to improve Greek relations with Turkey. Towards this end he dissolved various national organisations which had stirred up Greek movements in Crete, Epiros, and Macedonia, often to the extreme embarrassment of the government. At the same time he attempted to put down bandits and lawless men who were frequently involved in these movements. In June 1883 he made a bid for Austrian friendship—a move which he repeated towards the end of 1884, because he believed that Greece would need an ally to protect her from the machinations of the Slavs. This policy came in for constant opposition from the demagogue Deliyannis, a popular and striking man, who found considerable response to his eloquent and chauvinistic appeals to the masses.

It so happened, however, that Deliyannis was in office when in September 1885 a revolution broke out in Philippoupolis—an event which was to have critical consequences. The revolutionaries proclaimed the union of eastern Rumelia with Bulgaria—a *fait accompli* which Alexander of Battenberg, the first prince of Bulgaria, had to accept or to face dethronement. This union, if only because it had the 'blessing' of Alexander, whom Tsar Alexander III detested, was not to the liking of Russia. By way of contrast Great Britain, who seven years previously had been chiefly responsible for the separation of eastern Rumelia from Bulgaria, now favoured their union. Since Bulgaria had refused to be a Russian satellite and since eastern Rumelia had not become a barrier to a possible Russian advance because the Turks had failed to man the passes in the Balkan mountains, the British had come to calculate that eastern Rumelia was likely to become a more effective check to Russia if it were joined to Bulgaria.

Deliyannis, supported by the Serbs, protested against Bulgaria's infraction of the treaty of Berlin and demanded compensation. Prince Milan, in danger of being overthrown, went further. He had been advised by the Austrians that, if he must go to war, he should attack Bulgaria and not Turkey. On 13 November he declared war. He hoped to gain an easy victory, for the Bulgarians were short of officers and were mainly concentrated on the Turkish frontier. Victory, however, eluded him and he was soon faced with defeat. Weak Bulgarian detachments based on Sofia halted the Serbian advance. The main Bulgarian army came up from Rumelia. On 17–19 November it routed the Serbs at Slivnitza and shortly afterwards invaded Serbia; but Austria came to the help of the hard-pressed Serbs: she informed Alexander that if he advanced further she herself would occupy Serbian territory, and he, knowing that if this happened, then Russia would occupy Bulgaria, halted, accepted an armistice, and in March 1886 agreed to the restoration of the *status quo*.

Meanwhile the Greeks, having demanded the rest of Epiros to compensate for what seemed a certain acquisition of territory by Bulgaria, had mobilised on 25 September 1885, following demonstrations in Athens. Deliyannis had informed the powers that Greece had no intention of making war, and although three of the Greek ministers—Antonopoulos, Zigomalas, and Romas—had subsequently begun to press for the invasion of Epiros and the engineering of a revolution in Crete, the majority of the cabinet had decided that it would be inopportune to defy the powers, who had given strong warnings to Greece not to intervene. These warnings the powers followed up on 30 December by demanding the demobilisation of the Greek army, a course which Trikoupis favoured on financial and military grounds. On 12 January the powers repeated their demand. Behind the scenes, however, the French and the Russians encouraged Deliyannis to resist. This he did. In February he attempted direct negotiations with the Turks for territorial acquisitions. But these negotiations failed and on 14 April the powers (with France abstaining) delivered an ultimatum to Greece, demanding that she should demobilise forthwith. In reply Deliyannis offered demobilisation in stages, explaining that there would be revolution in Greece if the armies were dispersed immediately. The powers refused to accept this. On 8 May they imposed a blockade of the Greek coasts (with France again abstaining). The irony was that the officer commanding the British squadron was the duke of Edinburgh, who, some twenty-three years earlier, as Prince Alfred, had been elected king of Greece in succession to Otho.

Deliyannis was forced to resign, many of his supporters having gone over to the opposition. On 21 May Trikoupis returned to power. For a brief moment there was trouble on the frontier. Non-commissioned officers whose only hope of promotion was to show bravery in the field had begun to skirmish. But the fighting died down within five days, the army was demobilised, and on 7 June the blockade was raised. The cost to Greece had been about 133 million drachmai, and this time there was nothing to show for it. The nation was sorely disappointed and divided. One half regarded Trikoupis as a traitor and Deliyannis as a hero: the other looked upon Trikoupis as the saviour of Greece and upon Deliyannis as an irresponsible politician. It says much for Deliyannis, however, that he frustrated plans to assassinate his rival. He himself was not to be so fortunate. Some twenty years later he perished at an assassin's hand.[8]

---

[8] He was the first Greek statesman to be assassinated since Kapodistrias: his assassin was seeking vengeance, not against his foreign policy, but against his attempts to close down gambling dens.

CHAPTER 10

Party Politics and Internal Reform
1866-90

I. Koumoundouros, Trikoupis, and Deliyannis

During the parliamentary period of Otho's reign (1843–62) there had been eleven administrations. In the first twenty years of King George's reign (1863–83) there were no less than thirty-nine different governments. Voulgaris spanned both periods and in all he formed eight administrations. Koumoundouros (who had first held cabinet office in July 1856) was prime minister on ten occasions, the first in 1865. That same year the young Deligiorgis—the idol of the liberal youth and a street-corner orator of great eloquence—formed, at thirty-six, the first of his six ministries. That year was memorable, too, because Charilaos Trikoupis first entered parliamentary politics as a deputy for Mesolonghi. A less demagogic character than Deligiorgis, he had studied in Paris and in London, and like Mavrokordatos in an earlier age, he was the most westernised of the Greek politicians of his day. He quickly obtained ministerial office as foreign minister in the third of Koumoundouros's administrations of 1866–67, but it was not until 1875 that, having broken away from Koumoundouros, he formed the first of his seven administrations spread over two decades. If in the first part of his career he provided an alternative administration to that of Koumoundouros, in the second part his great rival was Theodoros Deliyannis, a descendant of the wealthy primates of the Morea. Deliyannis first took office as foreign minister in the Kiriakos government of 1863. Later, having struggled for a time with his own small party, he succeeded, after Koumoundouros's death in March 1883, to the leadership of the major part of the Koumoundouros following.

The fierce party conflicts, first between Trikoupis and Koumoundouros and later between Trikoupis and Deliyannis, gave Greek politics the semblance of a two-party system and, since all three were eloquent, something

140

of the Homeric grandeur of the conflicts of Gladstone and Disraeli. Tri-koupis himself deliberately aimed at creating a two-party system, and, as far as he could, he endeavoured to break with the past of personal parties and to expect of his followers, not a scramble for favours and office, but a steadfast adherence to liberal principles. To a greater extent than Deligiorgis (whose successor he was) he managed to bring under his leadership men from the growing professional and commercial classes and a certain number of independent liberals like Lomvardos who led small groups of friends. He could even, like Gladstone, command support of a more radical following, which included a small 'democratic' group. This group, which first ap-peared in 1881, was anti-dynastic, and it was the forerunner of parties which were to acquire importance in the twentieth century.

What is true of Trikoupis is to some extent true of Koumoundouros and Deliyannis. Although these two continued the tradition of personal parties and of employing the state administration and the distribution of offices to promote party interest, they both had a strong sense of service, and they saw the need to improve government, to develop the natural resources of Greece, and to organise better military forces, if only to make feasible the policy of the Great Idea. They both showed sincerity and devotion at least to the letter of the constitution; and they were both far removed from the political practices of Kolettis and Voulgaris. But both had to come to terms with the traditions of the *kotza bashis* of the Peloponnese, whence they de-rived their principal support, in contrast to Trikoupis, who found his fol-lowing in Rumeli, in the Ionian and other islands, and in the cities (except for the lower orders who associated his policies with high taxation and pre-ferred the patriotic demagogy of the Great Idea). There is a sense, then, in which Koumoundouros and Deliyannis represented Greek conservatism, and this is particularly true of Deliyannis, who, as a matter of course, op-posed or made a show of opposing every measure that Trikoupis sponsored. On one occasion he said, 'I am against everything that Trikoupis is for'. There was therefore a sense in which his collection of groups, which could sometimes be made to pull together, constituted a party of principle, at least when in opposition—in the negative form of opposing the more con-structive and Western-inspired programmes of Trikoupis. But Deliyannis was not without his own philosophy: he defended his conservatism, and in particular the spoils system, curiously enough on the Benthamite principle that it promoted, unlike liberalism, the greatest happiness of the greatest number. He defended it also on the grounds that it prevented nepotism and even the evils of bureaucracy.

Despite the semblance of a system of two parties based on principles, many, if not most, of the essentials of such a system were entirely lacking. Even though Trikoupis could expect the loyalty of a large proportion of his following, even though, so to speak, his measures gave cohesion to his men, there were groups and individuals who deserted him from time to time;

while on the other side, which retained the old traditions, men were always much more important than the measures, the party following being essentially a coalition of groups, some of which might even at times go over to Trikoupis. In the 1870s there were at least five main parties (each a coalition) led respectively by Voulgaris, Koumoundouros, Deligiorgis, Zaimis, and Trikoupis. In the terminology of the day that of Trikoupis was known as the 'Fifth Party'.

The existence of these groups and individuals with changing loyalties led to ministerial instability and frequent changes of government. When an administration was defeated there was little that the king could do but to ask one of the leading politicians (all of whom led only minority groups) to form a government by negotiation. In making his choice the king, for want of any clear indication of the national will, acted partly from personal preference, partly from the need to maintain what he considered to be a reasonable foreign policy, and partly from his own guess of what grouping stood a chance of survival. Needless to say, he was always under pressure from the foreign envoys and courtiers, and he was not insensible to the whole intense political environment of Athens—the newspapers, rumours, and popular demonstrations. Needless to say, too, he was always open to the accusations by men of all parties that he ignored the constitution, or that he chose ministries that failed to represent national opinion. Like the Whigs and Tories of late seventeenth- and eighteenth-century England, the Greek politician spoke and acted differently when in office from when in opposition. They were, as Trevelyan would have said, the merciless men of all parties.

Once a ministry was formed, either it carried on with the existing parliament, the prime minister modifying his programme to command support, or it went to the country, the prime minister hoping to remedy an intolerable position by a victory at the polls. Quite often the king was unwilling to grant a dissolution, for it meant he might be saddled with a prime minister who, though not totally unacceptable when controlled by groups other than his own, might be thoroughly objectionable if he successfully rigged an election and was returned to power with a following to carry out a policy which aroused conflicts and was unacceptable to the king himself. Nevertheless, at times when a parliament was nearing the end of its normal existence or when an impasse was reached in a ministerial crisis, the king would sometimes give way and sanction new elections. This happened in March 1872. On this occasion Deligiorgis rigged the elections, and Voulgaris was unseated. But when in 1874 Deligiorgis fell over the Lavrion financial scandal, Voulgaris formed a minority government (an event which brought much odium on King George) and he too went to the country to win what was to prove his notorious last election. It was on this occasion that Trikoupis wrote a scathing leader for the newspaper *Kairi* (*Times*), denouncing the Greek political system and, by implication, the king's irresponsibility in appointing minority governments. He followed this up with a second article in *Kairi* on 9 July. For his audacity he was imprisoned for four days, but was released on bail and finally acquitted. He remained firm to his principles. Although he himself formed a minority government on 8 May 1875 after the king had been obliged to dismiss Voulgaris because of rapidly developing anti-dynastic agitation, he did so only on condition that fair elections should be held and that the king should announce his intention not to call on minority parties to form administrations. As we have seen, he failed to win the July elections. These gave a clear majority to Koumoundouros, who managed with two short interruptions to survive until the Eastern crisis in the summer of 1877, when the king appointed an all-party government under the aged Admiral Kanaris. With great reluctance and because of the crisis Trikoupis joined that 'oecumenical' administration (national coalition) as foreign minister. It included Koumoundouros, Deligiorgis, Zaimis, and Deliyannis but not Voulgaris. On the demise of that administration, he gave way to Koumoundouros who won the elections of October 1879[1] and continued in office until March 1880 when changes in allegiance resulted in his downfall. Trikoupis, who now returned, suffered a similar fate in October 1880 and once again Koumoundouros took over until March 1882.[2]

II. The Rise of the Trikoupists

That same month Trikoupis formed a government which had a substantial majority and the support not only of certain independents, but also of many of the old followers of the deceased leaders Zaimis, Deligiorgis, and Voulgaris, and of the small democratic party.[3] This government lasted three years and forty days—until its crushing defeat at the elections of April 1885.[4] In this period it carried through a large and increasingly unpopular legislative programme,[5] which came under constant attack from Deliyannis, who on the death of Koumoundouros had become the eloquent and popular leader of the disgruntled Peloponnesian peasants and of the lower middle classes which in Greece, unlike in most of Europe, were conservative and traditionalist. In May 1885 Deliyannis formed his first government, but it was to last only one year, falling, as we have seen, because of its failure in foreign policy. During its term several of the Deliyannist groups went over

---

[1] The voting was: Koumoundouros-Deliyannis 93, Trikoupis 60, Independents 16, Deligiorgists 9 (Deligiorgis had died), Zaimis 7, Voulgarists 7. For the state of parties when parliament met, see Appendix IV.

[2] Koumoundouros was defeated in the elections of January 1882. For the state of parties following the elections see Appendix IV.

[3] At attempt was made by this group, by certain independents, and by sympathisers in other parties to set up a left-wing party under Lomvardos. Lomvardos, however, remained faithful to Trikoupis and thus kept his radical following within the Trikoupist party.

[4] Trikoupis's immediate following secured only 40 seats.

[5] See below, pp. 145–8.

to Trikoupis and on 20 May 1886 a Trikoupist candidate, Stefanopoulos, was elected president of the chamber by 139 votes to 78. The next day Trikoupis formed his fifth administration and in January 1887, with the constituencies enlarged and membership of the chamber reduced to 150, he won a comfortable victory at the polls.[6] The new parliament was the first to run its full term (1887–90) and Trikoupis's fifth administration, like his previous one, was able to carry through an extensive legislative programme.[7] Once again, however, his government came in for fierce attacks. Deliyannis and his friends resorted to filibustering tactics and on several occasions there were ugly scenes in the chamber. Trikoupis's biographer, D. Pournaras, goes so far as to say that political passions equalled those generated by the conflicts of Venizelists and Constantinists. Indeed the *dichasmos* (the split) of the twentieth century may not only have resembled the strife of the age of Trikoupis but may well have had its origins in that period.

In October 1890 Deliyannis turned the tables on Trikoupis, defeated him at the polls,[8] and formed his second administration (November 1890– February 1892). With Deliyannis, however, King George became highly dissatisfied, partly because of his poor showing in financial matters (for which he tried to blame his predecessor) and partly because of his irresponsible foreign policy. In the end the king dismissed him despite his majority and an overwhelming vote of confidence in the chamber. Troops with direct orders from the palace defied instructions from Deliyannis's minister of war and surrounded the parliament house. In vain did Deliyannis call out supporters, many of them anti-royalist, to demonstrate in the streets, to which came also Trikoupist counter-demonstrators to show their loyalty to the crown. Trikoupis himself, although he later admitted that the whole procedure was unconstitutional, agreed to Deliyannis's dismissal, but he would not take office himself unless elections (to be held under a caretaker government) should demonstrate that he had the backing of the country. These elections, held in May 1892, were hard fought, and the king himself came in for much abuse, especially from the Deliyannist press. Once again, however, Trikoupis triumphed and in June embarked upon his sixth premiership. This time he too came up against the king's displeasure over matters of economic administration and in May 1893 resigned in favour of Sotirios Sotiropoulos, a financier and economist. But by November 1893 Trikoupis was back in office with his seventh and last administration. As we shall see, he took over the control of what was virtually a bankrupt state. His relations with the king were bad and many of his followers had become anti-dynastic. The financiers, both Greek and foreign, had turned against him, and popular demonstrations denouncing his government were a common occurrence. In January 1895, following the intervention of Prince

---

[6] The figures were: Trikoupists 90, other parties 60.

[7] See below, pp. 145–8.

[8] The results were: Deliyannis 100, Trikoupis 15, Independents 35.

Constantine in a demonstration against taxation, he resigned, and a care-taker government was formed pending new elections. A violent electoral campaign by Deliyannis ensued, in April the Trikoupists were defeated,[9] and Trikoupis himself failed to hold his seat at Mesolonghi. At that point Trikoupis retired from political life, which he had certainly graced by his fundamental honesty and patriotism. He was one of the greatest of Greek statesmen, and though he failed before the onslaughts of men who as sheer politicians were cleverer than himself, he certainly left his mark upon his country to which he had devoted his undoubtedly great talent.

III. The Military and Economic Policies of Trikoupis

During his fourth and fifth administrations (March 1882–April 1885, and May 1886–November 1890) Trikoupis made a determined effort to main-tain public order and to improve the administration, finances, economic situation, and armed forces of Greece. In June 1882 he reduced compulsory military service (which in November 1878 Koumoundouros had attempted to extend to three years) from two years to one, his intention being to em-ploy the saving on the maintenance of troops for the provision of better training and equipment. Towards this end in 1883 he sent twelve officers under General Koroneos to attend military exercises of the French army and he invited a French military mission to Greece. In the same year he raised a loan of 40 million drachmai for expenditure on equipment for the army and navy. He reorganised the school of military cadets (the *Evel-pidhon*); improved the training of naval officers; and established schools of navigation in several seaports for officers of the mercantile marine. One of his principal aims was to introduce a better discipline into Greek military affairs by creating an officer class with a sense of service. It was with the same aim that he attempted to put down the 'patriotic organisations' which not only interfered with the conduct of Greek foreign policy but which also recruited adherents in the armed forces. These organisations, however, cut both ways. Although Trikoupis may have considered them a constant source of embarrassment, other Greek governments found them useful, and indeed had close connections with them.[10]

The French military mission arrived in Greece in 1884 and remained till 1887. In 1885 Trikoupis adopted its general recommendations, which he embodied in a military establishment (*organismos*). A French naval mission had already arrived and nineteen torpedo-boats had been obtained from France. In 1887 an order was placed with the shipyards of Cherbourg for three warships, the *Spetzes*, *Idra*, and *Psara*, the first of which reached

---

[9] The results were: Deliyannists 140, Trikoupists 18, Rallists 16, Independents 33. For the state of the parties when parliament met, see Appendix IV.

[10] This is particularly true of the period of the Macedonian struggle (see below, Chapter 12).

6

Greece in November 1890. These purchases and the slight improvement in the military services were of some importance, but no one could say that Trikoupis had succeeded in giving Greece either a well-organised army or indeed an adequate navy.

Much the same is true of his attempts to economise on and improve the efficiency of the civil service. In 1882 he passed a law establishing the qualifications for employment in the government services, aiming to get rid of useless office-holders appointed by favour and to provide a body of well-trained officials holding permanent office. Also in 1882 he endeavoured to eradicate corrupt practices from the administration of justice, to stamp out banditry which interfered with police and judicial processes, and to give judges security of tenure. He tried also to organise an independent police force to replace the gendarmerie, the manning of which had tended to deplete the units of the regular army. True, brigandage declined in Greece, but this decline had already set in before Trikoupis had attempted to deal with this long-standing problem: it had declined because the structure of Greek social and economic life was slowly changing. Lawless men there still were in Greece, but they were fewer, and those who remained were more strictly controlled by those who employed them.

In one field, however, Trikoupis met with a success that was plain to all and easily measured—the provision of better communications. In 1882 he introduced bills for the Peloponnese, Lavrion, Thessaly, Pirgos railways. He also began an extensive programme of road-building[11] and the development of posts and telegraphs. He was largely responsible, too, for the inauguration of works for the Korinth canal, which had been under discussion for some time. For his road-building programme he employed thirty-two engineers from France and Switzerland, and kept the general control of it in the hands of the state. For the railways he adopted a similar plan: instead of granting concessions to foreign companies, he vested control of the railways in the Greek state. In 1888–89 he began a second railway-building programme and this, when completed, provided along with his earlier programme almost the entire railway network that exists in Old Greece today.[12]

IV. Trikoupis's Financial Administration

Trikoupis's reforms proved to be costly and therefore unpopular in many quarters. In 1882 he increased taxation by 12 per cent, the principal increases resulting from state monopolies, higher customs, consumption duties, and a tax on farm animals.[13] But even then he failed to balance the budget: expenditure amounted to 80 million drachmai, while the state

---

[11] For details of railway and road development, see below, p. 247.

[12] For details, see below, pp. 246–7.

[13] On the other hand, Trikoupis abolished the tithe.

revenue remained at only 68 million. Despite his promise that by the end of 1883 there would be a surplus, the deficit continued to increase and in 1885 stood at about 60 million. On taking over the government that year, Deliyannis, in an attempt to balance the budget, cut down drastically on expenditure, even on education, and he abolished the unpopular monopolies in matches and cigarette papers and reduced the consumption tax on tobacco and wine. He likewise abolished Trikoupis's civil service reforms and filled the administration with the nominees of his party friends. His measures, however, were insufficient to restore the finances, on which his mobilisation of the army in September 1885 placed a severe strain, raising the deficit to 66 million. On his return to office in 1886 Trikoupis made matters worse by restoring the cuts in expenditure effected by Deliyannis and by reintroducing the taxes which had been abolished. For the next five years the Greek finances were in a deplorable condition. Between 1879 and 1890 Greece raised no less than six loans amounting in all to 630 million drachmai. Of this sum Greece received only 459 million for the loans were raised at 25 to 30 per cent below par. Most of that sum was spent abroad either on armaments or on interest[14] on the total debt. Only about 100 million drachmai were available in Greece and much of that sum was required to meet budgetary deficits, leaving very little for productive investment. The total result was that the national debt, despite a twofold increase in taxation during the period 1873 to 1893 and despite a favourable trade treaty with England in March 1890,[15] continued to mount. By the end of that period it was absorbing nearly one-third of revenue, which had risen from about 30 million to nearly 100 million. The situation was aggravated when in 1893 the market for Greek currants collapsed. The country was faced with bankruptcy. To meet the situation Trikoupis, who had failed to raise a new loan, reduced, much to the consternation of the foreign bondholders, the interest on the old loans by 70 per cent. Long and tedious negotiations followed, and it was not until February 1897 that Deliyannis managed to reach a compromise with Greece's creditors. But although he found the British bondholders fairly reasonable, the other Europeans, headed by the Germans, were demanding nothing short of an international commission to supervise Greek finances.

While it is true that Trikoupis overrated the productive capacity of the Greek economy, it is also true that in attempting to carry out his programmes he was faced with tax evasion and with crises in foreign affairs which placed a great strain on the treasury. One thing at least was certain: Greece had not the means to pursue successfully a vigorous foreign policy hostile to the powers in concert. Alone she was no match for Turkey, who was taking

[14] In 1886 the annual charge of the debt was 36 million drachmai.

[15] Great Britain reduced the tariff on Greek currants from 7 shillings to 2 shillings per 100 lbs in return for a reduction in Greek tariffs on herrings and textiles. This agreement gave rise to rumours, spread by the Deliyannists, that Trikoupis had 'ceded' Crete to Great Britain.

steps to improve her own military organisation. Nevertheless, Trikoupis gave Greece an important asset—the rudiments of a road-system and a railway network. Moreover, under his control, Greece was beginning to develop in industry, shipping, and agriculture, a development reflected in the great increase in revenue since 1873. But this was due not to government action: it was due to the impact of European capital, which was noticeable on the Balkans in general and also on Turkey in Asia.

CHAPTER 11

The Second War of Independence in Crete: The Second Phase

I. The Outbreak of the Revolt in Crete, 1896–97

During Trikoupis's fifth administration the Christian Cretans once again became restive. For ten years under the regime of the Halepa pact they had devoted themselves to fierce local politics, and had formed into two main parties, the conservatives (*karavanades*) and the liberals (*xipoliti*, the bare-footed). In 1888 these liberals won a majority in the Cretan chamber and this was the signal for unruly clashes between the two parties. The Turks despatched an army under General Sahir Pasha to the island to restore order and to curtail the liberties enjoyed under the Halepa pact. This action led the Cretans to prepare a revolt which the patriotic organisations in Greece encouraged, denouncing Trikoupis who, in view of the international situation, counselled moderation. In August 1889 the Cretans sent the European consuls a demand that the provisions of the Halepa pact should be observed; and Trikoupis requested the powers to ensure that the Turks withdrew their armed forces; but beyond that he would not go. In December the Porte abolished altogether the civil liberties of Crete. This action provoked only mild protests from Great Britain and Russia, and none at all from the other powers. It gave rise to unruly scenes in Athens, where Dimitrios Rallis, an excitable demagogue whose following came chiefly from Attica, denounced Trikoupis and the dynasty. But on taking up office in November 1890 even Deliyannis found it politic to attempt to silence the Cretan committee in Greece. Thereafter the tension decreased both in Athens and in Crete, and in May 1895 the Turks sent to the island the Christian Karatheodory Pasha as governor. Karatheodory, however, aroused the opposition of the Moslem Cretans and in December he resigned. Meanwhile in September there had been formed in Athens the 'National Association' (*Ethniki Eteria*) based on the old *Filiki Eteria*. This body had been first founded in 1894 as a military society with sixty members, but later extended membership to civilians. In September, too, the Cretan Christians had formed a committee under the leadership of Manousos Koundouros. They hoped to take advantage of the situation created by the Armenian massacres which had begun earlier in the summer.

In December 1895 the Porte sent a Moslem governor to Crete, Tourchan Pasha, whereupon the Cretan committee transformed itself into a revolutionary assembly. It received money and arms from the *Eteria* in Athens, and encouragement to demand *enosis*. Koundouros, however, belonged to a Cretan party which favoured not *enosis* but autonomy, an aim considered more realistic and one more likely to receive support from Britain. But an even stauncher conservative than Koundouros was Eleftherios Venizelos, then a young lawyer; he considered that a revolt would be useless, an attitude which enraged the extremists, who demanded his trial and execution.

By the spring of 1896 the 'National Association' had fifty-six branches in Greek cities and eighty-three among the Greek communities abroad, with a total membership of over 3,000. Supported by other patriotic clubs and by opposition politicians like Rallis, who was building up his own personal party, it placed Deliyannis's government under considerable pressure, accusing it of failing to aid the Cretans and of neglecting the army, in which the *Eteria* was daily gaining more adherents among the non-commissioned officers. The *Eteria* had become virtually a state within a state, and its activities were not confined to Crete, but extended to Macedonia and Epiros. Such was the situation when on 18 May 1896 the Cretan committee took action and surrounded 1,600 Turkish troops at Vamos. The Turks retaliated and massacred Greeks at Chania. In spite of popular demands for action, the Greek government did nothing, for the powers had sent their warships to the island. But when the Turks began to disembark further troops in Crete, arms and volunteers began to flow from Greece. This was the work, not of the Greek government, but of the *Eteria*. Although Smolenskis, the minister of war, proposed that the government should come to an understanding with the *Eteria* in order to control it, Deliyannis remained timid and even strengthened the northern border posts in the hope of preventing the *Eteria* from sending bands into Macedonia. He was waiting to see what became of the Cretan request to Britain to occupy the island and of the proposal of the powers, initiated by Austria, that the Porte should restore the Christian governor, convoke the Cretan assembly, execute the provisions of the Halepa pact, and grant a general amnesty. The Porte gave way, whereupon the powers made a *démarche* in Athens on 6 July, demanding that the flow of money, arms, and volunteers to Crete should cease forthwith.

When that same month the Cretan assembly met, the Christian delegates demanded for Crete a status similar to that of Samos, which from 1832 had enjoyed autonomy under a prince-governor and since 1852 a democratic constitution. About this time, however, the Turkish military began to over-rule the Christian governor. The struggle was renewed; further massacres occurred; the Greeks protested; and the Turks, in replying to the powers, accused the Greeks of running arms and sending volunteers not only to Crete but also to Epiros and Macedonia. The charge was not unfounded. Naoum Spanos, with Mitros and Hadji, old klefts of Thessaly, had crossed into Macedonia, where local bands were being organised, the most famous being that of Broufas, a chief from Grevena.

II. The Intervention of the Powers

It was at this point that Goluchowski, the Austrian foreign minister, pro-posed a peaceful blockade of Crete: but to this—as also to a German pro-posal for naval action against Greece—Lord Salisbury was resolutely opposed. On 25 August the Turks came forward with their own proposals: a Christian governor, approved by the powers and appointed for five years; two-thirds of offices for the Christians; a biennial assembly to vote a budget and discuss legislation; and foreign commissions for judicial reform and the reorganisation of the gendarmerie. The Greek government and the Cretan committee did not reject these proposals out of hand, but the Greek consul Gennadis and the opposition leaders in Athens, Rallis, Simopoulos, and Theotokis, began to act independently in Crete, thus giving the Turks the opportunity to retaliate and demonstrate to the powers that the Cretans were unreasonable. Further revolts and massacres followed. Under popular pressure Deliyannis sent naval vessels to Cretan waters. This encouraged the extremists to hoist the Greek flag at Halepa and to proclaim *enosis*. On 10 February 1897 Alexandros Skouzes, the Greek foreign minister, appealed to the powers, stating the case for union of Crete with Greece, and three days later a Greek force under Colonel Vassos, the king's aide-de-camp, was despatched to take possession of the island in the name of King George. On 15 February the powers landed marines, put the island *en dépôt*, and called on Greece to withdraw her forces. The Greek government, however, not only refused to comply with this request but designated Gennadis as royal commissioner—an act of defiance which produced a strong reaction from Germany, the Emperor William calculating that if King George were pressed hard he would abdicate in favour of Crown Prince Constantine, who was thought to be more pro-German than his father. But the British rejected the German proposal to blockade Piraeus and other Greek ports, and out of the ensuing negotiations a French proposal, taken up by Russia, became the programme of the powers: Crete should have an autonomous regime while remaining within the Ottoman empire. The Turks agreed in principle; but the Greek reply was ambiguous: Greece was willing to with-draw her ships but wished her forces to remain in Crete to preserve order: the powers should not impose a regime which like its predecessors would only be a failure: what was needed was a plebiscite. This reply had the approval of King George, who was beginning to lose patience with the tortuous diplomacy of the powers. Britain, he complained, had seized Cyprus; Germany had taken Schleswig-Holstein; Austria had laid claim to Bosnia and Herzegovina; surely Greece had a better right to Crete.

The British government found the Greek reply not altogether unacceptable, but Germany still advocated stern measures which should be executed by France and Italy. Germany was trying to set Britain against both France and Russia. But France worked steadily for a concerted solution and at length even Salisbury agreed to a blockade of Crete, which was announced on 18 March. Five days later the powers landed 3,000 troops. But these measures only exasperated the Cretan extremists and the sole restraint was that imposed by the presence of Vassos's troops. Meanwhile the powers discussed the choice of a governor-general. The Russians proposed Prince George, the Greek king's second son, but the Turks insisted that the office should be given to a Turkish subject.

The Porte, determined to settle with the Greeks once and for all, prepared for war. The Greeks too prepared. They began to concentrate troops in Thessaly; and the *Eteria* infiltrated, or were ready to infiltrate, no less than thirty-four bands of irregulars, which included Italian volunteers, into Macedonia. Russia now took alarm and proposed a blockade of Volos. (Though not unfavourable towards Greek aspirations in Crete, she wished to keep the Greeks out of the Slav preserves in the north.) This proposal was opposed by the British, who suggested instead that the Turks and Greeks should be asked to keep their troops 50 miles from the Greek northern frontier. If Greece refused this request, then Britain would agree to a blockade of Volos: if the Turks refused then Britain would join in coercive measures, which, it was presumed, would be initiated by Austria and Russia.

III. The Greco–Turkish War of 1897

As usual the tortuous diplomacy of the powers prevented quick decisions, and during the delay Prince Constantine, who had been named commander of the troops in Thessaly, embarked on 27 March for Volos. On 6 April the powers warned both Greece and Turkey that the aggressor would have to face the consequences. That was all they could agree on by way of concerted action. All this time the Germans were encouraging Sultan Abdul Hamid II to go to war. In contrast Russia and Austria, neither ready for a disturbance of the *status quo*, were intent on preventing the Slavs from intervening in the Greco–Turkish dispute. They achieved their aim: Serbia, Bulgaria, and Montenegro all assured the Porte that they would observe a strict neutrality.

On 9 April the Turks learned that Greek bands numbering one thousand men had crossed the frontier towards Metzovo. They protested to the powers, but Skouzes, when approached by the foreign envoys, claimed that the men in question were Macedonians who were returning to their home-land. This was nearly true, for with one or two exceptions the bandsmen were all natives of Macedonia. Meanwhile the Greek and Turkish armies faced one another along the frontier. Following incidents at Analipsi on 17 April hostilities began.

After a few initial successes the Greeks, badly supplied and poorly led, found themselves outnumbered by well-armed Turkish units which had benefited from their training by German officers. Soon they were thrown into great confusion, and someone (it is not known who) gave the order to retreat, even though at the time the junior Greek officers and the better-trained Greek units were still fighting strongly. So disorderly was the ensu-ing retreat that the Turks, thinking it a stratagem to mask the movement of the main Greek forces, occupied the abandoned towns and villages with excessive caution, and it was not until 25 April that they entered Larisa.

When the news of the retreat reached Athens there was great conster-nation. Prince Constantine was made the scapegoat. The king himself was accused of negligence in failing to employ the fleet and the palace was be-sieged by hostile and angry crowds. On 27 April Skouzes implored the protecting powers to intervene. As usual there was some delay, during which the king replaced Deliyannis by Rallis as prime minister, Stefanos Skouloudis succeeding Skouzes as foreign minister. The new government withdrew the Greek troops from Crete and on 11 May, with the road to Athens open to Turks, requested mediation. Tsar Nicholas II and Queen Victoria were determined that Greece should not be crushed and on 20 May their efforts resulted in an armistice. In the negotiations that followed Great Britain and Italy, with some support from France, Austria, and Russia, and in face of the hostility of Germany, saved Greece from any loss of territory except for salients on either side of the river Nezero to the east, in the region to the north-west and west of Larisa, and in the upper reaches of the Pinios. Greece, however, was to pay an indemnity of 4 million Turkish pounds, and, to facilitate prompt payment, the Greek finances were to be subject to a degree of international control. Finally, both Greece and Turkey undertook not to allow on their soil any agitation likely to threaten security and order in a neighbouring state.

The definitive peace was not signed until 4 December at Constantinople. During its negotiation, the Turks, with the continued encouragement of Germany, attempted to revise the preliminaries and, but for the support of Great Britain and Russia, Greece might have been forced to sign a humiliating treaty. Greece, however, had one great asset—King George's threat of abdication, which, if carried out, might have thrown the whole

Near East into turmoil. It was this danger that prompted the protecting powers to work for Greek advantage. During the crisis Austria deserted Greece and moved into line with Germany. Like Germany she strongly opposed the nomination of Prince George as governor of Crete—a proposal revived by Russia.

Despite the signature of peace, the Turks delayed the withdrawal of their troops not only from Thessaly but also from Crete and even attempted to reinforce them, with the result that further troubles arose in late summer. On 6 September 500 Christian Cretans and fourteen British troops were killed. The local British naval commander took firm action and early in October his initiative was followed up when Great Britain, France, Russia, and Italy (Germany and Austria had virtually washed their hands of Crete) demanded that the Porte should evacuate the island within a fortnight. The Turks, counting on German support, procrastinated, but on 9 November the four allied admirals delivered an ultimatum to the Turkish commander. Six days later the Turkish troops left Crete and on 30 November the four powers notified the Porte of their choice of Prince George as governor of that island.

Crete thus became an autonomous province and all that remained as a symbol of the Sultan's suzerainty was the Turkish flag. Irksome though this reminder was, Crete was to all intents and purposes earmarked for Greece, who, though defeated, had gained on balance. For this she was chiefly in debt to Great Britain and Russia who, despite their rivalries, had combined once again against Germany in south-eastern Europe. But this Anglo–Russian co-operation had, as far as the interests of Greece were concerned, reached its limits. The Greek gains in Crete (as King George had always foreseen) might lead Russia to attempt to compensate brother-Slavs in Macedonia. For the moment, however, she preferred to maintain her agreement of May 1897 with Austria to preserve the *status quo*, but in the event of any disturbance of it she would then favour the Slavic states. Greece therefore must ultimately look to Austria, who certainly would have preferred to see Greeks in Albania rather than Italians, and Greeks in Thessaloniki rather than Slavs. She could count in Macedonia on little or no support from France or Great Britain. France was occupied in other quarters and in preserving her ties with Russia. Britain, too, had preoccupations in all parts of the world; and, in any event, if there was indeed a British policy, it was to encourage reform within the Turkish empire even though this meant unpopularity in Constantinople and hostility to British economic interests.

IV. The Restoration of the Finances, 1898–1909

After the defeat of 1897 Greece recovered quickly. True, she had lost the major part of her equipment; but that equipment was nearly all obsolete.

On her simple economic structure the war had no lasting effects. During the absence of the men the women, who even in peacetime did much of the agricultural work, had tilled the fields. Except for part of Thessaly, the Greek soil had not been fought over, and even in that province the destruction of crops, animals, and homesteads had not been considerable. But on the finances, already in a perilous state, the war, which cost 52 million drachmai, had a disastrous effect. Yet within a few years, the financial position was vastly improved: it was better than it had ever been throughout the nineteenth century.

The financial recovery was due in part to the improved economic condition of the country[1] and in part to the work of the international financial commission established by the powers. To this commission were assigned the revenues from monopolies, stamp duties, tobacco tax, and import duties levied at Piraeus, the last of which were estimated to produce 39,600,000 drachmai annually. (If the yield fell below that sum, then the import duties of four other ports, estimated at 7,200,000 drachmai, could be assigned to make good the deficiency.) The revenues assigned were to be used to service the foreign loans of 1833 and 1881–93 and also a new loan which was to be raised to meet the indemnity to Turkey and certain other liabilities. The internal debt was to remain under the control of the Greek government and the costs of service were to be covered by any surpluses not required by the commission. Of any increase beyond 28,900,000 drachmai (*plus-values*) in the yield of the assigned revenues a part, 30 per cent, was to provide for an increased interest rate on the loans, another part, 30 per cent again, for amortisation, and the remainder, 40 per cent, for a contribution to the treasury. For the administration of the revenues a *société de régie* was to be set up and over it the commission was to have a tight control. All these arrangements were embodied in a law which was glumly voted in the Greek parliament on 11 March 1898. That same month the protecting powers agreed to a loan of 170 million drachmai, of which the greater part, 125 million, was to be offered immediately for public subscription.

Over the period 1898–1907 the Greek finances showed an improvement. At the end of 1905 the gold debt was £29,037,580 and the internal debt £6,286,792. By the end of 1907 both figures had been reduced. During 1905 a loan of 20,080,000 drachmai was raised and in 1905 a further 10 million paper-drachmai loan was floated. In the same year Greece raised a £800,000 gold loan at 4 per cent—a very good sign. So too was the increased dividend declared by the National Bank of Greece. Throughout 1906 and 1907 the revenue yield improved. But in 1908 there was a deficit of 9,800,000 drachmai which rose in 1909 to 24 million. Nevertheless, the temporary improvement of 1906 and 1907 had enabled Greece to increase expenditure on the army and navy.

[1] See below, Chapter 17.

V. The Reconstruction of the Army, 1904–09

Between April 1897 (when Rallis succeeded Deliyannis) and December 1905 there were ten changes of government. Trikoupis had left no successor of his own calibre. His followers supported Theotokis, and though they eschewed Deliyannis's mixture of heavy-handed conservatism and demagogic foreign policy, they were content with timid and halting measures; and they enjoyed no substantial leases of power until in December 1905 Theotokis formed his fourth ministry, which lasted up to July 1909. A Corfiot and old Trikoupist, Theotokis was honest but indolent. He left the management of his party chiefly to Anargiros Simopoulos, his able minister of finance. Although he won a considerable majority at the polls in February 1899 (thus defeating Zaimis whose government had negotiated the humiliating peace), he attempted no major reforms. He increased judges' salaries and made minor changes in the consular service. But fearing defection among his followers he dropped his plan (Trikoupis's old plan) to replace the gendarmerie by a civil police. Even then he lost the confidence of the chamber and was replaced by Zaimis (November 1901–December 1902), who in turn gave way to Deliyannis (December 1902–June 1903).

Deliyannis worked his way back to office by his usual method of organising demonstrations against the increase in taxation which between 1899 and 1902 reached an annual average of 16,500,000 drachmai. Obliged to live up to those precepts he had voiced when in opposition, he announced his intention to curtail expenditure by close on 10 million drachmai annually: to achieve this reduction he proposed to axe superfluous bureaucrats, to reduce the number of parliamentary deputies, and to cut down consular expenditure. His programme, however, encountered fierce opposition and he was superseded by Theotokis (June–July 1903) and Rallis (July–December 1903). In December 1904 he was back in office, only to be replaced by Rallis the following June.

All these short-lived governments swept and reswept the civil service, the judiciary, and the military establishment with the same old broom, the spoils system, and they were all mainly concerned with the thankless task of prolonging their own existence. Moreover, they all directed their attention to that other thankless task—reconstructing and expanding the army. To achieve this even on a very moderate scale an initial outlay of at least 100 million drachmai was required. But any government which embarked on a really adequate programme was likely to arouse hostility, even from those who were critical of the lack of military preparations. The Theotokis ministry of 1899–1901 was therefore content to carry through purely minor measures: it attempted to establish a general staff and to place it under the direction of a foreign military expert; and it appointed Crown Prince Constantine as commander-in-chief. This appointment raised an outcry. It was alleged that Constantine had been given responsibilities incompatible with the constitution. Tension grew when Constantine persuaded the government to appoint Colonel Sapountsakis as chief of staff, the German government (concerned for their relations with Turkey) having refused a request to supply a military expert. Like Constantine himself, the new chief of staff, who was highly unpopular in certain army circles, was accused of being responsible for the military disasters of 1897.

During his fourth ministry, when financial conditions had improved, Theotokis was able to pay more attention to the army. In 1906 he introduced a new military law. This measure reduced the forces with the colours, thus freeing money for the purchase of rifles, field-guns, horses, engineering material, and barrack-room accommodation. He also began to build a force of well-trained reserves, to improve the administrative arrangements for their mobilisation, and to provide for them to take part in annual manoeuvres. The result was that by the end of 1906 Greece had a standing army of some 70,000, about 30,000 of whom were equipped with Mannlicher rifles. A further 70,000 rifles were on order and these, along with 5 million cartridges, arrived the next year. Following international artillery trials in Greece in the spring of 1907, the Greek government ordered 144 7·5 mm Q.F. Schneider-Canet mountain guns. These did not arrive until the period 1909–10. Nevertheless, the army showed a vast improvement and the manoeuvres held in 1908 certainly impressed foreign observers.

By that date Greece had gone a long way to improving her naval forces. A decade earlier, the Greek navy, except for the ironclads acquired in 1890 and for the torpedo-boats purchased by Trikoupis, had become obsolete. To improve matters, in 1900 the government established a fleet fund. This fund subsequently benefited to the extent of 2,500,000 francs from the bequest of George Averov (a Greek–Vlach who had made a fortune in Egypt) and from budget revenues amounting to 925,000 drachmai annually. Hoping to increase and speed up naval expenditure, early in 1901 Theotokis sounded the international financial commission about a loan, only to be met with a rebuff. In July 1901 he approached the British firm of Armstrong with a view to buying a £400,000 cruiser on instalments. Nothing came of this move, and it was not until the Greek financial position had improved that Theotokis was able to find the money for a substantial naval programme. In 1908 he was able to order eight new torpedo-boat destroyers, all of which were delivered before the end of 1909. In November 1908 he purchased a cruiser of the Italian *Pisa* class, but this famous vessel, the *Averov*, did not arrive until 1911. In the meantime the Turks, alarmed at the increase in Greek naval strength, bought in 1910 two German cruisers. But Greece still enjoyed a naval supremacy over Turkey: the Turkish naval administration was so chaotic that it is doubtful whether the Turkish fleet could have put to sea.

The decade 1898 to 1908, despite political instability, was for Greece a period of recovery and progress.[2] It was also the period of the third War of

[2] See below, Chapter 17.

Independence—a struggle fought out in Macedonia. Although the issue of that struggle did not secure Macedonia for Greece, it prevented that province from becoming absorbed by Bulgaria.

CHAPTER 12

The Third War of Independence:
The Macedonian Struggle 1897-1908

I. Macedonia

Whatever the term Macedonia may have meant in earlier times, at the end of the nineteenth century it connoted a region stretching from Lakes Ochrid and Prespa in the west to the river Mesta in the east, and from the Shar mountains, Rila, and Rhodope in the north to Pindus, Olympos, and the Aegean in the south. An agglomeration of mountain-ranges, lakes, and river basins, it was a land of three principal routes—the first two the Vardar and Struma valleys connecting central Europe to the Aegean, and the third the old Roman *Via Egnatia* running through Monastir and Thessaloniki to Constantinople. As a consequence it was a region which successive peoples —Persians, Romans, Byzantines, Bulgarians, Serbs, and Turks—had attempted to dominate.

When towards the end of the nineteenth century the Ottoman empire seemed on the verge of collapse, the modern powers, Austria, Russia, Germany, and Italy, became aware of their somewhat ill-defined interests in Macedonia, which, in the railway age, assumed great importance. But, owing to international rivalries, no single power could simply annex that province: all that the great powers could do was to maintain influence at Constantinople as long as Turkey lasted and be ready to back one or more of the likely successors to Turkish rule—the Serbs, Greeks, Bulgarians, and Albanians, or indeed the Macedonians, whose chances of establishing an independent nation were not completely hopeless. All these peoples could put forward, on historical, ethnic, sociological, linguistic, cultural, and religious grounds, claims either to the whole or at least to extensive areas of Macedonia. The region had figured in the Serbo–Greek negotiations of

1866–67[1] and, as we have seen, after the treaty of Berlin and the Greek acquisition of Thessaly, all the Balkan powers had come to direct their irredentist aspirations to it and to claim the Macedonians as long-lost brothers. With the Macedonian Slavs, the Serbs and Bulgarians had certain racial, linguistic, and cultural links, but both disputed fiercely the degree of affinity. The Greeks could point to the greater antiquity of their historical claims. Furthermore, there were in Macedonia flourishing Greek-speaking communities in the townships, which had a firm grip on all the professions, on trade, and on commerce. There were, too, numerous villages, especially in the south, which were linguistically Greek: and even though the Bulgarian Exarchate had expanded, the Greek Church remained supreme in a considerable part of the purely Slav-speaking regions.[2]

Throughout the nineteenth century the Greeks had built up in Macedonia a 'national' organisation, which had come into play at the time of the Crimean War and again at the time of the treaty of Berlin. This organisation, in view of the expansion of the Exarchate and the establishment of a Bulgarian state, they began to make more efficient and to adapt, to enable it the better to withstand the competition of Slavism. Both the Patriarchate and the national kingdom began to pay more attention to the Greek schools. These, thanks to the care of the communities and to wealthy benefactors, were already numerous, but they needed to be increased, and, although the effort fell short of the needs, by 1902 there were just over one thousand Greek schools in Macedonia with 70,000 pupils and a number of private establishments providing for a further 8,000.[3] Exarchist schools, founded and maintained with money from Russia and Bulgaria, numbered 592 with a total of about 30,000 pupils. The Serbs too had returned to the educational field. In 1886 they had founded the educational society of St Sava and by 1901 they had, besides four lycées for boys and three for girls, 226 primary schools. One interesting thing about all these figures is that they correspond roughly to the Turkish population figures of 1905, which gave the number of patriarchists in Macedonia as 647,962 and of exarchists as 557,734. It was generally admitted, however, that many inhabitants were exarchists under duress and not by conviction. It was precisely in those regions where Greek schools were numerous that Hellenism was strongest and it was precisely in those regions where the exarchist and patriarchist school populations were evenly matched that the struggle between the two Churches was fiercest. Both the weakness and the strength of Hellenism in Macedonia

[1] It figured also in the Greco–Serbian negotiations of 1890–93. The Serbs laid claim to the greater part of Macedonia. The Greeks on that occasion rejected a Serbian offer of an alliance, calculating that the Bulgarians and Serbs could never come to terms and that a Serbo–Greek alliance would lead only to a Bulgarian–Turkish alignment, which would be detrimental to Hellenism in Macedonia.

[2] See above, pp. 121–2. By 1904 there were six exarchist bishoprics, of which two were Serbian. In some places, however, the Bulgarians had appointed *protojereji* (rural deans) who were bishops in all but name.

[3] Cf. the figures for the national kingdom: 3,123 schools with close on 190,000 pupils.

corresponded precisely to the position of Greek education. Many in western Europe doubted whether Hellenism really existed in Macedonia and regarded it solely as the invention of the Greek national press. Such people were proved wrong. Hellenism, though severely challenged, managed to survive; and it could not have survived had it not existed. What strength it had was the result partly of Greek education and partly of the innate conservatism of the majority of Macedonians, whether Slav-, Vlach-, or Greek-speaking.

Exarchist education had the advantage of being free and also of the existence of several boarding schools which provided bursaries. Moreover, although it was less thorough, it emphasised languages and useful knowledge, and it therefore had some appeal. But Greek education, if somewhat antiquated, had social standing and the more well-to-do Slavs preferred it for that reason. There were very few openings for the products of the exarchist schools. The professions and trades remained in the hands of Greeks, Vlachs, and Jews. Almost as soon as an élite was created by the schools, it migrated to Bulgaria or to distant lands. Hence the exarchist dream that Macedonia could be won by education did not come true. All that the exarchist schools had succeeded in doing was to make inroads into the weaker fringes of Hellenism at a cost of producing a class which was to become hostile to the Bulgarian Church.

II. The Internal Macedonian Revolutionary Organisation

In the course of time the exarchist educational system fell largely into the hands of irreligious social revolutionaries and the exarchist movement itself became harnessed to two conflicting causes—Bulgarian nationalism and Macedonian autonomy. While Stepan Stambulov was in power in Sofia (1887–94), Bulgarian policy was to co-operate with the Turks, who were hostile to Hellenism, and to obtain further bishoprics for the Exarchate; but Stambulov's successors began, somewhat timidly it is true, to encourage the movement for Macedonian autonomy, hoping that once autonomy had been secured, then, like eastern Rumelia, Macedonia could be gained for Bulgaria. Nevertheless, the movement for Macedonian autonomy had its own life and devoted adherents, who, though quite happy to get funds from Bulgaria and the Exarchate, wished to establish a separate state based on political and social principles quite different from those that obtained in the Bulgarian principality.

The secular movement for Macedonian autonomy had existed before the establishment of the Exarchate and it was this movement that later organised revolutionary bands in 1879–81 and again in 1885–86. In Macedonia the Turkish beys, mainly Albanians, in their dual capacity of landlords and tax-farmers, robbed both the peasantry and the Turkish treasury. The wretched peasants, too, had to compound with brigands for defence against other brigands and unscrupulous officials—costly, but not ineffective. Moreover, they suffered much if they had the misfortune to come before a Turkish court. Macedonia had all the social evils likely to bring recruits to a revolutionary movement. But it was not until 1893 when Gruev and Tatarchev founded the I(nternal) M(acedonian) R(evolutionary) O(rganisation)—I.M.R.O.—that a subversive movement of any importance existed. This organisation, which in theory was to include Macedonians of all creeds, adopted the slogan 'Macedonia for the Macedonians', and although it was fundamentally hostile to the exarchist movement, it worked alongside it; for it was found easier to create groups in villages which were exarchist or which contained exarchist parties than in the solidly patriarchist communities.

In 1895 a supreme Macedonian committee was formed in Sofia. Its aim was to reinforce and even take over the internal organisation by sending into Macedonia bands formed chiefly from the Macedonian immigrants. Bands were likewise formed in Bulgaria by the internal organisation, which, as it grew within Macedonia, had also begun to enlist the services of the local *haiduks*. This somewhat confused band activity increased considerably after the Greek defeat of 1897, and it was not long before it became anti-Greek as well as anti-Turkish. The aim was to support exarchist parties in the villages and thus to force these communities to declare for the Bulgarian Church. Against these disorders the Turkish garrison and gendarmes (drawn chiefly from the Gheg Albanians) began to take action and they were certainly guilty of repressive measures, reports of which provoked much sympathy for the revolutionaries in Europe. The idea of 'Macedonia for the Macedonians' had already found considerable support in Europe, chiefly among ill-informed liberals who in their ignorance imagined that there existed a Macedonian nationality.

In the villages the *grecomanes* (as the fervent patriarchists were called) acted as informers to the Turks. At the same time the Greek organisations throughout Macedonia began, somewhat belatedly, to defend Hellenism against revolutionary Slavism. Their task, though considerable, was not, however, so formidable as appeared at first sight. The Bulgarian–Macedonian movement was endlessly divided: there were rivalries and differences within the bodies competing to direct it, and, at the local level, it was a strange mixture of banditry, parish vendetta, social unrest, religious conflict, and an almost incomprehensible struggle between local leaders. Money and arms were hard to come by and most of the villagers were apathetic. Nevertheless, the Greek counter-organisation found it difficult enough to protect the Greek priests, schoolmasters, and patriarchist notables in the towns and villages where the struggle was fiercest. These communities lay principally in a broad band of territory composed of the *kazas* (districts) of Monastir and Florina in the west; of Gevgeli, Vodena (Edhessa), and Yanitsa in the central region; and Serres and Zihna in the east— the region through which the frontier was subsequently drawn.

III. The Greek Organisation

Foremost among the defenders of Hellenism in Macedonia was the metropolitan bishop Germanos Karavangelis who was appointed in 1900 by the Patriarch Konstantinos V to the see of Kastoria. He quickly saw the need to organise bands to protect the villages and to assist the Turks in destroying the I.M.R.O. and Bulgarian-Macedonian bands. His first choice fell on Christos Kota of Roulia, a Slav-speaking kleft who had quarrelled with the young lettered leaders of I.M.R.O. He later recruited Vangelis of Strebeno and Guelev of Tirsia (both of whom I.M.R.O. had attempted to employ) and later still the klefts Georgi of Negovani, Niko of Nereti, Karalivanos, and others. Furthermore, he had in his pay spies and agents within I.M.R.O. and also Turkish assassins. Needless to say, he kept the local Turks fully informed; and in return they supplied him with a bodyguard when he toured his diocese to celebrate communion and to carry on his political activities. When I.M.R.O. staged the abortive Ilinden rising of August 1903, it was Karavangelis and his henchmen who were in large measure responsible for its failure. Kota fought with a large band of 600 men. True, he fought largely on his own account, for he would never collaborate with the Turks, but his actions, like those of Vangelis,[4] who destroyed a large number of I.M.R.O. bands, greatly facilitated the Turkish victory over I.M.R.O., which never fully recovered from its defeat. In all this work for the Church in Macedonia, Karavangelis was not alone. Bishop Anthimos of Florina, Bishop Foropoulos of Monastir, Alexandros, metropolitan of Thessaloniki, Chrisostomos of Drama, and Stefanos of Vodena, all played distinguished roles in the Macedonian struggle. How far they were working solely for the Patriarchate or for the Hellenism of Athens (the two were not totally in conflict) it is difficult to say. While they took care as far as possible to maintain good relations with the Turks, they were not averse to obtaining help from Greece, and even to the Turks themselves the help that came from Athens was not altogether an unmixed evil.

Karavangelis had from the outset been receiving funds from Athens and he sent reports to Zaimis and Deliyannis. On the occasion that he reported the enlistment of Guelev he asked Zaimis to send him fifty Cretans, but Zaimis, mindful of the bands of 1896 and the defeat of 1897, said to his colleagues: 'Let us get rid of Karavangelis, for he will do great evil.' Zaimis's successors, however, were not so timid. From 1903 onwards considerable state funds, disguised in the budget as 'foreign expenses',[5] were sent to Macedonia. In any case, there were 'private' concerns with their own funds, and these, it seems, took charge of much of the Macedonian organisation on behalf of the government. For, despite the treaty with Turkey, and despite the formal disbanding of the notorious *Ethniki Eteria*, that

---

[4] Vangelis in fact had a licence from the Turks to maintain a band.

[5] The figure was probably somewhere in the region of 3 to 4 million drachmai annually, part of which sum was sent to Crete and Epiros.

association continued to exist in all but name, and counted among its members some of the young officers who still smarted under the defeat of 1897. These officers—Pavlos Melas, the brothers Mazarakis, and others—were in touch with Stefanos Dragoumis[6] (1842–1923) whose family came from Macedonia and who had been foreign minister in the fifth and sixth governments of Trikoupis. They were also in touch with Karavangelis and other bishops, and they used the cartographical service of the Greek army to run arms to Macedonia. In November 1902 one of their friends, the young Ion Dragoumis, son of Stefanos, was posted as vice-consul to Monastir, from which position he built up a defence organisation which was more elaborate than that of Karavangelis. To him the officers sent funds and to Karavangelis they sent in May 1903 a band of Cretans.

Meanwhile a Macedonian committee under the presidency of Dimitrios Kalapothakis, owner of the newspaper *Embros*, had taken shape in Athens. This committee was tolerated by Theotokis, who had become prime minister for the second time in June 1903. In 1904, under the pressure of public opinion and events, he began to send a new type of consular official to Macedonia to replace the somewhat easy-going and despondent officers who had tended to let matters slide. To Thessaloniki as consul-general he sent Lambros Koromilas, who was soon demanding that military officers should be attached to the consulate as intelligence agents—a plan favoured by Prince Constantine. This demand the Greek government met and it was not long before there were some sixty officers in Macedonia under the guises of schoolmasters, insurance touts, cattle-dealers, factory-managers, and so forth. (One of them even became the abbot of a monastery which occupied a position of strategic importance.) That same year the Greek government sent a four-officer commission to western Macedonia to study the problem in order to arrive at a decision whether the existing local effort was sufficient or whether bands should be sent from Greece. With some hesitation (for the commission reported with two voices) the government decided to act, but not on the scale envisaged by Dragoumis and his circle or by the Macedonian committee. In any case, though at first the government appears to have envisaged retaining a direct control over the bands, in the end, desiring to have an excuse *vis-à-vis* the great powers, it delegated the affairs of western Macedonia to the Macedonian committee. Operations in the *vilayet* (province) of Thessaloniki were placed under the control of Koromilas, who eventually, however, managed to persuade the government to vest in his consulate the strategic control of the struggle throughout the whole of Macedonia.

It fell to Pavlos Melas, who had been appointed commander-in-chief of western Macedonia, to take the first of these bands across the frontier. By the time he arrived Vangelis had been killed (May 1904) and Kota had been

[6] He had sent arms to Macedonia in 1871 and 1878.

captured (June 1904). Melas himself was soon to perish (October 1904). He was destroyed by Turks who were hunting not for him but for the famous I.M.R.O. leader Mitros Vlach. The tragedy made of him the Byron of the third War of Independence. His death achieved what even the chauvinist Athenian press had failed to bring about—the awareness that Greece had vital interests in Macedonia: that if these were not upheld Greece would be overshadowed by a more powerful northern neighbour; that the unredeemed islands would go by default; and that the cause of Hellenism outside the confines of the national kingdom would be irretrievably lost. Hitherto the Macedonian problem had been the concern only of a small section of the Greek people: it now became one of great national concern, and volunteers now came forward to avenge the death of a very gallant officer. Thereafter numerous bands (which included Cretans and Macedonians) were formed in Greece and made the perilous journey from the Greek frontier to the scene of action.

As the Greeks were soon to discover, only relatively small bands could survive in Macedonia. But even these small bands could never have survived without the elaborate organisation built up by Koromilas and his officers, who, needless to say, made good use of the existing organisations. At any given time there were not more than 2,000 Greek combatants in the field, but there were thousands of Greeks in the civilian service that made possible the operations of the bands—civilians who supplied intelligence, who arranged for the transport of arms, food, and ammunition, who carried messages, and so forth. This organisation worked quietly and in secret. Although important agents frequently visited the consulate-general (access was by way of a small door leading from the metropolitan church), Koromilas had aimed at creating an organisation which could function independently of the consulate, which, for political reasons, must not be too much in evidence. In Thessaloniki itself the organisation was fashioned by Souliotis, whose cover was a shop. He initiated agents for the six sections into which the town was divided and these initiated about ten assistants each. Money was collected as insurance premiums and failure to pay was severely punished by the so-called executive of the organisation (a select band of young men) who also had the duty of assassinating those people of importance who were working for I.M.R.O. or for the exarchists. One of the chief tasks of the organisation was to wage economic warfare against the exarchists who in recent years had increased in numbers in Thessaloniki. Greek shops were established and building-workers were brought in from Epiros, the aim being to drive the exarchists out of business. Greeks were encouraged and assisted to buy up exarchist property, and a general economic boycott was imposed upon all schismatics. The result was that Thessaloniki acquired more and more the appearance of a Greek city. Certainly, the Greeks were outnumbered by Jews and Turks, but they succeeded in reducing the number of Slavs and they prevented the city from harbouring hostile bands. Later this economic warfare was carried into other cities of Macedonia, all of which came to have organisations similar to that of Thessaloniki.

IV. The Military Operations of the Bands

The chief tasks of the Greek bands were to seek out and destroy the I.M.R.O.-exarchist bands (which were mainly composed of Macedonians), to protect the villages and small towns, to restore to the Patriarchate those communities which had been forced to declare for the Exarchate, to establish small local bands to hold 'territory' gained, and to keep open the supply-routes. To do all this it was essential that the bands should survive, that they should avoid clashes with the Turkish forces which were primarily interested in attacking I.M.R.O., that they should be able to roam far and wide, paying frequent visits to the villages. Freedom of movement was of greater importance than spectacular encounters, which, however, could not always be avoided, for bands were sometimes surrounded or ambushed in or near the villages, not infrequently by the Turks, who were never certain whether they were in contact with Greeks or I.M.R.O. Needless to say, many of the villages suffered damage or casualties.

To fulfil these aims the Greeks found that bands must include a large proportion of local men who knew not only the terrain but the enemies to be sought out. Neither the Greek officers and N.C.O.s nor the Cretans (who went to Macedonia in large numbers after fighting had died down in Crete) could have survived without the help of these local men, many of whom had lived under the kleftic conditions that had continued to exist in Turkish Macedonia. These klefts (or *haiduks* in Slav parlance) were to be found on either side, either as members of the large bands or as leaders of their own small units. They took sides in accordance with old enmities and affiliations, with their partialities for the patriarchic or exarchic Churches, with vague notions of political possibilities, and even with the attraction of pay, the Greeks being more generous than their enemies. These local men and indeed the Cretans sometimes created difficulties for the Greek leaders: they were often indisciplined, too harsh on the villages, and too much inclined to attack the Turks.

The plan of campaign was drawn up in Thessaloniki by Konstantinos Mazarakis. It was not carried out in every detail, but a reading of it makes intelligible the apparently confused military operations of the Greek formations. The plan was to concentrate on Morihovo to the north-east of Monastir, and to form a salient there for future operations. But to gain control of that region it was necessary to dominate a wide band of territory running from Kastoria and Monastir, to Gradesnitsa and Vodena (Edhessa), to the area lying north of Yanitsa, the plain and lake of Yanitsa (Rumlouki), Naousa, and east of the Vardar towards Doiran, Serres, and Drama. For these operations some eleven major bands (which could be split into smaller bands as required) were needed, and they must, as far as possible, maintain a continuous line of communication. As for the somewhat isolated Greek centres lying to the north of the area envisaged for operations (Krushevo and Meleniko for example), these must be left for the time being to fend for themselves.

Over the four years 1905–08 the Greek bands, many remaining in Macedonia to face the severe winters, roamed the mountains and villages, inflicting heavy casualties on the I.M.R.O.-exarchist bands, notables, and agents, and indeed sometimes on the Turks. Gradually they established a supremacy, evident from the ever-reduced scale of enemy operations. During that struggle they lost some 640 fighting men and agents (a figure which excludes the numerous victims, including women and children, who, though not officially in the Greek organisation, lost their lives in village battles). Of the I.M.R.O.-exarchist losses, no exact information is available, but they were certainly many times larger than the Greek. For seven years, Turkish troops took a heavy toll of the so-called *comitadjis* (committee men). In addition, I.M.R.O. suffered heavily at the hands not only of the Greeks but also of the Serbs who in the north established their own Macedonian organisation and sent numerous bands across their frontier.

The Greek (and Serbian) victory in the armed struggle in Macedonia did not win Macedonia or any part of it for Greece or Serbia; but it prevented what later became Greek and Serbian Macedonia from being lost. This victory the Greeks owed to their superior military and administrative organisation, to the intrinsic strength of Hellenism in Macedonia, to a degree of tolerance on the part of the Turks, and to the divisions in the Bulgarian–Macedonian movement, with its confused and conflicting aims and its strange mixture of sheer terrorism, social revolution, and religious propaganda. True, the Hellenism of Athens and the Hellenism of Macedonia were not always the same, but the conflicting aims did not materially weaken the Greek Macedonian movement. In Macedonia the two forces worked together in some sort of harmony: the leadership and supplies from Greece were vital to Hellenism in Macedonia, which the Turks tolerated, thus rendering the combined movement much less objectionable than Hellenism directed as a crusade solely from Athens. What is more, the Greek officers in Macedonia maintained a degree of discipline which was lacking in other quarters. Although they fought with much brutality and removed known enemies with merciless efficiency, they were on the whole much kinder to the villages. They had ample funds and they paid well for services (even for those rendered by needy Turks). Hence many villages came to side with Hellenism not so much because they preferred the Patriarchate as because they were hostile to the excesses of I.M.R.O., whose intervention the Exarch had every reason to deplore.

V. Greek Foreign Policy during the Macedonian Struggle

In view of the growing tension between Bulgaria and Turkey, and of the increasing attacks on Hellenism in Macedonia, Greece not only attempted to improve her relations with the Porte but in May 1899 renewed negotiations with Serbia. These, like the negotiations of 1890–93, foundered on the question of Macedonia. Greece had claimed a sphere of influence extending as far north as Nevrokopi, Strumitsa, and Krushevo in return for recognition of a Serbian sphere towards Dibra, Veles, and Radovishta, and for Greek support of the appointment of three Serbian bishops in Uskub, Prizrend, and Veles-Dibra. More substantive were the improved relations with Turkey, who had in some measure become reconciled to the virtual loss of Crete and who feared the Bulgarian–Macedonian propaganda much more than Hellenism. On their side the Greeks saw that, for the time being, the defence of Hellenism in Macedonia depended on Turkish goodwill and the continuation of Turkish rule. For that same reason they welcomed the attempts of the powers to restrain Sofia and to prevail upon the Turks to maintain order and introduce reforms in Macedonia. Furthermore, they improved their relations with Germany who had influence at Constantinople, and they displayed a growing aversion to Russia, whom they suspected of encouraging Bulgaria. They were suspicious, too, of the Russian–Austrian *entente* which perhaps foreboded a Balkan deal to the detriment of Greek interests. As for Great Britain, although they were grateful for past services, they were doubtful of services to come, and they were to find Lansdowne, the British foreign secretary, too neglectful of Greek interests and much too gullible to Bulgarian propaganda. He had the merit, however, of appearing to restrain Russia and of encouraging the Turks to keep order in Macedonia.

It was chiefly owing to British initiative that Austria and Russia were prompted, following the rising in Razlog in north-east Macedonia in October 1902,[7] to draw up and to watch over on behalf of the European Concert, the execution of what is known as the Vienna Reform Scheme, which was presented to the Porte in February 1903. This provided for an inspector-general of the Macedonian *vilayets*, the employment of foreign specialists in the police and gendarmerie, to which Christians should be admitted, certain budgetary and judicial reforms, and an amnesty—a programme which the Greeks welcomed because it maintained a *status quo*, because there was no provision for Macedonian autonomy which Lansdowne was known to favour, and because the inspector-general, Hilmi Pasha, who was a friend of Hellenism, was likely to reduce exarchist influence.

This reform programme, however, remained a dead letter. It was strongly opposed by the Albanians, who, already in revolt, tied down 50,000 Turkish

---

[7] This was hardly a rising, but an incursion of Bulgarian bands belonging to the external organisations. I.M.R.O. opposed it. It was put down by the Turks with a certain degree of severity much misrepresented in the European press.

troops that could ill be spared from Macedonia, where in the spring of 1903 I.M.R.O. had organised some ninety chief bands with a total membership of about 2,700. As we have seen, in August I.M.R.O. staged the so-called Ilinden rising in western Macedonia, which the Turks, with some assistance from the Greeks, put down with efficiency and severity. This action they followed up with a steady drive against the I.M.R.O. bands. In some 150 encounters they had, by the end of November, wiped out about 750 *comitadjis*.

The Ilinden rising had taken the Bulgarian government by surprise. At the time the prime minister, General Petrov, was trying to improve relations with Turkey and he had closed down the Macedonian committees. Under popular pressure, however, he had to make the best of the situation created by Ilinden by voicing protests, by producing exaggerated accounts of Turkish atrocities, and by ordering mobilisation. But all he succeeded in doing was to impress the powers with the need for further reform measures and not, as was hoped, a radical solution of the Macedonian problem.

The new reform programme of October 1903, known as the Mürzsteg programme, was, like its predecessor, chiefly the result of British initiative, and, like its predecessor, it rejected the scheme for a Christian governor, an idea which Lansdowne had put forward. Instead, two civil agents, one Austrian, the other Russian, were to be attached to Hilmi Pasha for two years, their function being to call his attention to abuses and to keep their own governments fully informed. The task of reorganising the Ottoman gendarmerie was to be entrusted to a foreign general in the Ottoman service: to him were to be attached foreign officers from the five powers, each nationality taking charge of a zone. Various other reforms were proposed, but the most important article of the programme was the one stating that as soon as some measure of pacification had been effected, the powers would demand of the Ottoman government 'a modification of the territorial boundaries and administrative units, with a view to a more regular grouping of the different nationalities'. This article was important because it was entirely misunderstood by the Bulgars, Serbs, and Greeks, who took it not as an intention to make minor local adjustments in administrative divisions, but as an invitation to stake out claims for consideration in the event of a partition of Macedonia. The Greek government certainly interpreted the article in this way and it was this interpretation which was a vital factor in its decision to intervene in Macedonia.

With the Mürzsteg programme, as with the Vienna programme, the Greeks had every reason to be satisfied, and it was fortunate for them that Lansdowne and the totally misinformed but influential London Balkan committee had been unable to prevail upon the Concert of powers to promote plans for Macedonian autonomy. It was also fortunate for the Greeks that the reform programmes were a failure, for the failure provided a very plausible excuse for the prosecution of the Macedonian struggle, which the new gendarmerie (despite its superficial efficiency) was totally unfitted to terminate. When in November 1905 Austria and Russia made protests in Athens, Belgrade, and Sofia against the band warfare, Skouzes, the Greek foreign minister, was able to reply that the Greeks of Macedonia were acting entirely in self-defence. This reply he was to give with monotonous regularity, and when it was pointed out to him that bands were being organised in Greece or that a Greek band was known to have crossed the frontier, he—a past master in irrelevant, desultory, and good-humoured conversation—would question the facts, talk about smugglers on the move, draw attention to the inadequacy of the Greek police and frontier forces, point out that Cretans and Macedonians were Turkish subjects, and invariably end up by producing a formidable list of crimes committed in Macedonia against the Greeks. He never found it so easy, however, to explain away the memorial services held in Athens for Greek officers who perished while fighting with the bands. All he could do was to promise to keep an eye on Greek military personnel and to punish them if they were caught crossing the frontier. His levity clearly showed that the dangers for Greece were less than in 1897. To the Turks the Greek bands were not unwelcome: not only did they help to neutralise the Slav movement, but they went a long way to proving the Turkish thesis that the disorders in Macedonia were not the result of Turkish tyranny but the outcome of the hatreds among the Christians and of the machinations of the Balkan powers.

During the year 1906, by which time the Greek bands had gained the upper hand and the danger from I.M.R.O. had receded, the Turks began to show greater hostility towards both the Greek government and the Patriarchate. In May 1906 the grand vizier requested the Patriarch to remove the metropolitan of Monastir and later that year, following representations from the British ambassador at Constantinople, he drew the Patriarch's attention to the subversive activities of the bishops of Grevena, Drama, and Kastoria. Against these activities the British had already protested at Athens, at the same time calling attention to the greater number of political murders perpetrated by Greeks than those for which I.M.R.O. were responsible. In his reply Skouzes had the better of the argument. He was able to supply the names of over 800 patriarchist victims, pointing out once again that the terrorist activities in Macedonia were originated by the exarchist-I.M.R.O. bands and that there were still hundreds of patriarchist villages which had yet to be freed from exarchist control. Nevertheless, the Greek government, in response to protests, withdrew Koromilas from the consulate-general at Thessaloniki, knowing full well that the organisation he had created could go on working without his control. Similarly the Patriarch withdrew the offending prelates, simply because it was politic to do so.

VI. The Cretan Question, 1890–1906

In representations made to the Greek government in November 1906,

Grey, who had replaced Lansdowne as British foreign secretary, threatened that if Greece were not reasonable on the Macedonian issue, then Great Britain would no longer support her in Crete. But this threat was not to be taken seriously. In Crete the danger for Greece was not so much the lack of support as the excess of support which might cause Greek gains in Crete to become a justification for Slav gains in Macedonia. The Greek king and his government knew perfectly well that Grey would not reverse the policy of keeping the Macedonian and Cretan questions apart in face of Russian efforts to bring them together. Much more alarming than Grey's empty threat was the opposition in Athens, which fiercely criticised Theotokis and Skouzes for their failure to take a strong line on both issues. What the opposition failed to realise was that affairs in Macedonia were going none too badly and that to raise the issue of Crete might place in jeopardy the Hellenism of Macedonia. What that same opposition also failed to realise was that the regular Greek military forces were as yet inadequately armed— a deficiency which Theotokis was doing his best to remedy.

In Crete the old demand for union with Greece was still being voiced by the Cretan assembly and by Prince George himself who had become much attached to his Cretans and a convert to their ideas. Under his rule, which began in December 1898, a constitution had been fashioned, a judicial code (the work of Venizelos) had been promulgated, and a gendarmerie had been established to keep law and order. The island had settled down quickly to peaceful habits and into this general pacification the Moslem population had entered with goodwill. But Prince George's mandate was designed in the first instance only for three years and there was a widespread conviction that it would be followed by *enosis* with Greece. Just over a year before his mandate expired Prince George, in a memorandum to the powers, advocated that Crete should become a part of Greece. This proposal the powers rejected: instead they expressed the hope that the prince would accept the renewal of his mandate for a further term. The prince then proposed that the Greek king should take over the provisional administration of Crete by an arrangement analogous to that existing between Austria–Hungary and Bosnia–Herzegovina. But this proposal, too, was rejected by the powers and the prince accepted a second term of office.

During these discussions Prince George came into conflict with Venizelos, the councillor for justice, with whom he had already had some difficulty. Venizelos, whatever he may have said at an earlier date, wanted for Crete not union with Greece but principality status with an elected prince or president. He expressed these views in an Athenian newspaper and Prince George, having consulted his father, dismissed him from office. This began a quarrel which, some four years later, was to bring the Cretan question again to the immediate notice of Europe and to raise the possibility of its becoming entangled with that of Macedonia. In March 1905, having failed to create in the assembly a strong opposition to Prince George's rule,

Venizelos retired with 600 armed followers to the mountains of Therissos to raise the standard of revolt. He had been supplied with money and arms from Greece. By then he had dropped his demand for principality status for Crete and under pressure from his supporters was again demanding *enosis*, hoping thereby to gain popular backing for the insurgents of Therissos. But the popular demand for *enosis* was very adequately represented by Prince George and by the majority of the Cretan assembly. On 20 April 1905 that assembly proclaimed *enosis* with Greece and requested Prince George to inform the powers. This he did: but the powers refused to recognise the declaration. Venizelos, hoping to steal a march on Prince George, dropped his demand for *enosis* and proposed to the consuls of the powers that Crete should be linked to Greece on the lines of eastern Rumelia's union with Bulgaria. Nothing came, however, of this proposal.

Prince George, who was loath to use his loyal gendarmes to spill Greek blood in putting down the rebels, thought of resigning, but, when he consulted the Greek government, he was advised to carry on as best he could. This he did despite the hostility of the European consuls, and the increasing self-confidence of the insurgents. Eventually, however, on 15 July 1905 the powers, holding out hopes of an amnesty, gave the rebels fifteen days to lay down their arms, while the Cretan assembly offered to admit a number of them to its deliberations, provided that these representatives did not raise the issue of the prince's powers. But neither the ultimatum nor the assembly's offer was acceptable to Venizelos, who virtually demanded that the insurgents of Therissos should be given a majority in the assembly at Chania. On 30 July the consuls proclaimed martial law and shortly afterwards the assembly formed a rural militia which the Cretans rushed to join. This measure the prince supported. He thus ignored the advice of Rallis, the Greek prime minister from June to December 1905, who throughout adopted an equivocal attitude. He likewise ignored Rallis's advice to ratify a bill permitting the Cretans to carry arms. Nevertheless, it was on Rallis's suggestion that he acted when he called upon the assembly to revise the constitution. The result of this revision (secret ballot, plural-member constituencies, elective mayors and local councils, freedom of the press, and the abolition of the prince's right to appoint ten deputies) deprived the insurgents (many of whom had already shown signs of weakening) of most of their pretexts; and on 2 November Venizelos reached an agreement with the consuls: the rebels would surrender 700 rifles and return to their homes provided the local militia were abolished. This agreement Prince George, who had not been consulted, accepted under protest. He was forced also to accept an international commission to report on the whole situation of the island.

It was at this point that Russia, hoping to prepare a case for the compensation of the Slavs in Macedonia, came forward (16 March 1906) with a proposal that the administration of Crete should be handed over to the Greek kingdom, provided that Greece recognised Turkish suzerainty over the island and gave an undertaking to withdraw all opposition to the Macedonian reform programme. But when Isvolsky succeeded Lamsdorf at the Russian foreign ministry, this proposal was allowed to lapse and shortly afterwards the international commission (exceeding its terms of reference) pronounced that the only solution of the Cretan question was the speedy union of the island with Greece. This was tantamount to saying that Prince George (who was indeed happier when in command of a ship) was totally incapable of ruling Crete under a constitutional regime.

The commission's proposal that Crete should be joined to Greece found little favour with the British government. They had consulted King George who was against it and they feared moreover that it was likely to play into the hands of Russia. They therefore put forward other proposals: the Greek king (not the government) should nominate another high commissioner in place of Prince George; Greek officers should reorganise the Cretan militia; the international troops should be withdrawn; and the Greek government should give an undertaking not to annex Crete without the consent of the powers. But these proposals satisfied neither Russia nor France. Further negotiations followed and these resulted in a collective Note submitted to Prince George on 23 July and on the following day to his father. This Note contained the following proposals: the reform of the gendarmerie; the creation of a militia in which Greek officers (not on the active list) should co-operate; the placing of both organisations under the orders of the high commissioner; a loan of 9,300,000 francs under the control of the financial commission in Athens; the complete equality of Moslems and Christians; and the appointment of a mixed commission to deal with religious administrative problems. But this Note satisfied neither the Cretan assembly nor the Greek king and government. The king advised Prince George to reject it, and the Greek government sent Boufidis to Crete to enlist the opposition of the Venizelists. But Venizelos saw that, given the international situation, the proposed settlement was the most that could be expected for the time being: he also saw that, as long as the support of Great Britain was retained, Crete would eventually gain union with Greece. In holding this view he was not alone. Both Queen Alexandra and Crown Prince Constantine (who was on a visit to London) sent telegrams to King George stressing the importance of not alienating Great Britain. The result was that King George advised his son to resign his office. This advice the prince, who had had an uncommonly bad deal, reluctantly accepted for the sake of his country and for the island which he had come to love and which he was loath to leave. In his place King George appointed Alexandros Zaimis, the former prime minister of Greece, who arrived in Crete on 1 October.

VII. Greek Proposals for an Alliance with France and Great Britain, June–July 1907

Although King George, Theotokis, and Skouzes had reason to resent

British policy in Macedonia and to be disappointed with her tendency to compromise on Crete, yet they were all well aware that Great Britain and to some extent France supplied, as indeed did Germany, a check to Russia. They had also sensed a change in Austrian policy. They were aware, from information given by the Turks, that Aehrenthal, who had replaced Goluchowski at the Austro–Hungarian foreign ministry in October 1906, was attempting to bring Bulgaria and Turkey together and was encouraging the Sultan to deal firmly with the Greek and Serbian bands in Macedonia. They suspected that he had initiated the *démarche* of 25 May 1907, when complaints were lodged against the activities of the Greek consular officers in Macedonia. They were also conversant with the changing situation in Europe; and although much of the detail was unknown to them, the principal lines of development were common knowledge, blurred and distorted though they might be by much speculation. Imagining that a Mediterranean league had been formed by Great Britain, France, Spain, Portugal, and Italy, in June 1907 Theotokis, with the king's approval, approached France, suggesting that Greece should become a member. A month later he made a similar approach to Great Britain. He pointed out to both powers the possibility of an Austrian–German–Turkish alignment and questioned the wisdom of encouraging Bulgarian aspirations, the implication being that Bulgaria was likely to join that alignment, whereas the friendship of Greece for the Western powers would be more rewarding and strategically more satisfactory.

The British response was cool: Britain could never bind herself by secret agreements; if Greece, however, wished to maintain British friendship, she must suppress her bands in Macedonia. But the French government showed much interest in the Greek proposals and sent to Greece Admiral Fournier, a naval expert, who had conversations with King George. The outcome was that the king asked him to submit his naval plans. These he discussed with the French foreign minister, Pichon, the following November. He then not only requested that Fournier should be placed at the disposal of the Greek government but that a loan should be made available to carry out both the naval plans and the reorganisation of the Greek army. On 12 November Pichon informed his minister in Athens that as soon as the Greek government stated officially its intention to entrust Fournier with the reorganisation of the Greek navy, he would then reply to Theotokis, employing a formula agreed on with the king, to the effect that although it was French policy to maintain the *status quo* in Macedonia, should the *status quo* be disturbed, then France would make every effort to safeguard the interests of Greece.

Fournier's view was that Greece should substitute for her weak and costly fleet a naval establishment more appropriate to her resources, national aptitude, geographical position, and strategic conditions. Her navy should consist of torpedo-boats and submarines, supported by small, well-armed cruisers or destroyers. If Greece possessed a fleet of this kind, the two Western powers would be bound to align with Greece and would, as a matter of course, ensure the protection of Hellenic interests in Crete and Macedonia. In other words, the Greek navy was to become a purely auxiliary force, and, since France would get the contracts for the construction of the vessels required, it would be so closely tied to the French naval system that it would be of little use to the central powers if by chance it fell under their control. But it was precisely for these reasons that the plan, news of which had leaked out, encountered fierce opposition in Greece and, much to the disappointment of Clemenceau, it foundered in the stormy seas of Greek politics.

Meanwhile, greatly to the chagrin of the king and Theotokis, Great Britain continued to nag away at the Macedonian issue and, what was worse, was co-operating closely with Russia following the Anglo–Russian *entente* of August 1907. This they feared foreboded a deal on Macedonia to the dis-advantage of Greece. Grey's speeches in the House of Commons were cer-tainly ominous. Although he did not accept the facile assumptions of the Balkan committee, although he said that Macedonia was not a unit but a geographical expression, he was canvassing the idea of a semi-independent governor (either Christian or Moslem) for a period of time—a proposal which he at length put forward in a circular Note of 3 March 1908. Against this idea Skouzes had already protested to the British minister in Athens: to appoint a governor for Macedonia was a 'tendency to the creation of a new Eastern Rumelia destined to have the same fate as the first'; the only solution of the Macedonian question was to divide the province into spheres of influence, shared by the Serbian government.

In point of fact, however, the British and the Russians were not so close together as the Greeks imagined. Neither Russia nor France for that matter took Grey's proposals very seriously: they both thought that Grey's move was a mere sop to liberal opinion in England. Russia promptly put forward counter-proposals, which she had discussed with Austria, and these became the subject of long, tedious, and inconclusive negotiations throughout the summer, during which the Greeks fought yet another successful campaign of the Macedonian struggle.

VIII. The Young Turk Revolution of 1908

This Greek campaign and the tedious Macedonian negotiations of the powers were suddenly cut short when the Young Turk revolution in Mace-donia issued, on 24 July 1908, in the restoration of the Turkish constitution of 1876 and the announcement of elections in which the Christian popu-lations were to take part. The fighting stopped as if by magic and many warring bandsmen came down from the mountains to fraternise with the Turkish troops in the towns and large villages. Even the Greek metropol-itan of Serres and the president of the Bulgarian revolutionary committee of that town are said to have met in fraternal embrace. There were banquets and much speech-making, which in Thessaloniki went on for several days. The prisons were emptied and prominent exiles were allowed to return. The Greek bishop of Monastir, after two years' absence, went back to his diocese escorted by bands of his flock. When Chrisostomos entered Drama he was greeted by 4,000 souls, and on being welcomed home by the chairman of the local Turk committee he enigmatically replied that he had come to reap the harvest of the good seed he had sown before he left.

From the warring Christians the Young Turk conspirators (as distinct from the intellectual Young Turks who had for a long while been working out their ideologies) learned that conspiracy could be successful and that resolute men could defeat the Sultan's espial system. In particular they had much admiration for the Greeks, and, like the old Turks, they saw that they had need of them. With Bulgaria they would happily have gone to war, but they had also seen the need to make use of the Bulgarian Macedonian organisation. They likewise established good relations with the Jews, Armenians, and Albanians. With the Greeks they had particularly close relations. Their committee in Thessaloniki met in a house belonging to a Greek; they were on friendly terms with Koromilas; and they used the Greek band organisation (which had a good grip on communications) to pass their agents through Macedonia. In return the Greek bands enjoyed the use of several *chifliks* (Turkish estates) where they could carouse and rest. How well the Young Turks had organised themselves it is difficult to say; but what is certain is that like all conspirators they were called upon to act before preparations had been completed. The Sultan, aware of subversion, had sent a commission to investigate it. One Enver Bey was invited to Constantinople 'to receive promotion'. Suspecting the worst, he took to the mountains, where he was followed by Major Niazi with a considerable body of troops. Officers sent to restore order were promptly despatched and thereafter the revolution spread like wildfire until on 21 July a demand, supported by threats, for the restitution of the constitution was sent to the Yildiz (the Sultan's palace).

When the constitution was proclaimed, not all bands made submission. Most Greek bands slipped quietly across the southern frontier. Most of the twenty-six bands (217 men) which submitted were entirely local. Of the fifty-five I.M.R.O.-exarchist bands (707 men) which came in, nearly all were composed of 'militia' peasants. The arms handed in were nearly all useless. The more treasured firearms and supplies of ammunition were hidden in readiness for another day. Those who surrendered had fought as Macedonian factions and not consciously as agents of Greek, Serbian, and Bulgarian nationalism. They had certainly welcomed pay from the Balkan capitals and assistance from intruders. But I.M.R.O. in particular had always been suspicious of Bulgaria and would have preferred autonomy within the Turkish empire to incorporation in the principality. Even among the

Greeks there were many whose aim, fantastic as it may seem, was to hellenise the Turkish empire rather than to aggrandise the Greek kingdom. Such was the aim of Souliotis who, having created the Greek organisation in Thessaloniki, went later to create an organisation, with the Patriarch's approval, at Constantinople. His view was that Athens should align with Constantinople: Greece must preserve Turkey: if Turkey were dismembered, then other powers would divide the spoils and Hellenism would be the loser. These ideas were shared by Ion Dragoumis, another chief architect of the Macedonian struggle, who like his friend Souliotis had gone on to work in Constantinople. His view was that the armed struggle in Macedonia was a necessary evil, which might have dangerous consequences, since it could easily lead to a dismemberment of Turkey by the Slavs. To him the Young Turk revolution offered a gleam of hope. If the Young Turks really intended to modernise the multi-racial state, the Greek élite would come back into its own: it would run the empire and restore to it many of the characteristics of its Byzantine predecessor. This too was the attitude of many of the clergy who played an important role in the Macedonian struggle. Whether this is true of Karavangelis of Kastoria it is hard to say. He gives no clear indication in his memoirs. Though the Turks had him removed from western Macedonia to satisfy the powers, he had never shown antagonism to Ottoman rule. It was he, probably, who betrayed Kota to the authorities simply because Kota was too much a kleft and too antagonistic to the local Turks, many of whom were Karavangelis's friends.

The clergy in the main had little use for the Young Turks. The Patriarch Joachim said they were merely a nine days' wonder. This remark he made to Rallis, the leader of the Greek parliamentary opposition who, after a visit to Thessaloniki, went on to Constantinople to confer with Greek circles there. At first he showed much enthusiasm for the new regime. At an official reception at the Young Turk committee in Thessaloniki, without having consulted the Greek officers at the consulate, he was stupid enough to say that, as Greece had the greatest faith in the new regime, the hundred Greek officers (there were only sixty) could now return home. He had betrayed the organisation. The Young Turks immediately ordered the officers to leave and began to exercise a surveillance that was infinitely stricter than under the old regime. When finally Rallis returned to Athens, he had quite changed his views: he was all for continuing the Macedonian struggle and even sending bands to Thrace and Asia Minor.

Despite the betrayal of the officers and many Greek agents by former accomplices who had been won over by the Young Turks, the Greek organisation remained intact and eventually succeeded in despatching those who had turned traitor. Likewise the I.M.R.O.-exarchist organisation continued to function and the armed struggle, resumed in October 1908, continued, though on a reduced scale, for the next four years. From this struggle the Young Turks endeavoured to remain aloof, hoping to divert efforts from what to them was a senseless vendetta to political channels provided by the constitution. They hoped that the parliamentary elections would substitute orderly rivalry for band warfare and political murders. In these elections, weighted in favour of the Moslems, the Macedonian factions indeed took part, each fearing to stand to lose if it abstained.[8]

During the preparations for these elections there developed, as a rival to the Greek, Serbian, and Bulgarian national democratic parties, a national federal party led by Macedonian socialists who had long been in conflict with I.M.R.O. and the exarchists, and who now aimed at gaining the support of socialists in other parts of the empire. This development alarmed the Young Turks who had fondly expected that the subject peoples would accept their leadership. Instead they found themselves confronted with parties aiming either at local autonomies or at taking over the Ottoman empire. As a ruling party they too had changed in outlook. After the failure of the Turkish counter-revolution of April 1909, a nationalist wing of the Young Turk party gained control. Gone entirely was the idea of a decentralised state in which people of the various creeds and races were to find freedom in equality of citizenship. The new policy was to ottomanise the empire, to abolish the nationalist organisations, and to disarm the warring factions. By the end of 1910 the Young Turk regime had become a tyranny more unbearable than the old Hamidian system. So severe indeed was their regime in Macedonia that 'Bulgarians' and 'Greeks' entered into a series of local truces and often settled their church problems by negotiation.

On the Cretan question the Young Turks were particularly stubborn and unimaginative. In October 1908 the Cretan assembly again demanded union with Greece. This demand was resisted by Great Britain, who had shown favour to the Young Turk regime. In August 1909, however, the new Young Turk government demanded from Athens written disapproval of the agitation in Crete and combined this demand with protests against Greek activities in Macedonia. Rallis, who had succeeded Theotokis in July 1909, replied that Greece would respect the decisions of the protecting powers, and the powers themselves informed the Turks that they had no right to address themselves directly to Greece on the Cretan question. There the matter rested until in May 1910 the Christian Cretans repeated their demand for *enosis*, having already attempted to impose on the Moslem deputies in the assembly an oath of fidelity to the king of Greece. Under pressure from the powers and in view of a boycott which the Turks had imposed upon Greek trade, the Greek government urged Venizelos to damp down the Cretans. This, with the aid of the consuls who threatened to occupy the customs-house at Chania, he succeeded in doing, but this action failed entirely to satisfy the Turks.

---

[8] For the *vilayet* of Thessaloniki there were 12 deputies (6 Moslems, 3 patriarchists, 2 exarchists, and one Jew). In the whole parliament there were 142 Turks, 60 Arabs, 25 Albanians, 23 patriarchists, 12 Armenians, 5 Jews, 4 exarchists, and one Vlach.

Turkish resentment increased when the Rallis party nominated Venizelos (who could claim Greek nationality) and five Cretans as candidates for the Greek elections for the new assembly which was to meet in September 1910. The Turks even threatened war. On 5 September the powers ruled that if Venizelos accepted election in Greece, he could no longer be recognised as a leader in Crete. Venizelos chose to transfer his activities to Greece, where for over a year fierce political storms had been raging.

CHAPTER 13

Constitutional and Administrative
Reforms of Venizelos

I. The Military Revolution of Goudhi, 1909

The improvement of the Greek armed forces was arrested during 1909 by a military revolution which began as a mutiny of non-commissioned officers against a bill restricting their promotion. But the whole affair had deeper roots. It was symptomatic of widespread hostility to the government and the king, which had increased when the full impact was felt throughout the country of the 1908 economic crisis in Egypt and America, the failure of the olive and tobacco crops, the fall in currant prices, and the increase in taxation. Radical reforms planned by Dimitrios Gounaris when he took over the finances in July 1908 had failed to materialise. Lacking support from his prime minister, Theotokis, and meeting with the opposition of vested interests, he resigned in disgust.

The opposition under Rallis, who had become a worthy successor to Deliyannis, took every chance to attack a government which had been in office since the end of 1905 and had survived long enough to pile up odium upon itself. A general feeling prevailed that Greece was adrift, that she was failing to make the material progress of other nations,[1] and that nothing was being done to protect the Greeks of Turkey from the hostility of the Young Turks. In March 1909 Theotokis, weary of the barren sittings of the chamber, grown more indolent with advancing age, and resentful of the king's lack of support, decided to resign. His pretext was the king's reception of a trade guild's deputation which he had ordered the police to disperse. Rallis, however, was unwilling, even unable, to form a government unless fresh elections were held, but these were to be avoided, for the Cretans had decided to hold elections simultaneously with the next elections in Greece

---

[1] See below, Chapter 17.

180

—a move which, if encouraged, would have provoked the hostility of Turkey and the powers. Theotokis eventually agreed to remain in office, on the understanding that Rallis would not impede the budget and cognate legislation. On 7 April 1909 the budget was passed and the chamber adjourned for Easter.

It was at this point that the non-commissioned officers mutinied, but although this mutiny was easily suppressed, there remained much resentment among regular and reserve officers who had sympathised with the mutineers. Early in July a clique of these officers drew up a demand for the resignation from the army of the crown prince, who was said to have shown favouritism. Theotokis, under fire in the chamber for allegedly mishandling the Cretan issue, resigned on 16 July. The king sent for Rallis, whose terms were: the abolition of the crown prince's post of commander-in-chief; the retirement of all the princes from their military offices; rigid economies; the increase of the army to 180,000 men; the reorganisation of the ministries of war and marine (exactly the proposals which the crown prince had long been advocating). But on taking office, having redistributed the spoils, he dropped his radical programme and began to inquire into army disorders. The result was that four officers were sent before a court of discipline. Certain fellow-officers drew up a manifesto which appeared in the press. Rallis for a while maintained an air of levity, but on 26 August he had several more officers arrested. The next day a deputation of officers, representing a military league of some 1,300, called on Rallis and presented a memorandum of the reforms they desired. This deputation Rallis refused to receive. The next morning at 2 a.m. the whole Athens garrison moved out to the suburb of Goudhi, where they were joined by a regiment of cavalry from Kifissia. From Goudhi the combined force (nearly 5,500 under the command of Colonel Zorbas) threatened to march against Athens if their demands were not accepted by 12 noon.

The demands were: a formal assurance that the chamber would not be dissolved; an amnesty for all those in the movement; the reinstatement of the non-commissioned officers who had been dismissed three months earlier; dismissal from the army of Lieutenant-Colonel Leandros Metaxas, Captain Andreas Kalinsky, and four named lieutenants (who had tried to stop the cavalry from proceeding to Goudhi); and a written acknowledgement of the memorandum on reforms. This contained the following propositions: that the royal princes should not hold responsible offices; that non-political appointments of serving officers should be made to the ministries of war and marine; that the government should introduce reforms in administration, justice, education, and finance; should put an end to jobbery and waste; and increase and improve the armed forces. These terms, though they closely resembled those he himself had put before the king, Rallis refused to consider and tendered his resignation. King George then sent for Kiriakoulis Mavromichalis, the leader of a minority party of twenty-five who had been in close touch with the officers' movement. The new government promptly accepted all the demands of the Goudhi leaders and even offered the post of minister of war to Zorbas, who, however, declined it, not wishing personally to profit from the revolution.

Like Zorbas, the officers as a body were not intent on taking over the functions of government. They had no plans for establishing a military dictatorship. All they wanted was a government which would carry out their programme, which was extremely moderate and conservative. They were not particularly anti-dynastic. Indeed nearly all of them hoped that the king would assist in putting an end to the aimless and futile manoeuvres of the politicians. Towards this end on 27 September they brought out the trade guilds of Athens (where they enjoyed considerable support) to hand resolutions to the palace. The king, whose first inclination was to abdicate, finally decided, on the advice of the French and British ministers and greatly comforted by the presence of British warships, to receive these resolutions and to make a bid for popular support. After all, he had already bowed to the junta by entrusting the government to Mavromichalis; and there was nothing to be lost by showing a kindly face to the populace. To them he said:

> I congratulate you because you express the desires of the people in a peaceable and law-abiding manner as befits constitutional citizens. . . . During the long period of my reign I have aimed at nothing save the interests of the nation, which are also the interests of the throne.

What surprised the extremists in the military league was the display of loyalty towards the king. Indeed the events of that day impressed its limitations upon the league as a whole. It had among its ranks no outstanding figure, and all it could hope was that Mavromichalis and his ministers would introduce satisfactory legislation.

Early in October Mavromichalis announced his programme, appealing to the legislature to legislate instead of talking and to sacrifice party interest upon the altar of patriotism. Eftaxias, the finance minister, called for an increase in revenue of 20 million drachmai to finance naval and military expansion and specific new taxes to finance new loans. When, however, bills concerning army promotions and providing for the abolition of the office of commander-in-chief and of the general staff met with opposition from Dragoumis and other politicians, the officers' league let it be known that if these bills were thrown out, then the government and the chamber would be swept away. The extremists held that even at the risk of the king's abdication, a military dictatorship was the only solution. Under this pressure the bills were passed and signed by the king, who also signed decrees placing Colonel Metaxas on the retired list and dismissing Captain Kalinsky from the service, the officers themselves having requested the king to do so. These dismissals led to a demand for others. Junior naval officers demanded the retirement of all senior officers (except for four post captains). Failing, how-ever, to get their way, they seized the naval arsenal and vessels at Salamis. But, at the request of the league itself, Greek battleships went into action and defeated the mutineers. Thus, the military league had forced the government to put down a naval mutiny. Within a short time it was com-pelling the administration to remove certain functionaries, ministers abroad, and even bishops. It also dictated economic policy, compelling the govern-ment to pass some 160 bills, most of which were badly framed and quite unworkable. Early in 1910 it demanded the dismissal of Mavromichalis, who had failed to render entire satisfaction. Nevertheless, the league itself was divided and in conflict with the marine, which had begun to resent the army's interference in naval matters.

II. The Advent of Venizelos

By that time the league had appointed Venizelos as its spokesman and negotiator with the political parties—a strange prelude to a strange and remarkable career, which was at once a series of inconsistencies and yet a ruthless and calculated pursuit of national aims. Venizelos remained always the opportunist he had been in Crete. Believing like most Greeks that he alone knew what to do and how to do it, he had changed his tactics even to the extent of what appeared to be a change of principles in order to retain leadership. Of principles, however, he was totally devoid. If he appeared to have any—constitutionalism, tolerance, monarchy, and honesty—it was because they all provided useful means which he was always clever enough to disguise as ends. As a politician he was in the first flight: quick and de-cisive in his moves, persuasive and eloquent in speech, a born leader of all those—and they were many—who chose to follow and the object of bitter enmity of those who did not. So commanding a position did he achieve in Greek politics—a position far exceeding that of Trikoupis, who himself had raised fierce hatreds—that those whom he kept out of office and leadership of the country were so bitter that the whole of Greek political life, which though unstable had not been particularly vicious, became venomous and ultimately a scene of undying hatreds. The nearer the Greeks approached a two-party system, the less became their political moderation.

Venizelos had moved to Greece because he saw that the key, or at least one of the keys, to the solution of the Cretan question lay in Athens. He saw, too, that Athens provided greater scope for his talents than did Chania. For some time, several of the officers who had met him in Crete and who were greatly impressed by his ability, had been negotiating for his services. These services he was anxious to render for he saw that, if left to them-selves, the military junta would do irreparable damage to Hellenism, and above all to Crete. It was for this reason that he chose to serve the league rather than join the party of Rallis, who had nominated him for election to parliament and who had hoped to monopolise his talents. In entering the service of the league, however, he let it be known at the outset that he would have nothing to do with a military dictatorship. If that had been the aim of the officers, they had missed their opportunity. What was needed was constitutional change.

By the time Venizelos had become the spokesman of the league, the idea of calling a national assembly to revise the constitution had gained general support. To this idea the king was strongly opposed: according to the constitution of 1864 he had no constituent powers whatever and therefore any would-be nomothete might devise constitutional laws which might deprive the crown not only of its rights under the constitution but of its influence and powers which rested on custom. Upon this matter he consulted Sir Francis Elliot, the British minister, who advised him to discuss the problem with the political leaders. This he did and as a result of these discussions it was agreed to call an assembly and to form, pending the elections, a caretaker government under Stefanos Dragoumis, with Kallergis at the foreign ministry and Colonel Zorbas as minister of war. Before taking office on 1 February 1910, Dragoumis, who had opposed the league and its attack on the princes and who favoured a policy of appeasement *vis-à-vis* Turkey, stipulated that the league must dissolve itself. Many in the league favoured this course, and Venizelos advised it, but in the event the league continued to exist and Dragoumis remained in office.

On 3 March the old chamber in an extraordinary session carried a resolution, 150 to 11, for the convening of a constituent assembly, which, in accordance with the constitution, was to be double the size of the ordinary chamber. At this point the league, according to agreements made, should have dispersed, but once again it failed to do so. It was no longer under the control of Zorbas, but of extremists; its tone had become anti-dynastic; and its aims confused. It tended more and more to defeat its own aims. Nothing was being done to improve the army, for most of the officers, having little better to do, were spending their time on politics. In any case, right from the outset the league's programme had contained a contradiction—the demand for an expansion of the armed forces and a drastic reduction in taxation.

On 29 March, however, the league, chiefly through the influence of Venizelos, was dissolved. It was not, however, until July that the king signed a decree for elections to be held on 21 August. When the day came 150 independents, who did not contest all the 362 seats, were returned. Theotokis and Rallis, who had agreed to divide seats, secured 150 victories between them. The remaining 58 deputies were followers of Zaimis and Mavromichalis. Venizelos, who had headed the poll in Attica-Boeotia, took no part in the campaign. He had returned to Crete where he had become premier following the March elections. His prestige in Greece was considerable. Many of the independents were inclined to follow his leadership, and though they were not a homogeneous group, they had gained a victory over the traditional parties. That victory aroused fears among the old society and in palace circles. It was assumed that if Venizelos attained power, he would straightway attack property and wealth, and display hostility to the monarchy.

On arriving in Greece in September, Venizelos had a great reception from his partisans. He spoke justifying the 'revolution'. Great was everyone's surprise, however, when he said that the assembly should be a revisionary and not a constituent body; that, although in his opinion the powers of the crown had not always been advantageously exercised, he himself believed in monarchy; that he would form a party of principles which would work for the material and moral elevation of Greece; and that he hoped the king would encourage a reform programme. Here indeed he showed his genius and his opportunism. Like any Whig or Tory he believed that monarchy, with himself behind the throne, was a reasonable form of government, and he therefore turned a revolutionary situation in which there were strong anti-dynastic undertones into a movement for constitutional reform. But the king too showed that he had political wisdom in abundance. He was quick to realise that Venizelos's opportunism did not rule out moderation. He saw, moreover, that Venizelos was the only man who would lead the officers back to their proper avocations; and he even had hopes that Venizelos would restore the princes to their posts in the army. He therefore gave Venizelos his full support, thus preserving the monarchy and avoiding a republican revolution which might have left the Greek state disorganised for many a year.

The old party leaders, Theotokis and Rallis, who were pledged to one another not to take office, attempted to bring about the fall of the Dragoumis administration in the hope of forcing Venizelos to form a government while he was in a minority. In this they succeeded. Dragoumis resigned on 12 October, whereupon Venizelos took office. There followed six weeks of recriminations. Arguing that the assembly was a revisionary and not a constituent body Venizelos demanded a vote of confidence, threatening to resign if he were defeated. But although he in fact gained a majority of votes he claimed to have been defeated, since 51 Theotokists had voted for him only conditionally. He therefore asked the king to accept his resignation. But although the king refused this, he granted him a dissolution, and at new elections of December 1910 for yet another double revisionary assembly he obtained at least 260 seats out of a total 362, the opposition parties (except for the Zaimists) having abstained from taking part. The total of votes cast, however, was only 8 per cent below that of the previous election. He may therefore be said to have gained a resounding victory. Not all his followers were new men: they represented that stratum in Greek society which had grown in size since Trikoupis's day and which was in revolt against the old oligarchic factions and the semi-patrician leaders.

The new party, which in the fully contested elections of March 1912 was returned again, this time with some 145 seats to 36, consisted chiefly of the growing trading and commercial classes (including many landowners), of men from the professions, and of a younger generation of service officers. The remainder consisted of agrarians from Thessaly, socialists (whose thunder Venizelos had stolen), republicans from the left wing of the old military league, a large sprinkling of men from the old Trikoupist connection, and *bona fide* converts from the more conservative groupings. To a large extent the so-called liberal party consisted of a personal following of Venizelos, or rather of an amalgam of the personal followings of lesser leaders who were either close to him or who chose to make their way by supporting him. What he fashioned was not so much a liberal party as a parliamentary dictatorship. Although he formed liberal associations in the constituencies, these did not provide an organisation which imposed control upon a central office and accepted direction from above. When all is said, they were not so vastly different from the local groups of friends composing the other parties. They added, perhaps, a semblance of strength and unity to the party, but beneath the surface there were divisions and rivalries. These Venizelos, like Trikoupis before him, kept under control, for he had that power which derived from his strong parliamentary position. He appeared even to be unassailable. But a strong parliamentary position cut both ways in Greece. The lack of strong opposition from without could give rise to conspiracy within. In any event, Venizelos did not represent the whole of Greece. In the constituencies there were large minorities of voters who were unrepresented, and if for the time being there was no sizeable opposition in the chamber, there were plenty of anti-Venizelists in the country at large.

III. The Reforms and Administration of Venizelos

Between October 1910 and the summer of 1912 Venizelos dominated Greece. During the first six months of 1911 he carried through fifty-three amendments of the non-fundamental articles of the constitution. He made no radical changes. Having insisted on a revisionary instead of a constituent assembly, he was able to preserve the essentials of the 1864 constitution and even to strengthen the position of the monarchy. Even in the process of revision the king had a place. In contravention of the letter of the 1864 constitution (Article CVII) the initiative for changes, instead of resting with the chamber of deputies, was assumed by a committee which the king often attended. In other ways too the procedure adopted differed from that laid down in 1864. The resolution to amend the constitution was passed only once in an ordinary chamber instead of in two successive sessions. What is more, the number of amendments promulgated exceeded the thirty which had originally been agreed in 1910.

Among the amendments were: measures to delineate and to safeguard the separation of the judiciary, the legislature, and the administration; the creation of a council of state, a consultative body for the preparation of bills and a court of appeal in administrative cases (which had been provided for in the constitution of 1864 but had been abolished shortly afterwards); exclusion of officers on the active list and public functionaries from serving as deputies; reduction of the parliamentary quorum from one-half plus one to one-third—a measure to put an end to a practice whereby opposition groups could hold up legislation; reduction of the age qualification of deputies from thirty to twenty-five; provision of a council of lawyers to verify returns, to save parliamentary time, and to avoid political sharp practice; disqualification of directors of banks and public companies from sitting in the assembly; security of tenure of judges and public officials; transfer of the administration of primary education (made compulsory and free) from the local authority to the central government; definition of the right of the state to expropriate private property on grounds of 'public benefit' instead of 'public necessity'; and powers to suspend in times of crisis guarantees against arbitrary arrest, right of public meeting, liberty of the press, trial by jury, and inviolability of domicile and correspondence.

More important than the constitutional changes were the 337 new laws which Venizelos and his ministers initiated. These introduced a whole range of reforms. Having got his own partisans into office (friends of his supporters and persons who by their talents promised to be useful), he abolished (at least on paper) the spoils system. That did not mean that it was swept away for all time. Nevertheless, the civil service was certainly vastly improved: recruitment was now by examination. It was, moreover, increased in size to deal with the administration of the great number of reforms. Among these were the introduction of factory and workshop regulations, the establishment of a ministry of agriculture, the break-up of the large Thessalian estates,[2] and the reorganisation of local administration, especially in its relations with the central ministries. Other reforms included the improvement in the administration of justice (there were in 1910 over 100,000 outstanding penal cases); abolition of scandalous conditions in the prisons; substitution in many cases of fines for terms of imprisonment; recognition of trade unions; reduction of interest rates; fixing of a minimum wage for women and children; revision of the chamber's standing orders with a view to giving the ministers more parliamentary time; entrusting of local administrative duties to unpaid parish councils; and the abolition outside the larger towns of the office of mayor, which in the past had been exploited for party ends.

---

[2] Approximately 300,000 stremmata (75,000 acres) were purchased and distributed among 4,000 families.

IV. Military and Naval Reorganisation

Venizelos, who himself took charge of the ministries of war and marine, made the improvement of the Greek armed services one of his principal aims. Here he was certainly committed to the officers, who had brought him into Greek politics. In any case, the expansion of the fighting services had long been an aim on which parties were agreed. They all realised that Bulgaria, Serbia, and Romania, like the great powers of Europe, had embarked upon military expansion,[3] and they had watched with anxiety the improvement and expansion of the Turkish forces. They saw too that Greek foreign policy was rendered feeble by the lack of armed strength. Where disagreement existed (and for over half a century every Greek government had been attacked on the twin issues of foreign and military policies), it had been concerned with ways and means, above all finance, for the demagogues had never seemed to understand that it was quite incongruous to catch votes by promising in one breath to reduce taxation and in the next to descant upon buying guns and expensive battleships in a market where prices were rising steadily.

In 1910 the Dragoumis government by economies reduced expenditure to 140 million drachmai, the total revenue (which had fallen below the budgetary forecast) being about 175,600,000. Koromilas (finance minister in the first Venizelist government) improved on this. His receipts were 240,100,000 and his expenditure 181,300,000. Hence in 1910–11 there was a surplus of over 94 million. During this period the credits for the ministries of war and marine were substantially increased and in July 1910 a loan of 150 million at 4 per cent was arranged[4] on the basis of an advance of 40 million at 5 per cent. This loan (later reduced by Venizelos to 110 million) was issued for subscription in June 1911 at $87\frac{1}{2}$ per cent. Its success demonstrated the financial rehabilitation of Greece. In February 1912 the Greek treasury had cash deposits of 77 million.

By October 1912 Venizelos had brought the mobilised strength of the Greek army up to 148,136 officers and men,[5] equipped with 115,000 Mannlichers (90 million rounds of ammunition), and 112,000 old types of rifle (20 million rounds). There were 144 quick-firing field guns (with 136,000 shells), and 36 mountain guns (with 35,000). There were uniforms for 125,000 and more were on order. There may indeed have been some truth in the crown prince's statement that the manoeuvres of May–June 1912 in

---

[3] Bulgaria had borrowed from France 245 million *leva* in 1904 and 1907 to purchase French armaments. She had the largest and best-equipped Balkan army. Serbia, who had increased the value of her average annual exports from 46,500,000 *dinars* in 1889–1903 to 94 million in 1908–12, had raised a loan of 95 million francs in France and Switzerland and had purchased 85 Creusot quick-firing batteries.

[4] The final negotiations were delayed by the crisis over the admission of the Cretan deputies to the Greek national assembly.

[5] With the return of many young Greeks from America and the call-up of further classes, the Greek army achieved early in 1913 a strength of about 200,000.

which 18,000 men took part showed that the army was not so good as three years previously, but this was not the view generally held by foreign observers who pronounced the army to be efficient. This efficiency was due in large measure to the work of the French mission under General Eydoux who had arrived in Greece in January 1911. Finding the senior officers of poor calibre and the army almost entirely deficient in good staff personnel, he sent several of the more junior officers to France for training. He established a staff college and various military schools for the separate arms. In February 1912 his scheme for the reorganisation of the Greek army was passed by parliament. All cadre units were abolished. Greece was divided into four military districts, each of which was to supply one division in peacetime and two on mobilisation. The standing army was to consist of twelve infantry regiments, six *evzone* (guards) battalions, three cavalry regiments, four regiments of field artillery, two regiments of mountain artillery, a battery of heavy artillery, and two regiments of engineers. Provision was to be made for an increase of reserve officers and warrant officers.

This army Venizelos endeavoured to keep out of politics and he attempted to ensure that postings were made according to need and merit. He insisted on the return of the princes to the army and the appointment of the crown prince to the post of inspector-general—an unpopular measure which, however, he forced through the assembly. He brought back I. Metaxas into active service, and released from prison Kalinsky and the four junior cavalry officers who had been arrested during the Goudhi revolution. These measures provoked hostility from many former members of the military league, but he managed, by making timely arrests of certain officers and N.C.O.s, to prevent a reoccurrence of the troubles of 1909.

During this period of reconstruction considerable attention was paid to the navy. Naval officers were sent to train in England, who provided a naval mission under Admiral Tufnell. This officer arrived in Greece in May 1911 and in July 1912 was appointed vice-admiral in command of the Greek fleet. In collaboration with the Greek ministry of marine he established schools of gunnery, signalling, and torpedo-firing, and reformed the system of naval cadet-training. In the summer of 1912 the fleet, which had been reinforced by a submarine, by six destroyers[6] (two from Toulon and four from Great Britain), and by four armed liners, undertook a strenuous training course, the heavy consumptions of coal and ammunition, however, causing many outcries from the parliamentary opposition. Other vessels— one battleship, two destroyers, and six torpedo-boats—were on order. By November 1912 the Greek fleet consisted of: one heavy cruiser, three ironclads (old vessels which had been repaired), six heavy and eight light destroyers, four torpedo-boats, eight gunboats, four armed liners, one submarine, and various smaller craft.

[6] One of these destroyers was paid for by the Greeks of America. Four of these vessels had been built in England for the Argentine government, which no longer needed them.

CHAPTER 14

The Balkan Wars 1912-13

I. Cretan Affairs

In November 1910 the Cretan assembly, to which the Moslem members were admitted without being required to take an oath, was opened in the name of King George of Greece, much to the annoyance of the Young Turks. By that time another problem had arisen. Zaimis, whose term of office expired in September 1911, spoke of returning to Greece. The Turks let it be known that his successor would have to be approved by the Porte. They also made known their intention of sending *kadis* (judges) to the island. The powers pointed out that this was contrary to the settlement. There the matter rested until August 1911, the month before Zaimis was due to retire. To avoid the problem of the appointment of a successor, the powers decided to leave the Cretan executive committee to carry on the government. In the assembly, however, it was proposed that Colonel Momferatos, Greek commandant of the gendarmerie, should administer the island as a royal commissioner, that the laws of Greece should apply to Crete, and that the assembly itself should be transferred to Athens and become a part of the Greek parliament. Venizelos frustrated these moves. In November 1911 he even secured the dissolution of the assembly itself. This gave rise to yet another agitation—the demand that Cretan deputies should be elected and sent to Athens, which demand Venizelos countered by announcing in the Greek parliament that he refused to be driven by the Cretans into war with Turkey. The following spring the Cretans took up the matter again: they stated their determination to elect representatives to go to Athens.

Venizelos made this an opportunity to implore the powers to settle the Cretan question. At the time the Turks were faced with difficulties in several quarters and he thought they would easily yield to pressure. But the Porte remained adamant and made it clear that the admission of the Cretan deputies to the Athens parliament would be a *casus belli*. Hoping to find a solution, the four protecting powers sought the co-operation of Germany and Austria. When, however, these two refused to help, the four decided to stage a naval demonstration to overawe the Cretans and their supporters in Greece, the British naval commander going so far as to arrest some twenty Cretan deputies on their way to Athens. Under pressure from the powers the Greek government postponed the meeting of the parliament, and Venizelos, while pointing out the dangers of this step to the dynasty of Greece, gave an undertaking that the Cretan deputies (who meanwhile had been released) would not be allowed to sit among the Greek deputies when they reassembled. Venizelos kept his word. When the Greek parliament was convened in June 1912, the Cretans were excluded. Meanwhile discussion had arisen about the revival of the high commissionership. The king was anxious for Prince Andrew to fill that office, but it seems that Venizelos, in view of external developments, dissuaded him from pressing the matter at that moment.

II. The Bulgarian–Serbian Alliance

In April 1904 Bulgaria and Serbia had made a secret alliance which on the Bulgarian side was aimed not only against Austria and Turkey, but also against Greece. They agreed to pursue a common policy in Macedonia, but exactly what the policy was to be they could not decide. By 1908 the alliance, for what it was worth, had ceased to exist. A similar fate befell certain Greco–Romanian negotiations which, though supported by Austria, had foundered completely by June 1906. That year the Greeks, as we have seen, endeavoured to join the Anglo–French *entente*, but failed to end their isolation. By then all the Balkan powers were isolated and remained so for some time to come. During the crisis of 1908–09 Serbia was humiliated when she protested against Austrian annexation of Bosnia and Herzegovina, and she received only cold comfort from Russia. Bulgaria, who had seized the opportunity of the crisis to declare herself a kingdom, was poised uneasily between Austria and Russia; like Serbia and Greece she had no moorings. In 1909, however, Russia, who had come to suspect Austria of aggressive Balkan designs (in fact Austrian policy was timid), not only made the Racconigi agreement with Italy but cautiously attempted to prevail on Serbia, Bulgaria, and Montenegro to work together to prevent Austria from profiting from their rivalries. The Slav states, Isvolsky instructed his agents, must unite, work together, and ultimately fulfil the principle: 'the Balkans for the Balkan states'. Here, then, is one of the underlying ideas of a Slav league under the patronage of Russia who would mediate between the conflicting claims of the Slav nations.

The need for that Slav league was emphasised when in September 1911 Italy declared war on the Ottoman empire. Had a Slav league been in existence, above all had it been linked to Greece, the Balkan powers might have seized all of European Turkey. As it was, each power separately tried to profit from the situation. Montenegro offered to assist Italy and proposed similar action to other Balkan states. Venizelos too made an offer to join Italy. Serbia and Bulgaria likewise made approaches but were restrained by Russia. The Italo–Turkish War both encouraged and alarmed the Balkan powers. Any action that weakened Turkey was welcome, but there was the danger that Italy might make acquisitions. Greece, in particular, feared that Italy might acquire not only the Dodekanese but also Chios, Mitilini, Samos, and other islands. The threat to the other powers was less direct. The danger was, however, that Italian gains would give rise to demands for compensation by Austria or even by France and Britain. Hence distrust of Italy combined with the fear that she might make peace too soon and the spectacle of Turkish mobilisation in European Turkey in October 1911 were to bring Serbia and Bulgaria into alliance.

Until the Italo-Turkish War the Serbo–Bulgarian negotiations, in progress for some time, had made little headway, owing to the inability of the two powers to agree on Macedonia. Eventually, however, it was decided to separate the Macedonian problems from the main treaty and to deal with them in a secret annexe. The treaty and the annexe were at length concluded on 13 March 1912 and were followed by a series of military conventions. The two parties agreed to come

> to each other's assistance with all their forces in the event of any Great Power attempting to annex occupy or even temporarily to invade any part of the Balkan territories which are today under Turkish rule, if one of the parties considered this as contrary to its vital interests and as a *casus belli*

and 'to succour each other with their forces, in the event of one of them being attacked by one or more states'. In the military agreement the likely attackers, Romania, Austria, and Turkey, were specifically named. Bulgaria was to provide at least 200,000 troops and Serbia 150,000. In the secret annexe it was stated that if Turkey became a danger, and one party thought military action necessary, that party should make a reasonable proposal, to which the other should give a reasoned reply. Any decision to take action should be referred to Russia. All territories acquired as a result of action should constitute common property. Nevertheless, 'Serbia recognises the right of Bulgaria to the territory east of the Rhodope Mountains and the river Struma; while Bulgaria recognises a similar right of Serbia to the territory north and west of the Shar Mountain'. As for territory lying in between, if the two parties became convinced that the organisation of this territory into an autonomous province was impossible, then Serbia was to undertake not to claim any territory beyond the line Mount Golem to Lake Ochrid. Bulgaria was to accept that line if Russia pronounced in her favour. The division of territory beyond that line, in the event of failure to reach agreement, was to be left to the arbitration of Russia, as were all disputes concerning any part of the treaty, annexe, and military convention.

No mention was made in the treaty of southern Macedonia. Over this region Bulgaria would eventually have to come to agreement with Greece unless she were able to seize it and hold it. Bulgaria therefore stood to gain most from the treaty. But Serbia had very little option. This was the price she had to pay. All she could hope for was to revise the bargain if her position subsequently improved.

III. The Bulgarian–Greek Agreement: the Serbian–Greek Negotiations

In February 1910 Venizelos unfolded to J. D. Bourchier, *The Times* correspondent, his ideas about the desirability of a Greek–Bulgarian alliance. He was thinking purely in terms of what he imagined to be the old policy of Trikoupis, whom he much admired—that of the Bulgarian–Greek defensive arrangement which might lead to better relations with Turkey, to the improvement of matters in Macedonia, even to a solution of the Cretan problem. He had no conception of the alliance as an aggressive instrument and he had no expectation that the Serbs would join it. Bourchier acted as go-between, but King Ferdinand of Bulgaria was advised by Russia to negotiate first with Serbia. In any case, Ferdinand had no desire to be drawn into war on the question of Crete. Indeed, it was not until he had decided to negotiate with Serbia that he showed any willingness to enter *pourparlers* with Greece, who, if completely ignored by Bulgaria, might enter an Albanian–Austrian–Romanian combination; and it was not until 6 February 1912 that Bulgaria through Bourchier made a definite approach to Greece. Bourchier had obtained from the Patriarch and the Exarch their approval of the project.

On 27 April 1912 Greece presented to Bulgaria a draft of treaty. But to Bulgaria this draft was unacceptable since it contained no mention of autonomy for Thrace and Macedonia and no reference to Article XXIII of the treaty of Berlin dealing with the privileges of the Christian provinces of Turkey. During subsequent negotiations Greece not only refused to concede autonomy to Macedonia but insisted on safeguards of those patriarchal rights which derived not from international treaties but from the decrees of the Sultan. While these inconclusive negotiations were proceeding, the situation in the Balkans became more critical. Both powers hastened to patch up an agreement, Bulgaria, because there was no knowing which way Greece might otherwise turn, Greece because she was aware that a Serbo–Bulgarian treaty existed, that she had everything to gain if she entered that agreement with her hands untied, and everything to lose if the Serbs and Bulgarians waged a successful war without her. The treaty was signed on 30 May and dated 29 May. The two powers set forth their object of preserving peace in the Balkans and of securing the peaceful existence of the Balkan nationalities and their rights 'whether they derive from the treaties or have been conceded in a different way'. If the one party were attacked by Turkey, either on its territory or through systematic disregard of its rights, the other would assist with its armed forces. An annexed declaration stated that the treaty did not apply in the event of war breaking out over the entry, against the wish of Turkey, of the Cretan deputies into the Greek parliament—a provision subsequently annulled after the decision had been taken to begin hostilities. There were no territorial clauses in the treaty, though Greece subsequently tried to obtain from Bulgaria recognition of her claims in Macedonia. On 28 September (two days before mobilisation) Serbia unilaterally revised her bargain with Bulgaria. Indeed, right from the outset each of the three powers was determined to grab what it could and to exploit whatever military or diplomatic situation should develop.

Meanwhile throughout the summer negotiations had been proceeding between Greece and Serbia, but it was not until 22 October (when hostilities had already begun) that the Greeks submitted to Belgrade a draft of treaty. This proposed treaty was hardly a complement to the Serbo–Bulgarian treaty: the two powers were merely to assist one another and to secure the rights belonging to the Serbian and Greek nationalities. Nothing came immediately of this negotiation, which was not resumed until the spring of 1913.

In spite of their intense rivalries, the three Balkan powers arrived, during a period of mounting crises, at a decision to fight together. These crises were: the spread of the Italo–Turkish War to the Aegean; the likelihood of its sudden termination; the Turkish constitutional struggle of the spring of 1912, followed by the fall of the Young Turk government in July; the mutiny of the Turkish garrison at Monastir; the Albanian revolt of July 1912; the demands of the Albanians for the *vilayets* of Uskub (Skopije) and Monastir; the purging of the Turkish army which, as a result, was virtually rendered militarily useless; the Austrian Note of 13 August 1912, which, in encouraging the Turks to decentralise their empire, foreboded the establishment of a large independent Albania; and the popular demands for war in Sofia, Athens, and Belgrade.

This bellicosity in the Balkan capitals was not shared by Venizelos. He considered that Greece was insufficiently prepared. He was still endeavouring to negotiate with Turkey a settlement of Crete. Men like Ion Dragoumis and Souliotis shared his caution. They believed that Greece (and there was much to be said for their views) would run a poor third in acquiring the spoils—and that the 'frankish' (westernised) nationalists in Athens, though they might at the best make small, uneasily defensible territorial gains, would only bring destruction to Hellenism in its wider sense. They feared not only the loss of Greek cities in Macedonia, but also the extermination of Hellenism in Asia Minor. They put their views to Venizelos, who was inclined to agree with them, and they advocated an alliance with Turkey against Bulgaria. They repeated their representations to Venizelos when war was on the point of breaking out. Again he was inclined to agree with them, but he was counting on the powers to prevent hostilities and to impose a diplomatic solution. Even after hostilities had broken out, he continued to believe that the powers would read the riot act and impose their own solution of the Turkish question. What he expected to gain for Greece was the formal acquisition of Crete. Unlike the 'frankish' nationalists in Athens he seems to have been reluctant to play for high stakes in Macedonia.

IV. The First Balkan War

About the middle of September, Bulgaria informed Russia of her intention to go to war unless Russia could induce the Porte to implement Article XXIII of the treaty of Berlin. Russia (even though Poincaré had in August 1912 interpreted the old Franco–Russian alliance in a form which underwrote Russia) was in no position to fight a war with Austria, who would probably be strongly supported by Germany. She feared moreover that Bulgaria might come to dominate the Straits. She therefore initiated the collective action of the powers who on 8 October let it be known in the Balkan capitals that they would tolerate no modification of the territorial *status quo* of European Turkey. That same day Montenegro, according to plan, began hostilities against the Turks and on 13 October Athens, Sofia, and Belgrade gave a defiant answer to the powers: they would address themselves directly to the Porte stating their terms. These they embodied in a memorandum. In effect they delivered to Turkey an ultimatum, and, expecting no reply, on 18 October (the day Turkey signed peace with Italy) they went to war.

In anticipation of hostilities the Greeks had already called up 250 of their old Macedonian irregulars: these were to raise the country, organise native fighters, seize important strongpoints, repair bridges which the Turks might destroy, cut enemy lines of communication, act as guides to the regular forces, and arrange for supplies and animals. These tasks they performed so well that the VIIth Greek division was able to advance rapidly to Katerini, where it defeated the Turkish forces, and thence to Tekeli (Sindos) some 6 miles outside Thessaloniki, which it entered on 8 November a few hours before Bulgarian forces, 3,000-strong, reached the outskirts. Already other Greek forces had taken Elassona (23 October) and Kozani (25 October), while, away to the west, Greek formations had invaded Epiros and had laid siege to Jannina. Meanwhile, contrary to the forecasts of most European military experts,[1] Greece's allies had carried all before them. Serbian and

---

[1] These experts failed to realise that the armies of the Balkan powers, which had reached a total strength of 1,297,000 men (Bulgaria 620,000, Serbia 467,000, and Greece 210,000), had been vastly improved, that they had an excellent morale, and that the Turkish forces, barely 400,000, consisted of a large proportion of raw recruits and irregulars, the trained reservists of the Italo–Turkish War having been disbanded. Nor did the experts allow for the shortage of officers in the Turkish forces, for the need of the Turks to fight on several fronts, and for the lack of supremacy at sea. (The Greek fleet, strengthened by 85 steamers, some of which were armed, not only enabled Greece to seize the islands, but to transport supplies and reinforcements to various bases in the north Aegean.)

Montenegrin forces overran the sanjak of Novibazar, while the main Serbian army, thanks largely to the Greek movements which drew off strong enemy forces, won on 18 November a great victory north of Monastir and pushed on towards the Adriatic, occupying Durazzo on 30 November. Montenegrin troops besieged Scutari. The Bulgarians, who because of their geographical position had to meet the main weight of the Turkish armies, likewise achieved remarkable successes. They scored great victories at Bunar Hissar and Lule Burgas. By early November they had forced the Turks back to the Chataldja lines outside Constantinople, having detached forces to contain the strongly held Turkish position of Adrianople. The relative ease with which they overcame the main but highly disorganised Turkish forces was in the end to contribute to their undoing. Their victories, which surprised them (at the time the Bulgarian foreign minister was negotiating with the Russians for mediation), led them to expand their lines of communication. The amazing thing is that, with so primitive a transport system, they managed to reach the Chataldja lines at all. Their attacks on these lines on 18 November failed completely: cholera began to take a greater toll of them than did the notoriously inefficient Turkish gunnery; and by tying up forces there and at Adrianople (areas in which Russia would never have tolerated Bulgarian expansion) they deprived themselves of all chance of dominating Macedonia, which was their original aim.

On 3 December, following an approach from Turkey, the three Slav Balkan states signed an armistice. Greece refused to enter this arrangement for the Turks would not surrender Jannina. Moreover, she was intent on continuing the war upon the sea. She did, however, send representatives to a peace conference which the great powers had arranged to open in London on 16 December. The powers were adjusting themselves to a new and unforeseen situation. Austria was waiting for the Balkan alliance to disintegrate, hoping to establish good relations with Bulgaria and to reconcile Bulgaria with Romania. She would allow Serbia and Montenegro some increase of territory provided they would enter into an economic union with her, provided Romania were given compensation, and provided Serbia were denied expansion to the Adriatic, in which region an independent Albania should be established. These aims led to tension with Russia, who planned to mobilise. Eventually, however, Austria accepted the idea that Serbia should be given a commercial outlet in the Adriatic and in return for Serbia's abandoning her pretensions to the Adriatic coast, she offered to support Serbian claims to the whole Vardar valley including Thessaloniki. These proposals had the support of Italy, who had originally suggested them. In making this offer Austria hoped to hasten the disintegration of the Balkan alliance. But Serbia, highly suspicious of Austria, did not respond to this attempt to detach her from her allies. Instead she continued to press her claims for a port in the Adriatic. Here, however, she received only lukewarm support from Russia. So feeble was Russian policy at this time that

Poincaré began to fear a decline in the prestige and deterrent power of the Triple *entente*.

The outcome of the negotiations among the powers was a decision to hold in London an international conference, which began its sessions a few days before the peace conference of the Balkan powers and Turkey. On this conference Grey, as chairman, exercised a moderating influence and it eventually decided that an autonomous Albania should be established under Turkish suzerainty and the control of the European powers. The question of her boundaries, however, and particularly whether she should include Scutari which the Montenegrins refused to relinquish, caused great tension until Russia, again showing caution, persuaded the Montenegrins to evacuate that city. But on other questions the powers made little headway, for much depended upon the outcome of the negotiations between Turkey and the Balkan states.

The Balkan allies demanded the cession of Adrianople and the Aegean Islands. The Turks refused. On 6 January 1913 negotiations were suspended. On 22 January, however, the Young Turks, as a result of a *coup d'état*, returned to power: under diplomatic pressure they offered to cede a part of the Adrianople *vilayet* and to place the islands at the disposal of the European conference on condition that they did not go to Greece. But these offers were of no avail. On 3 February the Balkan allies resumed hostilities. Bulgaria concentrated on an attack on Adrianople; the Greeks, whose navy had already enabled them to seize control of the Aegean, renewed operations against Jannina and occupied further parts of Epiros; and the Serbs, having little else to do, sent help to the Bulgarians at Adrianople and to the Montenegrins at Scutari. On 26 March the Bulgarians took Adrianople—a victory which encouraged them to take a firm line in their negotiations with Romania, who was demanding the Turkukaia–Balchik line as her frontier.[2]

Meanwhile, on 22 March, the European powers had presented peace preliminaries to the Balkan Courts. All Turkish territories (except Albania) west of the Enos–Maritsa–Ergene–Midia line and all the Aegean Islands were to be ceded to the allies; Turkey was to renounce her interest in Crete; the Balkan powers were to have a voice in the settlement of the Ottoman debt. But it was not until 30 May that the preliminaries were signed. When, however, the European powers came to deal with the problems reserved for their decisions, they found themselves at loggerheads and even the Triple Alliance failed to speak with one voice. Germany supported Greece on the question of the Albanian southern frontier, favouring a northerly line starting at Cape Kefali. Italy advocated a more southerly line beginning at the mouth of the Kalamas; and Austria tried to get a compromise. On the question of the islands Germany again favoured Greece, while Italy did what she could to prevent Greek expansion in the Aegean. All this time Koromilas, who had become Greek foreign minister, skilfully bid for support both from

[2] Nevertheless, in May 1913 Bulgaria agreed that Romania should have Silistria.

Germany and from the *entente* powers. In June he concluded in company with Serbia separate negotiations with the Turks and even contemplated making with them an alliance, which was favoured by Germany. His aim was to encourage the Turks to keep the Bulgarians occupied on the Chataldja lines.

Meanwhile the Greeks and Serbs, using to the full their old interior organisations, were getting a firm grip on Macedonia. On 4 May they signed an agreement to divide all territory west of the Vardar and to have a common frontier. On 1 June they signed a treaty and a military convention. They would divide Macedonia 'on the principle of effective occupation' and their common frontier was to run from Ochrid passing south of Monastir to Gevgeli. The Serbo–Bulgarian frontier was to run from Gevgeli to the confluence of the Bojimia–Dere and then eastwards to the old Bulgarian frontier. The two powers would support each other with all their armed forces to impose this settlement. If, having been obliged to fight, they were victorious, then they would take more territory, Serbia a region lying north and north-west of the Vardar–Perelik line, Greece the area to the south and south-east. Serbia was to have a corridor to the sea. Each power was to win for itself the territories staked out.

Koromilas, who had a much better understanding than Venizelos of the Macedonian question, had rightly calculated that Russia did not favour a powerful Bulgaria, and that with the help of Serbia and the blessing of Romania, Greece could acquire a lion's share of Macedonia. As early as October 1912, during certain Greco–Bulgarian discussions, he had claimed a population in Macedonia of 2 million, leaving to Bulgaria some 1,300,000 souls. But all along Bulgaria had shown no willingness to pay a price either to Greece or to Romania. Even the moderate Geshov, who had opposed the futile attack on the Chataldja lines, miscalculated on the attitude of Romania. On 30 May he resigned. Danev, his successor, tried to persuade Russia to bring the Serbs under control and to make an award favourable to Bulgaria. Danev, however, was hardly a master in his own house. Savov, the commander-in-chief, with the support of the Bulgarian–Macedonian organisations, was clamouring to occupy the Macedonian areas earmarked for Bulgaria in the Serbo–Bulgarian treaty of 1912; and on 28 June, with King Ferdinand's approval, he ordered an attack for the following day on the Greek and Serbian positions. Danev, while endeavouring to clear himself of all responsibility for this move, yet welcomed it, hoping it would force Russia quickly to announce a favourable arbitral award. This hope was shared by King Ferdinand. At the same time he reckoned on Austria's coming to his assistance. All along he had based his policy on much wishful thinking. In July 1912 he had communicated to Vienna a plan through which Bulgaria would make use of Russia to obtain alliances with the Serbs and Greeks, would overcome Turkey, then annihilate Serbia with the help of Austria–Hungary, and finally vanquish Greece. He had boasted to Chirol, *The Times* correspondent, that he had the key to Macedonia, and even to Constantinople, in his pocket. What he failed to reckon on, however, was Austrian timidity and the reluctance of his Bulgarian politicians to appease Romania.

V. The Second Balkan War: the Treaty of Bucharest

In the face of Savov's attack Greece and Serbia moved quickly into the offensive. On 1 July the Greeks overcame the Bulgarian garrison in the region of Thessaloniki and then advanced to occupy Drama, Serres, and Kavala. On 8 July, following their victory at Bregalnitsa, the Serbs entered Ishtip. On 11 July Romania occupied the Dobrudja quadrilateral without opposition. The following day the Turks entered the war and by 22 July had retaken Adrianople—an easy victory which enabled the Young Turks to pose as saviours of the empire. On 15 July Ferdinand had appealed for help to Austria who, having decided to wait upon events, referred him to King Carol of Romania. Carol consented to halt his own advance and proposed to Bulgaria, Greece, and Serbia an armistice to be followed by a general peace. This proposal did not suit Greece. She feared that an armistice alone would afford Bulgaria time to concentrate an army against her and insisted that preliminaries should be signed on the field of battle. Later, however, Greece, under strong pressure from Serbia and being none too sure of Austria and Russia, agreed to send negotiators to Bucharest, where on 30 July a five-day armistice was signed. Greece and Serbia then put forward extensive claims. Serbia claimed the Struma frontier, but finally accepted a frontier on the watershed of that river, thus leaving Strumitsa to Bulgaria; but she held out, in spite of Austrian pressure, against relinquishing Kotchana and Ishtip. Greece claimed the Aegean coast with an ample hinterland as far as Makri to the east, thus leaving Bulgaria some 25 miles of coastline. The real trouble rose over Kavala and here Venizelos was prepared to compromise, but France and Germany, each wishing to gain Greek friendship, insisted that Kavala should go to Greece. On this issue Germany and Austria, like France and Russia, were in conflict: Britain tended to side with Germany and France, having reverted to her old view that a large Bulgaria was a danger, since she might get to Constantinople on her own account or on behalf of Russia later on.

The treaty of Bucharest (10 August 1913) was brief: to it were annexed three protocols on boundaries. Romania was to have the Turkukaia–Balchik line. Serbia was to have the Vardar north of and including Gevgeli with Ishtip and Kotchana, but not a corridor to the Aegean. Greece was to have Crete and Kavala, and a northern boundary running from just north of Koritsa, between Monastir and Florina, to Doiran, then south of Strumitsa, Petrich, Nevrokopi, to the mouth of the Mesta. Thus Bulgaria had signed away the major part of Macedonia to Greece and Serbia. She did this in the hope (raised by Austria and Russia) that the great powers would revise the treaty. But France and Germany opposed revision, while Italy and Great Britain were prepared to accept it only if it were unanimously agreed.

Although Greece and Serbia had done well for themselves in Macedonia, they still had outstanding claims on northern Epiros and Albania. Serbia had obtained Pech, Prizrend, Jakova, and Dibra, but the Albanians had entered the last-named place. In retaliation the Serbs invaded Albania and demanded boundary rectifications. For once Austria acted firmly. She delivered an ultimatum to Serbia (18 October) and the Serbs, under pressure from Russia, withdrew on 25 October to the boundary fixed by the London conference. Greece, too, encountered opposition in southern Albania (northern Epiros). The powers fixed the boundary, Ftelia to Lake Prespa, thus awarding Koritsa and Argirokastro to Albania, and in February 1914 informed Greece that she would not get the islands until she withdrew her troops south of that line. Greece agreed to evacuate Albania, but proposed boundary rectifications around Koritsa and in the Argirokastro valley. On 28 February 1914, however, northern Epiros declared its independence and established a provisional government. To forestall possible Italian intervention, Venizelos ordered a blockade of Santi-Quaranta. In the negotiations that ensued between the Albanian control commission and the provisional government, the provinces of Koritsa and Argirokastro were given autonomy, while Chimara was granted its old Turkish privileges. This arrangement was sanctioned by the powers in July 1914. Greece had withdrawn her regular troops the previous April, but irregular Greek levies remained to take part in the disorders of the next few years. The whole problem of northern Epiros was to come up at the peace conference of 1919 and later still it was to occupy the attention of the League of Nations.

As for the islands, in December 1913 Grey proposed that all of them, including those held by Italy, but excluding the Dodekanese, Tenedos, and Imvros (which were to be returned to Turkey), should be awarded to Greece. The powers agreed in principle, but ruled out all idea of enforcing the award or of expediting the Italian evacuation of the Dodekanese. It was further agreed that Greece should not fortify the islands and that she should prevent their use for smuggling. Greece naturally demanded a guarantee of the islands she was not to fortify. Meanwhile the Turks were loud in their demand to retain Chios and Mitilini and offered to Greece compensation in the Dodekanese, still held by Italy. Venizelos hoped to appease Turkey, thus preventing a Bulgarian–Turkish alignment. He offered to cede Chios and Mitilini in return for a mutual guarantee of possessions on the European mainland. But this problem, like many others arising out of the Balkan Wars—the question of debts, contracts, financial claims, and railways—remained unsolved at the outbreak of the 1914–18 War.

CHAPTER 15

Greece during the 1914-18 War

I. Greece after the Balkan Wars

The Balkan Wars, in bringing together in a final phase the Cretan and Macedonian struggles for independence, brought them both to a successful conclusion. Outside Macedonia and Crete, Greece had made gains in Epiros, and was in effective occupation of numerous Greek-speaking islands. The net result was that she had increased her territory by 68 per cent (from 25,014 to 41,993 square miles) and her population from approximately 2,700,000 to 4,800,000. Her population was as a consequence greater than that of Bulgaria, who had added only 130,000 to her existing population of 4,300,000. Greece's achievement, like that of Serbia, who had almost doubled her territory and increased her population from 2,900,000 to 4,500,000, was astounding. A decade earlier it had seemed as though Bulgaria might stake out unassailable claims to the whole of Macedonia and perhaps also to the whole of Thrace. Events, however, had taken an unexpected turn, and for a second time Greater Bulgaria had failed to come into existence.

The Greek victory had not been won without considerable cost. Between 1905 and 1911 Greece had spent on her armed forces the sum of 193,700,000 drachmai, thus diverting expenditure from internal development. The cost of the war, including expenditure on prisoners-of-war and refugees, was about 411 million drachmai. But these burdens the Greek economy and the improved finances had been able to bear without great difficulty, part of them (124 million) being met from the ordinary resources of the treasury and the rest by internal and external loans. For this expenditure Greece not only increased the potential strength of her army and navy to nearly 250,000, but also her revenues. These in 1914 amounted to 204 million drachmai, of which 72 million derived from the new provinces. Moreover, Greece acquired an increase in cultivable land from 8,600,000 stremmata (2,150,000 acres) in 1911 to 13,300,000 (3,325,000 acres) in 1914, the value of the agricultural output rising from 262 million drachmai in 1912 to 413 million in 1914.[1]

But if these were the solid gains, they were not unaccompanied by serious problems. The long northern frontier, badly drawn in several places, was not easily defended. Further, Greece had acquired a large non-Greek (non-patriarchist) population. In Greek Macedonia there were only 528,000 Greeks (including Vlachs) as opposed to 465,000 Moslems. In the territory gained in Epiros (according to a Greek estimate of 1907) there were 166,000 Greeks (including Christian Albanians), 38,000 Moslems, and 10,000 Jews and Vlachs. True, the Aegean Islands were almost entirely Greek, but on Mitilini and Limnos there were nearly 9,000 Moslems. Altogether there was in Greece in 1914 a non-Greek population of some 750,000, most of it near the long northern frontier and therefore a danger in the event of war.

In 1913 the Young Turks agreed to exchange 48,750 Moslems for 46,764 Bulgarians (largely the recognition of a *fait accompli*). In July 1914 they compelled Greece, by forcing some 150,000 Asia Minor Greeks to emigrate, to accept in principle an exchange of the Greeks of Thrace and Smyrna for the Moslems of Macedonia and Epiros. In this projected deal, over one million people were concerned, nearly all of them peaceful peasants and traders who in the normal way would have had no wish to leave their home-lands. Left to themselves (and in theory they were free to emigrate or remain) they would for the most part have chosen not to move. It was per-fectly clear, however, that the Turks intended to force an exchange, for they were already transferring Greeks from the valleys of the Smyrna *vilayet* to inhospitable lands in the Anatolian mountains. The project raised an outcry in Greece. It had not been ratified when Turkey entered the First World War.

Events in Asia Minor, coming as they did hard upon the victories of 1912–13, intensified Greek irredentist aspirations. Outside the kingdom (in Macedonia, Albania, Thrace, Cyprus, the Dodekanese, Constantinople, Anatolia, and Pontus) there were still about 3 million unredeemed Greeks, and it was hoped that eventually most of these could be brought within the Hellenic fold. But the *megali idhea* of the 'frankish' nationalists of Athens had undergone a subtle change, and the prevailing desire was to build up a powerful state, which, though containing foreign elements both in race and religion, might be unified by Hellenic education and by an official Greek language. Like other Balkan powers, Greece had become conscious of her strength. The Balkan Wars had shown that the action of the European Concert was intermittent and that the Concert itself tended to disappear in face of the two opposing alignments, the Triple Alliance and the Triple *entente*. Throughout the negotiations of 1912–14, the great powers had shown some eagerness to compete for Greek support. Greece had therefore

[1] For the economic development of Greece, see below, Chapter 17.

achieved some freedom of choice, but in the field of foreign affairs the free-dom to choose was, where Greece was concerned, compulsion to engage in fierce internal strife. Differences over foreign policy were to intensify the party conflict and to give rise to constitutional and dynastic issues. Had King George continued to reign, it is possible that the troubles of the next decade would have been avoided. But in March 1913 he perished at the hand of a mad assassin in Thessaloniki. He had refused to leave the city he had so recently won while his armies were engaged in Macedonia. He was succeeded by Crown Prince Constantine, who lacked his father's experience and flexibility and was prone to allow his favourites in the army to influence his decisions.

II. Greece and the Serbian Alliance

During the Asia Minor crisis of June 1914 Venizelos inquired of Serbia what her attitude would be in the event of war between Greece and Turkey. Serbia replied that she was not ready for war: she would, however, exert diplomatic pressure on Turkey and use her good offices with the great powers. In the event, no hostilities broke out between Greece and Turkey. There were rumours that Turkey, with German connivance, was planning to exterminate the Greeks of Asia Minor. Venizelos risked further outcries from the opposition and arranged to see the grand vizier in Brussels to dis-cuss not only the question of the islands but also the problem of the Greek populations in Turkey. On his way to Brussels he heard the news of the Austrian ultimatum of 23 July to Serbia.

It was only natural that Serbia should ask Greece for assistance under the terms of the alliance of 1 June 1913. Venizelos, with King Constantine's concurrence, instructed Streit,[2] the Greek foreign minister, to state that while Greece would not tolerate a Bulgarian attack on Serbia, she neverthe-less reserved the right to interpret the treaty in the light of any develop-ment. On 31 July and again on 4 August the German Kaiser appealed to his brother-in-law King Constantine to support the central powers against Serbia, but the king replied on both occasions that it was in the Greek in-terest to remain neutral since Greece was vulnerable to the *entente* fleets. Venizelos, however, surmising that Turkey and Bulgaria were committed to the central powers, wished Greece to offer her services to the *entente*. To the German ambassador's request that Greece should join Bulgaria in attacking Serbia, he replied that Greece was 'too small a state to commit such a big infamy'. On 18 August he offered Elliot, the British minister, 'all the navy and military forces of Greece', adding that he had authority for this from the king and cabinet. Grey turned this down, not only because Russia had no enthusiasm for it but also because to have accepted it would

[2] Georgios Streit (1869–1948), a Greek of Bavarian ancestry, and formerly Professor of Law in the University of Athens.

have led Bulgaria and Turkey, whom he fondly hoped to wean from Germany, immediately to join the central powers; and he would not even pledge support to Greece, should she be attacked by Turkey alone. Venizelos therefore continued to pursue his negotiations with Turkey, which were resumed at Bucharest on 22 August. Although Germany stiffened the Turks, the *entente* powers advised Greece to be accommodating, and Venizelos offered to accept a fifty-year lease of the Aegean Islands in lieu of sovereignty. Greece learned, however, that Turkey and Bulgaria were planning to attack her. Venizelos consulted Grey, who could only state that any Turkish squadron emerging from the straits would be treated as though it were the German fleet. Mallet, British ambassador at Constantinople, reported that there was a peace party in Turkey which would prevail over the pro-Germans Enver, Talaat, and Djemal. This misled Grey. He continued to hope that Turkey could be detached from Germany, despite the closing of the Straits on 27 September, the sale of the German warships *Goeben* and *Breslau*, the virtual expulsion of the British naval mission, and the arrival of German military personnel in Constantinople.

On 29/30 October Turkish torpedo-boats entered the Black Sea and bombarded Russian ports. This brought an ultimatum from the *entente* and on 5 November Turkey entered the war on the side of the central powers, the British annexing Cyprus that same day. Thereafter the *entente* powers began to make greater efforts to win over the Balkan states. Here again, however, Grey was misinformed, this time by his agent at Sofia, and he concentrated on Bulgaria to whom he offered, without being specific, 'important territorial advantages'. These 'advantages' were bound to involve concessions of territory from Greece and Serbia, and it was precisely for these concessions that Russia was pressing. This same policy was advocated strongly by the still misinformed London Balkan committee. Noel Buxton, who had gone on a semi-official mission to Sofia, proposed in a memorandum to Grey (January 1915) that the concessions should consist of the 'uncontested zone' of Macedonia which Serbia, on being denied access to the Adriatic at the time of the Balkan Wars, had refused to cede to Bulgaria. They should also include the districts of Kavala, Drama, and Serres, which had been acquired by Greece. It was further proposed that Bulgaria should expand in Thrace as far as the Enos–Midia line. To Greece the *entente* offered expansion in northern Epiros—which, in Venizelos's view, was poor compensation for losses in Macedonia. On 24 January 1915 the *entente*, realising that Greek help for hard-pressed Serbia was urgent and having in mind their long-contemplated expedition to Gallipoli, improved their offer, vaguely defined as 'important territorial concessions on the coast of Asia Minor'.

Venizelos was prepared to gamble on the possibility of obtaining substantial gains in population in Anatolia for the loss of some 30,000 in Kavala, Drama, and Serres—part of the price the *entente* was ready to pay for Bulgarian neutrality. From Politis in Rome he had already learned that the *entente* powers were making offers to Italy of gains in Asia Minor and that they had in mind a partition of much of the Ottoman empire. If this was the case, then surely Greece, who had better claims than Italy, should be in on this deal. It was an offer no patriotic Greek could possibly spurn. In a memorandum to the king he advised the acceptance in principle of the *entente* offer. The king raised difficulties. On 30 January Venizelos argued the case in another memorandum. This time Constantine and the Greek general staff agreed to accept the offer provided a definite promise was given of Greek expansion in Asia Minor. In reply to the *entente*, Venizelos demanded that the Allies should send a force to the Balkans to ensure Bulgarian neutrality. He continued, moreover, with his negotiations with Romania in the belief that, if Greece and Romania were allied, Bulgarian neutrality would be assured and that then there would be no need to cede Greek soil in eastern Macedonia. Grey, however, would make no precise promise of territory in Asia Minor: at the time he was negotiating with Italy and therefore reluctant to tie his hands. Nor did anything come of the Greek–Romanian negotiations. Hence when Venizelos learned later that Bulgaria had raised a loan in Germany, he promptly withdrew the offer of the concession of Kavala, Serres, and Drama.

The *entente* powers realised at last that deeds and not words were required to win over the Balkan powers. On 15 February they made a fresh approach to Greece and offered to send one French and one British division to Thessaloniki to fight together with the Greeks in assisting Serbia. Venizelos and the Greek general staff turned this down on the grounds that two divisions were not enough. What the *entente* hardly realised was that while the Greeks would have been happy to fight the Turks, they were most reluctant to assist the Serbs against the Austrians. This came out clearly a few days later (19 February) when Anglo–French naval units began bombarding the Dardanelles. In this operation both Venizelos and the Greek army were keen to join and Venizelos initiated a British request made on 1 March for the assistance of the Greek fleet. In yet another important memorandum (2 March) to the king, he argued that participation would give Greece a voice in the final settlement of the question of Constantinople and the Straits and would ensure substantial gains in Asia Minor. If Bulgaria and not Greece should join in the allied venture at the Dardanelles, then Greece would be in danger. With these views the king and a council of ex-prime ministers agreed, but the acting chief of staff, Colonel Metaxas, resigned, having submitted a memorandum pointing out that if Greek forces were committed to operations either in Serbia or at the Dardanelles, Greece would be at the mercy of Bulgaria. He also pointed out that Greece could never hold territory in Asia Minor.

This resignation necessitated another meeting of the crown council, in which the chief of staff, Dousmanis, who had been recalled, strongly supported Metaxas. Venizelos offered to reduce the forces from an army corps to a division, to be put at the disposal of the Allies. With this suggestion Rallis and Dragoumis agreed, and Theotokis advised the king, in view of the popular demonstrations in favour of war, to accept Venizelos's plan. On 6 March, however, the king came down on the side of the general staff: he accepted their view that the Dardanelles expedition was likely to fail and that even if it succeeded, Russia would never allow Greece to have Constantinople. The king and general staff had their own sources of information, and they were right. The British and the French at the time were trying to get Russia to agree to Greek participation, under conditions which the Greeks, even Venizelos himself, would never have accepted. When at length on 12 March Russia agreed to Greek participation in the Dardanelles operation, she did so on the strict understanding that she herself should on the termination of hostilities acquire Constantinople and the Straits.

On 6 March, the day that Constantine backed the general staff, Venizelos resigned. So began a series of events leading to constitutional issues and eventually to the division of Greece into what were practically two separate states. Up to that point, although there were some differences of outlook, Constantine and Venizelos had much in common—hostility to Turkey, fear of Bulgaria, the desire to make an agreement with Romania, and appreciation of the dangers of renouncing neutrality. Where they disagreed was in their calculations of the point at which it might be necessary to set a new course and in their views of which direction that new course should take. Constantine, a military expert in his own right and no doubt biased by his German connections and by his failure to appreciate the value of seapower, was inclined to think that the central powers would win the war. Venizelos, a civilian with a larger but less precise vision and perhaps too inclined to neglect military considerations, believed that the *entente* allies would eventually be victorious and that Greece, both a continental and maritime power, must stake her future on the sea, and, at all cost, keep company with France and Britain. Greece was not alone in having to face the great decisions at which point and on which side to enter the war. Italy, Bulgaria, and Romania were in the same predicament. Their politicians, like those in Greece, were divided on the issues facing them. Unlike Greece, however, they arrived at their decisions, for good or for evil, without going through a process of revolution.

As Venizelos refused to give parliamentary support to Zaimis, the king entrusted the Greek government to Dimitrios Gounaris, a lawyer from Patras who had as his foreign minister Zografos, leader of the northern Epiros provisional government of 1913–14, a politician well disposed towards the *entente*, and particularly to the French. On 22 March they offered Greek assistance to the *entente* on condition that Bulgaria attacked Turkey, or alternatively that Greece should be guaranteed against Bulgarian treachery. What they were not prepared to do (and it was here they differed from Venizelos) was to make concessions to Bulgaria in eastern Macedonia —which, as Venizelos was to state in public, Constantine had agreed to.

The Greek offer was genuine. The king and government had sent Prince George (married to a Bonaparte) to Paris to press its acceptance and to propose that Constantinople should be internationalised. But the *entente* powers were still pursuing their futile policy of winning over Bulgaria, about whom they continued to be misinformed, and they not only refused the Greek demand for a guarantee but gratuitously gave Greece a warning against attempts to drive Bulgaria into the camp of the central powers. In vain did Constantine himself point out that there was some understanding between Bulgaria and Turkey since Turco–Bulgarian bands were active in Macedonia, and in vain did he demand a definite alliance with the *entente* powers, whom he strongly suspected of trying to reimpose Venizelos upon him. Following further futile negotiations on 10 May the Greek government made it clear that concessions to Bulgaria were out of the question. Whether Constantine or his new advisers were merely seeking excuses to maintain neutrality is a point open to dispute; but what is certain is that they were genuinely concerned about Bulgaria; and they much resented British policy which from Athens seemed to be particularly off-hand and which indeed was based on an assumption that Bulgaria could be won over and that Romania and Greece, and certainly Greece who was exposed to the allied fleets, would be bound to follow suit. What the British were counting on (and the French too) was that the pro-*entente* opposition in Sofia would gain the upper hand. So eager were the *entente* powers to win over Bulgaria that they were prepared to agree that she should acquire not only the contested and uncontested zones in western Macedonia, but also eastern Macedonia and the Dobrudja which she had ceded to Romania. Indeed, the *entente* was prepared to offer to Bulgaria, in return for an immediate declaration of war on Turkey with all her forces, a territorial expansion almost as large as that contemplated at San Stefano in 1878. Needless to say, when they heard of this design, the Serbs and Greeks were incensed; and they both let it be known that they would sanction no alienation of their national territory.

On 13 June 1915 Greece went to the polls and Venizelos was returned with 185 seats out of 316. Nevertheless, the king (who was ill) continued to keep Gounaris in office and it was not until 24 August that Venizelos formed a government. In the meantime the *entente* had made further efforts to entice Bulgaria, who was merely playing for time and at the same time negotiating in Berlin. Moreover, the *entente* continued to make demands of Greece to cede eastern Macedonia, which drove many of the pro-*entente* Greeks into the ranks of the neutralists. These demands were again repeated when Venizelos resumed office, but even he could no longer hold out much hope that the Greeks would agree. All he could promise was to do his best, at the same time intimating that his path might be easier if the Western

Allies would make Greece a loan. This loan he obtained, but he was quite unable to persuade Constantine to part with Kavala or to convince him that sheer neutrality—neutrality in isolation—laid Greece open to constant danger from Bulgaria.

On 21 September Bulgaria ordered mobilisation, having already, unknown to the *entente*, signed on 6 September a treaty of friendship and alliance and a military convention with the central powers. King Ferdinand, surmising that Serbia was nearing defeat, had decided to make a bid for Macedonia and to acquire Thessaloniki, which otherwise might pass to Austria–Hungary. Serbia, fully realising how critical the situation was, proposed to the *entente* that she should make a preventive attack on the Bulgarians before their mobilisation was complete. This the *entente* powers refused, for they did not want Serbia to become the aggressor, thus depriving herself of Greek support under the terms of the Greco–Serbian treaty. In any case, Russia had vetoed this proposed move on more general grounds: if the Serbs attacked Bulgaria, there was every possibility that, despite the letter of the Greco–Serbian treaty, the Greeks would join them in a local war against a common enemy—a development little to the liking of St Petersburg.

Whether the Greeks would have joined the Serbs in a preventive war on the Bulgarians, no one can say. All that can be said is that Bulgaria's decision to mobilise caused great alarm to all parties in Athens. But although Constantine granted Venizelos's demand for Greek mobilisation, he laid it down that Greece should not depart from her neutrality and he even assured the Bulgarians that Greece would not intervene if they attacked the Serbs, they in return assuring Constantine that they had no designs on Greece.

The *entente*, realising at last that they had been fooled by their so-called Balkan experts, now began to panic and took up again a scheme earlier advocated by Lloyd George and Briand of opening a front at Thessaloniki. This scheme, when it was put to him, Venizelos favoured, but he pointed out that if it were executed, he would have to make a protest, explaining that he could not, in view of the position in Greece, give the Allies a formal invitation to land. The position was that on the question of the Serbian treaty the Greeks were divided. For Venizelos and his followers it was not only politic but also obligatory to assist the Serbs. For the neutralists, however, that treaty had been in its origins a purely Balkan treaty: it imposed obligations on Serbia and Greece only if Bulgaria alone and not in alliance with Germany and Austria made an attack on either Greece or Serbia. In any case, Serbia was obliged to put into the field 150,000 men—an obligation she was unable to fulfil. This was a valid point, but Venizelos suggested to the Western Allies—and they immediately adopted this suggestion —that they themselves should provide the troops on behalf of Serbia. To this plan Constantine reluctantly agreed, merely stipulating that the troops should not be colonial levies. Venizelos then hastened to invite the *entente* powers to land their troops. Shortly afterwards, however, Constantine, not imagining that Venizelos would act so quickly and having learned from the German military attaché that the Allies would certainly find the troops, wanted to change his mind, arguing that if the troops landed, and if Bulgaria had not attacked, the neutrality of Greece would have been compromised. But the king was too late; he therefore accepted the situation only to learn of the landing at Thessaloniki on 1 October, without prior notification, of a party of British officers and men. This landing gave rise to much rumour. It was generally thought in Greece, especially in view of Grey's statement in the British House of Commons a few days earlier to the effect that Bulgaria and Britain remained traditional friends, that these troops were an advance party of a force which would occupy Kavala in order to hand it over to the government of Sofia. Needless to say, Venizelos was obliged to lodge a protest with the Allies, whose reply was that these troops, which were destined to help the Serbs, had been sent on their own responsibility, the implication being that as protecting powers of Greece, they could legally land troops on Greek soil whenever they considered there was a need to do so. Venizelos accepted these explanations and on the night of 4 October (the day the Bulgarians declared war) asked the Greek parliament to sanction the despatch of Greek troops to aid Serbia not only against Bulgaria but also, if necessary, against the central powers. For this policy he obtained 147 votes out of 257—a majority of 37. Next day, however, Constantine called him to the palace and asked him to resign.

III. The Constitutional Position in Greece

As he had recently won a general election and had maintained his majority in parliament, Venizelos considered that this, his second dismissal, was unconstitutional. His first dismissal had been another matter: Constantine had the right to test the feeling of the country, but, having done so, and having found that the Liberal party had a majority, he had no cause whatever to go through the same procedure. On this issue the constitution was not perfectly clear. The king had indeed a right to dismiss a government, but the spirit of constitutional government demanded that this should be done only to enable the popular will to prevail. Constitutional practice, however, was not so simple. In the past Greek political parties had normally left the king much discretion in matters of foreign policy, and there is no doubt whatever that King George, during his long reign, had exercised considerable influence in the making of Greek foreign policy. On the other hand, he was a man who knew when to yield. Had he lived, there is little doubt that he would have come closely into line with Venizelos, whose task of dealing with the *entente* Allies would have probably been made easier by the absence of a ruler who was suspected (quite wrongly) of being committed to the central powers. Nevertheless, Constantine, like his father, was

8

a great patriot, and he could claim to represent Greece and Hellenism as truly as Venizelos. He had won popularity in the Balkan Wars and had contributed more to the triumph of Greece than had Venizelos, who throughout had displayed timidity and readiness to make unnecessary concessions. Indeed Constantine, who had mystic and divine concepts of kingship, besides a first-hand knowledge of military matters, considered himself more fit to decide on issues of war and peace than a sheer politician whose parliamentary majority had been built up on domestic issues and perhaps in a way not entirely above suspicion. As in all conflicts of this kind there was much to be said for both protagonists. But if it was in the interests of Greece not only to defend the Greek populations she had already won but also to attempt to extend her boundaries to include other Greeks of the dispersion, then there is no doubt that Venizelos was right in his belief that Greece must join the *entente* powers. His assessment that the Western Allies would win the war, even though at the time it may not have been much more than guesswork, was proved correct. Judged by other criteria, which dismiss the *megali idhea* as an absurdity, then Venizelos was certainly wrong.

In October 1915 it seemed that, as far as the interests of Greece were concerned, King Constantine had taken a right decision. The war was going badly for the *entente* powers. The Allies, unable to spare troops for the Western front, were transferring forces from Gallipoli to Thessaloniki, thus suggesting that they had given up all hope of forcing the Straits. At Thessaloniki the allied forces were feeble and were totally inadequate to save Serbia, the Bulgarians having on 23 October cut the railway to Nish.

On 12 October the *entente* requested the Zaimis government, which had replaced that of Venizelos, to go to the help of Serbia, it being hoped that Romania would also join the *entente* camp. Certain Venizelists had already advised the *entente* (through the British minister) simply to coerce Greece into entering the war, and thus to counteract the intensive propaganda of the central powers, who had not only obtained a grip on the Athenian press but had also sent to Greece no less than 3,000 agents. For the Western Allies, however, coercion was out of the question and the British government preferred to try and tempt Greece with the offer of Cyprus. This offer the Greeks turned down, replying on 20 October that they preferred neutrality. Shortly afterwards the Zaimis government, which had been defeated in parliament, resigned, and on 5 November the octogenarian Stefanos Skouloudis formed an administration. He at once stated that the *entente* troops at Thessaloniki should be disarmed in accordance with the Hague Convention. This statement aroused the wrath of Venizelos, who himself began to advocate the coercion of Greece; and it certainly intensified the suspicions of France and Britain, who both demanded an assurance that the *entente* troops would not be molested by the Greeks. This they followed up with further demands—the retirement of Greek troops from the region of Thessaloniki, the use by the allied forces of the railway to Monastir, the establishment of a defensive zone on the boundary of Chalkidiki, facilities to search Greek vessels, and the right to destroy all enemy submarine bases in Greek waters. Shortly afterwards the French and British occupied Limnos (where the British built a naval base at Mudros) and also Kastelorizo, Mitilini, Argostoli, and Suda Bay. Following a German air raid on Thessaloniki, General Sarrail, the French commander of the allied forces, arrested, without informing the Greek government, the consuls of the central powers and sent them to Marseilles. In January 1916 *entente* forces occupied Corfu in order to accommodate (in violation of the treaty of 1863) the survivors of the defeated Serbian army, and that same month Sarrail, despite an undertaking to the contrary, took over the fort of Karabouzou which guards the approaches to the harbour of Thessaloniki. He next blew up bridges between Kilinder and Demir Hissar, thus cutting the land supply-route to the Greek forces in eastern Macedonia. But despite these acts of provocation Sarrail had a good reception when he visited Athens the following month, and the coercive activities of the Allies found loud applause in *Estia* and other organs of the Venizelist press.

By this time the Venizelists had formed an extra-parliamentary opposition. Fearing defeat, but arguing that yet another dissolution followed by an appeal to the country was quite unconstitutional, they had abstained from the elections of 19 December 1915 and as a result they had been removed by the government from the armed forces and the civil administration. This development intensified the conflict and gave rise to bitter hatreds which were inflamed by the increasing propaganda of the *entente* and the central powers, and by the activities of their intelligence agents and secret police, who took into their pay common informers and misguided patriots. Submarine sightings were reported by the score either through love of gain or through sheer hallucination, and brother Greeks denounced one another to gullible amateurs of the central and *entente* powers who imagined they were serving their countries better by being mixed up in the political intrigues of Athens than by dying in the trenches on the Western front.

Throughout 1916 the relations between the royal government and the *entente* powers grew steadily worse. What particularly annoyed the Allies was the refusal to allow the re-formed Serbian forces to be transported by the land-route from Corfu to Thessaloniki, where they were needed to build up a front. This refusal came in for fierce attacks in the Venizelist organ *Kirix*. On this issue the Greek government (who feared that the Serbs might join the Venizelists and bring off a *coup d'état*) remained adamant. The result was that the Allies, at the risk of losses from German submarines and putting a great strain on their shipping resources, had to send the Serbian troops by sea. It was conceded, however, that they could use the Korinth canal.

No sooner had the Serbian forces arrived at Thessaloniki than the Allies learned that on 28 May the royalist Greeks had surrendered to the Bulgarians and Germans the fort of Rupel[3] which, commanding the defile of the Struma river, was the gateway of eastern Macedonia. The order to surrender had been given by Skouloudis, who defended his conduct by saying that this was the only way to maintain a strict neutrality. Needless to say, this incident, which caused certain royalist officers to go over to the Venizelists, led to bitter recriminations in Greece, while to the Allies it was convincing proof of the unfriendliness and untrustworthiness of the Greek government.

IV. The Provisional Government of Thessaloniki

By May 1916 Venizelist officers had begun to form an organisation known as the 'National Defence' and it was this movement that prompted Venizelos to take up with the Allies the possibility of his setting up a provisional, pro-*entente* government in Thessaloniki. Both Elliot and his French colleague, Guillemin, favoured the idea but their governments disliked it. The British government considered that a movement of this kind, to be successful, would need considerable military support which, they felt, could not be mounted; while the French government favoured a naval demonstration at Piraeus as a more effective means of bringing the Greek government to heel. On this issue the French had strong Russian support, and it was at length agreed that an allied Note should be presented in Athens and backed by the menace of an allied fleet under Admiral Dartige du Fournet at Faliro Bay. This Note was presented on 21 June before the fleet arrived. It demanded the demobilisation of the Greek army, the formation of a new ministry which would dissolve the chamber and hold new elections, and the replacement of certain police officials by persons named by the *entente* powers. This intervention the *entente* exercised as the protecting and guaranteeing powers: they claimed that the 1864 treaty (which did nothing of the sort) gave them the right to restore a constitutional regime in Greece.[4] But by the time the Note was handed in, Skouloudis had resigned, his place having been taken by Zaimis, who was friendly towards the *entente*. By changing his government Constantine hoped to avoid carrying out the other demands and, although under pressure he subsequently disbanded the army, the ex-royalist officers were organised into a 'League of Reservists' under the direction of Metaxas. The aim of this league was to put down Venizelists

[3] On 14 May, Sarrail had occupied without resistance the fort of Dova-Tepe, north of Doiran. The Germans, by way of retaliation, had informed the Greek government of their intention to enter Rupel.

[4] Italy, not being a protecting power, associated herself with the *entente* demands in a separate Note. Throughout she had been hostile to Greece. Favouring strong measures on the grounds that Greek bands were invading the Italian-occupied territory of Valona, the Italians had begun in March 1914 to occupy northern Epiros. Subsequently, Italy had tried to promote a plan for detaching Bulgaria from the central powers by the offer of concessions to be enforced on Greece.

and generally to use intimidation in support of the cause of royalism. By way of retaliation, the Venizelist officers formed their own league under the leadership of General Danglis. The situation became one only just short of civil war. To both Constantine and Venizelos it was intolerable. The king, believing that he was being slandered by the Venizelists and by the *entente* representatives and agents, sent one of his brothers, Nicholas, to plead with the Tsar and another, Andrew, on a mission to London, Paris, and Rome. They were to try and convince the four powers that Constantine was genuinely neutral and not the instrument of Germany. This they failed to do, although it may be said that, as a result of their visits, the three *entente* Allies for a time endeavoured to prevent their agents from being too completely identified with the Venizelist cause.

It was not long, however, before the situation deteriorated still further. At the end of July in response to a Bulgarian attack against Greek central Macedonia, the Greek government ordered the VIth division to withdraw to the region Serres–Drama–Kavala, leaving the *comitadjis* free to commit atrocities against the Greek population. On 18 August the Bulgarians, having followed up the retreat of the VIth division, began operations in eastern Macedonia, just at the time when Sarrail had at long last completed preparations for an offensive in western Macedonia. This offensive he hoped to co-ordinate with Romania who, after long negotiations, agreed on 17 August to join the Allies. What he could no longer count on was any Greek resistance in the region of Kavala. Indeed, it was generally known that VIth division was under orders not to call up reservists but to wait until it could be evacuated by the fleet to some other part of Greece. Amid all this confusion Venizelos organised a demonstration on 27 August in the streets of Athens, and in a public speech implored the king to cease to be a party leader and to lead the country as a whole. Next day the royalists held a counter-demonstration, during which Rallis, Gounaris, and Stefanos Dragoumis denounced the follies of Venizelos. All this time Zaimis endeavoured to carry on some form of administration, and when on 29 August Romania declared war, he had some hopes, as did General Moschopoulos, the new chief of staff, that Greece might come in on the side of the Allies. These hopes were shared by the *entente* ministers, who advised their governments to reduce pressure on Greece and to postpone for the time being a contemplated naval demonstration. At the time they were engaged in secret negotiations with Zaimis, who conceded to the *entente* (a French demand) the control of the Greek posts and telegraphs and agreed to expel Baron Schenk and other German agents. But the French agents, above all de Roquefeuil, were intent on speeding matters up. They arranged with Venizelist *agents provocateurs* a demonstration against the French embassy. This gave them the pretext to land French marines, ostensibly to guard French property. Needless to say, this incident rendered Zaimis's position intolerable. He resigned on 10 September.

Meanwhile events in the north were adding to the general confusion. Here Sarrail was backing the Venizelist 'National Defence', which on 31 August proclaimed open revolt. Venizelos at the time was in Athens, and he did not make up his mind immediately to identify himself with this movement. On 11 September, however, the Greek forces defending Kavala surrendered to German troops without firing a shot and on the following day Bulgarian troops took possession of the town.[5] This capitulation had been arranged by Colonel Hadjopoulos who in fact was not in communication with Athens. At the last moment the British had offered to evacuate his force, which was totally inadequate to resist. On discovering, however, that the British intended to take him to Thessaloniki where he would be expected to join the 'National Defence', he decided that the only course open was to surrender to the Germans. The British had indeed offered to transport him to Volos and the Greek war ministry had agreed this plan; but the shipping available was inadequate to evacuate his force all at once. Rather than leave men behind, he preferred to carry through his arrangement with the Germans, though some of his men found their way into British ships and later joined the movement at Thessaloniki.

This event precipitated a crisis. The *entente* refused to recognise the short-lived administration of Kalogeropoulos, who had on 16 September replaced Zaimis. Venizelos embarked at Piraeus on 25 September and, escorted by a French destroyer, sailed for Crete where he raised a revolt. He then toured the islands to gain further support and at length proceeded to Thessaloniki, where on 5 October he established a pro-*entente* provisional government.

Greece thus became virtually two separate states, each with its own army. There was every danger of civil war and it was for that reason that the *entente* powers (mainly owing to the British attitude) refused to recognise the Thessaloniki government. To have done so, it was thought, would have driven royalist Greece into the arms of the central powers. Instead Bénazet, a French deputy, went on a mission to try to reconcile the 'old' Greece with the 'new'. This mission, carried out with threats and not in a spirit of conciliation, failed completely and the French began to press for stringent measures against the Athens government. To these the British government with some reluctance agreed. The result was that on 16 November Admiral Dartige du Fournet demanded the disarmament of the larger Greek warships, the control of the arsenal and of the railway to the north, and the expulsion of the diplomats and agents of the central powers. He also demanded, as compensation for the artillery and supplies surrendered to the

---

[5] It should be noted that the Germans made no attempt to invade Greece, or to attack Greek forces. They were quite content to give merely technical assistance to the Turks and Bulgarians. They were thus able to tie down an allied army which had reached a strength of 300,000 and which earned for itself the title 'The Gardeners of Salonika'. This army had at first been built up at the expense of the ill-fated Gallipoli forces. Under Sarrail it achieved nothing. His attempt to assist the Romanians in August 1916 was a costly failure and his advance up the valley of the Vardar in April 1917 was likewise a fiasco.

Germans and Bulgarians at the fort of Rupel, that ten batteries of mountain artillery should be handed over. This demand the Greek government formally refused. On 23 November the admiral, with the consent of the allied ministers, sent a new demand calling for the mountain guns to be surrendered by 1 December and for the rest of the material to be given up by 16 December: failure to do so would mean a landing of allied troops.

These demands were intolerable to Constantine, who realised that they would be resisted by his government, his officers, and the populace. He did what he could to get them reduced. On 30 November, the day before the allied ultimatum expired, he sent two of his brothers to the military club to persuade the officers to show restraint and explored the possibility of forming another cabinet which would yield to the allied demands. He sent his chamberlain, Count Mercati, to see Admiral Dartige and to explain that the officers were hostile, that no politicians would undertake the responsibility of surrender, and to request more time to get the acquiescence of those he was obliged to consult. But the French admiral could only say that his instructions from his government must be carried out and he asked Mercati to advise the king to give strict orders to his troops not to fire. This Constantine did. Nevertheless when the Allies landed detachments, they suffered heavy casualties, a body of marines was taken prisoner, and the survivors were forced to retire in disorder to their ships. The French fleet in retaliation fired on the palace. More serious, however, than this peevish gesture was the blockade of royalist Greece declared by the Allies on 7 December. For over three months not a single cargo of wheat reached the royalist ports. Old Greece, moreover, was completely deprived of coal. To run the railways and to generate electricity the only fuel available was lignite and timber from the forest of Tatoi, which had been partially destroyed by fire the previous July. Greek merchant ships were requisitioned only to be lost to enemy submarine action. Greek royalist troops were ordered to march into the Peloponnese and the garrison of Athens was forced on 29 January 1917 to salute the allied flags. 'And those', wrote Constantine in disgust to his friend Paola, princess of Saxe-Weimar, 'are the Powers who are supposed to be fighting for Justice and the rights of small nations.'

During the dark months that followed thousands of unemployed Greeks were thrown on the streets to beg for food. Even in the villages there was starvation and much illness, for money was lacking and most of the younger workers were with the armies. Nevertheless, there is no doubt whatever that the populace of Old Greece remained loyal to Constantine, feeling instinctively that he had had a bad deal at the hands of the Allies.

Constantine was not actively pro-German. At no time did he contemplate joining the central powers. For good or evil he genuinely believed that neutrality was the best policy for Greece. 'Just imagine', he wrote, 'what would have happened if I had joined the Entente. They would not have sent troops in sufficient numbers . . . and I alone against the Germans, Austrians, and Bulgarians should have been crushed . . .' What he also realised was that had he joined the central powers, the crippling allied blockade of Greece would have been imposed at a much earlier date and the whole of Greek shipping would have been confiscated.

V. The Deposition of Constantine

By midsummer 1917 the provisional government of Thessaloniki was firmly established and the Allies had plans, despite Sarrail's earlier failures, to open a Macedonian front. For a time they had been negotiating with Bulgaria, Austria, and Turkey for a separate peace, but once all hope of achieving this was past they began to realise that an advance from the southeast into central Europe might shorten the war. They still feared, however, that while Constantine remained on the throne, there was a danger to their base. For some time the French had been pressing for his deposition and on 11 June Jonnart, as high commissioner of the protecting powers, presented to Zaimis, who was again in charge of the government, the demand that Constantine should abdicate in favour of one of his younger sons, it being considered that the eldest, the future George II, was too pro-German. A crown council was summoned, and the king announced to his nervous ministers that he would go into exile for his country's sake. He made no formal abdication, but stated his willingness to hand over the reins of government to his second son, Alexander. Two days later he embarked at Oropos, despite the pleadings of the crowds that he should stay. Only by a stratagem did he manage to get away without incident. In a message to his sorrowing and bewildered people he said:

> It is necessary to obey, and I must leave. I am fulfilling my duty to my country. I am leaving you Alexander and beg you to resign yourselves and accept my decision; trust in God, whose blessings I invoke on you.

The Allies, who had landed troops, arrested leading royalists. Metaxas, Gounaris, and others they interned in Corsica. On 27 June Venizelos was installed as prime minister, and he immediately demanded the recall of the chamber elected in June 1915, claiming that the elections held the following December by Skouloudis had been unconstitutional. There soon followed a return of Venizelists to posts in the army, navy, and civil service and the dismissal of those who had been closely identified with the Constantinist regime—a process which led to increased bitterness, since it was accompanied by much retaliatory action from the Venizelist police. Meanwhile the Allies had raised the blockade and it had not been long before foodstuffs and war materials began to flow into Greece. To Venizelist Greece the Allies made a loan. This enabled Venizelos ultimately to equip ten divisions which were to fight alongside the Allies against the central powers with whom he had broken off relations immediately on taking office.

VI. The Campaign in Macedonia, September 1918

Long before the provisional government (a triumvirate of Venizelos, Danglis, and Koundouriotis) had been established at Thessaloniki the Greek army of the north had been taking shape. Officers and men who had escaped from the clutches of the right-wing league of reserve officers had made their way via the islands to Thessaloniki; remnants of the Greek forces which had retreated from Kavala had gone there too; and the local commander, Colonel Zimbrakakis, had, much to the annoyance of the local population and the Church, conscripted levies. By November 1916 there were three Greek battalions serving under British command in the Struma section of the Macedonian front. These troops had taken part in the unsuccessful spring offensive of 1917 which had cost the army of the Orient 14,000 casualties and for which there had been nothing to show except the acquisition of a few outposts. By the end of May that army had established itself again on a defensive line running from Lake Prespa in the west to the Struma in the east. It was certainly in a sorry condition. The Serbian contingent was disheartened and politically divided. The Russian brigades, with the arrival of Bolshevik agitators, were insubordinate and in March 1918 mutinied. The French troops, too, were in poor shape and were extremely hostile to the commander-in-chief, Sarrail. Only the British and the Greeks were in fighting condition and even they had been depleted by malaria. So serious was the situation along the whole length of the Macedonian front that the question whether to maintain the army of the Orient in being had become, even more than previously, a highly controversial question both within and between the allied cabinets. At the Rome conference early in 1917 Lloyd George, now prime minister, had favoured the continuance of the Macedonian front, but after the failure of the spring offensive he had come to have doubts of its value. Eventually, however, he turned against the so-called 'westerners' (those who wished to concentrate all forces on the Western front) and favoured a plan to use the Balkan front to knock away the props of Germany, to tie down German forces in the East, and to invade central Europe from the South-East. He also saw the value of having British forces in easy reach of Constantinople and although he was committed to detaching a division to Palestine, he counted on the Greeks to supply eventually one of the chief contingents on the Macedonian front.

Lloyd George's plans were unlikely to mature while General Sarrail remained in the supreme command. The Italians, the Serbs, and the Greeks were hostile to him and the British, too, looked upon him with profound distrust. Even many of the French would have liked to replace him or simply to close down the Macedonian front. But Sarrail had powerful friends in France. In March 1917 he had the support of the war minister Painlevé, who the following September became French premier. Not until November when Clemenceau formed a government and began his attack on

Sarrail's old friend and protector Caillaux, was Sarrail replaced by General Guillaumat. The new commander, who established good relations with his allies, soon had the 'gardeners' digging new roads and improving generally the lines of communication. But even then it was the very weakness of his troops which prevented their being transferred to the Western front. They therefore remained and were even reinforced. Of the Greek troops Guillaumat certainly had a good opinion and he attached to them considerable importance. To the old national army of Zimbrakakis he was able to add, mainly through the good offices of King Alexander, some 20,000 or more royalist troops from Athens, Larisa, Lamia, and Patras. It was these troops who with French support attacked the Bulgarian salient of Skra di Legen at the end of May, taking the Bulgarians by surprise and eliminating a whole enemy regiment and capturing 1,800 prisoners (including 200 Germans). This victory was important: it brought in a flow of volunteers, many of them from former royalist circles.

No sooner had Guillaumat won this much-publicised minor victory than he was recalled by Clemenceau to be at hand to take over the Western front should Foch or Pétain be found wanting. In his place Franchet d'Espérey, who had previously been under consideration for the command, was sent to Thessaloniki. He arrived on 17 June. The new commander was immediately on good terms with the subordinate national commanders and his presence brought, even more than his predecessor's, a sense of purpose on the Macedonian front. But the allied cabinets, under the influence of 'westerners' on their military staffs, continued to hesitate and the British war office not only withdrew twelve battalions from Macedonia for the Western front but looked askance at General Milne's demand for reinforcements and war materials. Nevertheless, at a military conference at Versailles on 3 August it was agreed that while effort should not be diverted from western Europe, d'Espérey should be instructed to launch an offensive when he considered the moment opportune. For that offensive he was almost ready. He had unobtrusively moved heavy guns to dominate from a height of over 7,000 feet the Dobropolje and the Vetrenik. He had, moreover, reorganised the front. The Serbs under their able General Mishich were to break through on the 6-mile sector between the Sokol and the Vetrenik. Six Greek divisions were under the command of General Milne, it being understood that at a later stage General Danglis would take command on the Struma. Two other Greek divisions were placed under the French General d'Anselme and a ninth division under his colleague General Henrys. The remaining Greek division was held in reserve.

Even at this stage the allied and particularly the Italian and British cabinets were hesitant. On 4 September, however, Guillaumat attended a conference at Downing Street and then went on to Rome. Both Lloyd George and the Italians agreed to an offensive, which d'Espérey decided to launch on 14 September. Early that morning he began a heavy bombardment of the sector between the western Vetrenik and the Sokol. Next day the Serbs stormed the western and eastern slopes of the Vetrenik while French colonial troops carried the strongpoint of Dobropolje. In the evening French and Serbian troops reached the summit of the Sokol. On 16 September the Serbs, now on home territory, attacked Kozyak. By the next day they had made a salient some 6 miles deep along a front of some 20 miles and by 18 September they were driving towards the Crna.

On the morning of that day the Greek and British troops began to move forward on the front at Doiran and within less than an hour Greek units had entered the town. Meanwhile British units took the Petit Couronné. Another Greek unit took 700 prisoners. It then advanced up the steep slopes of the Grand Couronné to the west of the town and lake, which other troops, chiefly British, also managed to ascend. But here the attackers were greatly outnumbered and were met with heavy machine-gun fire from the well-concealed and strongly defended Bulgarian posts. The going was certainly more difficult than on the Dobropolje and the Vetrenik sector, and the British and Greek forces failed to take the Grand Couronné. Meanwhile, however, the Cretan division and certain British formations were attacking from the Krusha range to the east of Lake Doiran, but that enterprise too failed, largely because of a lack of co-ordination. The same fate befell an assault the following day (19 September) on the hills north of Doiran, made by British troops and two Greek regiments of the Serres division. But although General Milne's casualties were high and although he had nothing much to show for two days' fighting, he had nevertheless fulfilled his role of preventing the enemy from transferring troops to fill the gaps made by the French and Serbs to the west.

It was at this point that the Bulgarian command made the extraordinary decision to retire from the Doiran defences, having been deterred by the Germans from carrying out their original desire to counter-attack at Doiran and to advance towards Thessaloniki. This advance would have been supported by the second Bulgarian army on the Struma. It had been calculated that d'Espérey, who was committed on the Crna, would be unable to come to the assistance of the British and Greek forces. This plan General von Steuben considered sheer madness. He wanted the Bulgarians on the Doiran sector to operate on the flank and supply-lines of d'Espérey's forces. General Todorov, the deputy Bulgarian commander-in-chief, much annoyed because the Germans had failed to send reinforcements to Macedonia, decided that if the Bulgarians could not advance, they had better fall back to a natural defence-line stretching from south of Sofia to southern Serbia. He had therefore, much to the disgust of the local commander, Nerezov, given the order for retreat. British aircraft, without any interference from the German air force, inflicted heavy losses on the retreating Bulgarian forces, and in their hurry to get away the Bulgarians, whose morale was broken, simply abandoned their guns and supplies. Milne followed up the retreat with all possible speed. British troops advanced into the Belasica Planina and the Cretan division advanced through the hills north-east of Doiran. By 25 September British cavalry had crossed the Bulgarian frontier.

Meanwhile to the west General d'Anselme with Greek support had on 19 September broken the Bulgarian IIIrd division on the mountain of Dzena. By 22 September the Serbs had reached the Vardar. On 25 September French and Serbian troops took Gradsko, the German supply-centre for the Macedonian front, and then continued through the Babuna pass where the Serbs had put up stout resistance in their retreat of 1915. Their next objective was Velesh. It was at this point that the French cavalry under Jouinot-Gambetta swung round Velesh to the left and covering nearly 60 miles of difficult terrain in less than a week, rejoined the Vardar valley just south of Skopije. They captured this important town on 29 September. By that date enemy resistance had almost everywhere ceased. On the previous day Bulgaria, in a state of revolution, had sent delegates to Thessaloniki to sue for peace. D'Espérey's terms were certainly severe: Greek and Serbian territory must be evacuated; Austrian and German troops must leave Bulgaria; Bulgaria must demobilise, surrender arms, and allow her territories and railways to be used by the Allies for the prosecution of the war. That same day Hindenburg and Ludendorff at Spa had arrived at the decision that, with the collapse of the Macedonian front, the war was lost.

D'Espérey had hoped to strike towards the Danube and enter Romania, but the British insisted that Milne should advance on Constantinople—a plan favoured by Foch. At an allied conference of 4 October a compromise was reached. An international force, mainly Greek and British, was to march on Constantinople under d'Espérey's supreme, but Milne's immediate, command, while another international force, including British and Greeks, should remain for operations towards the Danube. Milne's forces, however, were not called to fire a shot. On 30 October, the day his advance guard reached Dedeagatch, the Turks signed the Mudros armistice.

CHAPTER 16

The Fourth War of Independence:
The Struggle in Thrace and Asia Minor

I. Greek Claims at the Peace Conference

By bringing in Greece to fight on the Macedonian front, Venizelos assured for himself and Greece a good hearing at the European peace conference. He went to Paris in December 1918 virtually committed by his wartime pronouncements in his struggle against the Constantinists to bring the un-redeemed Greeks within the national kingdom. He did not, however, base his claims upon the vague offers made by Great Britain in 1915, for these had not been accepted: instead, he based his case on the services rendered to the Allies by Greece and upon one of President Wilson's fourteen points —that which laid down that the minorities of the Ottoman empire should 'be assured an undoubted security of life and an absolutely unmolested opportunity of autonomous development. . . .' Many have doubted the wisdom of the extensive claims to be made. Some, Ion Dragoumis, for example, were entitled to do so, for they had an historical philosophy and a vision quite different from that of Venizelos. Others, too, who had at the time pointed out the military problems involved in holding a Greek empire, were again entitled to their expert opinion. But most of Venizelos's critics were wise only after the event. What they forget was that at the end of 1918 the victorious Allies had three fallen empires—the German, the Austro-Hungarian, and the Ottoman—on their hands. These they were committed to carving up: they were obliged to recognise the liberation movements of the nationalities; they had made promises of sorts either by treaty or by declarations to one another and to various subject peoples; and they had made self-determination one of the principles of peacemaking. There were as a consequence many competing claims, and to deal with these there was a strong tendency to look upon the Ottoman empire, which no one had ever succeeded in reforming and which seemed to be completely moribund, as a fund from which compensations might be provided.

221

When Venizelos had first taken up the idea of acquiring gains in Asia Minor (and it should be remembered he was prepared to barter away Greeks of Macedonia), he had done so, as we saw, mainly because he knew that the Allies had ambitions in the region.[1] In 1918–19 the position was the same. It was not a question of Greece's going it alone. It was a question of taking part in a general share-out under a variety of arrangements—succession states, mandates, and spheres of influence—in company with America, Great Britain, France, and Italy. Of all these powers, Greece was the only one who could advance the additional claim that in the regions she coveted there was a large population which was Greek Orthodox and within that population a large proportion which spoke the Greek language, living in communities that had their own schools and a Greek way of life.[2] Moreover, Greece was contiguous to the regions in which she hoped to expand. In any event, Venizelos considered that Greece needed to expand in order not to be outdistanced by a considerably increased Serbia and Romania.

Not only did Venizelos conceive of Greek expansion into Asia Minor as part of an international arrangement, but he was prompted to bid high because he calculated that regions unclaimed by Greece would be swallowed up by Italy. After all, Italy was already in possession of the Dodecanese, almost entirely Greek-speaking. At the treaty of Lausanne of 18 October 1912 she had undertaken to evacuate them as soon as Turkish forces and civil servants had left Tripoli and Cyrenaica; but she had found a pretext to remain in occupation. By the treaty of London (April 1915) the *entente*, to bring her into the war, had agreed that she should receive 'entire sovereignty' over these islands and also Adalia with its hinterland. Two years later at the conference of Saint Jean-de-Maurienne (April 1917) Italy's sphere of interest in Asia Minor was extended to the district of Smyrna—an agreement which at the peace conference Lloyd George contended had been conditional upon Russian agreement (which had not been forthcoming) and upon a considerable Italian military effort against the Turks. Italy, moreover, by backing a viable and independent Albania, which, now that Austria was defeated, would fall under her influence, was in conflict with Greece in northern Epiros. Here during the war Italy had proclaimed 'the unity and independence of all Albania', and she had occupied Jannina.

Given all these conditions, the claims that Venizelos put forward at the peace conference were not unreasonable. Working on the assumption that Turkey in Europe would be abolished, he asked for the whole of western and eastern Thrace up to the Chataldja lines. At the time of the Balkan Wars, and even in 1915, he had been willing to forego these territories in order to appease Bulgaria. But in 1919 matters were different. Bulgaria had shown no willingness to be appeased, and there was now no Turkey with

[1] As indeed had the Triple Alliance powers before 1914.

[2] Other European communities were small, except in Smyrna town, which was cosmopolitan.

whom she could ally against the Greeks. All that he was prepared to give to Bulgaria was a commercial outlet to the Aegean seaboard. As for Constantinople and the Straits, he realised that, owing to Italian opposition, a Greek mandate was entirely out of the question, and he would have been satisfied with an international organisation or a mandate exercised by America. (He assumed that an arrangement of this kind would be made.) Under such an arrangement the Greek populations and the Patriarchate would be secure and would even play an important role in the internal government of the city and the province. At the conference he also demanded the *vilayet* of Aidin (Smyrna) less the sanjak of Denizli, but including a corridor reaching to the south coast of the Marmara. For this demand there was much to be said. Just before the war and during the war the substantial Christian populations of Asia Minor had been maltreated and it was essential they should be concentrated under friendly rule—the Armenians under American mandate and the Greeks of Aidin under Greece. Given exchanges of population (a principle already admitted), a concentration of Greeks in Aidin could be achieved and a Turkish minority, even though substantial, could be safeguarded under international treaty. The territory in question was not large, and given fair play by her allies, who would be her neighbours in Constantinople, in Syria, Palestine, and Anatolia, she could reasonably hope to develop; and what is more, being in possession of the offshore islands, she would be able to defend that region.

It is nonsense to say that Venizelos had lost his old statesmanship. On the contrary, he had grown in stature and had ceased to be the somewhat narrow-minded rebel of Therissos. It is nonsense, too, to say that he was forced to seek adventure by the necessities of Greek internal politics. Always an opportunist, he simply could not let an opportunity go unexploited. At no time in Greek history had the international situation been so favourable to Hellenic aspirations, which after all were not any more fantastic than those of Poles, Romanians, Czechs, Yugoslavs, and Italians. Venizelos did indeed become the victim of Greek politics, but sheer politics had nothing at all to do with his determination to realise the *megali idhea*. That vision was a common heritage and at no time did the Constantinists seriously consider reversing Venizelos's policy, the aims of which were generally acceptable to all Greeks, except those few who all along had favoured the maintenance of Hellenism within Turkey rather than the expansion of the Greek kingdom—an ideal for which ever since the rise of the Young Turks and the persecutions of the period 1914–18 there was very little to be said. The Constantinists did indeed consider, under the force of circumstances, the possibility of reducing the commitment in Asia Minor; but then Venizelos would have done the same. Their accusation, however, that Venizelos had committed them to a venture which was basically unsound and which they themselves would have avoided was merely an excuse for their failure. What they might more justifiably have said was that, given their policy of neutrality during the war, the opportunity to fulfil Greek aspirations would never have arisen if they had remained in power. The fact remains, however, that if they accepted a policy which they themselves could never have initiated, that policy was nevertheless in accordance with their own aspirations.

II. The Greek Landing and Greek Operations in Asia Minor

On 29 March Italian forces began a military and naval occupation of Adalia and moved north-westwards towards Smyrna. Greatly alarmed, Lloyd George raised the matter at the supreme allied council and accused the Italians of encouraging the Turks to persecute the Greek populations. At the time, the Italian delegation had withdrawn from the Paris conferences owing to their disagreement with their allies over Adriatic questions. On these questions they had come up against strong opposition from President Wilson. Hence when Lloyd George proposed that Greek troops should be sent to Smyrna in readiness to land, in order to protect the Christians, he was strongly backed by Wilson who proposed that these troops should be landed straight away. With this proposal Clemenceau agreed and on 7 May the three allies authorised Venizelos to land troops immediately. This landing at Smyrna, covered by allied warships, was carried out on 15 May.[3] Before long the Greeks, with the express approval of their allies, extended their bridgehead. In the course of these operations Greek troops committed certain atrocities, under great provocation, against the local Moslem population. The supreme council, however, instead of ordering the Greeks to withdraw, set up a commission of inquiry[4] to investigate matters and at the same time instructed General Milne to demarcate boundaries between the Greeks, the Italians, and the Turks. In the Greek zone the Greek high commissioner, Stergiadis, previously governor-general of Epiros, quickly established a stable and well-run administration. He organised the revenues, a gendarmerie, and a judicial system; and he certainly gave a better deal to the normal law-abiding Moslems than the Greeks had received at the hands of the Turks. He repatriated some 120,000 Christian refugees and deportees and gave them loans to re-establish themselves. He provided them with seeds and ploughs. He established an experimental farm and, with the help of Professor Karatheodoris, he founded a university. Nevertheless, both he and the Greek military authorities were faced with the activities of guerrilla bands which frequently infiltrated into the Greek zone. To deal with these the Greeks organised bands among the Christians, and, as time went on,

[3] In notifying this landing to the Turks, the Allies cited Articles 5, 7, and 20 of the armistice of Mudros which had terminated hostilities between the Turks and the Allies.

[4] The American Admiral Bristol was president. Venizelos took objection to the *Bristol Report* on the grounds that no Greek officer had been allowed to attend the inquiry and that the names of the witnesses had been withheld. The supreme council upheld this objection and refrained from publishing the report.

disturbances and crimes became more frequent. Moreover, under the pressure of military needs, the Greek authorities requisitioned the services of Moslem peasants, many of whom, to escape this burden, migrated to territories held by the Turks. Needless to say, their lands were confiscated and were given to Christian refugees who had returned to the safety of the Smyrna zone.

One result of the Greek landing and occupation was to strengthen Turkish resistance to the Allies. This resistance had already taken shape when it was realised that the armistice of Mudros, the terms of which at the time seemed less severe than those generally expected, was a prelude to a dismemberment of the Ottoman empire and a vigorous control of any territory that might be spared. Although the Allies could count on subservience from the pro-*entente* governments at Constantinople, these governments were ceasing to exercise authority in Turkey at large. A Turkish nationalist movement was taking shape in Anatolia, and Mustafa Kemal (the future Atatürk), a general who had been sent to the provinces to facilitate demobilisation, was attaining the leadership. The allied occupation officers were rapidly losing control of the situation. Rifles and munitions were no longer being handed in and the army which had at one time been reduced to 20,000 was beginning to expand. In January 1920 the Turkish nationalists proclaimed their final version of the so-called 'National Pact' in which they designated those territories which they would not relinquish. In view of this, and of general hostility, in March 1920 the Allies (including the Greeks) occupied the city of Constantinople (which under the armistice had been nominally exempt) and deported prominent Turkish nationalists to Malta. In April they dispersed the new Ottoman parliament which had become overwhelmingly nationalist and defiant.

III. The Treaty of Sèvres, 10 August 1920

The drawing-up of the peace terms had been long delayed, for the peacemakers had been faced with countless problems in Europe. What is more, the plans for the disposal of the Turkish empire had led to disputes among the Allies, who were unwilling to strike bargains in the Near East until they were certain of the reconstruction of the West. Throughout the negotiations both Italy and France endeavoured to deprive Greece of Smyrna by supporting her claim to Thrace—a policy which up to a point Lord Curzon favoured. In February 1920, however, Lloyd George, ignoring the protest of Millerand, the French prime minister, appointed a commission to hear Greek claims. Closely bound up with these matters was the Italo–Greek conflict over Epiros and the Dodekanese. On 29 July 1919, Tittoni, the Italian foreign minister, and Venizelos, both of whom were trying to improve Greek–Italian relations, arrived at an agreement whereby Greece waived her claim to northern Epiros, while Italy undertook to agree to the cession of the Dodekanese to Greece with the exception of Rhodes. But early next year Nitti, on coming to power in Rome, went back on this bargain and, although in April 1920 the powers reached agreement on the terms to be presented to the Turks, the British government was unwilling to proceed further until the Italians gave satisfaction on the question of the Dodekanese. At length the Italians, who had something at stake in the tripartite agreement (an arrangement on spheres of influence) to be signed at the same time as the Turkish peace, finally gave way and at long last the Turkish peace terms were signed at Sèvres on 10 August 1920. That same day Greece and Italy signed a treaty on the Dodekanese.

The terms of the treaty of Sèvres concerning Greece were based on the findings of the commission appointed by Lloyd George. This commission had delineated a zone around Smyrna and had recommended that it should be placed under Greek administration. It was claimed, on the basis of American figures, that the zone in question contained 375,000 Greeks and 325,000 Moslems.[5] Over this zone the Turks were to retain a nominal sovereignty. In return for this concession they were to cede to Greece eastern Thrace up to the Chataldja lines.[6] In Smyrna there was to be a local parliament, which, after a period of five years, would be called upon to vote on whether or not the zone should pass under Greek sovereignty. Like eastern Thrace, western Thrace,[7] ceded by Bulgaria to the Allies by the treaty of Neuilly, was transferred to Greece in full sovereignty under a separate treaty, with the proviso that Dedeagatch should be a port of 'international concern' and should contain a Bulgarian zone. The Greek army had been in occupation of both these territories since mid-1920. This occupation had been expressly sanctioned by the supreme council, which had once again called upon the Greeks for military assistance following Turkish hostility to the peace terms drawn up at San Remo and presented to the Turkish delegation on 11 May. On this occasion the Greeks had not only put down resistance in Thrace, capturing Adrianople, but they had also between 22 June and 2 July cleared the whole region between Smyrna and the Dardanelles, taking Brussa, the ancient capital of the Ottoman empire.

The treaty of Sèvres awarded to Greece the Aegean Islands. A number of these were to be demilitarised, since they fell within the demilitarised zone

---

[5] The zone consisted of the whole of the *kazas* of Kassaba and Manissa, about the whole of Aivali, and about half of Ak-Hissar. The American pre-war figures for this zone were 500,000 Greeks, 470,000 Moslems, 23,000 Armenians. According to A. A. Pallis there were 550,000 Greeks, 299,000 Moslems, and 92,000 other nationalities.

[6] There were to be general guarantees for minorities, for mosques, and for the observance of Moslem family law. All races in Adrianople were to be given representation on the town council.

[7] Western Thrace was less Greek than eastern Thrace. The composition of both areas had been greatly affected by the Balkan Wars. According to 1914 Turkish figures, in eastern Thrace there were 365,000 Turks, 235,000 Greeks, and 48,000 others. The Greek figures for 1912 gave 325,000 Greeks, 253,000 Turks, and 98,000 others. In western Thrace, according to Greek figures, there had been only 87,000 Greeks in 1912 (36·7% of the total). By 1919 that figure had been reduced by over one-half.

of the Straits, which was to include Gallipoli and a considerable area on either side of the Bosphoros and the Dardanelles. The Straits were to be controlled by an international commission of which Greece and indeed Turkey (when she should have joined the League of Nations) should have membership. For this zone, including Constantinople, there was to be a French, British, and Italian garrison and a local Greek and Turkish gendarmerie which was to be under allied command. As for Constantinople itself, it was to remain the capital of Turkey and the residence of the Sultan, the Allies retaining the right, however, to modify this arrangement should Turkey fail to carry out the treaty in general and the minority clauses[8] in particular. Of considerable importance were the military clauses. The Turkish army was to be reduced to 35,000 gendarmerie and 15,000 'special elements' to put down riots and defend the frontiers. The distribution of these forces, which were to be tied to specific districts, was to be under control of an allied military commission which was to supervise demobilisation and disarmament. To prevent the build-up of trained military personnel, the army was to be based on voluntary enlistment and not on conscription.

When Venizelos signed the treaty of Sèvres it was not unreasonable for him to expect, if words mean anything, that the allied powers would enforce the military clauses with that same severity that they were showing in the execution of the military clauses of Versailles in respect of Germany. Moreover, he worked on the assumption that the principal frontiers of his Greek empire of 'two continents and five seas' would run along a disarmed Bulgaria and a disarmed and European-controlled Turkey.[9] Other Greeks, indeed the vast majority of Greeks, made that same assumption. Though well aware that the treaty was to the liking neither of the French nor of the Italians, who regarded it primarily as an Anglo–Greek triumph, he made the further assumption that the influence of Great Britain, which had caused the terms to be agreed, would ensure that those terms would be carried out. That same assumption was made again by the majority of Greeks. All realised vaguely that France, in order to get her way in Germany, had to play second fiddle in the Near East, and that Greece was more favoured by Great Britain than was Italy. The general feeling was that British interests coincided with those of Greece—that it had suited Great Britain to tilt the treaty in favour of Greece in order to keep Italy in her place. It was not indeed generally thought among Greeks that Greece owed her triumph to Venizelos. Nor was it generally envisaged that Greece would

[8] These were based chiefly on the clauses concerning minorities in the European treaties, but there were special provisions thought to be necessary in the case of Turkey.

[9] He had thus theoretically at least fulfilled the conditions which in a memorandum of January 1915 Colonel Metaxas had laid down for a successful intervention in Asia Minor—that the Allies should participate in the intervention with sufficient forces and that Anatolia should be partitioned.

be called upon to fight, and fight alone, to hold the gains that the treaty gave her.[10]

IV. The Fall of Venizelos: the Return of Constantine

It was this mentality which played a dominating part in the events in Greece in the five months following the signature of the treaty of Sèvres, and which allowed sheer party politics to come into play precisely at that moment when all Greeks should have closed their ranks. But in the hour of triumph, fate removed King Alexander,[11] who, young as he was, had shown wisdom and forbearance. On 25 October he died from the bite of a pet monkey. Elections were pending, Venizelos having decided to renew his mandate from the people. For Greece this decision was most unfortunate. Having been absent so long in Paris dealing with matters of high policy, Venizelos had lost touch with the more humdrum aspects of Greek politics and was probably unaware that the old divisions, intensified by the tyranny of his political lieutenants, had made his regime an object of fierce hatred among those who failed to profit from it. The maintenance of an army of some 300,000,[12] many of whom had been with the colours for as long as eight years, the high rate of taxation to maintain that army, and the spectacle of the lucky few who were beginning to make money as trade recovered, all added to the discontent under which the election campaign was held. Alexander's death and Prince Paul's refusal of the throne on the grounds that neither his father nor his elder brother had renounced their rights transformed that campaign into a contest between Constantine and Venizelos. The opposition was better organised than the Venizelists bargained for and at the elections of 14 November they gained 260 seats out of 370, though in point of fact the Venizelists had 52 per cent of the total vote. Three days later Venizelos and several of his ministers went into exile. Their defeat did not mean that two-thirds or even one-half of the country had renounced the *megali idhea*: it merely meant that those who had been in the wilderness intended to profit from its realisation.

While the Italians hailed the defeat of Venizelos as an Italian victory, the

[10] Venizelos himself was not quite so naïve. He certainly realised that it would be in Greece's interest to take a major part in the enforcement of the treaty. In October 1920 he offered Greek assistance, providing that the Allies would give financial and military assistance, that a Pontine Greek state should be established, that the Turks should be expelled from Constantinople, and that Constantinople and the Straits should be established as an independent state. These proposals were still under consideration when Venizelos fell from power.

[11] Alexander was married to a Greek, Aspasia Manos, daughter of a divorced courtier. Venizelos was not personally opposed to that marriage, the conditions of which had been originally proposed by the British minister, Lord Granville. It had been finally agreed that 'Mme Manos' should be the king's legitimate wife but not his queen, that she should live in her own private house, and should never accompany the king on official occasions. This arrangement was generally accepted and the couple were certainly popular.

[12] The Greeks had in Asia Minor 8 divisions (150,000 men) costing 2 million drachmai a day.

French and especially the British were greatly perturbed. The French, who had already had serious misgivings over the treaty of Sèvres and who were inclined to be hysterical where Constantine was concerned, endeavoured to use the occasion to regain the ground they had lost in the Near East. At conferences held in London between 26 November and 4 December they demanded that should the Greeks decide to recall Constantine the Allies should refuse to recognise him, that they should break off diplomatic relations with Greece, terminate financial aid, and deny to Greece the possession of crucial strategic positions. Both Curzon and Lloyd George opposed this policy. Curzon, who had always objected to the principle of partition underlying the treaty of Sèvres, had no objection, given that principle, to the satisfaction of Greek claims. To Greece as a nation the Allies had obligations, no matter what government happened to be in power. Constantine, if he returned, should be given every opportunity of adhering to the policy and the international obligations of the previous regime. The presence of the Greeks at the Straits was in no way a threat to the Allies. In any case, it was quite impossible to expel the Greeks from Smyrna and the islands. Lloyd George, however, was less logical and was personally much more hostile to Constantine than was his foreign secretary. When on 3 December the French proposed that Smyrna should be returned to Turkey to appease Kemal, though he opposed this outrageous proposal, he agreed that if Constantine returned, the Allies should issue a formal warning that they would wash their hands of their responsibilities towards Greece and would begin by withdrawing all financial aid. This warning, issued on 4 December, seems not to have been made widely known in Greece. At all events, in a plebiscite held on 5 December Greece decided by 999,960 votes to 10,383 (the official figures) to recall Constantine, who on 19 December received a frantic welcome when with difficulty (the crowds were so large) he entered Athens. On 8 December the Allies had already informed Greece that they would no longer continue their financial support. In agreeing to this Lloyd George cut off his nose to spite his face. Thereafter he did nothing for the Greeks, upon whom he had based his Near Eastern policy, and it was left to Lord Curzon and the British foreign office to defend them as best they could. Any encouragement Lloyd George gave them was their own wishful thinking based on his somewhat philhellenic statements in which he answered Turcophils, busybodies, and political opponents.

Curzon had ascertained that the Constantinists (despite their election statements to the contrary) intended to maintain the Greek army in Asia Minor. In view of the increase of the Kemalists' power, he considered some modification of the treaty necessary. He therefore proposed that the Allies should invite both Greeks and Turks to an international conference in London. Venizelos, who was in constant touch with the British, objected. He urged Britain to assist Constantine rather than abandon Greece, or, alternatively, if collaboration was impossible, to offer Greece financial help on condition that Constantine abdicated. Lloyd George preferred, however, to make the best of Constantine and when in February 1921 the Greek prime minister, Kalogeropoulos, visited London, he asked him whether Greece was in a position to defend her new frontiers. Having received an assurance that Greece was confident that she could do this, he nevertheless warned Kalogeropoulos that he should be prepared to compromise, for it was important that responsibility for any breakdown in the conference should fall upon the Turks. On 21 February, however, Kalogeropoulos informed the conference that his instructions from Athens were that Greece would not abate her claims, and in reply to the French argument that Turkish forces were formidable, he stated that Greece was best fitted to judge the military situation. It was at this point that the Italians and French proposed an inquiry into the ethnographic composition of both Thrace and Smyrna. This proposal (which Lloyd George was not prepared to reject out of hand) the Greeks considered unjust and in view of past history quite irrelevant. As, however, the Turks with certain reservations had agreed to it Lloyd George suggested to the Greeks that they should accept administrative control of a reduced Smyrna zone under Turkish sovereignty. This the Greeks were prepared to do, provided the governor should be appointed by Greece with the consent of the League of Nations and provided administrative costs should be subtracted from any tribute to be paid to Turkey. The Turks made no reply. Hence when the French and Italians attempted to throw upon Greece the onus for the failure of the conference, Lloyd George and Curzon had good grounds for refusing to yield. They not only insisted that Greece should enjoy freedom of action: they proposed that the Allies should observe strict neutrality. But whatever the French and Italians may have agreed to in words, they had no intention of remaining neutral. While the conference was on, they both made agreements with the Kemalist element in the Turkish delegation. The French agreement not only conflicted with the provisions of the treaty concerning the frontiers of Cilicia, and with the tripartite agreement, but it also made available supplies of arms which eventually found their way to the Kemalists. The Italian agreement was an attempt to steal a march in the way of concessions, it being understood (but not expressly stated) that Italy would send arms to Turkey and generally support Kemalist claims. Indeed both powers had already begun to supply Kemal, their object being to defeat Great Britain by helping him to defeat the Greeks. This was but a prelude to the treachery that was to follow: in blatant disregard for their signatures on a treaty and of their frequent protestations of good faith, in blatant disregard, moreover, of the fate of both the Greek and Armenian Christians, France put her bondholders and her concessionaires before all else; and Italy, who played fast and loose between France and Great Britain, endeavoured to appease Kemal in order to gain what proved to be a disappointing mess of pottage.

On 18 March Lloyd George, on confirming to Gounaris (who had joined

Kalogeropoulos in London) that Greece retained freedom of action, went out of his way to warn him that a military failure might well prove irreparable. But the Constantinist government was determined to press on.[13] It realised that, during the time already wasted on inconclusive negotiations, the enemy, able to obtain supplies not only from France and Italy, but also from Russia, had been daily growing stronger.

V. The Campaigns in Asia Minor

In January 1921 the Greek third army corps made a reconnaissance towards Eskishehir where it overcame a Turkish force, but in accordance with instructions it retired to Brussa accompanied by 3,000 Greek and Armenian civilians who took the opportunity to escape from oppression. It was too early in the year to launch an offensive. In view, however, of the approaching spring and in case of the failure of the London conference, the Greek command in Asia Minor were making final preparations for an attack on the Turkish positions. At the time the Greeks had three army corps forming a crescent facing eastwards. On the right was the first army corps at Ushak and Bouladan. One hundred miles to the north (to the east of Brussa) was the third army corps, forming the left flank. In the rear, at a distance of about one hundred miles from the flanks, was the second army corps holding the Manissa–Panderma railway. Further in the rear at Smyrna was a division forming a reserve. This position was not thoroughly satisfactory. What was needed was either an advance or a withdrawal to form a shorter and more cohesive front.

In March, immediately upon the failure of the London conference, the Greeks attacked from both flanks. The first army corps advanced from Ushak and easily captured Afium Karahissar, but the third army corps encountered strong opposition and only with difficulty got back to Brussa. Kemal did not follow up in pursuit. Instead he turned south and attacked with eight divisions the first army corps' line of communication. The Greek 34th regiment defending that line fought stoutly until relieved by the main first army corps, which forced the nationalists to retreat with heavy losses. The Greeks now realised, however, that the enemy had grown infinitely more powerful and that only a crushing military defeat would make him come to terms. Throughout May and June they hastily increased their preparations and Constantine himself went over to Asia Minor to join his forces.

Meanwhile the diplomats had again become active. General Harington, the British commander-in-chief at Constantinople, had expressed the fear

[13] The British intercepted the Greek accounts of the London conference, and Curzon formed the impression that Lloyd George had encouraged the Greeks behind his back. Sir E. Crowe, the permanent undersecretary at the foreign office, discerned quite clearly, however, that the Greek delegation had misrepresented the situation in its reports to Athens.

that the Greeks might collapse and a British cabinet committee, accepting the advice of Venizelos, decided to revive the London (March) proposals in a slightly different form and to put forward the idea of imposing them on whichever belligerent refused to accept them. Briand, while willing to support fresh mediation, refused to contemplate any idea of coercing the Turks. It is not surprising therefore that Gounaris (who became prime minister on 7 April) refused to consider the allied terms. Had he been a wiser man, however, he would have accepted Curzon's offer (Smyrna under a Christian governor and an allied guarantee) in terms which would have thrown the responsibility for the Christian minorities fairly and squarely upon the Western Allies. By turning down the offer he did not exactly lose a friend (for a friend Curzon never was) but he weakened the resolution of a man who might have continued to fight hard for Greece: instead, he gave Curzon some excuse for his halting retreat under French pressure in the year that followed. But Gounaris was in a difficult position. The campaigning season was slipping away; the Greek army had been strengthened; changes in leadership had improved it; and it was essential it should strike without delay. Nevertheless, it was not until mid-July that the offensive began. This time the Greeks carried out a turning movement on the right and a flanking movement from Brussa on the left; and, although they failed to entrap the Turks between the two pincers, nevertheless on 21 July they won a pitched battle at Eskishehir. The great question was whether to hold the ground won or to push on to Angora which was only about 40 miles away. Dousmanis, the chief of the general staff, opposed any further advance. Papoulas, the commander-in-chief, favoured it, and King Constantine came down firmly on his side. Frantic preparations were undertaken to repair the railway supply-lines and to organise the necessary provisions. Despite this effort, the supply-system remained inadequate, and the Greek forces, having made heavy sacrifices on the Sakaria river, were obliged to pull back at the very moment when they were in sight of victory. Had the British only allowed the Greeks the normal belligerent right to purchase war supplies in Britain and helped them to raise a loan, at a time when they knew perfectly well that France and Italy were providing arms to the Turks, then the Greeks might well have finished off the war. As it was, the French and Italians even refused to recognise the Greek right of search in flagrant breach of the maritime law which they themselves had upheld during the war with Germany.

By 23 September the Greeks were back on the line Afium Karahissar–Eskishehir–Karakeui railway. In October they beat off a determined Turkish attack upon the first-named place. The military situation was therefore a stalemate and in view of this Curzon concluded that the time had come for a further attempt at mediation, particularly as Gounaris was anxious to visit London to discuss the situation and to raise a loan. The two met at the end of October. Curzon advised Gounaris to place himself in the hands of the powers, having intimated that the Greeks might have to withdraw from Smyrna and accept some frontier modification in Thrace. This advice Gounaris formally accepted on 2 November. Just at that moment, however, the news arrived that on 20 October the French, through the agency of that 'Levantine busybody' Franklin-Bouillon, had signed a separate agreement at Angora with Turkey. The French undertook to withdraw their troops from Cilicia in return for a vague promise of economic concessions. Later it transpired they had also agreed to leave behind military supplies and air-craft. This blatant act of disloyalty, though he denounced the French to their faces, Curzon nevertheless accepted, for despite constant provocation on many issues he could never bring himself to denounce the *entente*: if he sometimes threatened to do so, then he did so only as a means of preserving it.

During the last few months of 1921 Curzon persisted with his negotia-tions and in December produced a memorandum for consideration at a conference. That same month Lloyd George attempted a general settlement of all Anglo–French differences by offering British military aid in the event of German aggression against French soil. In return he hoped *inter alia* for a reasonable understanding on the Near East in accordance with Curzon's plans. But the conference, chiefly owing to Briand's replacement by Poin-caré in January 1922, did not meet till 22–26 March. In the meantime Curzon and Lloyd George saw Gounaris at Cannes and made it clear that no peace was possible while the Greeks remained in Smyrna. They advised an 80-mile withdrawal of the Greek army from the frontier of Thrace, promised that the Allies would protect the Christian minorities, and agreed that until a settlement was reached the Greek army should maintain its existing position in Asia Minor. They had already given their blessing to a Greek loan to be raised in London. For commercial reasons, however, this loan fell through, and despairing of the delays, Gounaris, who had again confirmed his willingness to place himself in allied hands, revealed to Cur-zon in a letter of 15 February that Greece had almost exhausted her re-sources. Curzon replied that he could only hope that the military position was less immediately critical than Gounaris's note suggested and that the patriotism and discipline of the Greek army would not be found wanting. Before he had received Curzon's reply Gounaris had warned the Greek high command that withdrawal and evacuation might be necessary. Whether Curzon's reply caused him to change his mind, we do not know. At all events, at his trial later in the year Gounaris cited Curzon's letter in his defence—as encouragement from the British to continue the war. Curzon's intelligence was that matters were not so black as Gounaris had painted them and he certainly hoped that the Greeks would stand fast on their winter line in order to give the Paris (March) conference a chance of success. At that conference he proposed to Poincaré that both sides should accept an armistice and that the basis of peace should be: withdrawal of the Greeks from Smyrna, which should be placed under the League of Nations; removal of the frontier in Thrace to a distance of 80 miles from Constantinople; limitation of Greek forces in the rest of eastern Thrace; conditional evacuation of allied troops from Constantinople; a League commission for the Straits; a reduction in the demilitarised zone; a national home in Cilicia for the Armenians; and supervision by the League of provisions for safeguarding the minorities. On these proposals Poincaré and Curzon, during ten tedious and polemical meetings, reached some agreement, but Poincaré let it be clearly understood that he would not use force against the Turks.

The Greeks, though willing to accept an armistice, reserved their reply to these proposals pending a reply from the Turks. The Turks, however, refused to accept any basic peace conditions and tried to secure the unconditional evacuation of the Greek forces before a peace conference began. This unconditional conference, with Poincaré's support, they wanted to hold in Asia Minor. Curzon threatened to wreck the *entente*. This brought Poincaré to London. Here Curzon was prepared to concede an unconditional conference in return for the recognition of the Greek right of search and a pledge by the powers to stand firm on the Paris proposals. But Poincaré flatly refused to recognise the Greek right of search—a refusal which led to further delays. Of these delays, obviously being engineered by the French while they supplied Kemal with arms, the Greeks complained, and on 29 July requested allied authority to enter Constantinople—a demand which was really a threat and which the Allies refused to countenance. Venizelos at this time was pressing Lloyd George to take firm action against the Turks. Lloyd George, however, let it be known that this was out of the question. Nevertheless, on 4 August he made in the Commons a rousing anti-Turkish speech, pointing out that while the Greeks were being prevented by the Allies from attacking Constantinople, the Turks were receiving arms from Europe. It was grossly unfair, he said, that the Greeks should be prevented from waging war to their best advantage. Whether or not it would have been of advantage to Greece to have shown open defiance at this juncture and to have rushed into Constantinople, risking possible conflict with the British (for the French and Italians were really powerless), is a matter on which one might endlessly speculate. At all events the Greeks were cautious, and Lloyd George's speech proved to be more an irritant to the Turkish nationalists than a stimulant to the Greeks. Kemal, fearing that the British would terminate their policy of neutrality, decided to attack the Greek positions. He had built up an army around Konia much stronger than that which the Greeks had failed to destroy on the Sakaria river, for the French evacuation of Cilicia had freed large forces and the supply of arms and ammunition from Russia and Europe had been considerable.[14]

The Greek main front was 200 miles in extent, covering the line Gemlik

---

[14] According to a British war office report this consisted of 36 guns, 304 machine-guns, 39,195 rifles, 197,164 shells, 15,595,440 cartridges, 1,500 aircraft bombs, etc.

(on the Marmara)—Eskishehir–Seidi Ghazi–Afium Karahissar–Savran–Chivril. From Chivril there was a 65-mile line of posts to Ortanja, the railhead of the Smyrna–Aidin railway. Along that railway was a southern defensive flank 115 miles in extent, which was extended in April when the Greeks occupied Sokia and Nuova Scala on their evacuation by the Italians. The Greek northern group, consisting of the third army corps (four divisions) with its headquarters at Eskishehir, held the sector Gemlik to Seidi Ghazi. The southern group, consisting of the first and second army corps (six divisions in all), occupied the sector Seidi Ghazi to Ortanja. The weak point was Afium Karahissar at the junction of the Kassaba and Baghdad railways, the latter of which was under Kemal's control. For this reason the Greeks had allocated two reserve divisions and a cavalry brigade to the commander of the southern army group. In April the southern group had repulsed with heavy losses a Turkish attack made with two divisions and artillery at Savran, but the Turks were beginning to show some superiority in the air, the Greek aircraft being old and hard to maintain, and the Greek anti-aircraft weapons were very poor. As for the southern flank, this was held by six regiments of line of communication troops.

In all sectors morale was good, the food simple but adequate, shelter and clothing satisfactory, and the defensive positions well prepared. On the other hand, the Greek troops, on learning of the allied March proposals, had become convinced that they would not be called upon to advance, and as a result they had lost their will to attack. The officers had discussed plans for pulling back to a shorter front covering the Smyrna zone. It was remembered, however, that the reason for the advance had been the very difficulty of defending a line further back; and everyone, particularly Constantine himself, was much concerned for the Christian populations which were showing signs of panic. There was some hope, however, that a local militia might be formed and the commander-in-chief had appealed to the Venizelist officers in the National Defence League in Constantinople under General Joannou to undertake this task. Joannou had agreed and for a moment the reconciliation of Venizelists and Constantinists seemed to be a possibility.[15]

In May 1922, following a complicated ministerial crisis (Stratos replaced Gounaris who was in turn replaced by Protopapadakis with Gounaris and followers of Stratos in his government), General Hadjianesti was appointed

[15] The National Defence League had been formed early in 1921 by Constantinople civilians and Venizelist officers who had left the army. It had hoped to create, with British support, a separatist regime on the lines of that established at Thessaloniki in 1916. The basic assumption was that the Constantinists would renounce the Venizelist policy in Asia Minor. Later the assumption was that the Constantinist forces were certain to fail. Hence in June 1921 plans were made to seize control of the army and to set up a provisional government under Stergiadis, the Greek high commissioner in Smyrna. These plans failed to materialise. Nevertheless, with the arrival in Constantinople of the Patriarch Meletios, an ardent Venizelist, the movement gathered strength and spread to Smyrna, the aim being to establish a 'Mikrasiatic' state. But no encouragement was forthcoming from Stergiadis; Venizelos was not enthusiastic; and Papoulas, the commander-in-chief, maintained a highly equivocal attitude. The movement petered out, its last flicker being an attempt to promote the return of certain Venizelist officers to the army.

to command the Greek troops in Thrace. Shortly afterwards, largely owing to the influence of Stergiadis, he was appointed to replace General Papoulas in Asia Minor. Although he was certainly somewhat eccentric, he was an honest, courageous, and devoted soldier. He was nevertheless narrow-minded, and he had a mania for centralisation. He had had no field experience since the Balkan Wars and it is doubtful whether he ever became conversant with strategic and tactical problems of the Asia Minor armies. Neither the chief of staff nor the deputy chief of staff had any confidence in him and these two experienced officers resigned. Having made a tour of his command and having returned to Athens to report, he was back in Smyrna by early July. He formed new regiments, combed the line of communication troops, and managed to build up the forces in Thrace to about four divisions to form the fourth army corps.[16] It was with this army corps that the Greeks threatened, at the end of July, to enter Constantinople. They hoped that this threat would entice the Turks to attack the Bosphoros and that, as a result, the Allies would call on the Greek troops to protect the allied forces. Failing this, they hoped that a threat from Thrace would cause Kemal to divert forces from Konia and thus facilitate a Greek withdrawal which otherwise would be a most hazardous undertaking.

On 26 August Kemal directed a main attack on a 30-mile front and broke through in the sector between Afium Karahissar and Savran. The Greeks fell back but found the Ushak road barred by Turkish troops. The second army corps and the reserve attempted to retire north of the Murad Dagh, but in the narrow valleys and mountain tracks lost cohesion and abandoned much material. Its commander, Trikoupis, who was cut off from the first army which he also commanded, was captured, only to learn from the Turks that he had been appointed to replace Hadjianesti. The main part of the second army corps fought in isolated positions. The first army corps, along with the XIIIth division of the second army corps, retired by the main road to Tonlu Bunar where it fought a stout rearguard action. It fought again with tenacity at Ushak. Thereafter it retreated, the retreat and the evacuation of Chesme being covered by substantial rearguard actions of the IInd Athens division (Colonel Gonatas) and the XIIIth division (Colonel Plastiras). On 8 September Greek headquarters, taking off most of the stores, evacuated Smyrna, which Turkish cavalry entered the following day. On 11 September the Turks massacred many Christians and two days later set fire to the town, destroying all of it except for two or three hundred buildings and the Turkish quarter. Over 25,000 people perished and over 200,000, without food or water, thronged to the shore, crying for help. Archbishop Chrisostomos did not live to see this unhappy sequel to French and Italian diplomacy. He had been martyred by Nureddin Pasha the day the Turks entered. He could easily have escaped, but preferred to die among his people. He had drafted a telegram to the archbishop of Canterbury: 'For

---

[16] At the time the Greeks had one division in Epiros and one in Macedonia.

Christ's sake, hasten to avert the calamity which we feel is approaching.'

Meanwhile the northern group (third army corps) had held its ground, but when the southern group lost Ushak and Gediz, on the river of that name, it had to retire. Its retirement, however, was mismanaged. The XIth division was cut off at Mudania and surrendered. The division at Seidi Ghazi was also cut off, but managed to get to the coast opposite Mitilini 260 miles away with its artillery intact. The rest of the group reached Panderma and was embarked for Greece.

Why a Greek army superior in numbers to the Kemalist forces and not decidedly inferior in equipment should have met with this disaster is a question which is still a matter of dispute. One theory is that Hadjianesti by centralising the command deprived its component parts of effective direction when the crisis came. Another view is that the reserve division was badly sited and could not be moved in time to the appropriate sector. Again, it is said that, when Trikoupis fell back with the first and second army corps, the leading division of these formations halted too soon, thus causing Trikoupis to be cut off from the Ushak road. Finally, it is said that Trikoupis, having been cut off, made the mistake of moving round to the northern side of the Murad Dagh. Generally speaking, the disaster must be attributed to a failure of command and not to any lack of fighting quality on the part of the Greek soldier. The Greeks had indeed inflicted very heavy losses on the Turks, who were tired, strung out, and hardly in a condition to take much more punishment. Like Waterloo, the great battle could have gone either way.

VI. The Revolution in Greece

In the months before the Anatolian fiasco Georgios Rallis had been attempting to form a new party, 'The National Awakening', drawn from moderate Constantinists and Venizelists, the two main parties having become considerably fragmented over the past year. Nothing, however, had come of Rallis's efforts and the national disaster again split the country from top to bottom. On 10 September the king dismissed his government, the real head of which was Gounaris, and, in spite of clamours on the one hand for Venizelos and on the other for Metaxas, he entrusted the administration to Triandafillakos, former Greek high commissioner in Constantinople. Soldiers were returning, refugees were flowing in, and the treasury was almost exhausted. There was much chaos, tempers ran high, but there were no riots or disorder. On 26 September, however, an aircraft dropped on Athens leaflets signed by Colonel Gonatas in the name of the army, the navy, and the populations of Chios and Mitilini, demanding the abdication of Constantine in favour of the crown prince. Shortly afterwards the battleship *Limnos* arrived at Lavrion with a revolutionary committee on board demanding that Gonatas's terms should be accepted before midnight. At noon next day the king abdicated, giving orders that no resistance should be organised. That afternoon Generals A. Mazarakis, Gargalidis, and Pangalos, constituting a provisional authority, installed themselves in Athens, and the following day revolutionary forces, 12,000-strong, made an orderly entry into the city. Later that day a revolutionary committee (Gonatas, Colonel Plastiras, and naval Captain Fokas) assumed authority. This committee arrested the ex-ministers and but for the intervention of the French and British ministers would have shot them out of hand. The triumvirate was not, however, hostile to King Constantine and it allowed the British naval mission to arrange for him, Queen Sophia, and their daughters, together with Prince Nicholas and his family, to proceed to Palermo. Thus for the second time Constantine, always a good patriot, left the land he loved and said farewell to his people whom he had tried to serve. In the country as a whole there was no bitterness against him, just as there was no enthusiasm for the revolution. With his successor, King George II, the masses were highly satisfied. Having been led to believe that the presence of Constantine had caused the isolation of Greece, they now looked for a change of attitude on the part of Great Britain and France, whom they expected to save for Greece her gains in Thrace and in the islands.

The revolutionary committee had promised the British minister to re-store civilian government and this they did, at least on paper, by announcing a government under the veteran A. Zaimis, with Nikolaos Politis, a Venizel-ist, as foreign minister. At the time Zaimis was absent from Greece, seeing his doctors in Vienna, and Sotirios Krokidas, formerly governor of Crete, now minister of the interior, was appointed acting prime minister. The majority of the government was moderate Venizelist. Venizelos himself, however, remained outside Greece and refused to give any advice on the internal situation. Nevertheless, he was willing to act as the Greek repre-sentative in Europe, and from that position he more or less conducted foreign policy. There is no doubt that his freedom from the party conflict facilitated his task of trying to rescue what he could for Greece from the Smyrna disaster. He was free also from the divisions within his old party following. In October some of his old left-wing associates attempted to set going a republican movement, much to the consternation of the moderate Venizelists and the leader of their party, General Danglis, who feared that to raise the constitutional issue would be tantamount to losing the elections which were expected to be held in the very near future.

Although the revolutionary committee had established a civilian govern-ment, it treated the ministers merely as heads of governmental departments. On 18 October it issued a revolutionary manifesto, stating that the revolu-tion was above party, that it would abolish all that had led to the national disaster, and punish those who had been responsible. Five days later it was announced that a court would be set up to try Constantine's ex-ministers and other persons. What exactly prompted this move, it is difficult to say.

No doubt the leaders and close supporters of the revolution feared that they would lose the elections if Gounaris remained alive; no doubt they were under pressure from army officers to find a scapegoat for the military disaster; and there is a strong suspicion that they were under the influence of the French representatives in Athens. At all events, the trial began on 3 November under the presidency of General Othonaios, a Venizelist, and eleven other military judges. The case, which was conducted with scant regard to rules of evidence, was concluded on 27 November, and the following morning Gounaris, Stratos, Protopapadakis, Baltatzis, Theotokis, and General Hadjianesti were condemned to death, the two other accused, General Stratigos and Admiral Goudas, being sent to life imprisonment. The death sentences were carried out that same morning.

Before and during the trial the British government had endeavoured to obtain assurances that death penalties would not be inflicted. The reply was that this might be done if Great Britain could guarantee that the accused should, if banished, never return to Greece. But this difficult undertaking the British government could not accept, and in refusing to do so threatened that if the accused were put to death, then diplomatic relations with Greece would be broken off. The Greek government, however, failed to get satisfaction from the revolutionary committee and resigned. On 27 November a new government was formed under Colonel Gonatas, with General Pangalos as minister for war and Apostolos Alexandris as foreign minister. Except for Colonel Plastiras, who remained outside as leader of the revolution, and for Captains Hadjikiriakos and Gerondas, the members of the former revolutionary committee were brought within the government. With this government the British minister made an eleventh-hour effort to save the prisoners. Throughout considerable pressure had been put on Venizelos to intervene. Eventually he sent Commander Talbot from Lausanne to Athens, but this friend of Greece arrived one hour too late. He was in time, however, to save Prince Andrew, who had been arrested in October, and he obtained from Pangalos a promise that no more political prisoners would be shot. This assurance was greatly welcomed by the British government who, while showing displeasure at the judicial murder of the unfortunate six by withdrawing their minister from Athens, did not completely break off (as is usually said) diplomatic relations with Greece.

The executions were a new experience in Greece. They brought upon the nation a sense of shame and, although they eventually served, along with the events out of which they had arisen, to perpetuate the fierce animosities of the Greek political scene, their immediate effect was a sobering one. Therefore it may be said that these men did not die in vain. Victims of their patriotism, of circumstance, and to some extent of their failings, which, like their patriotism, they shared with their murderers, their martyrdom probably prevented a civil war.

Throughout the year 1923 the principal conflicts lay not between two great parties but between different brands of Venizelists, between the leading military chiefs, even between Pangalos and Plastiras. With the creation of 'leagues of national safety' throughout the whole of Greece (extremist Venizelist organisations similar to the leagues of military reservists of Constantinist Greece) the republican movement grew apace, but both Plastiras and Venizelos continued to favour the 'crowned democracy'. All this time Zaimis, who might possibly have formed a civilian government to replace the rule of the military men, continued to dither, and demanded, before accepting office, that the allied governments should recognise George II—a not unreasonable request. One likely alternative was a *coup d'état* by Pangalos, but illness prevented him from taking this bold course. Now Venizelos broke his silence. On 8 August, while reiterating his 'irrevocable' decision never to return to Greece, he told the press that perhaps Greece was not unripe for a republic which was a less complicated form of government than a crowned democracy.

In October a military revolution broke out under the leadership of General Gargalidis and Colonel Ziras in the Peloponnese and Macedonia. This was directed against the existing revolution. The affair, however, did not last long. Pangalos and Plastiras took personal command of government troops, and assisted by General Georgios Kondilis they suppressed the revolt with very little difficulty. The chief result was to give the republicans the upper hand, for it was generally said (quite falsely) that the king was in league with the rebels. At any moment a *coup* was expected, but timely representations from the foreign ministers averted such a move for the moment. Hence the long-discussed elections came up for further consideration. In mid-November Venizelos, who was strongly against establishing a republic by force, advised his followers that no decision to abolish the monarchy should be made before elections were held. This advice was generally accepted, but the question remained whether a republican programme should be adopted at the elections. This issue split the Venizelists. Danglis appealed to Venizelos for further guidance and Venizelos came down firmly on the side of not making republicanism an election issue.

From these elections, held on 16 December, most of the old royalists abstained. The results claimed were: conservative liberals (General Danglis) 221, liberal republicans (Roussos) 97, republicans (Papanastasiou) 90, independent republicans 41, anti-Venizelists 7. The claims of the republicans were exaggerated, for the total adds up to 456, whereas the number of deputies was only 397. But no one quite understood what the election results portended. There was a general feeling, however, that George II should leave the country while the issue was being decided. This he did on 19 December. Great uncertainty prevailed. Eventually Danglis, Plastiras, Zaimis, and 279 deputies sent telegrams to Venizelos begging him to return to Greece. Similar action was taken by the league of officers, who stipulated, however, that he should not bring back the king. Venizelos decided to

return. Reaching Athens on 4 January 1924, the following day he was unanimously elected president of the chamber. When he arrived he had certainly retrieved his reputation. He had represented Greece at the conference
of Lausanne, where his presence had been most valuable and where he had
won the respect not only of Europe but also of his Turkish protagonist,
Ismet Pasha.

VII. The Armistice of Mudania and the Treaty of Lausanne

On 3 September 1922, when news of the collapse of the Asia Minor front
reached Athens, the Greek government requested British intervention. This
request the British government was prepared to meet. The British position
at the Straits had been endangered by the Greek collapse and it was
considered essential that no settlement should be made which ignored
vital British interests. The difficulty, however, was that France and Italy
might continue to undermine the British position in the Near East and
refuse to assist in holding Constantinople and the Straits. Curzon, who
complained bitterly of French treachery, nevertheless hoped to bring
France into line by winning the support of her Little *entente* allies.

On 7 September the British cabinet decided to uphold the March proposals and to send British forces to stiffen the weak French units holding
Gallipoli. A few days later they appealed to the Dominions for assistance
and publicly announced their intention to stand firm, having warned the
Turks to respect the neutral zone. They had decided to take fresh stock of
the Greek army which might be needed, but they were prepared, in the hope
of accelerating peace, to concede to the Turks eastern Thrace. General
Harington had already taken steps to secure Chanak and the Straits zone,
the French and Italian commanders having agreed to show their flags. But
on 21 September the French withdrew their troops to Constantinople and
the Italians followed suit. This gave rise to a slanging match between
Curzon and Poincaré, who were in conference in Paris. Curzon, recognising
that he had been again treacherously defeated, decided to play for time. He
agreed that the Turks should be invited to a conference with the intimation
that they would get eastern Thrace, Adrianople, and Constantinople as soon
as peace was signed. On 23 September the Turks advanced into the neutral
zone at Chanak. Kemal, however, was merely trying to improve his
negotiating position. He had no intention of fighting the British empire,
which could call upon the assistance of the Greek divisions in Thrace—an
army which was in good fettle and which only needed some British equipment to transform it into a formidable fighting force. Instead he agreed to
negotiate an armistice with General Harington at Mudania. While the
negotiations were going on, he relaxed pressure on Chanak and mounted a
threat to Ismid in the hope of obtaining an early entry into eastern Thrace
and the possession of Karagatch, a suburb of Adrianople. To Karagatch he

9

failed to stake a claim, but at the convention of Mudania signed on 11 October it was agreed that Greece should recognise Turkish claims to Smyrna and eastern Thrace and that Greek forces should retire to the west of the Maritza within fifteen days. Meanwhile on 6 October Curzon was again in Paris, fighting another round with Poincaré. Although he made it clear that Britain would, if necessary, make a stand alone, yet with Venizelos's agreement, he had given way on eastern Thrace. Poincaré, however, agreed to a provisional allied occupation of thirty days before the Turks moved in. Agreement had also been reached to hold a peace conference, which after much further negotiations met at Lausanne on 20 November. By that time the Lloyd George coalition government had fallen. Curzon, however, remained at the foreign office, and at the conference of Lausanne, he fought hard not only for British interests but for Greece. His greatest asset, and Venizelos's too, was the presence of the Greek army west of the Maritza, which, given British assistance (or even without it), might make a dash to Constantinople and drive the Turks out of eastern Thrace. Here the Turkish forces (though in excess of those permitted by the Mudania convention) were hardly in a position to stand up to four Greek divisions, which by May 1923 had been increased to nine.

During the first phase of the conference (which ended on 4 February 1923) Curzon saved for Greece western Thrace and Karagatch. Karagatch, along with a small triangle between the Maritza and the Arda, however, was subsequently conceded in the second phase of the conference by Venizelos, in return for the renunciation by the Turks of their claim to an idemnity from Greece. This question of an indemnity, which Greece could not possibly pay, had frequently threatened to bring about a breakdown in the negotiations. Venizelos persistently let it be known that if the Turks refused to yield, he could not restrain the Greek government from ordering an advance into eastern Thrace. On the other hand, he made it clear in Athens that he would resign from his mission if the Greek government failed to allow him to barter away Karagatch and the Arda–Maritza triangle.

At the treaty of Lausanne Greece lost to Turkey all that she had obtained in Asia Minor, the whole of eastern Thrace, including Karagatch and the Arda–Maritza triangle, and the islands of Imvros and Tenedos. She lost to Italy, besides Kastelorizo, the Dodekanese. Italy, hostile to the end, had denounced her agreements with Greece relating to these islands. The apparent loss to Greece in terms of Hellenic population was about 500,000.[17] But the real loss was considerably less, for during the first phase of the Lausanne conference, Venizelos had negotiated with Ismet Pasha, the Turkish representative, a convention, signed on 30 January 1923, providing for the exchange of the Greek population in Turkey with the Moslem population in Greece. Exception was made, however, in the case of Greek

[17] Greece had also lost a population of 150,000 as the result of the award of northern Epiros to Albania by the conference of ambassadors in November 1921.

inhabitants of Constantinople established there before 30 October 1918, and of Moslem inhabitants of western Thrace.[18] This exchange of populations was to be compulsory as from 1 May 1923.

Venizelos wished to make the exchange agreement independent of the treaty of Lausanne, which showed signs of being delayed. (He wanted to get rid as soon as possible of some 350,000 Moslems in order to make room for Greek refugees.) Yet he was strongly opposed to the principle of compulsion. The Turks, however, insisted that the exchange should be obligatory, and it was Curzon who persuaded Venizelos and through him the Greek government to give way on this issue. Curzon pointed out that if one accepted the policy of an exchange of populations (and he himself considered it a very bad and vicious one), it was immaterial whether the exchange were made legally voluntary or compulsory: in practice compulsion would be exercised by the Turks; and it would be to the advantage of the Greeks to have the legal right to expel the Moslems in order to free their land for the settlement of the displaced Greeks. Hence the principle of obligatory exchange was adopted.

The result of the convention, both in its retroactive aspect and in its immediate application, was that sparsely-populated Turkey received 354,647 Moslems for whom there was plenty of land, while overpopulated Greece was called upon to absorb some 1,300,000 souls, most of whom had already arrived completely destitute of movable property.[19] Thus in the hour of disaster, Greece, although her territory was reduced, achieved substantially her unification. Except for those who remained in Constantinople under Turkish rule, in northern Epiros under Albanian rule, in the Dodekanese under Italian rule, and in Cyprus which the British had annexed in 1914, all the Greek people had been brought within the confines of the Hellenic kingdom.

During the course of the discussions on the exchange of populations, the vexed problem of the Patriarchate had arisen. The nationalist Turks, who had in mind the eventual abolition of the caliphate, were demanding that the Patriarch should be expelled from their dominions. Both Meletios IV and his predecessor, the acting Patriarch Dorotheos, had favoured Greek irredentism. They had not only encouraged the Greek populations to continue their struggle against the Turks but had been in the habit of telegraphing congratulatory messages to the Greek commanders in Asia Minor.

[18] Later exception was made in the case of the Moslem Albanians to be found chiefly in Epiros.

[19] In the application of the convention the number of Moslems removed from Greece was twice that of the Christians who were ejected from Turkey. The exact number of Greek refugees from Turkey is not known. In 1928 there were 1,221,849 refugees in Greece, but by that date many had died and many had gone to Egypt, America, and elsewhere. About 152,000 had arrived between 1913 and 1922: just over one million had fled from Asia Minor and Thrace following the Greek defeat of 1922. During these troubled times more Moslems were displaced than Greeks: over the period 1912 to 1923 some 4 million Moslems left the territories which the Turks had lost.

Following the Greek defeat Meletios IV was eager to go either to Thessaloniki or to Mount Athos. The whole problem was complicated by the attitude of the Greek government towards Meletios and by a movement within Turkey to set up a purely Turkish patriarch who should have within his fold solely those Turkish Christian subjects (the 50,000 *karamanlis*) who spoke Turkish as their mother-tongue. This movement was associated with the name Papa Efthim, who, holding that the election of Meletios in December 1921 had been illegal, had set himself up in the autumn of 1922 along with four other prelates as the holy synod of the Turkish orthodox church with Turkish as the liturgical language. The basis of his church was destroyed, however, when at Lausanne it was decided to regard the *karamanlis* as Greeks and to include them in the exchange of populations. Instead of the *karamanlis* a considerable Greek-speaking population was to be left within the Turkish state, living in Constantinople itself. The question therefore arose whether this population should form an autocephalous Church in communion with a Patriarchate outside Turkey or whether it should form the patriarchal diocese, the Patriarch remaining in Constantinople. Meletios took the view that if the Patriarchate remained in Turkey, its position would be intolerable: it would be constantly interfered with by the Turkish authorities and it would fail to find suitable clerics with Turkish citizenship to provide for a holy synod and ecclesiastical administration. The majority of Greeks of all parties took a different view: they wanted the Patriarch to remain where he had always been. In any case, there were many Greeks who regarded the election of Meletios as illegal and the Constantinist governments had found his presence in Constantinople most embarrassing.

Born in Crete of Ottoman parents, Meletios had gone first to Jerusalem and then to Cyprus, where he was living when the British annexed the island. In 1918 he had been elected archbishop of Athens, a royal decree having been issued making him an Hellenic subject. An ardent Venizelist, upon the fall of Venizelos he had gone to America. Becoming a candidate for the patriarchal throne on the death of Dorotheos,[20] he had claimed to be an Ottoman, British, and Hellenic subject. The Greek authorities had already tried him. They accused him of being a foreigner who had usurped the archbishopric of Athens and of having promoted a schism in the Orthodox Church in America. But these charges were mutually destructive, for if he was not a Greek subject, the government had no right to take action against him. The holy synod deprived him of his archiepiscopal dignities, condemned him to forfeit his priestly rank, and ordered him to live as a monk at Strofades near Zante. This verdict, having been confirmed by royal decree, was communicated to the autocephalous Orthodox Churches

---

[20] After the armistice of 1918 the Patriarch Germanos was accused of having truckled to the Turks and was driven from office. Dorotheos was acting Patriarch until his death in London in 1921.

and to the prelates of Constantinople. In February 1922 the Greek government endeavoured to promote the election of a rival Patriarch, but the general situation in Constantinople did not admit of this. Hence Meletios remained as a centre of intrigue against the Greek government. He was associated with the independent Asia Minor movement and with the men who had prepared and carried out the revolution of September 1922. Following that revolution he had certainly enjoyed considerable popularity in some quarters in Athens, and he continued to hope that the new men in power would allow him to transfer the Patriarchate to Greek soil. At Lausanne in January 1923, however, Venizelos had assured Ismet that once the exchange of populations was settled and once it was agreed that the Patriarchate should remain in Constantinople, then Meletios would resign. This Meletios was certainly advised to do, but while he was prepared to withdraw from Constantinople, he refused to abdicate and he appointed Nikolaos, metropolitan of Caesaria, as his *locum tenens*.

During Meletios's absence from the *fanar* Papa Efthim made an attempt to get control of the Patriarchate. On 2 October, an hour or so before the allied forces evacuated Constantinople, accompanied by partisans and Turkish police, he thrust himself upon the holy synod and forced it to declare the deposition of Meletios IV. Then having changed the composition of the synod, he went to Ankara with the self-styled title of 'representative' of the Patriarchate. But the Turkish government, responding to a Greek approach to restore friendly relations between Ankara and Athens and to a Greek proposal to elect a new Patriarch strictly in accordance with the rules, on 12 October disavowed him, stating that as the Patriarchate was a purely religious institution, it could not be represented in the government. That same day Chrisostomos of Athens set out for Thessaloniki to obtain the abdication of Meletios, and to explain to him that the continuance of the Patriarchate in Constantinople was in the best interests of the Church. At length, after much hesitation, Meletios resigned and the Turkish government then invited the holy synod to elect a new Patriarch who must be a Turkish subject and friendly towards Turkey. The result was that on 13 December Grigorios VII, former metropolitan of Chalkidon, was enthroned. The following day Papa Efthim and his friends raided the *fanar* and called on Grigorios to resign. But the Turkish police put an end to this nonsense. For his unseemly behaviour, Papa Efthim was subsequently defrocked by the holy synod, and shortly afterwards Kemal and Grigorios exchanged friendly telegrams. As a consequence the Patriarchate remained in its ancient home: here it was to survive a crisis in March 1924 when, following the abolition of the caliphate, there were clamours in Turkey for the termination of the Patriarchate too; and it was to survive a further crisis following the alleged illegal election of Konstantinos VI in December 1924, an affair which brought Greece and Turkey almost to the point of war.

CHAPTER 17

The Economic and Intellectual Life
of Greece 1861-1923

I. Communications and Ports

During the second half of the nineteenth century, and more particularly in the last quarter, the economic expansion of western and central Europe began to impinge upon the Balkans with ever-increasing effect. The leading European powers were investing abroad a growing proportion of their national wealth and were competing with one another for foreign markets. The greater amount of investment, it is true, took place within the expanding colonial empires, which again were the chief source of raw materials and a market for goods produced in Europe. Nevertheless, both the Turkish empire and the succession territories provided an extensive field for the enterprises not only of the two Western colonial powers, France and Britain, but also of those—Germany, Austria, and Italy—who were less prominent in the colonial field. One sign of this penetration was railway-building, which began shortly after the Crimean War. British interests built two lines from the Black Sea to Cernavoda and Ruschuk on the Danube. In 1868 the Sultan gave a concession to Austrian interests for a line from the Austrian border to Nish, Sofia, Adrianople, and Constantinople—a line completed over the years 1872 to 1888. Meanwhile in Asiatic Turkey British interests began the development of the Smyrna–Aidin railway, in competition with a host of other schemes which continued to be put forward during the next three decades, the most grandiose being those connected with the Berlin–Baghdad line, for which the Germans obtained a concession in 1903. All this time railways were being built within the Balkan countries. In Greece the first development was the 6-mile line between Athens and Piraeus (1867–69). By 1914 Greece could boast of some 1,371 miles of railway,[1] the

[1] Some of this mileage had been built in what had previously been Turkish territory. In Macedonia Greece acquired 385 miles of railway.

last development being the 56-mile link between Thessaloniki (Gida) and the southern network,[2] which the Turks, so long as they held Greek Macedonia, had always, for strategic reasons, refused to sanction.

Side by side with railway development went the building of roads. In 1867 Greece had barely 250 miles[3] of paved highways fit all the year round for wheeled traffic. By 1914 the figure had risen to about 3,500, and by that date the lesser roads had undergone definite improvement. Many of the roads, like the railways,[4] served the ports, which, during this same period, were expanding under the influence of foreign capital invested in docks, sea-walls, piers, and warehouses. A short railway line opened up the plain of Ilia to the port of Katakolo and another line (the Attiki) connected the lead-mines at Lavrion to Athens and Piraeus. Two lines opened up the plain of Thessaly to the port of Volos and a fifth connected a hinterland north of the gulf of Korinth to Mesolonghi and Krioneri. More important, however, was the Piraeus–Athens Peloponnese railway which, after leaving Athens, ran along the coast (crossing the Korinth canal, which was opened in 1893) to the port of Patras and then along the west coast to Kiparissia. Branches linked this line up to the ports of Kalamata, Kalo Nero, and Nafplion. Similarly a small branch line linked Chalkis to the main line running from Piraeus and Athens towards Thebes and Larisa.

Of all these ports Piraeus, already well developed by about 1860, was the only one to attain considerable size, the rest for the most part handling only the small ships of the coastal trade. From 1861 to 1920 the population of Piraeus rose from 6,452 to 131,170, and by the end of that period the quays extended to almost a mile.[5] By 1922 Piraeus had outstripped Naples and Genoa, and ran close to Marseilles in the volume of its total shipping (5,789 steam vessels, 5,792 sailing ships) handled annually. Meanwhile the port of Patras also had grown, but in a less spectacular fashion: its population rose from 16,641 in 1870 to 52,174 in 1920, in which year it handled 523,386 tons. Much the same is true of several of the lesser ports. But of greater significance for the future was the acquisition of Thessaloniki during the Balkan Wars. At a time when Athens and Piraeus had been mere villages, Thessaloniki had become a flourishing city and trading centre. By 1750 it had a population of about 60,000 and its trade, mainly owing to Greek enterprise, had continued to expand up to and during the French revolutionary and Napoleonic Wars. Subsequently, the reduction of the Greek element at the time of the

[2] The line from Piraeus to Papapouli on the Turkish frontier had been completed between 1902 and 1912. The first Simplon Orient express from Paris to Athens ran in July 1920.

[3] This figure excludes the roads in the newly-acquired Ionian Islands. Here an extensive road-system had been made during the forty years of British occupation.

[4] Where, however, the road and railways ran together the road was usually allowed to fall into a state of disrepair.

[5] These quays were on the inner harbour and on the east side of the central harbour. Not until 1930, when the mileage increased to three, were the quays completed on the north sides of the central and outer harbours.

first War of Independence had brought about considerable recession, but gradually the city, despite frequent visitations of cholera[6] and fire,[7] had again begun to expand. Although in 1865 the population was rather less than it had been a century earlier, it had risen to 90,000 by 1880, to 120,000 by 1895, to 157,889 by 1913, and to 170,321 by 1920. This progress, however, had been restricted by political events. Trade had suffered to some extent from the fragmentation of the hinterland in 1878, and again in 1913, when on becoming Greek the city was almost completely cut off from the regions it formerly served. When Thessaloniki again recovered, it had become an essentially Greek port handling trade which was in the hands of Greeks.[8]

Earlier, Thessaloniki had not been primarily a Greek city. Most numerous were its Moslem inhabitants. After them came the Jews who, as refugees from persecutions in Spain, Sicily, southern Italy, and Portugal, had been settled there by Sultan Bayezid II (1481–1512). In the seventeenth century many of these had become outwardly Moslems and were known as *dönmes* (apostates). Thereafter the Jews had experienced a serious economic decline, their place as traders being taken by the Greeks and by colonies of Franks, and it was not until about 1850 that they again became prominent in commercial activity and finance. At the end of the nineteenth century the Jews, including the *dönmes*, numbered about 75,000. At that same time the Greek-speaking population was about 35,000, the Slav-speaking inhabitants, Europeans, and Levantines amounting to 10,000. During the Great War of 1914–18, the 'Bulgarian' element was greatly diminished, and the Greek element began to increase rapidly, reaching considerable proportions following the treaty of Neuilly (November 1919). With the exchange of populations between Turkey and Greece, Thessaloniki, rebuilt in the years following the fire of 1917, became a predominantly Greek city. The *dönmes* (some 18,000 of them) regarded themselves as Turks and were exchanged, but other Jews remained until exterminated by the Germans in World War II.

As a result of the allied occupation during the Great War of 1914–18, the new harbour of Thessaloniki (first opened in 1901) and the land communications leading to it were greatly improved. In 1923 the port handled 1,722 ships with a total tonnage of 1,068,625. Its rapid expansion, however, lay in the future. During the war Greece had lost over half of her steamship tonnage, and it was not until these losses had been made good that Thessaloniki as a port began to make its enormous contribution to the economic development of modern Greece. Between 1922 and 1929 its population was trebled. Side by side with that great port, though on a lesser scale, the port of Kavala developed as a tobacco-exporting centre, its mixed population

---

[6] There were outbreaks of cholera in 1832, 1857, 1893, 1911, and 1913.

[7] Fires took place in 1840, 1849, 1877, 1890, and 1910. The great fire of 1917 laid waste the major part of the city.

[8] From 1925 there was a Yugoslav zone in one section of the port.

having risen to 20,000 in 1914 and to an almost entirely Greek population of 49,980 in 1928.

II. Industrial Development

In all the ports, as indeed in a number of inland towns, there was some industrial development. In 1877 Greece had only 136 industrial concerns, employing only 7,350 workers. From 1880, however, owing to the influx of foreign capital, to the improvements in communication, and to tariff protection, a steady expansion of industry took place, only to be retarded by numerous factors (economic, fiscal, and political) during the last decade of the century. Progress was resumed after 1900. By 1911 the cotton industry had an investment capital of 50 million drachmai and an annual output valued at 17 million. It employed a labour force of 8,000, the total for the country being 26,206—which was larger than that of either Serbia (20,000) or Bulgaria (15,886). By 1913 Piraeus had 130 large factories and by 1917 Greece possessed over 2,000 industrial concerns employing close on 36,000 workers, of whom about 10,000 were to be found in the newly-acquired northern provinces.

Greek industry, apart from mining and shipbuilding, was confined chiefly to the production of consumer goods—flour, textiles, olive oil, tobacco, leather goods, soap, glass, and pottery. Alongside of it, and sometimes hardly distinguishable from the smaller industrial concerns, were the craft industries, supplying a whole range of consumer goods and services—clothes, shoes, jewellery, furniture, buildings, and so forth. There was a long tradition of handicraft skill in Greece and its output expanded slowly in response to the gradual increase in the nation's wealth and particularly to the needs of the growing commercial and administrative classes within the towns. Between 1879 and 1896 the urban dwellers (that is to say those living in settlements of over 5,000 inhabitants) rose from 18 to 22 per cent of the total population. During that time the organisation of industry was beginning to change, but not until the post 1914–18 War period were foreign capitalists and well-to-do Greeks at all eager to develop the heavier industries in Greece where coal, power, and iron were lacking. They much preferred to invest in small concerns producing consumer goods and quick returns, while foreigners preferred to invest in mining, railways, or docks which required chiefly unskilled labour, most of which was outside the towns. Hence until more recent times there was no great exodus of Greeks from the villages and, as a consequence, the Greek population remained predominantly rural.

III. The Rural Population

The Greek population, like the population elsewhere in the Balkans, had increased rapidly in the second half of the nineteenth century. By 1912 the total, which in 1829 had been only 750,000, had risen to 2,750,000, although the extent of the soil had increased only from 18,346 to 24,558 square miles. In effect the population had increased nearly threefold, as is shown by the increase of the density figure of 41 per square mile in 1829 to that of 114 in 1914. This increase was due primarily to a fall in the death-rate, which in turn was due to improved medical knowledge, to the increase of doctors and hospitals, to the absence of war, and to some increase in supplies of food.

Until about 1850 Greece had been underpopulated and much of the cultivable land left untilled. But by about 1880, owing to the limits to agricultural ameliorations and to the lack of industry, she was overpopulated. There was a shortage of land. On the land available a peasant propriety had become established, but eventually the number of landless men had greatly increased. What is more, owing to the inheritance laws and customs, the average size of holdings had dwindled, with the result that more often than not the patrimony failed to provide full employment for members of the family. If in Greece total unemployment was perhaps rare, underemployment was a universal feature.

The rapid increase of population would have been disastrous but for the improvement in agriculture which, owing to the development of industry and communications, underwent a transformation during George I's reign. Gradually the agricultural economy began to change from one which was predominantly pastoral and self-sufficient to one which aimed at making profits. The farmers began to grow more grain, tobacco, currants, fruit, grapes, and olives. Of these commodities, first currants and later tobacco were produced for export in response to a growing European demand. Exports of currants (the income of which enabled Greece to pay for the import of grain) rose in value from 13,600,000 drachmai in 1861 to 37,800,000 in 1875. In the next decade the export of currants (mainly through Patras) almost doubled and exceeded in value all other Greek exports combined. This increase was abnormal. In 1878 the phylloxera pest had reduced drastically the output of the French vineyards and the French wine-producers, in order to keep going, increased enormously their purchases of grapes from Greece until they were taking about one-third of Greek total export. This boom gave a considerable stimulus to the Greek economy and brought more and more land under viticulture. But by 1892 the French vineyards had been restored and in that year the French government imposed a high tariff on Greek currants. The result was that exports to France, which had been 70,000 tons in 1889, dropped by 1893 to 3,500, while prices fell to under one-third of their level. At first the growers attempted to produce more currants to offset the drop in price, but eventually they began to change over to tobacco production, the area devoted to which had already increased from 6,500 acres in 1860 to 16,000 in 1889. By 1911 the total acreage under tobacco was nearly 40,000. It was not, however, until after World War I, following the settlement of the newly-acquired provinces of Thrace and Macedonia, that a large-scale tobacco production and export was attained by Greece.

In the closing decades of the nineteenth century there was a steady but not spectacular increase in the production of grain. By 1912 about 6 per cent of the cultivable land was devoted to the production of cereals. But although improvements in cultivation had taken place on the better farms, the yield generally had not been vastly improved, and grain had to be imported to supply the nation's bread—imports which in the period 1900–12 accounted roughly for one-quarter of the total. Even the acquisition of Thessaly in 1881 had not boosted grain production as much as might have been expected, the area devoted to cereals in Thessaly having fallen by 17 per cent between 1896 and 1911. Here the land was held in large estates or *chifliks*,[9] which were bought from their former Moslem owners chiefly by wealthy Greek traders from Constantinople, Asia Minor, and Macedonia. These estates continued to be farmed by share-croppers in a most primitive fashion; only about one-third of the arable land was cropped each year; and huge tracts were leased for winter grazing to the sheepowners of Pindus. In 1912 just over half the Thessalian peasants were still share-croppers. Only gradually were improvements made. By 1918 about 150 of the original 466 *chiflik* villages had disappeared, the peasants, owing to legislation and the institution of an agricultural bank in 1907, having been enabled to buy their land. But the splitting-up of the great Thessalian estates (and this was to be true of those in Greek Macedonia, Thrace, and Epiros where the old Turkish *chiflik* system obtained as in Thessaly) probably in the long run impeded production by reducing the unit of cultivation: although small proprietors undoubtedly worked their land better than indolent landlords and share-croppers, they did not quickly amass sufficient capital to adopt machinery or to purchase fertilisers. How eventually during the past fifty years, and particularly in the last twenty-five years, modern methods were introduced is a story largely of the activities of the Greek ministry of agriculture, of the adoption of co-operative organisation, and of the increasing fund of capital in agrarian enterprise. The result was that in 1957 for the first time Greece produced a surplus of wheat.

IV. Emigration

Although the gradual expansion and improvement of agriculture went a long way to enable Greece to support her growing population, that expansion alone was not sufficient to avert disaster. So poor and famished indeed were many scattered regions throughout the whole of Greece that the young men began to emigrate. Whereas previously small numbers of the more

[9] The average size was about 750 acres, but there were some which were ten or more times as large.

enterprising had gone chiefly to Russia, Romania, and Egypt, in the 1890s large numbers found their way to America, the figure reaching 14,000 in 1903, over 10,515 in 1905, and thereafter 31,000 on an average every year until 1914, by which time over a quarter of a million had gone to that country. The stream of emigrants began to flow again after World War I until 1924, when American immigration laws reduced the number to a few thousands a year. Altogether close on half a million Greeks had emigrated since Greece first achieved independence, though many, perhaps about 40 per cent, returned later in life to a homeland which ever remained dear to them. Some of those who returned were relatively wealthy men, and they gave funds for schools, libraries, orphanages, and public buildings.[10]

Being overpopulated, Greece had been able to stand the loss of population. In the villages which suffered most the womenfolk did the work required. There was a sense, moreover, in which emigration favoured the economic development of Greece. The emigrants sent large remittances home, the total being 58 million drachmai in 1911. These enabled families to redeem their mortgages and other debts, and even to invest in land, the value of which rose. At the same time this influx of dollars, which accounted for a quarter of Greek 'export' earnings, improved the Greek balance of trade and reduced the rate of interest. Needless to say, a proportion of the money coming from abroad found its way into industrial and commercial enterprise, the more rapid expansion of which provided ever-increasing profits for agricultural production.

V. Greek Shipping and Trade

All this time, partly in response to the greater output of agriculture and of industry, but mainly independently of it, Greek shipping continued to expand. Only the Greek coastal trade was closely tied to the economic life of Greece. This trade provided work for sailors, dockers, and ships' carpenters; it transferred agricultural surpluses from one region to another (and above all to the rapidly growing town of Athens); and it had a place in the export trade with neighbouring countries. But the shipping carried on in large vessels was not so closely tied: it did indeed provide a livelihood for sailors from the islands and the coastal regions of the mainland; and it therefore provided a wage fund which was expended or invested on Greece, the figure being 10 million gold francs in 1904 and 20 million in 1912.[11] But the shipowners who invested in large vessels and derived profits from them tended to keep their money outside Greece, partly to avoid taxation and partly for convenience. Although a portion of it eventually found its way to Greece in the form of purchases of property and of charitable gifts, it remained chiefly in the field of international finance. This was particularly true when

[10] It is said that 40,000 young Greeks returned from America to fight in the Balkan Wars.

[11] i.e. 13,500,000 drachmai in 1904, and 20 million in 1912 when the drachma was at par with the franc.

the steam-age began. As we have seen, the steamships themselves were purchased abroad and although the smaller ones were maintained in the shipyards which began to develop in Greece, the maintenance of the larger ones and indeed the major repairs to the smaller ones had to be carried out in foreign ports. Nevertheless, the rapidly expanding steamfleet (8,244 tons in 1875, 144,975 tons in 1895, and 893,650 tons in 1915, representing a total of 475 ships) provided employment in 1923 for some 30,000 sailors. By 1912 Greek shipping was second only to that of Great Britain in the Black Sea, the Greeks being the principal carriers of Russian grain to Marseilles. By that time the Greeks had four trans-Atlantic liners and they were beginning to get a grip on the carrying trade in all parts of the world. Indeed Greek shipping, though it had owed something to the expansion of Greek import and export trade, was not dependent on it and that is why the Turkish boycott in 1912 of Greek trade had no appreciable effect upon the larger concerns.[12]

The expansion of Greek import and export trade in the fifteen years before the 1914–18 War was considerable. Annual exports increased from an average value of 90 million drachmai in 1899–1905, to 113 million in 1906–09 and to 143 million in 1910–12. In the last period imports had risen to 162 million drachmai. These figures, like those for the increase of customs receipts (30,600,000 in 1900, 47,600,000 in 1905, and 56 million in 1912), reflected the economic progress which had enabled Greece to furnish the adequate army and navy that took part in the Balkan Wars. Over that same period the value of shares[13] had risen and foreign investment had steadily increased.[14] Even the adverse trade balance, which in 1912 was about 11 million drachmai, was not so serious as appears at first sight, for it was covered several times over by invisible earnings, consisting of remittances from Greeks abroad and from the earnings of Greek shipping. Nevertheless, in spite of the progress that all these figures show, the total volume of trade remained that of an undeveloped nation.

VI. Education and Intellectual Life

Throughout this period there was a steady expansion in the number of Greek schools. In part the increase is to be accounted for by the incorporation of new territories within the Greek state and in part by the endeavours

[12] Even on the smaller concerns the effect was not very great. The trade in small vessels between Greece and Turkey was not considerable, being less than 5 per cent of the total volume of Greek trade.

[13] In the reign of Otho transactions were carried on in a room in the café *Orea Ellas*. The first stock exchange in Greece was established in Piraeus by a royal decree in 1875. This was abolished the following year when a new exchange was established in Athens. Not until 1918 did the Greek stock exchange become a state-controlled institution.

[14] The bankruptcy of 1893 had led to a fall in foreign investment and in the value of the drachma; but this devaluation, by reducing imports and expanding exports, ultimately led to the increase of foreign investment, and to a rise of 18 per cent in the value of industrial shares between 1896 and 1904. France was the chief foreign investor, being slightly ahead of Great Britain. By 1911 she had invested 319 million drachmai in state and municipal loans and close on 148 million in Greek public limited liability companies.

of the state, of benefactors, and of the local communities to provide schooling for a population which was rapidly increasing. In 1866 there were 1,067
primary schools attended by 44,102 boys and 8,481 girls; 123 Hellenic
schools[15] with a total 6,675 pupils; and 16 gymnasia (or grammar schools)
providing places for 1,908. The total school population was therefore just
over 60,000. By 1922 that figure had risen to just over 587,334, of which
88,250 were to be found in the 122 gymnasia. In addition to these gymnasia
there were a variety of private educational institutions and also state schools
for military, naval, and mercantile cadets, for ecclesiastics, and for commerce, crafts, and agriculture. Considerable improvement had undoubtedly
been made, but, according to the Greek census of January 1928, 66 per cent
of the women and 34·6 per cent of the men were illiterate.[16] At that date the
full impact of the provision in the constitution of 1911 for compulsory and
free primary education up to the age of ten had not been felt, and its effect
had been reduced by lack of funds, shortage of teachers, failure to enforce
the law, and by internal instability.

Of the quality of the primary education provided, it is hard to speak. It
had the merit of being religious, patriotic, and moral: it fitted the masses for
the work they did; and it afforded for some the opportunity to improve
their lot. Given in the demotic language, or rather in the written version of
that language, this primary education increased to some extent the reader-
ship of the Greek popular press which continued to expand throughout this
period not only in the number of newspapers published but also in the size
of their editions. Not all Greeks after a few years of primary schooling could
read newspapers with ease and many did not acquire the ability to read
them at all; but those who could get a start on reading the press found in
these lively newspapers the means of improving their knowledge and of
satisfying their thirst for news, information, and polemical argument.

Nevertheless, most Greek newspapers were written in the *katharevousa*,
an artificial language originally created out of Attic, Byzantine, and demotic
Greek by Korais, who gave to it a systematisation based upon a French
analogy. This language, which in the course of the nineteenth century was
developed by literary, academic, and administrative users to the extent that
it lost some of its uniformity, became the official language of modern
Greece. It was this language that was taught in the University of Athens and
in the military and ecclesiastical training schools. Hence it was chiefly from
the gymnasia that the reading public of the press derived and it was chiefly
from these schools that personnel for administrative office, for teaching, for
trading offices and banks were recruited.

From these same schools the University of Athens drew its students, who
in most subjects were given a four-year course or, in the case of medicine, a

---

[15] See Appendix VI, note 1.

[16] During the war in 1914–18 it was reckoned that 30 per cent of Greek soldiers could
neither read nor write.

six-year course. This institution, to which the old Ionian Academy had been added in 1864 and which in 1911 was renamed 'National and Kapodistrian University',[17] had increased its student body from 1,182 in 1866, to 3,358 in 1912, and 9,799 in 1922. Greece thus came to have a comparatively larger university population than France, Germany, Italy, or Great Britain. Spread over five faculties—theology, medicine (with dentistry and pharmacy), natural science, philosophy (i.e. arts), and law—over 40 per cent of these students were to be found in the faculty of law where they trained not only for the legal profession but also for administration. In this faculty, as distinct from those of medicine, natural science, and theology, there was always an excessive production of graduates. Hence in the legal profession there was much under-employment and the time not given to legal practice was inevitably devoted to politics and journalism. Indeed, along with the army and navy (which gave their personnel much leisure), the university provided Greece with a steady flow of politicians. By way of contrast, doctors, dentists, and teachers (who were very badly paid) were in short supply, especially in the provinces.

Before the Balkan Wars of 1912–13, large numbers of Greeks from the unredeemed lands—Constantinople, Asia Minor, Macedonia, Thrace, Crete, Epiros, Cyprus, and other islands—found their way to the University of Athens, whence they returned to their territories as apostles of the *megali idhea*. In that period, too, many Romanians, Serbs, and Bulgarians studied in Athens, which even more than ever was the Paris of south-eastern Europe. As for the quality of the education provided, again it is very hard to say. By English and American standards it was too diffuse, too bookish, too much a matter of learning by rote, and hardly practical enough in the scientific field; but though it may have failed to discipline, it certainly did not stultify the lively Greek mind, which remained inquisitive and highly speculative.

The university was not merely a generating house of Greek politics and modern Hellenism: it was also the centre of a vigorous intellectual life, to which other institutions contributed and to which those Greeks who had studied or sojourned outside their homeland provided variety and colour. Among those institutions were the National Library, originally based on the collections of Kapodistrias, of Sakellarios, and of the Bavarian regency and merged with the university library in 1903; the library of parliament which specialised in buying foreign books; and several learned societies including one devoted to archaeology.[18] Archaeology indeed, under the stimulus of the foreign archaeological schools,[19] continued to loom large

[17] On the expulsion of Otho it had changed its name from 'Othonian' to 'National'. In 1911 money left by Dombolis, a Greek merchant in Russia, became available for a university in memory of Kapodistrias. The new institution was joined to the existing university.

[18] The Academy of Athens, based on the lines of the French Academy, was not founded until 1926.

[19] Following the French School (1846), there were founded the German (1874), the American (1881), the British (1886), the Austrian (1897), and the Italian (1909).

in Greek education and to provide thousands of Greeks with an intellectual interest. Always desirous of discovering and preserving their classical heritage, the Greeks welcomed the activities of foreign archaeologists and with their help built up their own tradition and a trained personnel. As time went on, they extended their activities to Byzantine archaeology, Byzantine studies having at length won a place in the curriculum of the faculty of arts of the University of Athens.[20]

It is often said, and Greeks have said it too, that the Greek educational system placed too much emphasis on the study of classical civilisation, on the teaching of the purist language, and on religion. True, not much time was available in the gymnasia for the study of the many other subjects taken. It should be remembered, however, that openings for science graduates other than in medicine were very few indeed, and that the process of building up a supply of science-teachers was long and laborious. Greeks with a leaning towards a scientific or technical training often went to study in those countries where science and technology were much more advanced, and they usually remained abroad to find fitting employment. Hence, almost of necessity, the Greek gymnasia produced large numbers of students who went on to the university to read in arts or law, and it was generally considered that the appropriate basic education of these future citizens should be religion, classical Greek, Greek history, and the purist language.

The purist language (the *katharevousa*), though firmly entrenched, was not unchallenged, and as the challenge developed[21] the problem of language came to be as hotly disputed as any political issue. On occasions it even gave rise to political incidents. For example, in 1901 when the queen (with the help of the archbishop of Athens) translated the gospels into the vernacular, the opposition accused the government of condoning a subversion of the cultural heritage of Hellenism, which, it was said, would only rebound to the advantage of Slavdom. On 21 November 1901 demonstrations and clashes, in which students were involved, took place in Athens and these 'Gospel Riots' led to the fall of the government of Theotokis. Another disturbance took place two years later, the students having disapproved of the language used in a performance of the *Oresteia*.

So firmly entrenched was the *katharevousa* as the official language that not only nearly all the newspapers but even most literary works were written

[20] Byzantine studies were soon to find a place in the University of Thessaloniki which opened in November 1926 in the Villa Allatina and whose library began with a collection formed in 1919 for the proposed University of Smyrna. It was the intention that this university should devote much attention to applied science—agriculture, forestry, engineering—and to the study of folklore, the modern language, and Balkan history. During the last forty years the university has great achievements in these fields, and where Balkan history is concerned its achievements have been enhanced by those of the Institute of Balkan Studies.

[21] Opposition to the *katharevousa* was not new: there are signs of it even before the first War of Independence.

in it. Whereas Rigas and Solomos had used the demotic language—the language of the ballads and folk literature, a language which had developed from Byzantine Greek—their successors, Andreas Kalvos,[22] P. Soutzos, Rizos Rangavis, Rizos Neroulos, A. Soutzos, Koumanoudis, G. Paraschos, A. Paraschos, E. Roïdis, P. Kalligas, L. Melas, and others, had written romantic verse, novels, and essays, either in varieties of the artificial *katharevousa* of Korais or in the style of the fanariot tradition. Most of these writers were influenced by the French romantic school and by the debates on literature and art that went on in Paris. Their centre was the 'Parnassos' club of Athens where they discussed literary problems in the terms of Sainte-Beuve and Taine. They formed what came later to be known as the 'old school' of Athens.

The 'new school' of Athens was formed when in the last quarter of the nineteenth century there began a strong movement to restore the demotic language. This language in its written form had been developed at the Court of Ali Pasha, before the first Greek War of Independence. Much earlier, Sofianos (sixteenth century) and others had attempted to standardise it by analysing its grammatical forms, and many had subsequently endeavoured to enrich it by making compilations of vocabulary. The whole movement drew strength since its adherents were able to give a more plausible reply to the linguistic and racial theory of Fallmerayer than those who were using the artificial language. Demoticists could show that the demotic dialects were a natural evolutionary product of classical dialects and that the continuity of the Greek race was an indisputable fact. It drew strength also from among the ranks of those who were hostile to the patrician-led political parties.

Among these demoticists were Aristotelis Valaoritis, an Ionian, who entered the Greek parliament when the Ionian Islands were joined to Greece, and A. Laskaratos, an anti-clerical, who was excommunicated by the Church. More famous than these, however, was Kostis Palamas. Entering the University of Athens as a law student in 1875, he came into contact with the Parnassos club where he became involved in literary and philosophic discussion. He subsequently arrived at the conclusion that to write romantic verse and prose in an artificial language was an arid and self-contradictory pursuit, and that if Greece was to have a living literature of her own she must use her living language. At the same time Palamas (along with those whom he inspired, G. Drosinis, J. Griparis, G. Kampas, and others) rejected French romanticism and turned towards the young French Parnassian poets, who drew their inspiration from classical Greece. The demoticists could thus claim that far from betraying the Greek birthright, they were not only using a language which had a real continuity with the

---

[22] Kalvos, an Ionian, who lived for most of his life outside Greece, was little known at the time. He was discovered in the 1880s by Palamas, who admired him on account not so much of his language as of his choice of classical subjects.

classical past but that they were making classical subjects, and not an alien culture, the substance of their literature.

Another well-known demoticist was Yannis Psicharis, a Greek from a Chiot family and a teacher of philology at the Sorbonne. His controversial work *My Journey* appeared in 1888. In this work he not only challenged the literary and educational establishment of Greece, but sponsored an extreme form of demotic Greek. In doing this, however, it is doubtful whether he gained much additional support for the popular language, which was making its own way in literary circles: he merely provided an opening to the *katharevousa* school who could point out that Psicharis had no knowledge of Greece and that his so-called *dimotiki* was of purely academic manufacture. Nevertheless, Psicharis had a following, which if it did not blindly adopt his language, emulated his attempt to get away from the *katharevousa*. Among these were A. Pallis who translated the *Iliad*, and his cousin Eftaliotis who translated the *Odyssey* into demotic. Like Palamas, Psicharis and his disciples were all adherents of the liberal programme of Trikoupis. Likewise many of the supporters of Venizelos were ardent demoticists, among them M. Tsirimokos, A. Theros, and N. Kazandzakis. But not all the demoticists were politically to the left. A. Sikelianos, K. Varnalis, and Karkavitsas, although the first two later changed sides, were anti-Venizelists. So too was Ion Dragoumis, who regarded demotic Greek as a unifying element in the non-national Hellenism which he favoured.

The Greek literary world (and the same is true of that of Greek art and music) had a history of its own. If it was sometimes caught up in political and social issues, it had its own problems and its own development. Nevertheless, Greek literature, like all literature, was in some measure the mirror of its surroundings: at least it reflected in a multiplicity of broken and sometimes distorted images many of the enduring characteristics, the developments, and the conflicts of Greek intellectual, social, and religious life. Greek poetry, in particular, reflects the surviving traditions of the liturgical poetry of Byzantine times and of the popular folk-poetry of Turkish times —the lives of the saints, the deeds of the warriors, the struggle for freedom, natural surroundings, the seasons, birth, death, and fate. It reflects also attempts on the part of the disillusioned to substitute for the values of the Orthodox Church those of the classical pre-Christian era. Finally, and this is particularly true of the Greek novel, it reflects village life and, when Athens had become a city of some size, urban life as lived in Greece. But the purely literary sources have only a limited value for the study of a nation's history and where Greece is concerned, the press, in the great variety of its organs and the high standards of its journalists, gives a fuller picture of the modern Greek nation.

VII. The Orthodox Church in Greece

While problems of language and politics absorbed the attention of an intelligentsia in Athens and in the larger provincial towns, the Greek masses, though not untouched by and not disinterested in the political struggles, still found stability in their conservative, decentralised, and democratic Church, with its twelve annual feasts and its veneration of the saints. Village life—feastings, dancing, weddings, burials, all work and recreation—continued to be centred on the local church and shrines. Throughout Turkish and modern times Orthodox Christianity had been undisturbed by doctrinal or ritualistic dispute. Conflicts in the hierarchy, even the breaking-away of the Church in Greece from the Patriarchate of Constantinople, and its being placed under the control of the Greek state, had left the religious life of the Greek parish unchanged. Certainly, the antagonism of the Greek state towards monasticism had resulted, as we have seen, in some erosion of communal life. But the Greek state made no deliberate attempt to secularise the schools. Nor has it ever sanctioned marriage and divorce outside the Church. Hence up to 1923, while (as in other European countries) non-attendance at church and the neglect of fasting became more common, the Orthodox tradition remained strong in Greece. Although a whole century had passed since the day when the Oecumenical Patriarch had been the Ethnarch of all Greeks, yet even among the westernised and national Greeks—even among Greeks like Trikoupis and Venizelos—there remained a profound respect for the titular head of the Orthodox religion.

By 1923 the Patriarch, who was a less important personage than the archbishop of Athens,[23] was oecumenical only in the sense that the autocephalous Orthodox Churches recognised him as *primus inter pares* of the Orthodox hierarchy and looked to the great Church of Constantinople to provide the sacred oil for the anointing of bishops. Step by step, the extensive territory of the Patriarchate had been reduced. In July 1866 the dioceses of the Ionian Islands had been added to the autocephalous Church of Greece. In 1870 the Bulgarian Exarchate had been established. In May 1882 the dioceses of Thessaly, Arta, and a part of that of Jannina had been added to the Church of Greece. As for territories later acquired by Greece, these remained for a time under the Patriarchate. Not until 1928 was the administrative control of the dioceses in Greek Epiros, Macedonia, and Thrace, and those of the Archipelago, transferred to Athens. In the meantime autocephalous Churches had been established in Yugoslavia, Romania, and Albania. As for Crete, the seven dioceses here continued to enjoy the semi-autonomous regime established in 1900 under a local holy synod: they were independent of the Church of Greece and enjoyed a direct relationship to the Patriarchate, which, however, had merely the right to nominate the metropolitan of the island. Similarly the Patriarch continued to enjoy some control over Mount Athos. In 1920 the twenty monasteries of the Holy

---

[23] In 1889 all the archiepiscopal sees in Greece were reduced to bishoprics, but in 1922 all Greek bishops were given the title of metropolitan, the primate of Athens taking the title of archbishop.

Mountain were established as a theocratic republic under Greek sovereignty. This position was regularised by a constitution of 1927.[24] It was then laid down that the peninsula, though forming a part of the Hellenic state, should enjoy administrative autonomy and should depend ecclesiastically upon the Patriarchate. All monks, no matter whence they came, were to be deemed Greek subjects, the Greek state being represented by a governor who was to have under his control a force of gendarmes. Apart from Constantinople, only the Dodekanese remained directly dependent upon the Patriarchate, and they continued to do so when they were added to Greece in 1947.

[24] This, except for providing for Greek instead of Turkish sovereignty, differed very little from the constitution of 1783.

Conclusion

IT HAD TAKEN the Greeks well over a century to achieve their political unity. The Italians had been more fortunate: they had achieved their unification in just over two decades. Whereas Rome fell relatively easily into the hands of Italian nationalists, the new Rome, Constantinople, never came the way of the Greeks. On perhaps two occasions the Greeks might have entered their Holy City; first in July 1922, when, if instead of directing large forces against Kemalist Angora, they had mounted from eastern Thrace an offensive against the Chataldja lines; again in May 1923 when, after the disaster in Asia Minor, they might have advanced with their reorganised army in western Thrace against the Kemalists who were divided and in decline. But on both occasions they were hesitant, and they ended by accepting the dictation of France, Great Britain, and Italy, who, although militarily weak in the Near East, let it be known that, even if a Greek army entered Constantinople, it would not be allowed to stay there. In 1922 and 1923, as at many other times, the European political situation was unfavourable to the Greeks. But when Rome fell to the Italians, despite their earlier failures at Aspromonte, Mentana, and Porta Pia, everything was in their favour. The French troops of occupation had left Rome to fight the Prussians on the Rhine, only to be defeated at Sedan. Fortune had smiled (as it had often smiled) upon the Italians, and all they had to do was to overcome a feeble Papal army—a victory which cost them only forty-nine casualties. Once in Rome they were there to stay. Rome thus became the capital of a state of 27 million Italians, indeed nearly all those who spoke the Italian tongue, there being outside its confines only the Italians of Switzerland, of the Trentino, and of the communities of the eastern Adriatic coast.

This great and speedy achievement owed much to the skilful diplomacy of Cavour and his successors, to the sympathies of France and Great Britain, to their rivalries (these worked in favour of Italy but against Greece), and to the policies pursued by Bismarck. It cost the Italians not more than six thousand lives. By way of contrast, the Greek wars of liberation took a heavy toll of the Greek people. Moreover, the very existence of Greece was twice in jeopardy—first during the period of World War I and then again during the 1940s. On both these occasions the sacrifices were enormous.

They constituted, as it were, a surcharge on the costs of liberation; so that whereas one counts the bill of the Italian *risorgimento* in terms of thousands, that of the Greek *enopiisis* (unification) must be reckoned in hundreds of thousands. Even though one were to regard Italy's entry into World War I as the embarkation on a final war of liberation of the Italians in the Trentino and the Adriatic (the cost is sometimes reckoned as nearly 700,000 lives), the disparity remains considerable. It is doubtful, however, whether one should regard Italy's participation in the 1914–18 War as a war of liberation. Italy was out not merely to liberate Italians but to acquire better frontiers and to expand in the eastern Mediterranean. For Greece, however, the 1914–18 War was a continuation of the Balkan Wars. Her aim was to regain territories previously won, to acquire eastern Thrace, the Greek-speaking islands of the Aegean, and to liberate, if it were feasible, all Greek populations remaining in the Ottoman empire.

Throughout her struggle for political unity Italy had the advantage of having a large population concentrated on a terrain which was a geographical unity, bounded on three sides by the sea and to the north by the Alps. The Greeks, however, were not nearly so numerous nor so concentrated. In the regions where they first achieved political independence—the Peloponnese, continental Greece as far as the Arta–Volos line, and the Cyclades—they were only 750,000-strong. Their brethren in the western or Ionian Islands were not included within the first Greek kingdom. As we have seen, these seven islands had been established by the Congress of Vienna (1815) as a (theoretically) independent state under the protection of Great Britain. Had they become in 1815 independent in fact as well as theory, had they been more compact, richer, and more densely populated, they might have become the 'Piedmont' of Greece. As it was, Greece had no 'Piedmont' with which to begin her Unification—no Piedmont to make alliances with other states, no Piedmontese bureaucracy and diplomatic service, no well-equipped and well-supplied regular army. By 1833, however, if not before, those regions of Greece which had freed themselves had fashioned the bare rudiments of a Western state. Only then, and not till then, was there even the semblance of a Greek 'Piedmont'.

But the small Greek kingdom of 1833 had, as a salient of nationalism, one advantage over the Italian Piedmont: its Hellenism was much more intense than was the *Italianità* of the dominions of the House of Savoy. Those dominions, until the acquisition of Sardinia and Genoa, had been predominantly French-speaking; and for two decades during the Napoleonic Wars, they had been a colony of France. Nevertheless, after the Vienna Settlement of 1815, the kingdom of Sardinia–Piedmont had much to offer to Italian nationalists: its anti-Austrian foreign policy, much facilitated by the resurgence of France, found considerable support in the adjacent regions, where *Italianità*, in all its various forms, began to think in terms of getting rid of Austrian rule. But for the Greek 'Piedmont' circumstances were much less favourable. Russia, except for brief periods, did not pursue an aggressive anti-Turkish policy; and when she did, she invariably met with opposition from other great powers. Moreover, although Holy Russia was ever mindful of the Greek patriarchal Church, the Tsar and his ministers had no consistent, and certainly no altruistic, aim of encouraging the pretensions of the government of Athens. In the event of the collapse of the Ottoman buffer state, Russia was likely to favour the establishment, not of a new Byzantium, but of client states or autonomies, composed of brother Slavs.

Such states would necessarily impede the advance of Hellenism: any Greek expansion outside Crete, the eastern islands, and the mainland of Asia Minor must be to the north, into regions where Slavs and Albanians had pretensions. Thus there was no 'Lombardy', no 'Tuscany', and no 'Modena' to be acquired for Greece, unless it were Thessaly and Arta, territories of moderate extent which, as we have seen, were obtained in 1881 with relative ease. Beyond Thessaly, however, lay the elusive prize of Macedonia. Here the Slavs and Albanians had long been pressing; and in 1878 the province had seemed almost to be within the grasp of Bulgaria, whose liberation Russia had assisted. Macedonia was certainly no 'Naples'. Nor indeed was Crete. In both these regions the Turks could concentrate strong military forces. True, the Turkish troops lacked the efficiency of the Austrian army; but, in virtue of their numbers, they were more than a match for the Greeks, who being without allies (like the Italians in 1848), met their 'Custozza' at Domoko in 1897. Not until 1912 was the Greek 'Piedmont' (by then in uneasy alliance with the Slavs and vastly improved in military organisation) able to inflict heavy defeats in Macedonia and Epiros upon the somewhat disorganised Turkish forces. Even then, the extent of the territory overrun hardly matched Greek aspirations. Not only were the Serbs in possession of soil claimed by Greece, but the Bulgarians were in occupation of Thrace and of eastern Macedonia. These same Bulgarians were pressing hard on Thessaloniki, which the Greeks had entered only in the nick of time; and they had managed, having showed great courage and endurance, to reach the outer defences of Constantinople at Chataldja. So confident was their king, Ferdinand, that he would conquer the Holy City that he had ordered a mosaic to be made, depicting himself riding a white charger to the doors of St Sophia. But for once fortune smiled upon the Greeks. The Bulgarians, decimated by cholera, were halted by the Turks. Later, in the hour of their disappointment, they were foolish enough to attack the Greeks and Serbs, who, seizing the initiative and being indirectly assisted by the Romanians and Turks, defeated their former ally and together walked off with most of the spoils.

Whereas a few skirmishes had sufficed for the Italians to acquire Umbria, the Marches, and the Two Sicilies, battles on a considerable scale had been fought by the Balkan allies of 1912 against the Turks. For the Greeks, moreover, there had been war upon the sea. Their task had been much more difficult than that of the Italians, who had merely to ferry a thousand men across the Straits of Messina. Again, when after the World War of 1914–18 the Greeks advanced into Asia Minor, they became engaged in large-scale military and naval operations. There was no one else to fight their battles for them: there was nothing comparable to Königgrätz (Sadowa), which presented Venetia to united Italy.

At no time during the *risorgimento* did Italians have to face military problems of the same order as those with which the Greeks were constantly confronted. Once the lesson of Custozza had been learned, the Piedmontese managed to avoid a military effort on a scale involving such great sacrifices in men and materials as those which the Hellenes were called upon to make. Certainly, for the Italians there were always great risks. At any moment the population of 22 million forming the kingdom of 1861 might have found themselves at war with their erstwhile ally, France, or with Austria seeking revenge. But owing to the favourable European diplomatic situation, and to the correct appreciation of its nuances by Cavour and his successors, external threats to Italian unification did not materialise.

The main obstacles to Italian nationalism were internal. Each of the provinces eventually incorporated in United Italy had its own historical traditions, its own systems of law and land tenure, its own coinage and customs barriers, and its own dialect, not easily understood by inhabitants of other provinces. The south was backward and squalid. Lombardy, the home of industrious peasants, was a garden studded with flourishing cities and townships. The Grand Duchy of Tuscany was a time-honoured cultural centre with an outlook vastly different from that of other regions. Turin was a northern-type city, not very distinguishable from Paris. In all the Italian provinces, as in the provinces and states of Germany, local patriotism was strong. Consequently, despite the existence of a common Italian literary language and a national consciousness, the positive urge to unification was not, except upon the part of individuals or groups, either intense or single-minded. Napoleon I, while momentarily imposing on the Italian peninsula a single system of law and a uniformity of heavy taxation, had not created political unity; nor had he inspired a longing for it. And when at length the idea of unity found some support, the variants of the idea and the diversity of its supporters were considerable. For the idea itself derived from many sources—from the European Enlightenment, from the commercial ambitions of the growing middle classes, from historical and literary sentimentality, from the example of the Latin Americans and Greeks, from a love of conspiracy, from economic discontent, and from sheer politics. Each stressed, according to his fancy, or to his position, some particular aspect of the idea. Hence the plans put forward were numerous, and the actions proposed were conflicting. But in the end a divided yet energetic minority managed somehow to achieve, if not a common aim, at least a centralised, united Italy.

The Greek liberation movement in its ideological and internal aspects, while displaying some of the characteristics of the *risorgimento*, was in many ways very different. There was indeed the same diversity of ideological origins. Like the Italians, the Greeks were heirs of the Enlightenment; they were spectators of the French Revolution; and, even more than the Italians, they placed some hope in the call to oppressed people to throw off their shackles. Although they had never come under the heel of Napoleon, Napoleon's name was a legend among them, and was all the more respectable for being a legend only. Again, the Greek middle classes were growing at an ever-increasing pace. Social and economic discontent was rife. Like the Italians, the Greeks, as we have seen, had a long history of conspiracy behind them. Within the limits that their thraldom prescribed, they enjoyed a kind of political life in which intrigue and excessive finesse were to be reckoned as virtues. They had a vague picture of and some illusions concerning their pre-Christian past: like the Italians they had learned from the travellers to have respect for, and even pride in, their classical ruins; and they had experienced a literary renaissance. They spoke a language which was closer to ancient Greek than the Italian dialects were to Latin. Indeed, where language was concerned they had some advantage over the Italian nationalists. The Greek demotic language was fairly uniform. The small Greek trader from Constantinople or Smyrna, the Greek sailor from the islands, the Greek share-cropper from Macedonia or Thessaly had little difficulty in conversing with a tradesman in Attica or a peasant farmer in the Morea.

The uniformity of the Greek language had been in part preserved by the Greek Church which had survived the downfall of the Byzantine Empire, the Greek liturgy being conducted in a language which was more intelligible to the Greek peasant than was the Latin of the Roman Church to the unlettered Italian. Moreover, everywhere in the Greek homelands of the Ottoman empire, the Greek Church and the Greek communities had maintained schools where even the Slav-speaking Orthodox could acquire a knowledge of Greek—the cultural and commercial language of the Levant. Indeed, the long use of Greek for trading purposes was perhaps an even more important influence than that of the Church in preserving linguistic uniformity. Through trade the Greek communities had kept in touch with one another. The constant comings and goings made the Greek trader less provincial than the Italian. Whether he came from Smyrna or Jannina, from Thessaloniki or Candia, he was above all a Greek. The Italian, on the other hand, was first and foremost a Venetian, a Neapolitan, a Tuscan, Sicilian, or Sardinian. He did not trade primarily with other Italians. Each Italian trading state had its own national trade, and two of them, Genoa and Venice, had built up overseas empires. By way of contrast, the Greek traders handled much of the internal trade of a large dominion; they handled also by means of their ships and through the Greek communities in other countries a large proportion of its external trade. One may even say that Greece had a commercial empire before she had a nation-state. One may also say that because of their trading and commercial activity, the Greeks acquired, before their unification, a form of unity which had been denied to the Italians—a unity made all the more real because they lived under the rule of a common oppressor.

Although parts of Italy had passed under foreign rulers, there was not for the Italians as for the Greeks a common oppressor of alien faith. Only for a relatively brief period in modern times (during the time of Napoleon) had the whole of Italy been overrun and even then no attempt had been made to create a single state. In the Greek lands, however, all the Christian peoples had been ruled for centuries by men of different faith. But what is equally important is that the Turks from the outset had tolerated the existence of the Greek Orthodox Church and had even given it a privileged position within their empire. The Church, which included the non-Greek-speaking Christians, formed a kind of theocracy, the hierarchy of which in its upper ranks was Greek, the bishops whatever their racial origins thinking of themselves as Greek. There existed indeed local and separatist tendencies within this Church, especially among the lower clergy; and these were to assume considerable importance when, during the nineteenth century, the Slav-speaking regions began to develop a nationalist outlook. But the very existence of this theocracy preserved for the Greeks, and indirectly for the Slavs and other peoples, their national identity. Indeed, so closely knit was the national existence of the Greeks with their Church that in their liberation movement there was no hostility to the Greek Patriarchate at all comparable to that which the majority of the Italians displayed towards the Papacy. Certainly, there were conflicts. On the one hand, early ideologists of the Greek revolution, like Rigas and Korais, were anti-clerical, as were the westernised Greeks. On the other hand, most of the higher clergy disapproved of the activities of the revolutionaries; and the Patriarch himself opposed the movement towards a Greek national, autonomous Church within liberated Greece. Such a Church was eventually established in 1833 by the Bavarian regency. But this action was regretted by most Greeks, even by most of those who had just been liberated. Here, nevertheless, was one of the great problems of the Greek liberation—a problem vastly different from the Roman question, which was fundamentally a matter whether the Pope needed to retain, in order to fulfil his spiritual duties in the world at large, a temporal power within the Roman city and its environs. The Greek problem was less simple: it could be argued with some force that the aims of Hellenism might be better served by preserving intact the Ottoman empire, in order that the Greek patriarchal Church might, as the survivor of the old Byzantine Empire, become the precursor of the new—an ideal (one form of the *megali idhea*) which conflicted with the nationalist aspiration of gathering the Orthodox, Slavs as well as Greeks, into a Greek national kingdom ruled from Athens or even from Constantinople itself.

As time went on, the development and reorientation of Serbian national-ism, together with the rise of ethnic-linguistic nationalism in Romania and Bulgaria, rendered the narrower, nationalist Hellenism of Athens more practical politics than the oecumenical Hellenism of the Patriarchate and its supporters. This was certainly true of the regions which the Slavs were staking out for themselves. But in Asia Minor, there was no challenge from the Slavs. Here, then, was a dilemma. Either these Asia Minor Greeks must remain, along with those in Constantinople, a privileged theocracy within the Ottoman empire (being hostages, as it were, for the good conduct of the Greek nationalist state), or Greece must expand to link up European and Asiatic Greece by gaining control of Constantinople and the Straits.

Although the two forms of Hellenism were basically antagonistic to one another, the conflict was predominantly theoretical. As we have seen, Con-stantinople and Athens were able to arrive at working arrangements. Not that these arrangements resulted from any Greek propensity for compromise and moderation: they were the results of the restraints imposed upon the nationalists of Athens by the sheer physical difficulties of embarking upon a policy of expansion—the sparsity, dispersal, and poverty of the Greek people, the consequent weakness of their military forces, and, above all, the pressure from the European powers which, from their various standpoints, worked towards the preservation of the Ottoman empire and consequently imposed restraining hands on Greece. So great were the difficulties, when viewed from Athens, in the way of an expansionist policy, it is not surprising that many otherwise realistic Greeks sought refuge in the dreams of reach-ing Byzantium, not by force of arms, but by hellenising the Turkish dominions.

Apart from these obstacles to unification there existed for the Greeks, as for the Italians, other difficulties which were the legacy of their past. For the Italians, the legacy consisted of that self-sufficient provincialism which to many had more to offer than national unity: for the Greeks the legacy was one of deep-rooted hostility to secular and central authorities—a hostility which they yet combined with a high degree of subservience to their spiritual rulers. Liberty to the Greek was, and still is, the constant yearning to throw off oppression, to escape the shackles of government, and to defy the law. A Greek recognises obligations to his family; he will obey the officer who fights by his side and leads him in battle; but, a politician him-self, he is critical of political leaders and will change his allegiance over-night. He is hostile to the officials of the state who do not directly and even exclusively promote his interests. He expects to be rewarded for his political support; and although he may speak eloquently of moral causes (echoing the precepts of his Church or the tenets of Western philosophy), he is an individualist, combining uneasily with his fellows to promote some design or conspiracy whose end may or may not happen to be laudable. So lacking is he in ready obedience to the organs of the secular state that he tends to conceive of the function of government as one of granting favours to win and retain supporters, or of a ruthless seeking-out of conspirators, and of the punishment of those who cannot be won over. It is this conception of government which goes far to explaining that political instability of Greece during and ever since the first war of liberation.

Nevertheless, the Greeks, who had found a kind of freedom even under Ottoman rule, have always, under self-rule, enjoyed a political liberty, which though stormy and on occasions curtailed, has been of no mean order. This was a point noticed by the English historian George Finlay, a hundred years ago. His words, written in 1868, hold good today: 'No one could witness the behaviour of the people without feeling that there exists in Greece a good foundation for free institutions. . . .' The Greeks, he said on another occasion, are 'unfitted both by nature and circumstances for any but constitutional government'. What indeed Finlay had discerned (and he had lived for half a century in Greece) was that the Greeks had such a passionate belief in liberty and such a high order of intelligence that they could make parliamentary institutions work, albeit in a way somewhat peculiar to themselves. It is true that they may have been lacking in some of the traditions that make parliamentary government stable, but unstable government is not necessarily bad government from every point of view; and, as we have seen, the Greeks were on the whole happier politically under short-lived coalition governments based on a multiple party system than under strong governments founded on parliamentary dictatorship.

All the same, the instability of Greek governments contributed in part to the failure of the Greeks to provide the means for the uninterrupted pursuit of Hellenism. Whether indeed a more constant pursuit would have made much difference to the result (so unfavourable were external circumstances) is a matter for speculation. What, however, is perfectly clear is that the strong government of Venizelos (1910–15) enabled Greece to fight successfully and reap great benefits from the Balkan Wars of 1912–13. What is also perfectly clear is that the feuds in Greek political life engendered during World War I, and the intensification of those feuds when in November 1920 the Greek electorate threw over Venizelos and recalled King Constantine, produced the greatest disaster in Greek history since the fall of Constantinople in 1453. Just when the promised land seemed to be in their grasp, the Greeks, divided politically, divided into two nationwide factions, were able neither to manoeuvre on the diplomatic front nor to produce the necessary military efforts that would have left nothing to chance. The result was that in the late summer of 1922 they suffered ignominious defeat.

But Greece, as on all occasions, bore her cross bravely. She gathered in her children, not by conquering the soil on which they had laboured for centuries, but by receiving them—a million or more—within the existing Greek homeland. No nation has achieved so much as Greece on this occasion. With the help of friendly powers and of the League of Nations, she transformed the moment of disaster into her finest hour. For her many sacrifices she was to reap great rewards. The Asia Minor and east Thracian Greeks brought with them, if very little money or possessions, intelligence and skills. They were settled principally in Greek Macedonia and western Thrace, great care having been taken to see that strong settlements were made in the frontier regions. Their influx, combined with the exodus of the Slavs and Moslems, gave to Greece linguistic and ethnic homogeneity. Whereas the Greece of the treaty of Sèvres (if one includes Smyrna) contained heterogeneous elements amounting to 23 per cent, Greece after the exchange of peoples had minorities amounting to only just 6 per cent of the total population of 5,820,000,[1] the linguistic minorities being slightly larger, for some of the refugees did not know Greek.

Of the economic impact of the refugees upon Greece, although it was obviously considerable, it is not easy to speak with precision. At first the newcomers were a burden of great magnitude.[2] They later became an economic asset of enormous value—an asset which cannot be stated in figures because their economic contribution to Greece became indistinguishable from the development of the national economy as a whole under the impetus of a general economic expansion in Europe and the world at large. What is certain, however, is that as they settled down they began to make productive every inch of soil in the regions where they lived. They were, in the main, more enterprising, harder-working than the native Greeks, and more willing to introduce better agricultural methods. They began to grow a greater variety of crops and in the cultivation of tobacco (two-thirds of which in 1926 was in their hands) they introduced better strains. Even more than the native Greeks (and this was because they were bound more closely by their common misfortunes) they adopted co-operative methods. Much the same enterprise was displayed by the refugees who went into industry and trade. They brought new processes, above all in textiles, including silk, in carpet production, and in certain domestic crafts (embroidery, pottery, silverware, and enamel). Nevertheless, for many of these unfortunate people the struggle was hard. They were often housed in shacks either near their fields or in the outskirts of the towns, and many years had to elapse before the new villages of Macedonia, Thrace, and other regions began to take a tidy and a pleasing shape.

Needless to say, there was much discontent among these newcomers to Greece and it was not long before they were in the thick of Greek politics. Their political impact (at least in the short term) is easy to measure. They

---

[1] Cf. Romania, 28·3 per cent; Czechoslovakia 32·6 per cent; Yugoslavia 15·1 per cent. In Greece the largest minority (about 102,000) was Turkish. The Slav minority, which included 16,000 Pomaks, was about 80,000. The Moslem Albanian minority was just over 20,000.

[2] The cost has been variously estimated: Venizelos, £80,773,417; Tsouderos, £72,400,000; Loverdos, £78 million.

added some 300,000 votes to the 800,000 voting strength of Greece. Almost to a man they were Venizelists, for they associated their whole misfortunes with Venizelos's enemies. Many among them were anti-monarchist: in Turkey they had been used to a degree of self-government in their communities: the former traders had lived in the cosmopolitan centres of Constantinople, Smyrna, and other towns, and their outlook was liberal and often republican. Monarchy they associated with the name of Constantine and not with the fifty years of constitutional rule of George I. In the plebiscite held on 13 April 1924 the refugee vote was decisive. On that day 758,472 Greeks voted for the republic and 325,322 for the monarchy. But though the refugees had a decisive influence on Greek politics, they never succeeded in creating their own party. Instead they became gradually merged in the existing parties and in the new political groups that took shape. The same merging eventually took place in the social and intellectual life of Greece. They brought new dishes which became part of the Greek cuisine, new musical instruments, new standards of behaviour, their ignorance and dislike of the *katharevousa*, new literary themes, and new ideas. The story of that merging is a long and complicated one. But eventually the two populations settled down. After all, they had a common language, a common religion, and a common heritage of great antiquity.

Bibliographical Note

Works in English, French, and German

The most comprehensive account of the period 1821–1923, although on some topics it is out of date, remains Driault, E. et Lhéritier, M., *Histoire diplomatique de la Grèce, 1821–1923*, 5 vols., Paris, 1925–26 (with extensive bibliography). Another much older work, which certainly repays reading, both for its literary value and, despite its inaccuracies, for its insight into Greek political life up to 1864, is George Finlay's *History of the Greek Revolution* which comprises vols. vi and vii of F. H. Tozer's (Clarendon Press) edition of Finlay's historical works (1877). A photoprint edition of these two volumes, bound in one volume, was published in 1971 by Zeno, Booksellers and Publishers, Denmark Street, London.

Among modern works the following may be mentioned:

Alastos, D., *Venizelos: Patriot, Statesman, Revolutionary*, London, 1942.

Arnakis, G. (Editor), *Samuel G. Howe, An Historical Sketch of the Greek Revolution*, Austin, Texas, 1966.

Arnakis, G. and Dimitracopoulou, E. (Editors), *George Jarvis: his Journal and related documents*, Thessaloniki, 1965.

Botsaris, N., *Visions Balkaniques dans la préparation de la Révolution Grecque (1789–1821)*, Genève and Paris, 1962.

Bower, L. and Bolitho, G., *Otho I, King of Greece*, London, 1939.

British Documents on the Origins of the War, 1914–1918 (Editors G. P. Gooch and H. W. V. Temperley), H.M.S.O., London, 1926–30, vols. V, IX.

Campbell, J. and Sherrard, P., *Modern Greece*, London, 1968.

Crawley, C. W., *The Question of Greek Independence, 1821–33*, Cambridge, 1930.

——, *John Capodistrias: Unpublished Documents*, Thessaloniki, 1970.

Dakin, D., *British and American Philhellenes during the War of Greek Independence (1821–33)*, Thessaloniki, 1955.

——, *British intelligence of events in Greece, 1824–27*, Athens, 1959.

——, *The Greek struggle in Macedonia, 1897–1913*, Thessaloniki, 1966.

Dixon, C. W., *The Colonial Administration of Sir Thomas Maitland*, London, 1939.

Documents Diplomatiques Français, 1871–1914, Paris, 1929, etc.

Documents on British Foreign Policy (First Series), H.M.S.O., London, vol. I (ed. Rohan Butler), vol. III (ed. Rohan Butler), vol. IV (ed. Rohan Butler), vol. VII (ed. Rohan Butler), vol. VIII (ed. J. P. T. Bury), vol. XIII (ed. J. P. T. Bury), vol. XV (ed. J. P. T. Bury), vol. XVII (ed. Douglas Dakin). (Vol. XVII is devoted entirely to Greco–Turkish affairs, as is vol. XVIII (ed. Douglas Dakin), now in preparation.)

Dontas, D., *The Last Phase of the War of Independence in Western Greece*, Thessaloniki, 1966.

——, *Greece and the Great Powers, 1863–1875*, Thessaloniki, 1966.

Forster, E., *A Short History of Modern Greece, 1821–1956* (third edition, revised and enlarged by Douglas Dakin), London, 1958.

Frangoulis, A., *La Grèce et la crise mondiale*, 2 vols., Paris, 1926.

Frazee, C., *The Orthodox Church and independent Greece, 1821–1852*, Cambridge, 1969.

Georgescu, V., *Mémoires et projets de réforme dans les Principautés Roumaines, 1769–1830*, Bucuresti, 1970.

Greece: Foreign Ministry, *Recueil des Traités, Conventions et Accords*, Athènes, 1912, etc.

Greece: Statistical Service, *Annuaire statistique de la Grèce*, Athènes, 1930, etc.

Howard, H., *The Partition of Turkey*, New York, 1966.

Jenkins, R., *Dionysios Solomos*, Cambridge, 1940.

Kaltsas, N., *Introduction to the Constitutional History of Modern Greece*, New York, 1940.

Kitsikis, D., *Propagande et pressions en politique internationale. La Grèce et ses revendications à la Conférence de la Paix, 1919–20*, Paris, 1963.

Kofos, E., *Nationalism and Communism in Macedonia*, Thessaloniki, 1964.

Korizis, H., *Die politischen Parteien Griechenlands, 1821–1910*, Hersbruck/Nürnberg, 1966.

Levantis, A., *The Greek Foreign Debt and the Great Powers, 1821–98*, New York, 1944.

Mavrocordato, J., *Modern Greece, 1800–1931*, London, 1931.

Miller, W., *Greece*, London, 1928.

——, *A History of the Greek People, 1821–1921*, London, 1922.

——, *The Ottoman Empire and its successors*, Cambridge, 1928.

Moschopoulos, N., *La Presse dans la renaissance balkanique*, Athènes, 1931.

Mustapha Kemal, *A speech delivered by Ghazi Mustapha Kemal . . . in October 1927*, Leipzig, 1929.

Ostrogorsky, G., *History of the Byzantine State* (tr. by Joan Hussey), New Brunswick, N.J., 1969.

Pallis, A. A., *Greece's Anatolian Venture—and after*, London, 1937.

Papadakis, B. P., *Histoire diplomatique de la question Nord-Epirote, 1912–57*, Thessaloniki, 1958.

Papadopoulos, G., *England and the Near East, 1896–1898*, Thessaloniki, 1969.

Pentzopoulos, D., *The Balkan Exchange of minorities and its impact upon Greece*, Paris, 1962.

Petropulos, J. A., *Politics and statecraft in the Kingdom of Greece, 1833–1843*, Princeton, 1968.

Polyzos, N., *Essai sur l'émigration grecque*, Paris, 1947.

Prevelakis, E., *British policy towards the change of dynasty in Greece*, Athens, 1953.

Psomiadis, C., *The Eastern Question: the last Phase*, Thessaloniki, 1968.

Stavrianos, L., *Balkan Federation: A History of the Movement toward Balkan Unity in Modern Times*, Northampton, Mass., 1944.

——, *The Balkans since 1453*, New York, 1963. (Contains a good bibliography.)

Svoronos, N., *Histoire de la Grèce Moderne*, Paris, 1964.

Tsakonas, D., *Geist und Gesellschaft in Griechenland*, Bonn, 1965.

Tsourkas, C., *La vie et l'œuvre de Theophile Corydalée, 1563–1646*, Thessaloniki, 1967.

Vasdravellis, J., *The Greek struggle for Independence. The Macedonians in the Revolution of 1821*, Thessaloniki, 1968.

Venizelos, E., *The Vindication of Greek National Policy*, London, 1918.

Woodhouse, C. M., *The Greek War of Independence*, London, 1952.

——, *The Battle of Navarino*, London, 1965.

——, *The Story of Modern Greece*, London, 1968.

——, *The Philhellenes*, London, 1969.

The following Memoirs are available in translation:

Kolokotronis, Th., *The Greek War of Independence* (translated and edited by E. M. Edmonds), reprint, Chicago, 1969.

Makriyannis, I., *Memoirs* (translated and edited by H. A. Lidderdale), London, 1966.

The following works which contain much statistical material are valuable for the study of Greek economic, social, and administrative history:

Bickford-Smith, P. A. H., *Greece under King George*, London, 1893.

Leconte, C., *Étude économique de la Grèce*, Paris, 1847.

Mansolas, A., *Renseignements statistiques sur les établissements industriels à vapeur en Grèce*, Athènes, 1876.

Martin, P., *Greece of the Twentieth Century*, London, 1913.

Moraitinis, P., *La Grèce telle qu'elle est*, Paris, 1877.

Sergeant, L., *Greece in the Nineteenth Century*, London, 1897.

Strong, F., *Greece as a Kingdom*, 1842.

Thiersch, F., *De l'état actuel de la Grèce et des moyens d'arriver à sa restauration*, 2 vols., Leipzig, 1833.

Tsouderos, E., *Le relèvement économique de la Grèce*, Paris, 1919.

Articles in English, French, German, and Italian

Numerous periodicals contain from time to time articles on Greek history. Special mention, however, should be made of *Balkan Studies* (Thessaloniki), a bi-annual publication which first appeared in 1960. This is devoted to articles on Greek history and reviews of current historical literature. A new venture of which the first volume appeared in 1970 is *Neo-Hellenika* (Editor, G. Arnakis), Annual publication of the Center for Neo-Hellenic Studies, Austin, Texas.

Important works in Greek (titles translated)

Anastassopoulos, G., *History of Greek Industry, 1840–1940*, 3 vols., Athens, 1947.

Andreadis, A. M., *National Loans and the Greek Economy, 1821–93*, Athens, 1925.

Aspras, G., *Political History of Modern Greece, 1821–1921*, 3 vols., Athens, 1922.

Dafnis, G., *Greek political parties*, Athens, 1961.

Dimakopoulos, G., *The Administrative organisation of Greece during the War of Independence*, Athens, 1966.

Dimaras, K., *History of Modern Greek Literature*, 2 vols., Athens, 1948–49.

Evelpidis, C., *Economic and Social History of Greece*, Athens, 1950.

Greece: General Staff, *History of the Organization of the Greek Army, 1821–1954*, Athens, 1957.

Greek Government Gazette, 1833–1923.

Greek Parliament: Parliamentary Debates, 1885–98.

Kandiloros, T., *The 'Filiki Eteria'*, Athens, 1926.

Karolidis, P., *History of Contemporary Greece, 1821–1921*, 7 vols., Athens, 1922–29.

Kofos, E., *The Revolution in Macedonia in 1878*, Thessaloniki, 1969.

Kordatos, Y., *History of Modern Greece*, 5 vols., Athens, 1957–58.

Kyriakidis, E., *History of Contemporary Hellenism, 1832–92*, 2 vols., Athens, 1892–94.

Kyriakopoulos, E. (Editor), *The Constitutions of Greece*, Athens, 1960.

Lascaris, S., *Diplomatic History of Greece, 1821–1914*, Athens, 1947.

Mager, K., *History of the Greek Press*, 3 vols., Athens, 1957–60.

Markezinis, S., *Political History of Modern Greece*, 4 vols., Athens, 1966–68. (This work is superbly illustrated.)

Mazarakis, A., *Historical Study, 1821–1907, and the War of 1897*, 2 vols., Athens, 1950.

Moschopoulos, N., *History of the Greek Revolution according to Turkish Sources*, Athens, 1960.

Mylonas, G., *Electoral Systems*, Athens, 1946.

National Assembly of Greece, *Minutes*, 3 Sept. 1843–18 March 1844.

National Assembly of Greece, 1862–64, *Official Gazette*, Athens, 1862–65.

Notaris, I., *Unpublished documents from the Archive of Stefanos Dragoumis*, Thessaloniki, 1966.

Pangalos, Th., *Memoirs*, Athens, 1959.

Papadopoulos, S. I., *Educational and Social activities of Macedonian Hellenism during the last century of the Ottoman occupation*, Thessaloniki, 1970.

Petrakakos, D. A., *The Parliamentary History of Greece*, 3 vols., Athens, 1935–46.

Pournaras, D., *Charilaos Trikoupis*, 2 vols., Athens, 1950.

Prevelakis, E. and Plagianakou-Bekiari, V. (Editors), *The Cretan Revolution (1866–69)*, 2 vols., Athens, 1967 and 1970 (ed. of the Academy of Athens).

Protopsaltis, E., *The 'Filiki Eteria'*, Athens, 1964. (ed. of the Academy of Athens).

——, *The Archive of Alexandros Mavrokordatos*, 2 vols., Athens, 1963–65 (ed. of the Academy of Athens).

Sakellariou, M. B., *The Peloponnese during the second Turkish occupation*, Athens, 1939.

Tsirintanis, N., *Political and Diplomatic History of the Cretan National Revolution, 1866–69*, 3 vols., Athens, 1950–52.

Vasdravellis, J., *The Macedonians in their struggle for Independence, 1796–1832*, Thessaloniki, 1950.

Vendiris, G., *Greece in 1910–20*, 2 vols., Athens, 1931.

Vranousis, L., *Rigas*, Athens, 1953. (Contains all the works of Rigas.)

Zegellis, E., *Parliamentary Law*, Athens, 1912.

Bibliographies

Many of the above-mentioned works contain good bibliographies. For further bibliographies, see the following:

Brown, A. D. and Jones, H. D., *Greece: a selected list of references*, Washington, 1943.

Gines, D. S. and Mexas, B. G., *Greek bibliography (1800–63)*, 3 vols., Athens, 1939–57. (In Greek.)

Greece: Press and Information Ministry, *Greek bibliography*, Athens, 1960, etc. (In English and French.)

Institute for Balkan Studies (Thessaloniki), *List of Publications*.

Institut Français d'Athènes, *Bulletin analytique de bibliographie Hellénique (1945, etc.)*, Athènes, 1947, etc.

Legrand, E., *Bibliographie Hellénique* (up to 1790), 11 vols., Paris, 1885–1928.

——, *Bibliographie Ionienne* (1494–1900), 2 vols., Paris, 1910.

Miller, W., Bibliographical articles in: *History*, X (July 1925), 110–23; *Cambridge Historical Journal*, II (1928), 229–47 and VI (1938), 115–20; *Journal of Modern History*, II (Dec. 1930), 612–28 and IX (March 1937), 56–63; *American Historical Review*, XXXVII (Jan. 1932), 272–79 and XL (July 1935), 688–93.

Papadopoulos-Vretos, A., *Neohellenic philology, 1453–1830*, Athens, 1854. (In Greek.)

Phousaras, G. I., *Bibliography of the Greek bibliographies, 1791–1947*, Athens, 1961. (In Greek.)

Royal Research Foundation, *Quinze ans de bibliographie historique en Grèce, 1950–1965*, Athens, 1966.

Royal Research Foundation, *Cinq ans de bibliographie historique en Grèce, 1965–69*, Athènes, 1970.

Topping, P. W., Bibliographical articles in: *Byzantine-Metabyzantine*, I (1949), 113–27; *Journal of Modern History*, XXXIII (No. 2, June 1961), 167–73.

Weber, S. H., Bibliographical article in: *Journal of Modern History*, XXI (Sept. 1950), 250–66.

Appendices

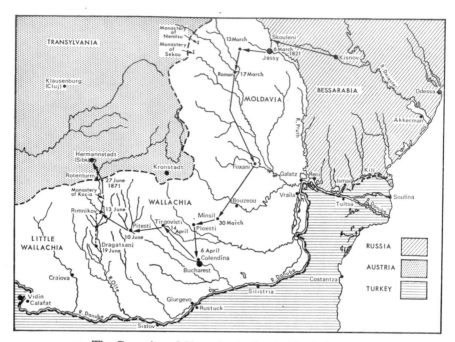

1   The Campaign of Alexander Ipsilantis, March–June 1821

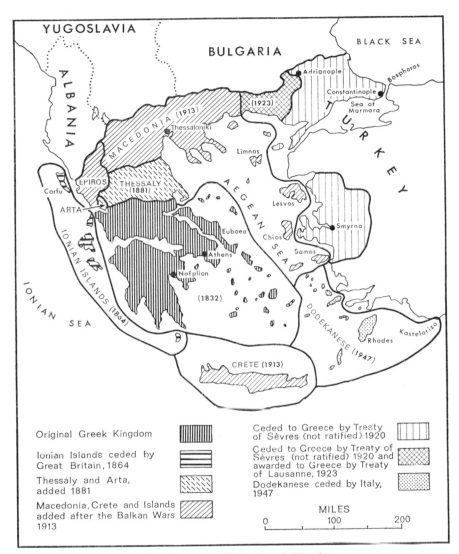

2   The Expansion of The Greek Kingdom

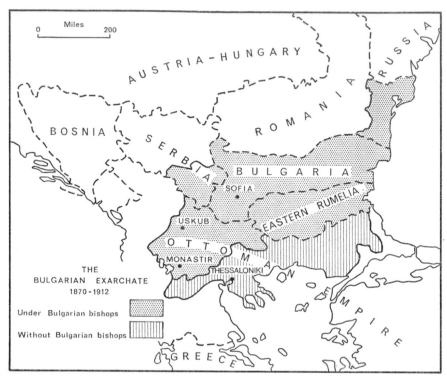

3   The Bulgarian Exarchate, 1870–1912

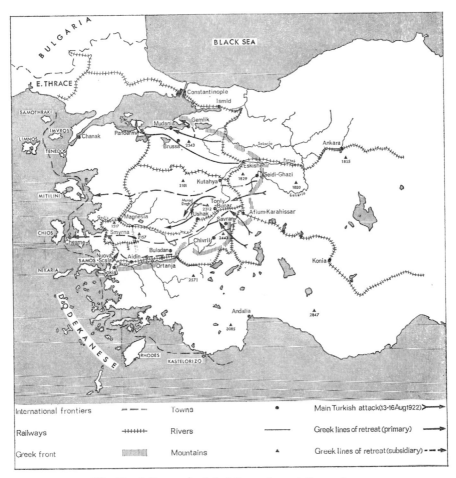

4   The Greek Retreat in Asia Minor, August–September 1922

GREECE

5   Greece and the Aegean

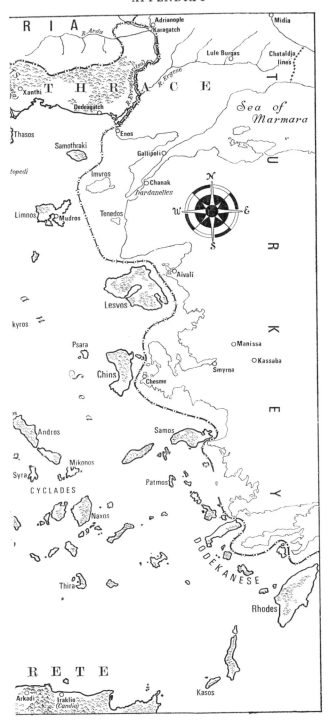

APPENDIX II: The Greek Kingdom: Dynastic Table

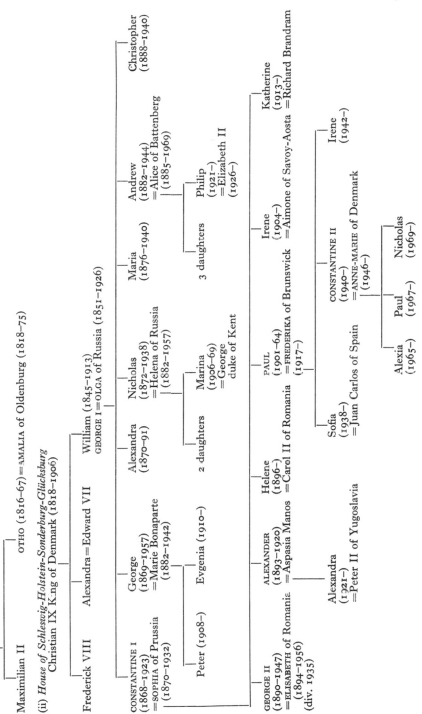

Date	President of the Council	Foreign Affairs[1]	Justice	Interior
6 Feb. 1833	S. Trikoupis (1st admin.)	S. Trikoupis	C. Klonaris	D. Christidis
15 April 1833	S. Trikoupis (2nd admin.)	S. Trikoupis	G. Praidis	G. Psillas
24 Oct. 1833	A. Mavrokordatos (1st admin.)	A. Mavrokordatos	K. Schinas	J. Kolettis
12 June 1834	J. Kolettis (1st admin.)	I. Rizos-Neroulos	K. Schinas G. Praidis (20.viii.34)	J. Kolettis
1 June 1835	J. von Armansperg	I. Rizos-Neroulos	G. Praidis I. Rizos Neroulos (25.ii.36)	J. Kolettis G. Praidis (vii.35) D. Mansolas (25.ii.36)
14 Feb. 1837	I. von Rudhart	I. von Rudhart	I. Rizos-Neroulos A. Paikos (24.iv.37)	D. Mansolas A. Polizoidis (24.iv.37) G. Glarakis (11.xii.37)
20 Dec. 1837	King Otbo	K. Zografos A. Paikos (16.xi.39) K. Zografos (20.iii.40) A. Paikos (28.v.40)	A. Paikos	G. Glarakis N. Theocharis (11.i.40)
22 Feb. (6 July) 1841	A. Mavrokordatos (2nd admin.)	A. Mavrokordatos D. Christidis (6.vii.41)	A. Paikos L. Melas (6.vii.41)	N. Theocharis A. Mavrokordatos (6.vii.41)
22 Aug. 1841	A. Kriezis (1st admin.)	I. Rizos-Neroulos	G. A. Rallis	D. Christidis
15 Sept. 1843	A. Metaxas (1st admin.)	A. Metaxas	L. Melas	R. Palamidis A. Lontos (i.44)
28 Feb. 1844	K. Kanaris (1st admin.)	D. Mansolas	L. Melas	A. Lontos
11 Apr. 1844	A. Mavrokordatos (3rd admin.)	S. Trikoupis	A. C. Lontos S. Trikoupis (8.viii.44)	A. Lontos

Cults and Public Instruction	Finance	War	Marine
I. Rizos-Neroulos	A. Mavrokordatos	K. Zografos	D. Voulgaris
S. Trikoupis	A. Mavrokordatos	A. Mavrokordatos C. von Schmaltz (13.vi.33)	J. Kolettis C. von Schmaltz (22.vii.33)
K. Schinas	N. Theocharis	C. von Schmaltz W. Lesuire (23.iii.34)	A. Mavrokordatos
K. Schinas I. Rizos Neroulos (20.viii.34)	N. Theocharis	W. Lesuire	W. Lesuire
I. Rizos-Neroulos	N. Theocharis (K. Lasanis 25.ii.36 Director of Finances)	W. Lesuire C. von Schmaltz (22.vi.35)	W. Lesuire C. von Schmaltz (22.vi.35) I. Rizos-Neroulos (9.ii.36) A. Kriezis (25.ii.36)
I. Rizos-Neroulos A. Polizoidis (24.iv.37) G. Glarakis (11.xii.37)	(K. Lasanis) N. Botasis (2.iv.37)	C. von Schmaltz	A. Kriezis
G. Glarakis N. Theocharis (11.i.40)	N. Botasis G. Spaniolakis (4.i.38) A. Paikos (16.x.39) (G. K. Tisamenos 28.x.39 Director of Finances)	C. von Schmaltz	A. Kriezis
N. Theocharis S. Valetas 6.vii.41)	(G. K. Tisamenos)	C. von. Schmaltz A. Metaxas (14.vii.41)	A. Kriezis
I. Rizos-Neroulos	(G. K. Tisamenos) N. Silivergos (21.xi.42) A. Kriezis (7.xii.42) G. A. Rallis (30.xii.42)	A. Metaxas A. Vlachopoulos (10.ix.41)	A. Kriezis
M. Schinas	D. Mansolas	A. Lontos	K. Kanaris
L. Melas	D. Mansolas	A. Lontos	K. Kanaris
S. Trikoupis	A. Mavrokordatos	P. Rodios	A. Mavrokordatos

Date	President of the Council	Foreign Affairs	Justice	Interior
18 Aug. 1844	J. Kolettis (2nd admin.)	J. Kolettis K. Tzavellas (14.xi.46) J. Kolettis (28.xii.46) G. Glarakis (12.viii.47)	Z. Valvis L. Krestenitis (26.i.46) J. Kolettis (31.i.46) K. Kanaris (14.iii.46) J. Kolettis (27.i.47) K. Kolokotronis (17.iv.47)	J. Kolettis N. Poniropoulos (14.xi.46) J. Kolettis (28.xii.46) R. Palamidis (17.iv.47)
17 Sept. 1847	K. Tzavellas	G. Glarakis	K. Kolokotronis	R. Palamidis
19 Mar. 1848	G. Koundouriotis	D. Mansolas K. Kolokotronis (14.vi.48)	L. Krestenitis G. A. Rallis (7.vii.48)	L. Krestenitis B. Roufos (7.vii.48)
27 Oct. 1848	K. Kanaris (2nd admin.)	K. Kolokotronis A. Lontos (14 i.49) G. A. Rallis (13.iii.49) G. Glarakis (29 iv.49)	G. A. Rallis I. Antonopoulos (17.v.49)	A. Lontos G. Glarakis (25.i.49) D. Christidis (29.iv.49) L. Krestenitis (9.viii.49)
24 Dec. 1849	A. Kriezis (2nd admin.)	A. Lontos P. Deliyannis (4.viii.50) A. Paikos (5.v.51)	Z. Valvis N. Chrisogelos (22.v.50) G. Notaras (4.viii.50) A. Paikos (16.viii.50) I. Damianos (5.vi.51) K. Provelengios (5.ii.52) A. Paikos (22.vii.52) S. Pillikas (10.ix.53)	G. Notaras D. Meletopoulos (5.vi.51) A. Danopoulos (5.ii.52) R. Palamidis (22.vii.52) I. Amvrosiadis (8.iii.53)
28 May 1854	A. Mavrokordatos (4th admin. K. Kanaris acting head of government until arrival of Mavrokordatos 29.vii.54)	P. Argiropoulos A. Mavrokordatos (29.vii.54) P. Argiropoulos (20.vi.55)	P. Kalligas A. Lontos (29.vii.54) P. Varvoglis (13.vi.55)	R. Palamidis A. Mavrokordatos (10.xii.54)
4 Oct. 1855	D. Voulgaris (1st admin.)	N. Silivergos M. Potlis (15.x.55) A. Rizos-Rangavis (26.ii.56)	M. Potlis M. Skalistiris (28.ii.56)	D. Voulgaris

Cults and Public Instruction	Finance	War	Marine
J. Kolettis	A. Metaxas	K. Tzavellas	A. Metaxas
K. Kanaris	Z. Valvis		K. Kanaris
(14.xi.46)	(21.viii.45)		(6.i.45)
J. Kolettis	N. Poniropoulos		D. Voulgaris
(27.i.47)	(26.i.46)		(17.iv.47)
G. Glarakis	J. Kolettis		
(17.iv.47)	(28.xii.46)		
	N. Poniropoulos		
	(27.i.47)		
	N. Korfiotakis		
	(17.iv.47)		
G. Glarakis	N. Korfiotakis	K. Tzavellas	D. Voulgaris
D. Mansolas	V. Christakopoulos	P. Rodios	G. Koundouriotis
A. Mavromichalis	T. Manginas		
(7.vii.48)	(7.vii.48)		
D. Kallifronas	D. Voulgaris	A. Mavromichalis	K. Kanaris
	L. Krestenitis	K. Tzavellas	
	(29.iv.49)	(29.iv.49)	
	I. Antonopoulos		
	(17.v.49)		
	Z. Valvis		
	(9.viii.49)		
	I. Antonopoulos		
	(19.xi.49)		
	Z. Valvis		
	(9.xii.49)		
N. Chrisogelos	Z. Valvis	I. Staikos	A. Kriezis
P. Deliyannis	A. Lontos	Spiromilios	
(4.viii.50)	(22.v.50)	(16.viii.50)	
N. Korfiotakis	P. Deliyannis	S. Soutsos	
(16.viii.50)	(4.viii.50)	(17.x.53)	
A. Paikos	D. Christidis		
(2.ix.50)	(16.viii.50)		
P. Varvoglis	K. Provelengios		
(5.vi.51)	(17.x.53)		
S. Vlachos			
(5.ii.52)			
G. Psillas	P. Argiropoulos	D. Kallergis	K. Kanaris
P. Argiropoulos	L. Krestenitis		D. Kallergis
13.vi.55)	(13.v.55)		(6.iii.55)
			A. Zigomalas
			(13.vi.55)
M. Potlis	N. Silivergos	L. Smolenitz	A. Miaoulis
A. Miaoulis	D. Voulgaris		
(15.x.55)	(15.x.55)		
C. Christopoulos	A. Kontostavlos		
(17.x.55)	(17.x.55)		
	A. Koumoundouros		
	(14.vii.56)		

Date	President of the Council	Foreign Affairs	Justice	Interior
25 Nov. 1857	A. Miaoulis (From 3.ii. to 7.iii.62 A. G. Koundouriotis was acting head of government)	A. Rizos-Rangavis A. Miaoulis (11.iii.59) A. G. Koundouriotis (10.vi.59) T. Zaimis (24.i.60) A. G. Koundouriotis (31.iv.60)	G. A. Rallis M. Potlis (26.v.60)	K. Provelengios R. Palamidis (10.vi.59) A. G. Koundouriotis (24.i.60) L. Krestenitis (3.vii.60) A. G. Koundouriotis (7.xii.60) N. Papalexopoulos (19.xii.60) C. Christopoulos (23.v.61)
7 June 1862	G. Kolokotronis	N. Theocharis E. Iliopoulos (23.vi.62) N. Dragoumis (1.viii.62)	E. Iliopoulos	G. Kolokotronis
22–23 Oct. 1862	D. Voulgaris (2nd admin.)	A. Diamantopoulos P. Kalligas (20.ii.63)	A. Koumoundouros Z. Valvis (20.ii.63)	T. Zaimis A. C. Lontos (20.ii.63)
24 Feb. 1863	Z. Valvis[2] (1st admin.)	D. Mavrokordatos	I. Papazafiropoulos	A. Avgerinos
9 Apr. 1863	D. Kiriakos	T. Deliyannis	I. Paleologos	G. Petmezas
10 May 1863	B. Roufos (1st admin.)	T. Deliyannis	K. Platis	A. C. Lontos
3 July 1863	B. Roufos[2] (2nd admin.)	P. Kalligas	P. Mavromichalis	A. Petmezas
6 Nov. 1863	D. Voulgaris (3rd admin.)	P. Deliyannis	A. Diamantopoulos T. Petrinos (4.iii.64)	D. Voulgaris
17 Mar. 1864	K. Kanaris (3rd admin.)	T. Deliyannis	A. Koumoundouros	T. A. Zaimis
28 Apr. 1864	Z. Valvis (2nd admin.)	P. Kalligas Z. Valvis (28.v.64)	I. Papazafiropoulos	A. Avgerinos
7 Aug. 1864	K. Kanaris (4th admin.)	T. Deliyannis D. Boudouris (10.xii.64)	A. C. Lontos	A. Koumoundouros
14 Mar. 1865	A. Koumoundouros (1st admin.)	D. Boudouris P. V. Armenis (28.iii.65) D. Boudouris (14.iv.65)	A. Koumoundouros L. Krestenitis (28.iii.65) P. Kalligas (6.x.65)	A. Chatzianargirou A. Koumoundouros (18.viii.65) K. Lomvardos (6.x.65)
1 Nov. 1865	E. Deligiorgis (1st admin.)	E. Deligiorgis	E. Deligiorgis	T. A. Zaimis
15 Nov. 1865	D. Voulgaris (4th admin.)	C. Christopoulos	N. Papamichalopoulos	D. Voulgaris

Cults and Public Instruction	Finance	War	Marine
C. Christopoulos T. Zaimis (10.vi.59) M. Potlis (30.iv.60)	A. Koumoundouros E. Simos (3.vii.60)	L. Smolenitz Spiromilios (10.vi.59) D. M. Botsaris (22.vi.59)	A. Miaoulis D. M. Botsaris (3.ii.62) A. Miaoulis (7.iii.62)
D. Chatziskos	D. Levidis I. Varvoglis (7.viii.62)	Spiromilios	N. Mexis
E. Deligiorgis V. Nikolopoulos (divided ministry)	T. Manginas E. Kehayas (20.ii.63)	D. Mavromichalis A. Michos (20.ii.63)	D. Kallifronas A. Michos (20.ii.63)
K. Dosios	D. Charalambis	L. Smolenitz	D. Boudouris
D. Kallifronas	A. Koumoundouros	D. Botsaris	N. Boudouris
D. Kallifronas	A. Koumoundouros	D. N. Botsaris P. Koroneos (30.vi.63)	M. Kanaris
V. Nikolopoulos	E. Kehayas	I. Klimakas	G. Bouboulis
A. Petsalis	D. Drosos	L. Smolenitz V. Petmezas (30.xii.63) D. Trigetas (4.iii.64)	A. Diamantopoulos A. Rondiris (4.iii.64)
A. Koumoundouros	D. Christidis	P. Koroneos	K. Kanaris
I. Papazafiropoulos	Z. Valvis	C. Zimbrakakis	M. Kanaris
A. C. Lontos	S. Sotiropoulos	A. Karnalis	K. Kanaris
A. C. Lontos K. Lomvardos (28.iii.65) P. Kalligas (6.x.65)	S. Sotiropoulos A. Koumoundouros (28.iii.65)	A. Karnalis T. Lazaretos (6.x.65)	D. Boudouris T. Lazaretos (6.x.65)
D. Kallifronas	D. Christidis	D. Grivas	A. Mavromichalis
A. Koundouriotis	D. Drosos	D. Kallergis	S. Antonopoulos

Date	President of the Council	Foreign Affairs	Justice	Interior
18 Nov. 1865	A. Koumoundouros (2nd admin.)	A. Koumoundouros	P. Petrakis	A. Koumoundouros
25 Nov. 1865	E. Deligiorgis (2nd admin.)	E. Deligiorgis	E. Deligiorgis S. Antonopoulos (8.xii.65)	T. A. Zaimis E. Deligiorgis (2.xii.65)
10 Dec. 1865	B. Roufos (3rd admin.)	I. Valassopoulos	B. Roufos	V. Nikolopoulos
7 Feb. 1866	B. Roufos (4th admin.)	S. Valaoritis	B. Roufos T. F. Tipaldos (15.ii.66)	K. Provelengios B. Roufos (6.vi.66)
21 June 1866	D. Voulgaris (5th admin.)	E. Deligiorgis	E. Deligiorgis	D. Voulgaris
30 Dec. 1866	A. Koumoundouros (3rd admin.)	C. Trikoupis	A. Koumoundouros K. Lomvardos (5 Jan. 1867)	A. Koumoundouros
1 Jan. 1868	A. Moraitinis	A. Moraitinis P. Deliyannis (16.i.68)	A. Moraitinis	I. Messinezis
6 Feb. 1868	D. Voulgaris (6th admin.)	P. Deliyannis	P. Varvoglis S. Antonopoulos (23.ix.68)	A. Mavromichalis
6 Feb. 1869	T. A. Zaimis (1st admin.)	T. Deliyannis P. Soutsos S. Valaoritis (8.i.70)	A. Petsalis T. A. Zaimis (23.xii.69) D. Saravas (8.i.70)	T. A. Zaimis
21 July 1870	E. Deligiorgis (3rd admin.)	E. Deligiorgis M. Antonopoulos (3 ix.70)	N. Leopoulos	E. Deligiorgis
15 Dec. 1870	A. Koumoundouros (4th admin.)	C. Christopoulos A. Koumoundouros (7.iii.71) P. Petrakis (3.iv.71)	A. A. Kontostavlos	A. Koumoundouros
9 Nov. 1871	T. A. Zaimis (2nd admin.)	T. A. Zaimis	I. Papazafiropoulos	T. A. Zaimis
6 Jan. 1872	D. Voulgaris (7th admin.)	D. Voulgaris	A. Metaxas G. Bouboulis (12.vii.72)	V. Nikolopoulos
20 July 1872	E. Deligiorgis (4th admin.)	E. Deligtiorgis I. Spiliotakis (11.viii.72) E. Deligiorgis (8.xi.72)	D. Christidis E. Deligiorgis (10.viii.72) P. Chalkiopoulos (6.i.73)	E. Deligiorgis D. Drosos (13.xii.72) E. Deligiorgis (27.v.73)
21 Feb. 1874	D. Voulgaris (8th admin.)	I. A. Deliyannis	V. Nikolopoulos	D. Voulgaris

Cults and Public Instruction	Finance	War	Marine
K. Lomvardos	S. Sotiropoulos	T. Lazaretos	T. Lazaretos
S. Antonopoulos	D. Christidis	D. Grivas	A. Mavromichalis
K. Dariotis	S. Sotiropoulos	V. Skaltsodimos	N. Boudouris
B. Roufos S. Antoniadis (6.vi.66)	P. Yannopoulos	V. Petmezas	D. Sachtouris
D. Drosos	D. Christidis	A. Michos C. Zimbrakakis (13.vii.66)	D. Drosos
C. Christopoulos	E. Kehayas	D. M. Botsaris	K. Lomvardos D. Grivas (5.i.67)
I. Messinezis	P. Yannopoulos	Spiromilios	D. Sachtouris
E. Simos	E. Simos I. Valassopoulos (23.ix.68) S. Valaoritis (31.xii.68)	Spiromilios	M. Kanaris
D. Saravas A. Avgerinos (8.i.70)	A. Avgerinos T. Deliyannis (8.i.70)	S. Soutsos S. Valaoritis (25.iv.70) L. Smolenitz (29.iv.70)	D. Trigetas G. Tombazis (8.i.70)
M. Antonopoulos	D. Christidis	C. Zimbrakakis	D. Drosos
P. Petrakis A. Petmezas (14.ii.71)	S. Sotiropoulos	A. Koumoundouros L. Smolenitz (14.ii.71)	P. Petrakis
F. Filonos	T. Deliyannis	C. Zimbrakakis	A. Avgerinos
A. Notaras	N. Papamichalopoulos	I. Drakos	G. Bouboulis
D. Drosos D. Mavrokordatos (10.viii.72) D. Drosos (29.x.72) D. Kallifronas (6.i.73) I. Valassopoulos	D. Christidis N. Papamichalopoulos V. Nikolopoulos (16.x.74)	D. Grivas K. Trigetas D. Grivas (9.v.74)	D. Drosos S. Petmezas (6.i.73) D. Drosos (27.v.73) V. Nikolopoulos K. Trigetas (9.v.74)

Date	President of the Council	Foreign Affairs	Justice	Interior
8 May 1875	C. Trikoupis (1st admin.)	C. Trikoupis	K. Lomvardos	C. Trikoupis
27 Oct. 1875	A. Koumoundouros (5th admin.)	A. A. Kontostavlos	I. Papazaphiropoulos	A. Koumoundouros
8 Dec. 1876	E. Deligiorgis (5th admin.)	E. Deligiorgis	D. Voulpiotis	I. N. Deliyannis
13 Dec. 1876	A. Koumoundouros (6th admin.)	A. A. Kontostavlos	A. Koumoundouros	A. Koumoundouros
10 Mar. 1877	E. Deligiorgis (6th admin.)	E. Deligiorgis	S. Antonopoulos	E. Deligiorgis
31 May 1877	A. Koumoundouros (7th admin.)	A. Koumoundouros	A. Koumoundouros	N. Papamichalopoulos
7 June 1877	K. Kanaris (4th admin.) on death of Kanaris 15.ix.77, ministers took turns to preside)	C. Trikoupis	T. A. Zaimis	A. Koumoundouros
23 Jan. 1878	A. Koumoundouros (8th admin.)	T. Deliyannis A. Koumoundouros (8.vi.78) T. Deliyannis (23.viii.78)	N. Papamichalopoulos	A. Koumoundouros
2 Nov. 1878	C. Trikoupis (2nd admin.)	C. Trikoupis	T. A. Zaimis	T. A. Zaimis
7 Nov. 1878	A. Koumoundouros (9th admin.)	T. Deliyannis A. Koumoundouros (15.ix.79)	A. Koumoundouros G. Bouboulis (26.iv.79) A. Koumoundouros (10.x.79) N. Valsamakis (20.i.80)	A. Koumoundouros
22 Mar. 1880	C. Trikoupis (3rd admin.)	C. Trikoupis	A. Petmezas	K. Lomvardos
25 Oct. 1880	A. Koumoundouros (10th admin.)	A. Koumoundouros A. Rikakis (18.vii.81)	S. Sotiropoulos A. Koumoundouros (7.vi.81) A. Rikakis (16.vi.81) N. Papamichalopoulos (21.xi.81)	N. Papamichalopoulos
15 Mar. 1882	C. Trikoupis (4th admin.)	C. Trikoupis A. A. Kontostavlos (11.iv.83)	D. G. Rallis A. A. Kontostavlos (24.vii.83)	C. Trikoupis K. Lomvardos (19.v.83)

Cults and Public Instruction	Finance	War	Marine
D. G. Rallis	A. Petmezas	P. Gennatas	P. Gennatas G. Servos (15.vi.75) K. Lomvardos (18.viii.75)
G. Milisis	S. Sotiropoulos	S. Karaiskakis	A. Avgerinos
T. Kanakaris	D. Levidis	S. Petmezas	G. Zochios
G. Milisis	S. Sotiropoulos	S. Karaiskakis	G. Bouboulis
T. Kanakaris	D. Levidis	A. Mavromichalis	G. Zochios L. Palaskas (16.v.77)
A. Notaras	S. Sotiropoulos	S. Petmezas	G. Bouboulis
T. Deliyannis	E. Deligiorgis	C. Zimbrakakis	K. Kanaris C. Zimbrakakis (19.ix.78)
T. Deliyannis G. Bouboulis (8.vi.78) A. Koumoundouros (4.vii.78) T. Deliyannis (23.viii.78)	N. Papamichalopoulos	S. Petmezas G. Bouboulis (4.vii.78) V. Sapountzakis (19.vii.78)	G. Bouboulis
N. Mavrokordatos A. Avgerinos	C. Trikoupis T. Deliyannis N. Papamichalopoulos (20.i.80)	S. Karaiskakis G. Bouboulis D. Grivas (30.xii.78) G. Bouboulis (28.vii.79) V. Valtinos (22.viii.79)	M. Kanaris G. Bouboulis
N. Mavrokordatos	C. Trikoupis	S. Karaiskakis	G. D. Voulgaris
N. Papamichalopoulos A. Koumoundouros (7.vi.81) S. Romas (16.vi.81) A. Koumoundouros (13.vii.81)	S. Sotiropoulos A. Athanasiadis (16.vi.81)	A. A. Mavromichalis V. Valtinos (23.iv.81)	G. Bouboulis
K. Lomvardos D. Voulpiotis 24.vii.84)	P. Kalligas C. Trikoupis (19.v.83)	S. Karaiskakis C. Trikoupis (31.iii.82)	G. Roufos G. Tombazis (21.vii.83)

Date	President of the Council	Foreign Affairs	Justice	Interior
31 Apr. 1885	T. Deliyannis (1st admin.)	T. Deliyannis	S. Antonopoulos A. Kontogouris (20.x.85) Z. Valvis (11.xi.85)	N. Papamichal-opoulos
12 May 1886	D. Valvis	E. Louriotis	D. Valvis	I. Papailiopoulos
21 May 1886	C. Trikoupis (5th admin.)	S. Dragoumis	D. Voulpiotis	K. Lomvardos C. Trikoupis (17.vii.88) S. Dragoumis (14.xi.88) G. Theotokis (11.viii.90)
5 Nov. 1890	T. Deliyannis (2nd admin.)	L. Deligiorgis	A. T. Zaimis	T. Deliyannis
2 Mar. 1892	K. Konstantopoulos	G. Filaretos L. Meletopoulos (6.iii.92)	G. Filaretos	K. Konstantopoulos
22 June 1892	C. Trikoupis (6th admin.)	S. Dragoumis	A. Simopoulos	G. Theotokis
15 May 1893	S. Sotiropoulos	A. A. Kontostavlos	S. Sotiropoulos	D. G. Rallis
11 Nov. 1893	C. Trikoupis (7th admin.)	D. Stefanou	D. Stefanou	N. Boufidis
24 Jan. 1895	N. P. Deliyannis	N. P. Deliyannis	S. Aravantinos	N. P. Deliyannis N. Metaxas (26.i.95)
12 June 1895	T. Deliyannis (3rd admin.)	A. Skouzes	P. Varvoglis	K. Mavromichalis
30 April 1897	D. G. Rallis (1st admin.)	S. Skouloudis	N. Triandafillakos	G. Theotokis
3 Oct. 1897	A. T. Zaimis (1st admin.)	A. T. Zaimis	A. Toman	G. Korpas
11 Nov. 1898	A. T. Zaimis (2nd admin.)	A. T. Zaimis	A. Momferatos	N. Triandafillakos
14 Apr. 1899	G. Theotokis (1st admin.)	A. Romanos	N. Karapavlos	G. Theotokis
25 Nov. 1901	A. T. Zaimis (3rd admin.)	A. T. Zaimis	K. Topalis N. Triandafillakos (26.ii.02) K. Topalis (23.iv.02)	N. Triandafillakos

Cults and Public Instruction	Finance	War	Marine
A. Zigomalas A. Kontogouris (20.x.85)	T. Deliyannis	A. Mavromichalis T. Deliyannis (29.iv.86)	R. Romas T. Deliyannis (18.x.85) G. Bouboulis (23.x.85)
M. Venizelos	A. Avgerinos	V. Petmezas	D. A. Miaoulis
P. Manetas G. Theotokis (27.ii.89) T. K. Roufos (11.viii.90)	C. Trikoupis	C. Trikoupis N. Tsamados (11.viii.90)	G. Theotokis
A. Gerokostopoulos	K. Karapanos T. Deliyannis (7.ix.91)	T. Deliyannis	K. Koumoundouros
K. Papamichalopoulos	K. Konstantopoulos S. Deimezis (7.iii.92)	C. Mastrapas	K. Sachtouris
K. Kossonakos	C. Trikoupis	N. Tsamados	S. Skouloudis
A. Eftaxias	S. Sotiropoulos	E. Kriezis G. Korpas (17.v.93)	E. Kriezis
D. Kallifronas	C. Trikoupis	N. Tsamados	G. Bouboulis
A. Vlachos	T. Ketseas A. Vlachos (5.vi.95)	I. Papadiamantopoulos	D. Kriezis
D. Petridis T. Deliyannis (5.xii.96)	T. Deliyannis	N. Smolenskis N. Metaxas (3.iii.97)	N. Levidis
A. Eftaxias	A. Simopoulos	N. Tsamados	D. G. Rallis
A. Panayotopoulos	S. Streit A. T. Zaimis (28.viii.98) S. Streit (28.x.98)	K. Smolenskis	K. Smolenskis K. Hatzikiriakos (6.x.97) G. Korpas (4.iv.98) D. A. Miaoulis (27.vi.98)
A. Momferatos	F. Negris	G. Korpas	D. A. Miaoulis
A. Eftaxias G. Theotokis (27.iii.00) S. Stais (9.vi.00) A. Momferatos	A. Simopoulos G. Theotokis (3.iv.01) A. Simopoulos (23.iv.01) F. Negris	K. Koumoundouros N. Tsamados (12.i.00) G. Korpas	V. Voudouris G. Korpas

Date	President of the Council	Foreign Affairs	Justice	Interior
6 Dec. 1902	T. Deliyannis (4th admin.)	A. Skouzes	A. Zigomalas	K. Mavromichalis
26 June 1903	G. Theotokis (2nd admin.)	G. Theotokis	N. Kalogeropoulos	N. Levidis
10 July 1903	D. G. Rallis (2nd admin.)	D. G. Rallis	P. Merlopoulos	K. Mavromichalis
18 Dec. 1903	G. Theotokis (3rd admin.)	A. Romanos G. Theotokis (26.vi.04) A. Romanos (5.ix.04)	N. Levidis	G. Theotokis
28 Dec. 1904	T. Deliyannis (5th admin.)	A. Skouzes	K. Karapanos	T. Deliyannis N. Gounarakis (14.vi.05)
22 June 1905	D. G. Rallis (3rd admin.)	D. G. Rallis	A. Christopoulos	M. Mavromichalis
20 Dec. 1905	G. Theotokis (4th admin.)	A. Skouzes D. Vokotopoulos (3.viii.07) A. Skouzes (ix.07) G. Baltatzis (4.vii.08)	D. Vokotopoulos D. Stefanou (4.vii.08) K. A. Lomvardos (30.i.09)	N. Kalogeropoulos N. Levidis (4.vii.08)
20 July 1909	D. G. Rallis (4th admin.)	G. C. Zografos	E. Deliyannis	N. Stratos
28 Aug. 1909	K. Mavromichalis	K. Mavromichalis	A. Eftaxias A. Romas (30.viii.09) K. Mavromichalis (8.x.09) P. T. Zaimis (24.xii.09)	N. Triandafillakos A. Eftaxias (2.i.10)
31 Jan. 1910	S. Dragoumis	D. Kallergis	G. Fikioris	S. Dragoumis E. Petmezas (4.ii.10) E. Mavrommatis (7.iii.10)
19 Oct. 1910	E. Venizelos (1st admin.) (Late in 1912 L. Koromilas was appointed acting head of government and took charge when Venizelos was abroad.)	N. Dimitrakopoulos I. Griparis (31.x.10) L. Koromilas (11.v.12) D. Panas (31.viii.13) G. Streit (4.i.14) E. Venizelos (13.ix.14)	N. Dimitrakopoulos K. Raktivan (31.v.12) A. Diomidis (26.x.12) K. Raktivan (28.ii.13) A. Diomidis (16.iii.13) K. Raktivan (3.vii.13)	E. Repoulis
10 Mar. 1915	D. Gounaris (1st admin.)	G. C. Zografos D. Gounaris (19.vii.15)	P. Tsaldaris	N. Triandafillakos

Cults and Public Instruction	Finance	War	Marine
A. Romas	T. Deliyannis	T. Libritis T. Deliyannis (1.iv.03)	T. Libritis K. Karapanos (11.xii.02)
K. A. Lomvardos	A. Simopoulos	K. Grivas	A. Stefanopoulos
T. Farmakopoulos	D. G. Rallis	I. Konstandinidis	I. Konstandinidis
S. Stais A. Simopoulos (4.vii.04) K. A. Lomvardos (10.vii.04) K. Karapanos	A. Simopoulos N. Kalogeropoulos (17.x.04) N. Gounarakis	K. Smolenskis K. Mavromichalis	S. Koumoundouros K. Mavromichalis
L. Kallifronas	D. G. Rallis	K. Mavromichalis V. Voudouris (31.vii.05)	V. Voudouris E. Deliyannis (31.vii.05)
A. Stefanopoulos S. Stais (4.vii.08)	A. Simopoulos N. Kalogeropoulos (3.ii.08) D. Gounaris (4.vii.08) N. Kalogeropoulos (27.ii.09)	G. Theotokis	K. Trikoupis D. Embirikos (4.vii.08)
K. Gerokostopoulos	D. G. Rallis	E. Manousoyannis	Ath. Miaoulis
P. T. Zaimis	A. Eftaxias	K. Mavromichalis L. Lapathiotis (31.viii.09) K. Mavromichalis (25.xii.09) I. Konstandinidis (30.xii.09)	I. Damianos
A. Panayotopoulos	S. Dragoumis	N. Zorbas	An. Miaoulis
A. Alexandris I. Tsirimokos (13.vi.12)	L. Koromilas A. Diomidis (30.viii.12)	E. Venizelos N. Stratos (8.xii.12) E. Venizelos (12.ii.13) (Subsequently ministry run by E. Venizelos, E. Repoulis, or K. Demertzis)	E. Venizelos N. Stratos (13.vi.12) K. Demertzis (22.xi.13) Ath. Miaoulis (22.xi.14)
C. Vozikis	P. Protopapadakis	D. Gounaris	N. Stratos

Date	President of the Council	Foreign Affairs	Justice	Interior
23 Aug. 1915	E. Venizelos (2nd admin.)	E. Venizelos	K. Raktivan	G. Kafandaris
7 Oct. 1915	A. T. Zaimis (4th admin.)	A. T. Zaimis	D. Rallis	D. Gounaris
7 Nov. 1915	S. Skouloudis	S. Skouloudis	D. Rallis M. Chadzakos (9.iv.16)	D. Gounaris A. Michelidakis (9.xi.15)
22 June 1916	A. T. Zaimis (5th admin.)	A. T. Zaimis	A. Momferatos	F. Negris A. Charalambis (24.vi.16)
16 Sept. 1916	N. Kalogeropoulos (1st admin.)	A. Karapanos	L. K. Roufos D. Vokotopoulos (18.ix.16)	L. K. Roufos
10 Oct. 1916	S. Lambros	E. Zalokostas	A. Tselos T. Iliopoulos (16.x.16) A. Tselos (20.xi.16) S. Tzanetouleas (28.xi.16) M. Soultanis (14.xii.16)	A. Tselos S. Lambros (1.v.17)
3 May 1917	A. T. Zaimis (6th admin.)	A. T. Zaimis	D. Eginitis K. Lidorikis (8.v.17)	F. Negris
27 June 1917	E. Venizelos (3rd admin.) (During frequent absences of Venizelos, E. Repoulis was acting head of government.)	N. Politis A. Diomidis (26.xii.18) N. Politis (3.xii.19) M. Negrepontis (8.xi.20)	I. Tsirimokos	E. Repoulis K. Raktivan (16.i.18)
17 Nov. 1920	D. G. Rallis (5th admin.)	D. G. Rallis	D. Rallis	P. Tsaldaris
6 Feb. 1921	N. Kalogeropoulos (2nd admin.)	N. Kalogeropoulos G. Baltadzis (10.ii.21)	N. Theotokis P. Mavromichalis (5.iii.21)	P. Tsaldaris
8 Apr. 1921	D. Gounaris (2nd admin.)	G. Baltadzis A. Kartalis (15.x.21)	D. Gounaris C. Vozikis (15.x.21)	S. Stais
15 Mar. 1922	D. Gounaris (3rd admin.)	G. Baltadzis	D. Gounaris	M. Goudas
16 May 1922	N. Stratos	N. Stratos	K. Likourezos	G. Karpetopoulos

Cults and Public Instruction	Finance	War	Marine
I. Tsirimokos	E. Repoulis	P. Danglis	Ath. Miaoulis
G. Theotokis	S. Dragoumis	I. Yannakitsas	P. Koundouriotis
G. Theotokis	S. Dragoumis D. G. Rallis (9 iv.16)	I. Yannakitsas	P. Koundouriotis
K. Lidorikis	G. P. Rallis	K. Kallaris	K. Kallaris I. Damianos (4.vii.16)
A. Kanaris	N. Kalogeropoulos	N. Kalogeropoulos	I. Damianos
S. Lambros	S. Tzanetouleas M. Soultanis (2.v.17)	N. Drakos I. Hatzopoulos (1.xii.16)	I. Damianos
D. Eginitis	G. P. Rallis	I. Hatzopoulos A. Charalambis (8.v.17) K. Demerdzis (1.vi.17) A. Charalambis (4.vi.17)	K. Demerdzis
D. Dingas K. Raktivan (5.x.20)	M. Negrepontis K. Raktivan (26.iv.18) M. Negrepontis (9.v.18) P. Vourloumis (9.x.18) M. Negrepontis (11.xi.18)	E. Venizelos A. Michalakopoulos (4.ix.17) I. Athanasakis (17.vi.18) M. Negrepontis (7.iii.20) A. Grivas (19.iii.20) Ath. Miaoulis (21.x.20)	P. Koundouriotis E. Repoulis (2.iv.18) P. Koundouriotis (18.v.18) E. Repoulis (22.i.19) Ath. Miaoulis (15.xii.19)
T. Zaimis	N. Kalogeropoulos	D. Gounaris	I. Rallis
T. Zaimis	P. Protopapadakis	D. Gounaris N. Theotokis (6.iii.21)	I. Rallis N. Theotokis (8.ii.21)
T. Zaimis	P. Protopapadakis	N. Theotokis	P. Mavromichalis
K. Poligenis	P. Protopapadakis	N. Theotokis	G. Baltadzis
D. Hadziskos	E. Ladopoulos	N. Stratos	K. Tipaldos

Date	President of the Council	Foreign Affairs	Justice	Interior
22 May 1922	P. Protopapadakis	G. Baltadzis D. Gounaris (4.vi.22) G. Baltadzis (12.vi.22)	D. Gounaris S. Yannopoulos (3.ix.22)	N. Stratos
10 Sept. 1922	N. Triandafillakos	G. Baltadzis N. Kalogeropoulos (21.ix.22)	S. Yannopoulos	G. Boussios
29 Sept. 1922	S. Krokidas	E. Kanellopoulos N. Politis (16.x.22)	F. Vasiliou	S. Krokidas
27 Nov. 1922	S. Gonatas	K. Rentis A. Alexandris (11.xii.22) S. Gonatas (31.iii.23) A. Alexandris (19.iv.23) S. Gonatas (9.v.23) A. Alexandris (11.vi.23) S. Gonatas (18.vi.23) A. Alexandris (14.vii.23) S. Gonatas (6.xi.23)	K. Rentis G. Sideris (29.xii.23)	P. Mavromichalis G. Papandreou (9.i.23) L. Sakellaropoulos (18.x.23)
12 Jan. 1924	E. Venizelos (4th admin.)	G. Roussos	G. Kafantaris	T. Sofoulis

Notes: (1) Up to October 1862 this ministry was designated Ministry of the Royal Household and Foreign Affairs.

(2) Between 21–24 February 1863 and 1–3 July 1863 there was no government. In the first period A. Moraitinis and in the second period D. Kiriakos (presidents of the assembly) assumed executive power.

(3) Between 1911 and 1917 new ministries were formed. The ministers appointed to them are shown below.

Date	Nat. Economy	Communications
14 Jan. 1911	E. Benakis E. Repoulis (17.iv.11) E. Benakis (19.v.11) E. Repoulis (16.viii.11) E. Benakis (3.x.11) A. Michalakopoulos (13.vi.12)	
2 July 1914		D. Diamantidis

Cults and public Instruction	Finance	War	Marine
K. Poligenis	E. Ladopoulos	P. Protopapadakis	I. Leonidas
T. Skoufos	A. Eftaxias	N. Triandafillakos	N. Triandafillakos
I. Siotis	G. Embirikos A. Diomidis (2.x.22) S. Krokidas (15.xi.22)	A. Charalambis	D. Papachristos
I. Siotis K. Gontikas (3.iv.23) A. Chadzikiriakos (18.x.23) A. Stratigopoulos (17.xi.23)	A. Prekas G. Kofinas (15.xii.23)	T. Pangalos S. Gonatas (25.xii.22) P. Mavromichalis (23.i.23) S. Gonatas (15.vi.23) P. Mavromichalis (18.viii.23) K. Manetas (3.xi.23)	S. Gonatas K. Voulgaris (2.xii.22)
I. Valalas	A. Michalakopoulos	K. Gontikas	I. Kannavos

Date	Nat. Economy	Communications
10 Mar. 1915	A. Eftaxias	G. Baltadzis
23 Aug. 1915	A. Michalakopoulos	D. Diamantidis
7 Oct. 1915	G. Theotokis	D. G. Rallis
7 Nov. 1915	G. Theotokis	D. G. Rallis
	P. Kalligas	
	(22.i.16)	
22 June 1916	P. Kalligas	F. Negris
16 Sept. 1916	T. Bassias	I. Kaftandzoglou
10 Oct. 1916	N. Apostolidis	P. Argiropoulos
		N. Apostolidis
		(4.iv.17)
		A. Tselos
		(29.iv.17)
3 May 1917	P. Kalligas	P. Argiropoulos
27 June 1917	A. Michalakopoulos	A. Papanastasiou
	K. Spiridis	
	(2.vii.17)	
17 Nov. 1920	P. Mavromichalis	P. Tsaldaris
6 Feb. 1921	P. Mavromichalis	P. Tsaldaris
8 Apr. 1921	I. Rallis	P. Tsaldaris
		X. Stratigos
		(15.ii.21)
15 Mar. 1922	L. K. Roufos	X. Stratigos
16 May 1922	L. K. Roufos	K. Drosopoulos
22 May 1922	L. K. Roufos	X. Stratigos
10 Sept. 1922	L. K. Roufos	A. Matsas
29 Sept. 1922	E. Kanellopoulos	P. Kalligas
	K. Manetas	
	(21.xi.22)	
27 Nov. 1922	K. Manetas	L. Sakellaropoulos
	A. Chadzikiriakos	
	(9.xii.22)	
12 Jan. 1924	K. Spiridis	E. Tsouderos

Agriculture	Welfare	Supplies
		K. Drosopoulos
		L. Embirikos
A. Michalakopoulos	S. Simos	M. Theodoridis
(and four others)	(and two others)	
P. Mavromichalis	T. Zaimis	N. Kalogeropoulos
G. Baltadzis	T. Zaimis	L. Embirikos
K. Tertipis	A. Kartalis	P. Protopapadakis
A. Argiros	M. Theodoridis	M. Theodoridis
E. Ladopoulos	I. Leonidas	I. Leonidas
A. Argiros	M. Theodoridis	S. Merkouris
T. Skoufos	S. Yannopoulos	G. Boussios
P. Kalligas	A. Doxiadis	G. Embirikos
A. Milonas		
(22.xi.22)		
G. Sideris	A. Doxiadis	G. Embirikos
G. Kofinas		
(26.iv.23)		
A. Doxiadis		
(18.x.23)		
A. Milonas	A. Doxiadis	

APPENDIX IV: Elections and Parties in Greece, 1843–1924

Note: (1) The figures showing the state of parties are approximate. Certain deputies did not reveal their allegiance until a government was formed or they changed their allegiance while parliament was in session.
(2) Extraordinary parliamentary sessions are denoted by an asterisk.

Elections	Number of Seats	State of Parties		Parliament	Session	From	To	President of Chamber
Oct.–Nov. 1843	243	Three-party alliance (Metaxas c. 30) Opposition (Palamidis group—30) (Makriyannis group—60)	120 90	National Assembly		20.xi.43	30.iii.44	P. Notaras
June–Aug. 1844	127	Metaxas Kolettis Mavrokordatos	55 20 28	I	1 2 3	19.ix.44 22.xii.45 19.xi.46	12.xi.45 12.xi.46 26.iv.47	K. Deliyannis R.Palamidis R. Palamidis
July–Aug. 1847	127	Kolettis (coalition) absolute majority		II	1 2 3	9.viii.47 9.xi.48 22.xii.49	30.x.49 9.viii.50	D. Kallifronas D. Chatziskos A. Georgantas
Oct.–Nov. 1850	131	Kriezis (coalition) Opposition	100 10	III	1 2 3	11.xi.50 12.xi.51 12.xi.52	10.viii.51 11.xi.52 8.xi.53	L. Yourdis L. Yourdis E. Parisis
Nov.–Dec. 1853	138	Kriezis (coalition) absolute majority		IV	1 2 3	11.xi.53 16.xii.54 12.xi.55	2.v.54 6.xi.55 10.xi.56	P. Varvoglis T. Zaimis A. Koumoundouros, I. Zarkos
Nov.–Dec. 1856	133	Voulgaris (coalition) absolute majority		V	1 2 3	19.xii.56 11.xi.57 11.xi.58	18.vi.57 11.v.58 5.vi.59	A. Kontostavlos D. Voudouris A. Avgerinos

Elections	Number of Seats	State of Parties		Parliament	Session	From	To	President of Chamber
Nov.–Dec. 1859	139	Miaoulis (coalition)	120	VI	1	10.xi.59	30.v.60	A. Londos
		Opposition (Opposition majority in second session)	11		2	15.xi.60	28.xi.60	T. Zaimis
Feb.–March 1861	138	Miaoulis (coalition)	absolute majority	VII	1	27.ii.61	23.viii.61	A. C. Anargirou
					2	2.x.61	31.iii.62	F. Filonos
				National Assembly	*	17.v.62	23.ix.62	L. Petmezas
						22.xii.62	28.xii.64	Z. I. Valvis
								A. Moraitinis
								D. Kiriakos
								I. Messinezis
								E. Deligiorgis
28 May 1865	170	Koumoundouros	95	VIII	1	9.vi.65	17.i.66	E. Kehayias
		Voulgaris (Deligiorgis)	40		*	22.vi.66	3.ii.66	E. Kehayias
					2	22.xii.66	21.iv.67	L. Krestenitis
		Othonists	35		3	7.x.67	2.i.68	E. Paximadis
2 April 1868	184	Voulgaris	114	IX	1	7.v.68	8.xi.68	D. Drosos
		Koumoundouros–Deligiorgis	70		*	20.xi.68	xii.68	D. Drosos
28 May 1869	c. 186	Zaimis (Deligiorgis—35)	100	X	1	17.vi.69	2.xii.69	D. Christidis
		Koumoundouros	50		2	23.xii.70	7.vi.71	K. Lomvardos
		Voulgaris	30		3	30.x.71		D. Hadziskos
9 March 1872	190	Voulgaris	65	XI	1	5.iv.72	2.vii.72	Spiromilios
		Koumoundouros	65					

Elections	Number of Seats	State of Parties		Parliament	Session	From	To	President of Chamber
		Lomvardos–Trikoupis	10					
		Zaimis	15					
		Deligiorgis	15					
		Independents	20					
Feb. 1873	190	Deligiorgis	85	XII	1	26.ii.73	2.viii.73	Deliyannis
		Opposition	95		2	31.i.74	8.v.74	T. Zaimis
		(Koumoundouros, Voulgaris, Lomvardos–Trikoupis, Zaimis)						
5 July 1874	190	Voulgaris	92–94	XIII	1	6.viii.74	15.xii.74	I. Zarkos
		Opposition	90–96		*	17.iii.75	9.iv.75	S. Kasimatis
		(Koumoundouros, Deligiorgis, Zaimis, Independents)						
30 July 1875	190	Koumoundouros	80	XIV	1	23.viii.75	3.i.76	A. Koumoundouros, T. Zaimis
		Zaimis	25					
		Deligiorgis	30		2	22.ix.76	20.iii.77	T. Zaimis
		Voulgaris	12		*	28.v.77	2.vii.77	A. Avgerinos
		Trikoupis	25		3	22.x.77	11.ii.78	A. Avgerinos
		Independents	18		4	12.viii.78	21.xii.78	S. Sotiropoulos
					**	17.vii.79	28.vii.79	N. Papamichalopoulos
5 Oct. 1879	207	Koumoundouros–Deliyannis	100	XV	1	1.xi.79	29.iv.80	S. Sotiropoulos
		Opposition	85		2	20.x.80	24.iii.81	A. Avgerinos
		(Trikoupis, Zaimis,						

Elections	Number of Seats	State of Parties	Parliament	Session	From	To	President of Chamber
		Deligiorgists, Voulgarists) Independents　20					
1 Jan. 1882	245	Trikoupis　125	XVI	1	30.i.82	11.vii.82	S. Valaoritis
		Koumoundouros–		2	30.x.82	5.iv.83	S. Valaoritis
		Deliyannis　100		3	8.xi.83	8.iii.84	P. Kalligas
		Deligiorgis, L.　6		4	6.xi.84	23.ii.85	P. Kalligas
		Independents　10					
		Democrats　5–7					
19 April 1885	245	Deliyannis　170	XVII	1	21.v.85	30.vii.85	D. Kallifronas
		Trikoupis　40		*	23.x.85	17.iv.86	A. Rikakis
		Independents　30		2	19.v.86	17.xi.86	S. Stefanopoulos
		Democrats　5					
16 Jan. 1887	150	Trikoupis　90	XVIII	1	3.ii.87	3.vi.87	A. Avgerinos
		Opposition　60		2	5.xi.87	29.xii.87	A. Avgerinos
		(Deliyannis, Karapanos,		3*	27.x.88	19.ii.89	A. Avgerinos
		Independents, Sotiropoulos,			11.iii.89	16.iv.89	A. Avgerinos
		Rallis, Papamichalopoulos)		4	21.x.89	3.iii.90	A. Avgerinos
				*	6.iii.90	12.vi.90	A. Avgerinos
26 Oct. 1890	150	Deliyannis　100	XIX	1	10.xi.90	6.iv.91	K. Konstantopoulos
		(Karapanos, L. Deligiorgis)		2	9.xi.91	2.iii.92	N. Georgiadis
		Trikoupis　15					
		Independents　35					
15 May 1892	207	Trikoupis　160	XX	1	5.vi.92	8.viii.92	V. Voudouris
		Opposition　47		2	10.xi.92	28.ii.93	V. Voudouris
		(Deliyannis, Rallis,		3	8.xi.93	24.iii.94	V. Voudouris

Elections	Number of Seats		State of Parties	Parliament	Session	From	To	President of Chamber
			Konstantopoulos,		4	8.xi.94	21.i.95	V. Voudouris
			Independents)					
28 April 1895	207	150	Deliyannis	XXI	1	27.v.95	2.viii.95	A. Zaimis
		20	Trikoupis					G. Petousis
		20	Rallis		2	20.i.96	2.iv.96	A. Romas
		4	Karapanos		*	5.xi.96	10.x.97	A. Zaimis
		6	Deligiorgis, L.		3	11.xi.97	4.iv.98	A. Romas
		7	Independents					
9 Feb. 1899	235	110	Trikoupists	XXII	1	16.iii.99	27.vii.99	N. Tsamados
		35	Zaimis		*	11.xii.99	15.iv.00	N. Boufidis
		35	Deliyannis		2	11.xi.00	4.viii.01	N. Boufidis
		20	Deligiorgis, L.		3	12.xi.01	16.iv.02	T. Retsinas
		3–6	Karapanos					
		4–6	Rallis					
		15	Independents					
29 Nov. 1902	235	110	Deliyannis	XXIII	1	21.xii.02	2.vi.03	D. Rallis,
		70	Theotokis		*	14.vi.03	19.vii.03	D. Rallis, N. Leonidas
		30	Zaimis		2	20.xii.03	12.v.04	N. Chadziskos
		10	Deligiorgis, L.		*	16.v.04	29.vi.04	N. Chadziskos
		4	Dragoumis		3	6.xii.04	3.i.05	N. Boufidis
		11	Independents					
4 March 1905	235	144	Deliyannis	XXIV	1	26.iii.05	17.vii.05	A. Romas
			(Dragoumis, Rallis)		*	12.xii.05	11.ii.06	N. Boufidis
		53	Theotokis					
		18	Zaimis					
		16	Independents					

Elections	Number of Seats	State of Parties		Parliament	Session	From	To	President of Chamber
7 April 1906		Theotokis	120	XXV	1	12.v.06	17.vii.06	N. Boufidis
		Rallis	47		*	23.xi.06	17.vi.07	N. Levidis
		Zaimis	7		2	10.xi.07	16.iv.08	N. Levidis
		Independents	6		3	11.xi.08	21.v.09	K. Koumoundouros
		Dragoumis–Gounaris	4–6		4	12.x.09	25.i.10	A. Romas
					*	12.ii.10	29.iii.10	N. Tsamados
21 Aug. 1910	362	Theotokis	75	Revisionary Assembly	1	14.ix.10	24.x.10	K. Eslin
		Rallis	75					
		Zaimis	15					
		Mavromichalis	43					
		Venizelos	20					
		Dimitrakopoulos	8					
		Benakis	2–3					
		Thessaly group	44					
		Independents	64					
11 Dec. 1910	346	Venizelos (Liberals)	260	Revisionary Assembly	1	21.i.11	25.vii.11	N. Stratos
		Zaimis	40		2	21.x.11	2.ii.12	I. Tsirimokos
		Thessaly group	23					
		Socialists	7					
		(Rallis, Theotokis, and Mavromichalis abstained)						
24 March 1912	181	Venizelos	145	XXVI	1	31.v.12	12.x.13	I. Tsirimokos, K. Zavitsianos
		Theotokists	15		2	12.xi.13	15.vi.14	K. Zavitsianos
		Rallists	6					

Elections	Number of Seats	State of Parties	Parliament	Session	From	To	President of Chamber
		Mavromichalis 6		3	27.ix.14	5.iii.15	K. Zavitsianos
		Zaimis 4					
		Independents 3					
		Socialists 2					
13 June 1915	316	Venizelos 185	XXVII	1	16.viii.15	11.xi.15	K. Zavitsianos
		Gounaris 95					
		Dimitrakopoulos 7					
		Theotokis 12					
		Rallis 6					
		Mavromichalis 7					
		Independents 2					
		Socialists 2					
19 Dec. 1915	332	Gounaris 230	XXVIII	1	24.i.16	21.vi.16	M. Theotokis
		Anti-Venizelist groups and Independents 100 (Venizelists abstained)					
		Reconvention of Parliament XXVII		1	28.ix.17	3.ii.18	T. Sofoulis
				2	28.ii.18	28.xii.18	T. Sofoulis
				3	12.xi.19	28.x.20	T. Sofoulis
14 Nov. 1920	c. 370	Anti-Venizelists 260 (Gounaris—75) (Stratos—60) (Dragoumis—30) (Rallis—25) (Independents and small	Third National Assembly		3.i.21	12.vii.22	K. A. Lomvardos

II

Elections	Number of Seats	State of Parties		Parliament Session	From	To	President of Chamber
16 Dec. 1923	397	groups—70) Venizelos		Fourth National Assembly	2.i.24	29.ix.25	E. Venizelos (5–21.i.24) K. Raktivan
		Liberals (Venizelists)	110				
		Democratic Union (Papanastasiou)	250				
		Democratic Liberals (Roussos)	120				
		Anti-Venizelists	6				
		Agrarians	3				
		Independents	18				
		(Anti-Venizelist parties abstained)					

APPENDIX V: Population, Emigration, and Occupations (Percentages)

Year	Total Population	Agriculture, Forestry, Fishery	Industry, Handicrafts	Trade, Finance, Transport	Professions	Personal Services	Public Service (including Army and Navy)	Emigrants
1821	938,765							
1838	752,077							
1861	1,096,810	74·0	10·0	6·1	1·6	3·9	4·4	
1870	1,457,894	74·8	10·3	6·3	1·4	3·8	3·4	22
1879	1,679,470	69·9	12·8	7·3	1·9	5·2	3·9	23
1907	2,631,952	66·3	12·8	11·1	3·2	3·4	3·2	29,619[1]
1920	5,016,889[2]	70·9	13·1	9·2	2·6	2·2	2·0	32,463[3]
1928	6,204,684	68·3	14·7	10·7	2·9	1·9	1·5	8,850

[1] 28,808 of these went to the U.S.A.
[2] This figure excludes the populations in Thrace and Smyrna acquired in 1920. In 1912 Old Greece (Peloponnese, Continental Greece, Euboea, Thessaly, Arta, Ionian Islands, Cyclades) had a population of 2,829,000. As a result of the Balkan Wars, 1912–13, Greece acquired, in Macedonia, Epiros, Crete, and the Aegean Islands, a population of 1,979,000. At the end of 1920 the population of Greece was approximately 6,500,000. Following the loss of western Thrace and Smyrna in 1923 and the influx of refugees, the population was approximately 5 million..
[3] During 1920–21, 33,737 former emigrants returned from the U.S.A.

APPENDIX VI: Public Education in Greece 1830–1922

| Year | University of Athens | Gymnasia | | Hellenic Schools[1] | | Primary Schools | | Literacy | |
		No.	Students	No.	Students	No.	Students	Men	Women
1830				39	2,528	71	6,721		
1840	159[2]	4	1,205	54	3,250	252	22,000	12·5%	
1869[3]	1,205	15	1,875	114	5,971	1,029	43,876 (boys) 8,824 (girls)	28·6%	6·3%
1910	3,300	41	6,500	338	24,500	3,551	177,396 (boys) 82,458 (girls)	50%	20%
1922[4]	9,799	122	88,250	—[5]		7,200	499,084 (boys and girls)	56·19%[6]	27·38%[6]

[1] Originally the Hellenic Schools provided a post-primary education in the 'purist' (katharevousa) form of Greek. Later they provided post-primary schooling up to the age of 13.
[2] The university had opened in May 1837.
[3] The Ionian Islands had been joined to Greece in 1864.
[4] By this date the Greek population was approximately double that of 1910.
[5] By this time Hellenic Schools were in the proces of becoming either Gymnasia or Primary Schools. They were formally abolished in 1929.
[6] These are the 1920 figures. Of the refugees who went to Greece in 1922–24, 62·24% of the men and 40·26% of the women were literate.

APPENDIX VII: Strength of the Greek Army and Navy

Year	Army	Mobilised Strength	Navy	Military Budget in Millions of Drachmai
1840	8,736		1,025	6·4
1861	10,911		1,225	9·0
1878	14,271		1,938	19·7*
1880	12,354	40,000		75·3*
1884	30,692		2,637	32·4*
1885	30,652	85,181	2,135	58·8*
1900	25,180		4,042	25·8
1912	26,518	150,000 (approx.)	4,061	400 (approx.)
1914	55,803			
1918			17,597 (mobilised strength)	
1921	52,609	200,000 (by the end of the year)	11,706	
1922	70,000	220,000 (approx.)	11,463	
1923		160,000	11,463	

* Including extraordinary credits.

APPENDIX VIII: Communications and Shipping

| Year | Roads Kilometres | Railways Kilometres | Mercantile Marine | | | | | | Employers |
| | | | Steam | | Sail | | Total | | |
			No. of ships	Tonnage	No. of ships	Tonnage	No. of ships	Tonnage	
1813[1]					413	119,950	413	119,950	17,500
1821[1]					600	150,000	600	150,000	
1830[1]	12·00				1,050	30,600	1,050	30,600	
1835	23·3				3,036	91,550	3,036	91,550	15,703
1852	168·3				4,327	247,751	4,327	247,751	
1867	412·6		11	5,240	5,368	321,911	5,379	327,231	31,168
1883	(1,050)	22	50	24,378	5,162	232,149	5,212	256,527	
1892	3,286	906	162	77,066	5,732	234,484	5,894	311,550	23,620
1912	4,800	1,585	389*	433,662	788*	136,639	1,177*	570,301	
1921	(8,000)	2,464	440*	685,000	1,093*	152,000	1,533*	837,000	25,000
1927	10,309	2,680	504*	1,111,052	726*	58,684	1,230*	1,169,736	

[1] These figures refer to ships based on the ports included in the Greek kingdom of 1833.
* Only ships of 60 tons and over are included in these figures.

APPENDIX IX: Public Finance and Foreign Trade

(Millions of drachmai)

Year	Actual Revenue	Actual Expenditure	Surplus or Deficit	Budget Estimates Army	Navy	Army & Navy	Imports	Exports	Export of Currants
1833	37·0	13·5	+23·5	8·0	0·9	8·9	12·3	5·5	
1834	16·8	29·1	−12·3	9·0	2·0	11·0	16·4	6·8	
1835	12·7	16·2	−3·5	6·4	2·3	8·7	16·2	9·8	
1836	13·0	15·7	−2·7	4·9	2·0	6·9	16·0	12·8	
1837	20·8	18·0	+2·8	3·9	2·6	6·5	18·4	7·5	
1838	17·1	15·6	+1·5	5·5	1·6	7·1	21·7	6·7	
1839	16·9	15·7	+1·2	5·4	1·6	7·0	18·6	7·3	
1840	17·9	16·2	+1·7	5·0	1·4	6·4	20·3	8·7	
1841	13·7	16·2	−2·5		1·6				
1842	14·9	16·0	−1·1						
1843	13·5	14·4	−0·9						
1844	12·8	13·8	−1·0						
1845	13·3	14·2	−0·9				22·3	11·0	3·5
1846	14·7	14·5	+0·2	4·4	1·1	5·5			
1847	14·0	15·4	−1·4						
1848	15·1	15·8	−0·7	4·6	1·3	5·9			
1849	16·4	15·8	+0·6	4·7	1·2	5·9			
1850	16·6	16·7	−0·1						
1851	16·3	16·0	+0·3				25·8	13·8	8·3
1852	16·5	16·4	+0·1	4·8	1·3	6·1	25·0	10·4	2·8
1853	17·2	16·3	+0·9	4·8	1·3	6·1	20·2	9·0	

Year	Actual Revenue	Actual Expenditure	Surplus or Deficit	Budget Estimates			Imports	Exports	Export of Currants
				Army	Navy	Army & Navy			
1854	18·2	17·6	+0·6				21·3	6·8	
1855	19·9	19·3	+0·6				26·4	10·8	
1856	21·6	19·4	+2·2				c. 30·0	c. 26·0	
1857	22·5	19·8	+2·7	4·9	1·6	6·5	36·6	24·4	13·5
1858	22·0	23·0	−1·0				40·4	25·0	11·8
1859	23·3	23·3	0				46·2	24·4	12·5
1860	25·3	23·5	+1·8				54·0	26·9	14·1
1861	23·0	25·3	−2·3	7·1	1·9	9·0	47·9	28·1	13·6
1862	19·7	25·6	−5·9	6·2	1·9	8·1	44·1	28·0	13·2
1863	22·8	23·6	−0·8				56·6	23·0	12·3
1864	24·3	24·6	−0·3	5·3	1·3	6·6	55·0	25·2	11·1
1865	26·2	28·5	−2·3	6·2	1·6	7·8	75·5	41·4	17·9
1866	27·2	28·1	−0·9	6·7	1·4	8·1	77·0	41·5	20·4
1867	41·3	38·2	+3·1	9·5*	1·5	11·0	75·1	48·8	21·0
1868	39·0	44·7	−5·7	10·4*	2·0	12·4	74·1	40·5	13·5
1869	41·2	37·4	+3·8	8·0	1·8	9·8	84·0	46·6	20·2
1870	41·2	36·0	+5·2	8·0	2·0	10·0	85·4	37·9	17·3
1871	37·4	37·0	+0·4	7·4	1·6	9·0	97·5	62·2	30·3
1872	33·2	33·1	+0·1	7·6	2·0	9·6	99·0	56·2	25·4
1873	31·4	32·5	−1·1	7·1	1·7	8·8	92·2	64·5	35·6
1874	54·9	45·6	+9·3	7·5	1·9	9·4	98·8	65·1	
1875	32·7	35·1	−2·4	7·8	1·8	9·6	114·5	75·7	37·8
1876	32·0	35·1	−3·1	8·1*	1·9	10·0	86·9	53·5²	
1877	40·2	35·3	+4·9	7·6	2·1	9·7	96·1	52·4	
1878	37·7	36·8	+0·9	7·6	2·1	9·7*	90·5	57·1	

Year	Actual Revenue	Actual Expenditure	Surplus or Deficit	Budget Estimates			Imports	Exports	Export of Currants
				Army	Navy	Army & Navy			
1879	73·1	96·1	−23·0	14·2*	3·7	17·9	101·5	55·6	
1880	45·4	88·8	−43·4	64·2*	11·1	75·3	97·6	60·2	
1881	107·2	102·6	+4·6	74·0*	5·3	79·3	116·3	69·9	
1882	71·6	64·4	+7·2	23·3*	4·3	27·6	142·5	76·3	
1883	58·5	67·8	−9·3	16·5	3·8	20·3	121·3	82·6	
1884	107·4	91·3	+16·1	21·9*	10·5*	32·4	115·9	73·6	
1885	61·4	122·8	−61·4	42·1*	16·7*	58·8	113·5	76·3	
1886	95·6	129·7	−34·1	23·6*	3·5	27·1	116·7	79·0	
1887	176·2	107·1	+69·1	18·0	10·3*	28·3	131·7	102·6	54·4
1888	93·7	108·1	−14·4	16·4	13·5	29·9	109·1	95·6	52·4
1889	183·0	168·7	+14·3	17·1	6·2*	23·3	132·6	107·7	55·5
1890	123·2	141·5	−18·3	18·4	8·0*	26·4	120·7	95·8	48·1
1891	106·4	122·8	−16·4	17·8	6·0	23·8	140·3	107·5	60·5
1892	106·5	107·7	−1·2	16·6	6·4	23·0	119·3	82·2	40·7
1893	96·7	92·1	+4·2	14·6	5·1	19·7	91·5	88·0	46·3
1894	102·9	85·2	+17·7	14·7	5·3	20·0	109·9	74·2	22·5
1895	94·6	91·6	+3·0	15·4	5·5	20·9	109·6	72·2	21·8
1896	96·9	90·8	+6·1	16·0	5·6	21·6	116·2	72·5	23·4
1897	92·4	137·0	−44·6	61·7*	13·0	74·7	116·3	81·7	33·6
1898	104·7	312·0	−207·3	19·8	6·3	26·1	138·2	88·2	37·1
1899	111·2	104·6	+6·6	22·3	7·6	30·3	131·2	93·8	37·9
1900	119·5	109·3	+10·2	18·0	7·8	25·8	131·4	102·7	52·5
1901	167·6	114·1	+53·5	17·3	7·1	24·4	140·5	94·0	40·8
1902	138·9	124·6	−14·3	17·8	7·3	25·1	137·2	79·6	22·4
1903	116·1	116·2	−0·1	18·4	7·3	25·7	137·5	85·9	24·8

Year	Actual Revenue	Actual Expenditure	Surplus or Deficit	Budget Estimates			Imports	Exports	Export of Currants
				Army	Navy	Army & Navy			
1904	133·5	116·1	+17·4				137·0	90·5	28·3
1905	129·7	116·3	+13·3				141·7	83·7	33·5
1906	133·0	121·5	+11·5	29·0*	7·6	36·6	144·6	123·5	42·5
1907	136·5	132·1	+4·4				149·0	117·6	39·5
1908	126·3	133·6	−7·3	45·0*	8·4	53·4	154·6	110·7	29·2
1909	125·0	136·9	−11·9	51·0*	8·5	59·5	137·5	101·7	32·7
1910	175·4	140·5	+34·9	83·5*	12·0	95·5	160·5	144·5	40·5
1911	240·1	181·3	+58·8	24·3	8·5	32·8³	173·5	141·0	46·7
1912	224·9	207·9	+17·0				157·6	146·1	40·6
1913	303·6	261·9	+41·7				177·9	119·0	34·2
1914	559·2	482·3	+76·9				318·8	178·5	39·0
1915	433·4	375·7	+57·7				289·3	218·3	36·9
1916	309·7	215·3	+94·4				399·4	154·8	43·2
1917	443·1	317·6	+125·5				223·0	112·6	7·1
1918	1,250·5	1,446·1	−195·6				733·9	296·8	96·7
1919	1,128·7	1,353·6	−224·9				1,552·1	764·2	163·5
1920	1,653·6	1,682·6	−29·0				2,177·5	686·3	
1921	1,622·5	2,257·8	−635·3				1,725·6	947·7	
1922	5,158·2	3,383·2	+1,775·0				3,085·4	2,485·0	
1923	3,992·2	4,950·7	−958·5				6,035·3	2,545·1	

* Including extraordinary credits.
1 Figures for 1833–40 are taken from F. Strong, *Greece as a kingdom* (London, 1842). Those for 1845 are taken from K. Leconte, *Étude économique de la Grèce* (Paris, 1847). Figures from 1851 are based on Greek official statistics.
2 From 1876 to 1919 values are given in gold drachmai.
3 From 1912 to 1923, owing to much extraordinary military expenditure, the budget bore little resemblance to the sums expended.

Index

Type set by Gloucester Typesetting Company Limited
Printed in Great Britain by The Pitman Press, Bath